Lecture Notes in Computer Science 6227

Commenced Publication in 1973
Founding and Former Series Editors:
Gerhard Goos, Juris Hartmanis, and Jan van Leeuwen

Antonín Kučera   Igor Potapov (Eds.)

Reachability Problems

4th International Workshop, RP 2010
Brno, Czech Republic, August 28-29, 2010
Proceedings

 Springer

Volume Editors

Antonín Kučera
Masaryk University, Faculty of Informatics
Botanická 68a, 60200 Brno, Czech Republic
E-mail: tony@fi.muni.cz

Igor Potapov
University of Liverpool, Department of Computer Science
Ashton Building, Liverpool L69 3BX, England
E-mail: potapov@liverpool.ac.uk

Library of Congress Control Number: 2010932672

CR Subject Classification (1998): F.3, D.2, D.3, F.4, F.4.1, F.1

LNCS Sublibrary: SL 1 – Theoretical Computer Science and General Issues

ISSN   0302-9743
ISBN-10   3-642-15348-8 Springer Berlin Heidelberg New York
ISBN-13   978-3-642-15348-8 Springer Berlin Heidelberg New York

springer.com

© Springer-Verlag Berlin Heidelberg 2010
Printed in Germany

Typesetting: Camera-ready by author, data conversion by Scientific Publishing Services, Chennai, India
Printed on acid-free paper   06/3180

Preface

This volume contains the papers presented at the 4th International Workshop on Reachability Problems, RP 2010 held during August 28–29, 2010 in the Faculty of Informatics, Masaryk University, Brno, Czech Republic and co-located with Joint MFCS and CSL 2010 (35th International Symposiums on Mathematical Foundations of Computer Science and 19th EACSL Annual Conferences on Computer Science Logic). RP 2010 was the fourth in the series of workshops following three successful meetings at Ecole Polytechnique, France in 2009 at University of Liverpool, UK in 2008 and at Turku University, Finland in 2007.

The Reachability Problems workshops series aims at gathering together scholars from diverse disciplines and backgrounds interested in reachability problems that appear in *algebraic structures, computational models, hybrid systems, logic and verification*, etc. Reachability is a fundamental problem in the context of many models and abstractions which describe various computational processes. Analysis of the computational traces and predictability questions for such models can be formalized as a set of different reachability problems. In general, reachability can be formulated as follows: Given a computational system with a set of allowed transformations (functions), decide whether a certain state of a system is reachable from a given initial state by a set of allowed transformations. The same questions can be asked not only about reachability of exact states of the system but also about a set of states expressed in terms of some property as a parameterized reachability problem. Another set of predictability questions can be seen in terms of reachability of eligible traces of computations, unavoidability of some dynamics and a possibility to avoid undesirable dynamics using a limited control.

The purpose of the conference is to promote exploration of new approaches for the predictability of computational processes by merging mathematical, algorithmic and computational techniques. Topics of interest include (but are not limited to): reachability problems in infinite state systems, rewriting systems, dynamical and hybrid systems; reachability problems in logic and verification; reachability analysis in different computational models, counter/ timed/ cellular/ communicating automata; Petri nets; computational aspects of algebraic structures (semigroups, groups and rings); frontiers between decidable and undecidable reachability problems; predictability in iterative maps and new computational paradigms.

The first venue of Reachability Problems was Turku, Finland in 2007, as a satellite event of *Developments in Language Theory DLT 2007*. The second was held at Liverpool University in 2008 and the third at Ecole Polytechnique, France in 2009.

The proceedings of the previous RP workshops appeared as follows:

- Mika Hirvensalo, Vesa Halava, Igor Potapov, Jarkko Kari (Eds.): Proceedings of the Satellite Workshops of DLT 2007. TUCS General Publication No 45, June 2007. ISBN: 978-952-12-1921-4.
- Vesa Halava and Igor Potapov (Eds.): Proceedings of the Second Workshop on Reachability Problems in Computational Models (RP 2008). Electronic Notes in Theoretical Computer Science. Volume 223, Pages 1-264 (26 December 2008).
- Olivier Bournez and Igor Potapov (Eds.): Reachability Problems, Third International Workshop, RP 2009, Palaiseau, France, September 23–25, 2009, Lecture Notes in Computer Science, 5797, Springer 2009.

The four keynote speakers at the 2010 conference were:

- Markus Holzer, "Descriptional Complexity of (Un)ambiguous Finite-State Machines and Pushdown Automata"
- Kim Guldstrand Larsen, "Symbolic and Compositional Reachability for Timed Automata"
- Alexander Rabinovich, "Temporal Logics over Linear Time Domains Are in PSPACE"
- Philippe Schnoebelen, "Lossy Counter Machines Decidability Cheat Sheet"

Each of the submitted papers received at least three reviews by members of the Program Committee, with the help of external reviewers. The full list of the 23 members of the Program Committee and the list of external reviewers can be found on the next two pages. The Program Committee is grateful for the highly appreciated and high-quality work produced by these external reviewers. Based on these reviews, the Program Committee decided finally to accept nine papers, in addition to the four invited talks.

We also gratefully acknowledge the support from the Czech National Research Center *Institute for Theoretical Computer Science (ITI)*.

It is also a great pleasure to acknowledge the team of the *EasyChair system*, and the fine cooperation with the *Lecture Notes in Computer Science* team of Springer which made possible the production of this volume in time for the conference.

Finally, we thank all the authors for the high quality of their contributions, and the participants for making this edition of RP 2010 a success.

June 2010   Antonín Kučera
                                                              Igor Potapov

Conference Organization

Program Chairs

Antonín Kučera
Igor Potapov

Program Committee

Parosh Aziz Abdulla	Uppsala, Sweden
Eugene Asarin	Paris, France
Christel Baier	Bonn, Germany
Bernard Boigelot	Liege, Belgium
Olivier Bournez	Palaiseau, France
Cristian S. Calude	Auckland, New Zealand
Stephane Demri	Cachan, France
Javier Esparza	München, Germany
Laurent Fribourg	Cachan, France
Vesa Halava	Turku, Finland
Oscar Ibarra	Santa Barbara, USA
Franjo Ivancic	Princeton, USA
Juhani Karhumäki	Turku, Finland
Joost-Pieter Katoen	Aachen, Germany
Antonin Kucera	Brno, Czech Republic
Michal Kunc	Brno, Czech Republic
Alexander Kurz	Leicester, UK
Slawomir Lasota	Warsaw, Poland
Alexei Lisitsa	Liverpool, UK
Luke Ong	Oxford, UK
Igor Potapov	Liverpool, UK
Wolfgang Thomas	Aachen, Germany
Hsu-Chun Yen	Taipei, Taiwan, China

Local Organization

Antonín Kučera
Igor Potapov

with the help offered by the Faculty of Informatics, Masaryk University
for the organization of the Reachability Workshop.

External Reviewers

Laurent Doyen
Ingo Felscher
Florent Jacquemard
Arnaud Sangnier
Pawel Parys
David Pichardie
Roman Rabinovich

Table of Contents

Descriptional Complexity of (Un)ambiguous Finite State Machines and Pushdown Automata

Markus Holzer and Martin Kutrib

Institut für Informatik, Universität Giessen,
Arndtstr. 2, 35392 Giessen, Germany
{holzer,kutrib}@informatik.uni-giessen.de

Abstract. Unambiguity and its generalization to quantified ambiguity are important concepts in, e.g., automata and complexity theory. Basically, an unambiguous machine has at most one accepting computation path for each accepted word. While unambiguous pushdown automata induce a language family strictly in between the deterministic and general context-free languages, unambiguous finite automata capture the regular languages, that is, they are equally powerful as deterministic and nondeterministic finite automata. However, their descriptional capacity is significantly different. In the present paper, we summarize and discuss developments relevant to (un)ambiguous finite automata and pushdown automata problems from the descriptional complexity point of view. We do not prove these results but we merely draw attention to the big picture and some of the main ideas involved.

1 Introduction

Finite automata are traditionally classified into deterministic (DFA), nondeterministic (NFA), and unambiguous (UFA) machines, and it is well known that all these devices are equally powerful and capture the family of regular languages. Here an NFA is *unambiguous* if for every word in the language there is at most one accepting computation. Clearly, any DFA is a UFA and every UFA is an NFA. The more complicated part of this equality is to show that every NFA or UFA can be simulated by a DFA without changing the accepted language. The construction is normally given by the *powerset construction* [56], but this simulation can also be interpreted as a reachability analysis on the configuration graph induced by the NFA with a device without nondeterminism. Here the "search algorithm" keeps track of all possible configurations (here states) the NFA may reach simultaneously by reading some word (see Figure 1).

Thus, given some n-state NFA one can always construct a language equivalent DFA with at most 2^n states [56], and therefore NFAs can offer exponential savings in space compared with DFAs. In fact, later independently in [49,51,52] it was shown that this exponential upper bound is best possible, i.e., for every n there is an n-state NFA which cannot be simulated by any DFA with strictly less than 2^n states. Exactly the same bound is reached when simulating UFAs

A. Kučera and I. Potapov (Eds.): RP 2010, LNCS 6227, pp. 1–23, 2010.

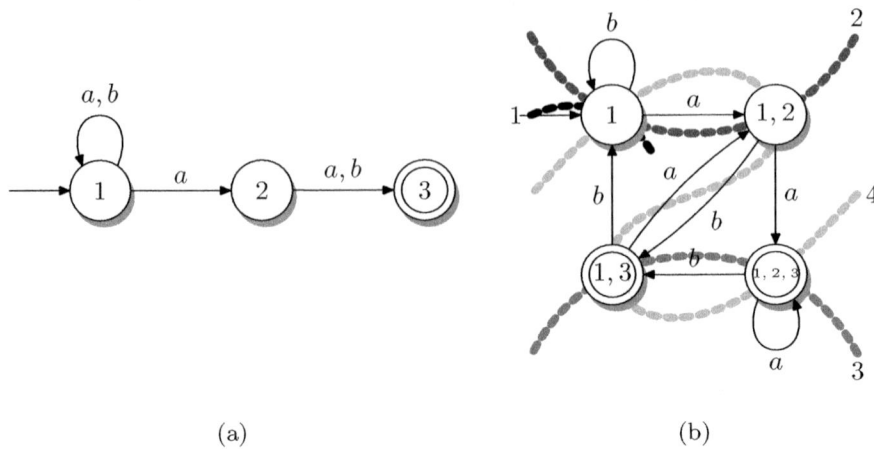

(a)   (b)

Fig. 1. Powerset construction: (a) NFA and (b) equivalent DFA with initial state $\{1\}$, visualizing the "search front" by numbers from 1 to 4 of an incremental powerset construction for the sub-automaton reachable from the initial state—in the drawing the curly brackets are omitted. The first search front 1 consist of the state $\{1\}$, the second of the states $\{1,2\}$ and $\{1\}$, the third of $\{1,2,3\}$ and $\{1,3\}$, and finally the fourth of all depicted states. Observe, that the NFA in (a) is actually also a UFA.

by DFAs [45,48], while for the simulation of NFAs by UFAs the upper bound drops to $2^n - 1$, which was also shown to be tight in [47].

These results are only three examples from a vast of different simulation results of various devices from automata theory that can be found in the literature; for some further readings we refer to, e.g., [24,25,26]. We tour a fragment of the literature summarizing simulation results of variants of NFAs and pushdown automata. In particular we pay special attention to unambiguous finite automata and pushdown machines, because we think that unambiguity deserves more attention since it is a valuable and important concept that appears in a lot of sub-fields of theoretical computer science such as, e.g., automata and formal language theory, complexity theory, etc. A size lower bound on a simulation can be interpreted as a succinctness gain, when changing from one description to the other description. In most cases tight bounds for the simulations (in order of magnitude) are obtained, but there are also situations, where the gain in succinctness in a simulation cannot be bounded by any recursive function. This latter phenomenon known as *non-recursive trade-off* appears when pushdown automata become involved. This is not entirely true in general, because for certain restrictions on pushdown machines such as, e.g., deterministic pushdown automata (DPDA) accepting regular languages only, or pushdown machines accepting unary languages, the simulation becomes recursive again. Moreover, we also draw a picture of the relations between higher degrees of ambiguity and nondeterminism. We do not prove these results but we merely draw attention to the big picture and some of the main ideas involved.

The paper is organized as follows: in the next section we introduce the necessary notations. Then in Section 3 we focus on finite automata presenting simulation results and complexity bounds on the minimization problem. The concept of higher degrees of ambiguity and nondeterminism is then discussed for finite automata in Section 4. Finally, similar questions on simulations, and the relation of ambiguity and nondeterminism are addressed for pushdown automata in Section 5.

2 Definitions

In connection with formal languages, strings are called *words*. Let Σ^* denote the set of all words over a finite alphabet Σ. The *empty word* is denoted by λ, and we set $\Sigma^+ = \Sigma^* \setminus \{\lambda\}$. For the *length of a word* w we write $|w|$; in particular, the length of the empty word is zero, i.e., $|\lambda| = 0$. A *formal language* L is a subset of Σ^*. One of the easiest devices in formal language theory are finite automata, which are defined as follows:

A *nondeterministic finite automaton* (NFA) is a quintuple $A = (Q, \Sigma, \delta, q_0, F)$, where Q is the finite set of *states*, Σ is the finite set of *input symbols*, $q_0 \in Q$ is the *initial state*, $F \subseteq Q$ is the set of *accepting states*, and $\delta : Q \times \Sigma \to 2^Q$ is the *transition function*, where 2^Q refers to the *powerset* of the set Q. The *language accepted* by the NFA A is defined as

$$L(A) = \{\, w \in \Sigma^* \mid \delta(q_0, w) \cap F \neq \emptyset \,\},$$

where the transition function δ is recursively extended to $\delta : Q \times \Sigma^* \to 2^Q$ by $\delta(q, \lambda) = \{q\}$ and $\delta(q, aw) = \bigcup_{p \in \delta(q,a)} \delta(p, w)$. A finite automaton is said to be *minimal* if its number of states is minimal with respect to the accepted language.

Special kinds of NFAs are *deterministic* and *unambiguous* finite automata. Let $A = (Q, \Sigma, \delta, q_0, F)$ be a finite automaton. Then A is *deterministic* (DFA) if $|\delta(q, a)| = 1$, for all states $q \in Q$ and letters $a \in \Sigma$. In this case we simply write $\delta(q, a) = p$ instead of $\delta(q, a) = \{p\}$ assuming that the transition function is a mapping $\delta : Q \times \Sigma \to Q$. Moreover the NFA A is *unambiguous* (UFA) if for every word $w \in L(A)$ there is at most one accepting computation path, i.e., the sequence of states seen during the accepting computation on the given word is unique. Clearly, every DFA is a UFA. Any DFA is *complete*, that is, the transition function is total, whereas it may be a partial function for NFAs and UFAs in the sense that the transition function of nondeterministic machines may map to the empty set. So, a *sink* or *dead state* is counted for DFAs, since they are always complete, whereas it is not counted for NFAs and UFAs, since these devices are not necessarily complete. For further details we refer to [29].

A natural generalization of finite automata are pushdown machines. A *nondeterministic pushdown automaton* (NPDA) is a 7-tuple $A = (Q, \Sigma, \Gamma, \delta, q_0, Z_0, F)$, where Q is the finite set of *states*, Σ is the finite set of *input symbols*, Γ is the finite *stack alphabet*, $q_0 \in Q$ is the *initial state*, $Z_0 \in \Gamma$ is the *bottom of stack symbol* which initially appears on the pushdown store, $F \subseteq Q$ is the set of *accepting states*, and *transition function* δ maps $Q \times (\Sigma \cup \{\lambda\}) \times \Gamma$ to finite subsets of $Q \times \Gamma^*$. An NPDA A is in *configuration* $c = (q, w, \gamma)$ if A is in state $q \in Q$ with $w \in \Sigma^*$ as remaining input, and $\gamma \in \Gamma^*$ on the pushdown store, the rightmost symbol of γ being the top symbol on the pushdown. We write

$$c = (q, aw, \gamma Z) \vdash_A (p, w, \gamma \beta),$$

if $(p, \beta) \in \delta(q, a, Z)$, for $a \in \Sigma \cup \{\lambda\}$, $w \in \Sigma^*$, $\gamma, \beta \in \Gamma^*$, and $Z \in \Gamma$. As usual, the reflexive transitive closure of $\vdash_A$ is denoted by $\vdash_A^*$, and the subscript A will be dropped from $\vdash_A$ and $\vdash_A^*$ whenever the meaning remains clear. The *language accepted* by A *with empty pushdown* is defined by

$$L(A) = \{ w \in \Sigma^* \mid (q_0, w, Z_0) \vdash^* (q, \lambda, \lambda), \text{ for some } q \in Q \}.$$

Equivalently, the *language accepted* by A *with final state* is defined by

$$L_f(A) = \{ w \in \Sigma^* \mid (q_0, w, Z_0) \vdash^* (q, \lambda, \gamma), \text{ for some } q \in F \text{ and } \gamma \in \Gamma^* \}.$$

As in the case of finite automata one can define deterministic (DPDA) and unambiguous pushdown automata (UPDA) in a straightforward way (cf. [19]). By definition every DPDA is a UPDA. NPDAs characterize the family of context-free languages defined by context-free grammars. This characterization carries over to UPDAs in the sense that the family of unambiguous context-free languages, generated by unambiguous context-free grammars, is equal to the family of languages accepted by UPDAs. Finally, the family of deterministic context-free languages are simply defined to be all languages accepted with final state by DPDAs (or equivalently by LR(k) context-free grammars). These three types of devices induce a strict hierarchy of language families [19].

3   (Un)ambiguous Finite Automata

Since regular languages have many representations in the world of finite automata, it is natural to investigate the succinctness of their representation by different types of automata in order to optimize the space requirements. Here we measure the costs of representations in terms of the states of a minimal automaton accepting a language. More precisely, the *simulation problem* is defined as follows:

  – Given two classes of finite automata C_1 and C_2, how many states are sufficient and necessary in the worst case to simulate n-state automata from C_1 by automata from C_2?

In particular, we are interested in simulations between DFAs, UFAs, and NFAs. In order to compare these simulations the following relation from the literature, see, e.g., [57] is of use: if the transformation from an automaton from C_1 to an equivalent automaton from C_2 is polynomially bounded, i.e., there is a polynomial p such that for any n-state automaton from C_1 one finds an equivalent automaton from C_2 with at most $p(n)$ states, then we write $C_1 \leq_p C_2$.

In this case we consider this transformation to be cheap. In case $C_1 \leq_p C_2$ but $C_2 \not\leq_p C_1$, we say that C_1 is *(polynomially) separated* from C_2 and abbreviate this by $C_1 <_p C_2$. In other words, while the transformation of an automaton from C_1 into an equivalent C_2 automaton is cheap the converse transformation is expensive and exceeds any polynomial bound. Note that the non-polynomial bound for the transformation from right to left is in most cases not explicitly specified. In what follows we will see that in most cases one obtains separation results for most combinations of classes of finite automata.

3.1   Simulations

It is well known that to any NFA one can always construct an equivalent DFA [56]. This so-called *powerset construction*, where each state of the DFA is associated with a subset of NFA states, turned out to be optimal in general. That is, the bound on the number of states necessary for the construction is tight in the sense that for an arbitrary n there is always some n-state NFA which cannot be simulated by any DFA with strictly less than 2^n states [49,51,52]. So, NFAs can offer exponential savings in the number of states compared with DFAs. This gives rise to DFA $<_p$ NFA or more precisely to the following theorem.

Theorem 1 (NFA by DFA Simulation). *Let $n \geq 1$ and A be an n-state NFA. Then 2^n states are sufficient and necessary in the worst case for a DFA to accept $L(A)$.*

The situation for UFAs is similar. A first result on UFAs was shown in [61] proving a $2^{\Omega(\sqrt{n})}$ lower bound on the trade-off between NFAs and UFAs and between UFAs and DFAs. Hence DFA $<_p$ UFA and UFA $<_p$ NFA. Since DFAs are also unambiguous both results led a large gap between the lower and the upper bound of $2^n - 1$ (as for the case of NFAs in general, the dead state can be saved for UFAs). Later the lower bound for the transformation of an NFA to an equivalent UFA was improved to $2^{\Omega(n)}$ in [65] and finally, for every n, an n-state NFA was exhibited in [47]—see Figure 2—whose smallest equivalent UFA cannot do better in the number of states than the smallest equivalent DFA besides the aforementioned saving of the dead state. Hence a $2^n - 1$ tight bound

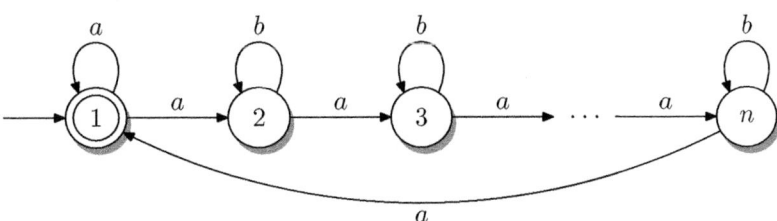

Fig. 2. Leung's NFA A_n with n states, for $n \geq 2$, accepting a language for which any equivalent UFA needs at least $2^n - 1$ states

on the trade-off between NFAs and UFAs was established. For the remaining UFA by DFA simulation it was mentioned in [65] that the well-known language $L_n = (a + b)^*a(a + b)^{n-1}$, that is the set of words over the alphabet $\{a, b\}$ whose nth last letter is an a, may serve as a witness for a 2^{n-1} lower bound (see Figure 3). Then this transformation problem was solved in [45] in a similar vain as the NFA to DFA transformation (providing UFAs with several initial states) obtaining a tight bound of 2^n in the exact number of states. Later this problem was reconsidered in [48] giving UFAs with a single initial state that reach the maximal trade-off when transformed into equivalent DFAs. Again exponential state savings in both cases are possible. These results are summarized as follows:

Theorem 2 (NFA by UFA and UFA by DFA Simulation). *Let $n \geq 1$ and A be an n-state NFA. Then $2^n - 1$ states are sufficient and necessary in the worst case for a UFA to accept $L(A)$. If automaton A is a UFA, then 2^n states are sufficient and necessary in the worst case for a DFA to accept $L(A)$.*

Proving lower bounds for NFAs is complicated in general. Several authors have introduced methods for proving such lower bounds; see, e.g., the fooling set technique [10], the extended fooling set technique [1,31], and the biclique edge cover technique [17]. Although the bounds provided by these techniques are not always tight and, in fact, can be arbitrarily worse compared to the nondeterministic state complexity, they give good results in many cases. For UFAs a lower bound method was already given in [61], which is based on a rank argument on certain matrices, which was further elaborated in, e.g., [47,48]. This method reads as follows—note that the rank technique shares the deficit of the previously mentioned lower bound techniques for NFAs that the provided bounds may not be tight in general:

Theorem 3 (Rank Method for UFAs Lower Bounds). *Let $L \subseteq \Sigma^*$ be a regular language and $\{\,(x_i, y_i) \mid x_i, y_i \in \Sigma^*$ with $1 \leq i \leq n\,\}$ a finite set of pairs of strings. Consider the $n \times n$ matrix $M = (m_{ij})$ over the field of characteristic 2 defined by $m_{ij} = 1$, if $x_i y_j \in L$, and $m_{ij} = 0$, otherwise. Then any UFA accepting L has at least the rank of M number of states.*

For the particular case of unary regular languages the situation is significantly different. The general problem of evaluating the costs of unary automata simulations was raised in [63], and has led to emphasize some relevant differences with the general case. For state complexity issues of unary finite automata *Landau's function*

$$F(n) = \max\{\,\mathrm{lcm}(x_1, \cdots, x_k) \mid x_1, \ldots, x_k \geq 1 \text{ and } x_1 + \cdots + x_k = n\,\},$$

which gives the maximal order of the cyclic subgroups of the symmetric group on n elements, plays a crucial role. Here, lcm denotes the least common multiple. Since F depends on the irregular distribution of the prime numbers, we cannot expect to express $F(n)$ explicitly by n. In [43,44] the asymptotic growth rate

$$\lim_{n \to \infty} (\ln F(n)/\sqrt{n \cdot \ln n}) = 1$$

was determined, which for our purposes implies the (sufficient) rough estimate $F(n) \in e^{\Theta(\sqrt{n \cdot \ln n})}$. The following asymptotic tight bound on the unary NFA by DFA simulation was presented in [5,6]. Its proof is based on a normalform (Chrobak normalform) for unary NFAs introduced in [5]. Each n-state unary NFA can be replaced by an equivalent $O(n^2)$-state NFA consisting of an initial deterministic tail and some disjoint deterministic loops, where the automaton makes only a single nondeterministic decision after passing through the initial tail, which chooses one of the loops.

Theorem 4 (Unary NFA by DFA Simulation). *Let $n \geq 1$ and A be an n-state NFA accepting a unary language. Then $e^{\Theta(\sqrt{n \cdot \ln n})}$ states are sufficient and necessary in the worst case for a DFA to accept $L(A)$.*

Surprisingly the corresponding simulation questions on unary languages involving UFAs was investigated only recently in [53]. Based on a refined transformation, presented in [34], of UFAs into Chrobak normalform without increasing the number of states, the precise number of states for converting a UFA accepting a unary language into an equivalent DFA is determined by a more complicated variant of Landau's function, which is defined as

$$\tilde{F}(n) = \max\{ \operatorname{lcm}(x_1, \ldots, x_k) \mid x_1, \ldots, x_k \geq 1, \text{ and } x_1 + \cdots + x_k = n \text{ and}$$
$$\exists f_1, \ldots f_k \text{ with } 0 \leq f_i \leq x_i - 1 \text{ such that}$$
$$\forall i, j \text{ with } i \neq j \text{ we have } f_i \neq f_j \bmod \gcd(x_i, x_j) \}.$$

Here the additional condition compared to Landau's function is the criterion that forces a unary NFA in Chrobak normalform to be unambiguous. By involved calculations the function $\tilde{F}(n)$ is asymptotically estimated by $e^{\Theta(\sqrt[3]{n \cdot \ln^2 n})}$, which gives the following result on unary UFA by DFA simulation.

Theorem 5 (Unary UFA by DFA Simulation). *Let $n \geq 1$ and A be an n-state UFA accepting a unary language. Then $e^{\Theta(\sqrt[3]{n \cdot \ln^2 n})}$ states are sufficient and necessary in the worst case for a DFA to accept $L(A)$.*

What concerns the simulation of unary NFAs by UFAs? In fact, in [53] it was shown that one cannot do asymptotically better than in the unary NFAs to DFAs transformation. This nicely contrasts the results on the NFA by UFA and UFA by DFA simulation in general, given in Theorem 2, where in both cases an exponentially tight bound is reported. Here in the unary case easy calculations show that the UFAs to DFAs transformation is asymptotically better than the NFAs to UFAs conversion since $\tilde{F}(n) \in o(F(n))$, which intuitively means that UFAs are somehow "closer" to DFAs than NFAs.

Theorem 6 (Unary NFA by UFA Simulation). *Let $n \geq 1$ and A be an n-state NFA accepting a unary language. Then $e^{\Theta(\sqrt{n \cdot \ln n})}$ states are sufficient and necessary in the worst case for a UFA to accept $L(A)$.*

Very often UFAs are compared to a slight extension of DFAs, namely multiple-entry DFAs (MDFAs), which were defined in [8,68]. Here the sole guess appears at the beginning of the computation, that is, by choosing one out of k initial states. So, the nondeterminism is limited in its amount and in the situation at which it appears—it is worth mentioning that MDFAs are a special case of ambiguous finite automata, which are discussed in Section 4 in detail. Converting an MDFA with k initial states into a DFA by the powerset construction shows immediately that any reachable state contains at most k states of the MDFA. This gives an upper bound for the conversion. In [27] it has been shown that this upper bound is tight resulting in DFA $<_p$ MDFA or more precisely:

Theorem 7 (MDFA by DFA Simulation). *Let $n, k \geq 1$ with $k \leq n$ and A be an n-state MDFA with k entry states. Then $\sum_{i=1}^{k} \binom{n}{i}$ states are sufficient and necessary in the worst case for a DFA to accept $L(A)$.*

So, for $k = 1$ we obtain DFAs while for $k = n$ we are concerned with the special case that needs $2^n - 1$ states. Interestingly, NFAs can be exponentially concise over MDFAs. The following lower bound has been derived in [36].

Theorem 8 (NFA to MDFA Simulation). *Let $n \geq 1$ and A be an n-state NFA. Then $\Omega(2^n)$ states are necessary in the worst case for an MDFA to accept $L(A)$.*

For the trade-off between MDFAs and UFAs a tight bound in the exact number of states was shown in [46,48]. This nicely fits into the known upper and lower bound results presented earlier, and shows that even very limited use of nondeterminism can induce a dramatic increase in the number of states.

Theorem 9 (MDFA by UFA Simulation). *Let $n \geq 1$ and A be an n-state MDFA. Then $2^n - 1$ states are sufficient and necessary in the worst case for a UFA to accept $L(A)$.*

Recently a variant of UFAs, so called *structurally unambiguous* finite automata were introduced and investigated in [46]. An NFA $A = (Q, \Sigma, \delta, q_0, F)$ is *structurally* unambiguous (SUFA) if for every word $w \in \Sigma^*$ and every state $q \in Q$ there is *at most one* computation from the initial state q_0 to state q reading word w. Observe, that compared to the original definition of unambiguity the computations need *not* be accepting. Thus, unambiguity is a semantic concept, while structurally unambiguity is a syntactic one, which is independent on the choice of the set of final states. However, if there is only one final state, that is, $|F| = 1$, then a SUFA is also a UFA, but in general SUFAs may differ from UFAs. But what can be said about the relation of SUFAs to DFAs, UFAs, and MDFAs, in general? First of all every DFA is a SUFA and it is easy to see that this two automata classes are separated from each other, i.e, DFA $<_p$ SUFA, since the automaton depicted in Figure 3 is structurally unambiguous, and any equivalent DFA needs at least an exponential number of states. But we can do slightly better as we will see below. Moreover, every MDFA can be transformed

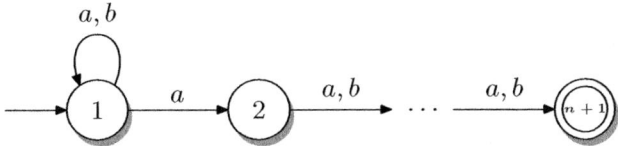

Fig. 3. UFA which is also a SUFA A_n with $(n+1)$-states accepting the set of all words having a letter a at the nth position, i.e., $L(A_n) = (a + b)^*a(a + b)^{n-1}$, which any equivalent DFA needs at least 2^{n-1} states

into an equivalent $O(n^2)$-state SUFA by simply making at most n copies of the MDFA and introducing a new initial state that is appropriately connected to these copies. It is easy to see that the constructed automaton is a SUFA, hence DFA $<_p$ SUFA and MDFA $\leq_p$ SUFA; recall that DFA $<_p$ MDFA holds true. The missing separations of MDFAs and SUFAs and of SUFAs and UFAs can be found in [46], and were proven by a single witness language only. In fact, the results presented there give tight bounds for the simulations in the exact number of states, and read as follows:

Theorem 10 (SUFA by DFA, UFA, or MDFA Simulation). *Let $n \geq 1$ and A be an n-state SUFA. Then 2^n states are sufficient and necessary in the worst case for a DFA to accept $L(A)$. Moreover $2^n - 1$ states are sufficient and necessary in the worst case for a UFA or MDFA to accept $L(A)$.*

3.2 Minimization Problems

We continue with some comments on a problem closely related to finding good lower bounds on the automata simulations for certain types of devices, namely the minimization problem. The study of the minimization problem for finite automata dates back to the early beginnings of automata theory—for further reading we refer to [35] and references therein. The decision version of the minimization problem, for short the *NFA-to-NFA minimization problem*, is defined as follows: given a NFA A and a natural number k in binary, that is, an encoding $\langle A, k \rangle$, is there an equivalent k-state NFA? This notation naturally generalizes to other types of finite automata, for example, the DFA-to-NFA minimization problem. It is well known that for a given n-state DFA one can efficiently compute an equivalent minimal automaton in $O(n \log n)$ time [28]. More precisely, the DFA-to-DFA minimization problem is complete for NL, even for DFAs without inaccessible states [4]. This is contrary to the nondeterministic case since the minimization problem for NFAs is known to be computationally hard [35]. The PSPACE-hardness result for NFAs was shown by a reduction from the union universality problem to the NFA-to-NFA minimization problem. For some further problems related to minimization we refer also to [17].

In order to better understand the very nature of nondeterminism one may ask for minimization problems for restricted types of finite automata such as, e.g., UFAs. Already in [35] it was shown that for UFAs some minimization problems remain intractable. To be more precise, the UFA-to-UFA and the DFA-to-UFA minimization problems are NP-complete. Later in [50] it was shown that the minimization of finite automata equipped with a very small amount of nondeterminism is already computationally hard. To this end, a reduction from the NP-complete minimal inferred DFA problem [11,35] to the the minimization problems for MDFAs with a fixed number of initial states as well as for NFAs with fixed finite branching has been shown. Prior to this, the MDFA-to-DFA minimization problem in general was proven to be PSPACE-complete in [27]. Here the minimal inferred DFA problem [11] is defined as follows: given a finite alphabet Σ, two finite subsets $S, T \subseteq \Sigma^*$, and an integer k, is there a k-state DFA that accepts a language L such that $S \subseteq L$ and $T \subseteq \Sigma^* \setminus L$? Such an automaton can be seen as a consistent "implementation" of the sets S and T. Recently, the picture was completed in [2] by getting much closer to the tractability frontier for NFAs minimization. Interestingly it turned out, that unambiguity plays an important role in this characterization. There a class of NFAs is identified, the so called δ-nondeterministic finite automata (δNFA), such that the minimization problem for any class of finite automata that contains δNFAs is NP-hard, even if the input is given as a DFA. Here the class of δNFAs contains all NFAs A with the following properties: (1) the automaton A is a UFA, (2) the maximal product of the degrees of nondeterminism over the states in a possible computation is at most 2, and (3) there is at most on state q and a letter a such that the degree of nondeterminism of q and a is 2. It is worth mentioning that for every n-state δNFA there is an equivalent DFA with at most $O(n^2)$ states.

4   Quantified Ambiguity

The concept of unambiguity implied devices whose mode of operation is somehow in between determinism and nondeterminism. On the one hand, UFAs can be seen as DFAs that are allowed to guess in rejecting computations. On the other hand, UFAs are NFAs that are not allowed to guess in accepting computations. A natural generalization is to relax the condition that forbids guessing in accepting computations to allow a certain amount of guessing in accepting computations. This idea and a formalization of what is a certain amount brings us to the concept of *quantified ambiguity* [57].

For an NFA A, we define the ambiguity of a word w, denoted by $\mathsf{amb}_A(w)$, to be the number of different *accepting* computations of w. Note that a word w is in the language $L(A)$ if and only if the ambiguity of w is not zero. The ambiguity function $\mathsf{amb}_A : \mathbb{N} \to \mathbb{N}$ is defined such that $\mathsf{amb}_A(n)$ is the maximum of the ambiguities of words that are of length n or less. Here $\mathbb{N}$ refers to the set of natural numbers. Observe, that amb_A is nondecreasing by definition. This definition fits that for UFAs previously given, because an NFA A is unambiguous if the ambiguity of any word is either zero or one; in the latter case we may also say that A is a 1-*ambiguous* NFA. Moreover, automaton A is called *finitely* (*polynomial*, *exponential*, respectively) ambiguous if amb_A is bounded by a constant (polynomial, exponential, respectively) function f such that $\mathsf{amb}_A(n) \leq f(n)$,

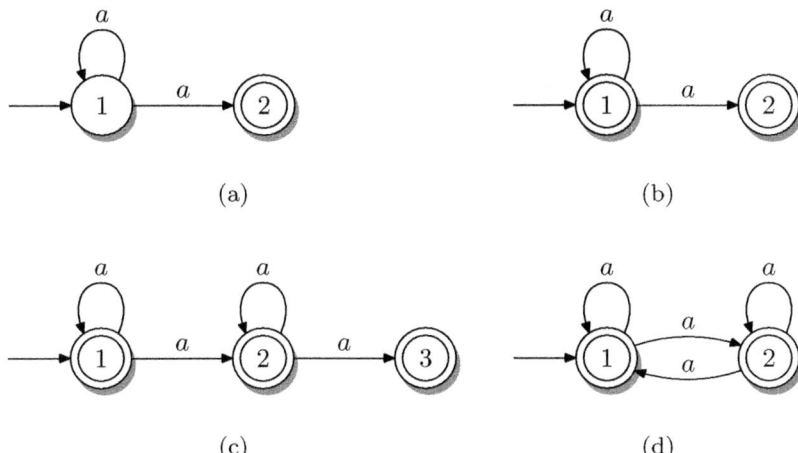

Fig. 4. NFAs A with different degrees of ambiguity: (a) UFA, (b) FNA with amb_A is constant 2, (c) PNA with amb_A is even linear, and (d) ENA. These automata drawings also nicely illustrate the structural characterizations of (strictly) polynomial and (strictly) exponential ambiguity presented in Theorem 11.

for every $n \in \mathbb{N}$—see Figure 5 for (unary) NFAs with different degrees of ambiguity. We abbreviate finitely (polynomial, exponential, respectively) automata by FNA (PNA, ENA, respectively). It is easy to see for any NFA A we have $\mathsf{amb}_A(n) \leq |Q|^n$, where Q is the state set of A, i.e., every NFA is exponential ambiguous. We mention in passing that in [4] necessary and sufficient structural conditions on NFAs were utilized to distinguish between exponential, polynomial, bounded, and k-bounded ambiguity, and it was shown that these *ambiguity problems*, i.e., determining whether the degree of ambiguity of a given NFA is exponential, polynomial, constantly bounded, k-bounded, where k is a fixed integer, or unambiguous are all NL-complete. These structural characterizations read as follows [33,57,71] (cf. Figure 4) An automaton is *strictly* ambiguous of a certain degree, if it is ambiguous of this degree, but not of any lower degree in the ambiguity hierarchy induced by the classes above.

Theorem 11 (Structural Characterization of NFAs Ambiguities). *Let A be an NFA with state set Q and input alphabet Σ, in which all states are useful.[1] Then we have the following structural characterizations of (strictly) finitely, polynomially, and exponentially ambiguities on finite automata:*

1. *Automaton A is strictly exponentially ambiguous if and only if there exists a state $q \in Q$ and a word $w \in \Sigma^+$ such that there is more than one computation from state q to q reading word w.*
2. *Automaton A is strictly polynomially ambiguous if and only if A is not exponentially ambiguous and there exists different states $p, q \in Q$ and a*

---

[1] A state q is *useful* if it is reachable from the initial state and one can reach at least one final state from q.

word $w \in \Sigma^+$ such that there are computations from state p to itself, from state p to q, and from state q to itself, all reading the same word w.

3. *Automaton A is finitely ambiguous if and only if A is neither strictly exponentially nor strictly polynomially ambiguous.*

Next we consider the relation between the types of ambiguity to the relative succinctness in the number of states for NFAs. This is still a vivid area of research, even after more than 30 years since one of the first results on UFAs simulations appeared in [62].

4.1   Ambiguity and the Succinctness of Representation

Once quantified ambiguity has come into play it is interesting to explore how several structural and computational parameters relate to the degree of ambiguity. Is a certain parameter independent of the ambiguity? If not, what are the precise relations? This subsection is devoted to discuss the connections between the degree of ambiguity and the succinctness of the representation, that is, the necessary number of states.

Recall that by definition

$$\text{DFA} \leq_p \text{UFA} \leq_p \text{FNA} \leq_p \text{PNA} \leq_p \text{ENA} =_p \text{NFA},$$

where $C_1 =_p C_2$ is a short hand notation for $C_1 \leq_p C_2$ and $C_2 \leq_p C_1$. The following separation results are known (not listing the already reported results on the relations between DFAs, UFAs, and NFAs): DFA $<_p$ UFA [45,48,61,65], UFA $<_p$ FNA [48,57,61], PNA $<_p$ NFA [32,47], and the intermediate relation between FNAs and PNAs turned out to be very complicated to separate. Several attempts to prove it failed, see, e.g., [32,57], until recently, where this long standing open problem was solved in the affirmative, resulting in FNA $<_p$ PNA [30]. These separation results can be summarized as follows:

Theorem 12 (Simulations of NFAs with Different Ambiguities). *The following separation results on NFA with different degrees of ambiguity are known:*

1. *For every $n \geq 1$, there is an n-state NFA A (having exponential ambiguity) such that any PNA accepting $L(A)$ has at least $2^n - 1$ states.*
2. *For every $k, r \geq 1$, there is a $k \cdot r^{O(1)}$-state NFA with ambiguity $O(n^k)$ such that any NFA accepting $L(A)$ has an exponential (in k and r) number of states, if ambiguity $o(n^k)$ or finite ambiguity is required.*
3. *For every $n \geq 1$, there is an n-state FNA A such that any UFA accepting $L(A)$ has at least $2^n - 1$ states. This also holds true when changing FNA to UFA and UFA to DFA.*

The given bounds in the first and last results are known to be tight.

Next we investigate the question whether there is a relation between ambiguity and the amount of nondeterminism used during the computation.

4.2   Ambiguity and the Amount of Nondeterminism

Nondeterminism has started to be seen as an additional limited resource at the disposal of time or space bounded computations in [7,37]. The concept of limited nondeterminism in finite automata is more generally studied in [12,38]. In the latter reference a bound on the number of nondeterministic steps allowed during a computation as well as on the maximal number of choices for every nondeterministic step is imposed. Since in a certain sense the degree of ambiguity restricts nondeterministic computations, it is suspenseful to explore the question whether there is a relation between the degree of ambiguity and the degree of nondeterminism.

Here, the nondeterminism is measured dynamically by counting the number of guesses an automaton has to make [13]. More precisely, for an NFA $A = (Q, \Sigma, \delta, q_0, F)$, the *amount of guessing* of a single move $\delta(q, a)$, for $q \in Q$ and $a \in \Sigma$, is defined to be $\log_2(|\delta(q, a)|)$. This concept is extended additively to computations by adding the amounts of the single steps. Then for each $w \in L(A)$ the amount of guessing, referred to $\mathsf{guess}_A(w)$, is the minimum over all accepting computations on w, and the guessing function guess_A is defined such that $\mathsf{guess}_A(n)$ is the maximum of the amounts of guessing of words in $L(A)$ that are of length n or less. Note that, in general, $\mathsf{guess}_A(n)$ is not an integer. If the NFA branches to at most two states in every step, then guess_A simply counts the number of nondeterministic steps. Moreover, guess_A counts a branch to 2^k successor states as equal to k branches to two successor states.

Concerning the relation between the amount of nondeterminism and the degree of ambiguity, it is illustrated in [13] that finite automata A with constant or linear nondeterminism, that is, guess_A is a constant or linear function, can be of all types UFA, FNA, PNA, and ENA. So, no prediction can be made about the degree of ambiguity. Figure 4 shows the four types of ambiguity in question for NFAs with a *linear* amount of nondeterminism, and Figure 5 depicts examples for NFAs with a *constant* amount of nondeterminism. The surprising result obtained in [13] revealed that the situation is different for the intermediate level of nondeterminism. The subtle relation between the two concepts is that an automaton with a non-constant but sublinear guessing function must have an infinite degree of ambiguity. Furthermore, it is shown that for each $k \geq 1$ there is, in fact, an NFA A with $\mathsf{guess}_A(n) \in \Theta(n^{1/k})$. The key result of [13] is the following trade-off lemma.

Lemma 13. *If A is an n-state NFA and $w \in L(A)$ is such that there is no word $v \in L(A)$ with $|v| < |w|$ and $\mathsf{guess}_A(v) \geq \mathsf{guess}_A(w)$, then*

$$\frac{n^{\mathsf{amb}_A(w)}(\mathsf{amb}_A(w)\, \mathsf{guess}_A(w) + 1)}{|w|} > 2^{-n}.$$

For a given NFA A the number 2^{-n} is a positive constant. So, the lemma can be interpreted such that an input that requires few nondeterminism at the same time causes a high degree of ambiguity. The next theorem [13] is an immediate consequence of the trade-off lemma.

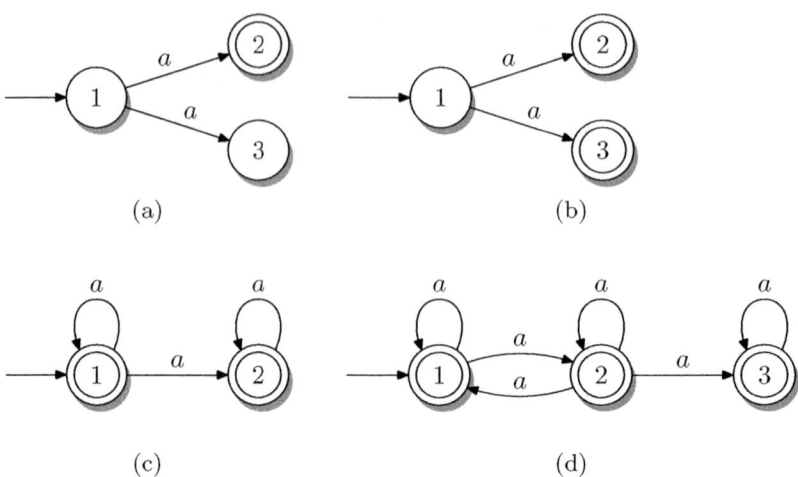

Fig. 5. NFAs A with a *constant* amount of nondeterminism and different degrees of ambiguity: (a) UFA, (b) FNA with amb_A is constant 2, (c) PNA with amb_A is linear, and (d) ENA

Theorem 14. *Every NFA with a non-constant but sublinear guessing function has an infinite degree of ambiguity.*

4.3   Finite Ambiguity and the Structure of Finite Automata

The characterizations of finite automata with different degrees of ambiguity already discussed in Theorem 11 are with respect to the inner structure of the finite automata. From this point of view the relation between the number of states and the amount of ambiguity are worth studying. Since the example given in Figure 4(d) shows that there is 2-state NFA with exponential ambiguity, the question for upper and lower bounds on the *finite* degree of ambiguity of n-state nondeterministic finite automata is of particular interest.

   In connection with the questions asking for the decidability of the finiteness of a finitely generated monoid of matrices with entries in the natural numbers $\mathbb{N}$, (or in a larger semiring), and for an algorithm which computes the degree of an NFA, rough upper bounds have been derived in the late seventies. In three papers it was independently obtained that the degree of ambiguity of a finitely ambiguous n-state NFA with input alphabet Σ is at most (1) $n^{2^{3^{3n^2}+1}}$, (2) $n^{f(n,|\Sigma|)}$, where f is a recursive function, and (3) $2^n n^{2n} 2^{4n^3}$. A systematic study of this problem started in [71], where the next theorem has been shown.

Theorem 15. *Let A be an n-state FNA. Then amb_A is at most $5^{n/2} n^n$.*

By reduction, Theorem 15 can be generalized to NFAs with λ-moves. The upper bound has slightly be improved in the context of formal power series. In [39] it was decreased to $2^{1+k_2 n} n^n$, where $k_2 < 0.7956$. In order to compare the results note that $5^{n/2} n^n = 2^{k_1 n}$, where $k_1 \approx 1.161$.

A so-called *chain-NFA* has a certain inner structure. Roughly speaking, the transition graph representing a chain-NFA consists of strongly connected components (SCC), say $Q_1, Q_2, \ldots, Q_k$ acting as chain links, such that there is a single initial state in Q_1, a single accepting state in Q_k, and exactly one transition from Q_i to Q_{i+1}, for $1 \le i \le k-1$. A chain-NFA can be seen as a sequence of modules which have to be passed through in a one-way fashion. The upper bound for chain-NFAs is much lower than for arbitrary NFAs [71]:

Theorem 16. *Let A be an n-state chain FNA. Then amb_A is at most n^n.*

Now we turn also to lower bounds. In order to capture classes C of NFAs defined with respect to their inner structures more generally, let $C_f \subseteq C$ denote the subclass including exactly all FNAs from C, and set

$$\mathsf{amb}_C(n, m) = \max\{ \mathsf{amb}_A(m) \mid A \in C_f \text{ and } A \text{ has } n \text{ states} \}.$$

By Theorem 15 $\mathsf{amb}_C(n, m)$ is at most $5^{n/2} n^n$. In Table 1 we summarize the results for several subclasses of NFAs. The proofs can be found in [70,71]. Notably, for several subclasses upper and lower bounds are tight (in the order of magnitude $2^{\Theta(n)}$).

5 (Un)ambiguous Pushdown Automata

In this section we consider the descriptional capacity of unambiguous as well as finitely ambiguous pushdown automata. In particular, the relative succinctness of those machines among each other and to finite automata are discussed. It turned out that the situation is completely different compared to the previously presented finite automata simulations. First, these pushdown devices induce a strict hierarchy of languages [19], which was not the case for finite automata. Moreover, and even more importantly, we will come across a qualitatively new

Table 1. Upper and lower bounds on the ambiguities for several subclasses of NFAs in relation to the number of states n

Automata class C	Ambiguity amb_A	
	lower bound	upper bound
NFAs	$2^{1.0221 \cdot n}$, for $n = 0 \bmod 64$	$2^{1.161 \cdot n} n^n$
chain-NFAs	$2^{1.0221 \cdot n}$, for $n = 0 \bmod 64$	n^n
chain-NFAs with 2 SCCs	2^{n-2}, for $n \ge 2$	2^{n-1}
NFAs for finite languages	$\binom{n}{\lfloor (n+1)/2 \rfloor}$	$\binom{n}{\lfloor (n+1)/2 \rfloor}$
NFAs for unary languages	2^{n-1}	2^{n-1}

phenomenon first observed in [51], the so-called *non-recursive trade-offs*. That is, there is no recursive function bounding the succinctness gap (for non-trivial simulations). Before we report on results we briefly have to discuss some issues on measuring the size of pushdown automata.

Measuring the size of a pushdown automaton by its number of states, as is done for finite automata, is clearly ineligible. It is well known that every pushdown automaton can effectively be converted into an equivalent one having just one sole state [29]. But, in general, one has to pay with an increase in the number of stack symbols, and determinism or unambiguity is not preserved. For DPDAs accepting by empty pushdown, the computational capacity is known to increase strictly with the number of states [19]. So, measuring the size of a (deterministic) pushdown automaton by its number of stack symbols is also too crude. In fact, it is also possible to reduce the number of stack symbols if one pays with an increase in the number of states. The precise relations between states and stack symbols have been shown in [15] and [16]. So, the number of states as well as the number of stack symbols have to be considered to measure the size of a pushdown automaton. But even their product is still insufficient. For example, for all integers $n \geq 1$ the language $L_n = (a^n)^*$ can be accepted by a pushdown automaton with two states and two stack symbols that, in one move, is able to push n symbols onto the stack. So, in addition, we have to take into account the lengths of the right-hand sides of the transition rules which can get long when a pushdown automaton pushes lots of symbols during single transitions. Therefore, the size of a pushdown automaton $A = (Q, \Sigma, \Gamma, \delta, q_0, Z_0, F)$ is measured as $|Q| \cdot |\Sigma| \cdot |\Gamma| \cdot h$, where h is the length of the longest word pushed in a single transition.

5.1 Simulations

Here we present some fundamental results in connection with the representation of *regular languages by pushdown automata*. In [64] the decidability of regularity for DPDAs has been shown by a deep proof. This effective procedure revealed the following upper bound for the trade-off in descriptional complexity when DPDAs accepting regular languages are converted into DFAs. Given a DPDA with $n > 1$ states and $t > 1$ stack symbols that accepts a regular language. Then the number of states which is sufficient for an equivalent DFA is bounded by an expression of the order $t^{n^{n^n}}$. Later this triple exponential upper bound has been improved by one level of exponentiation in [66].

Theorem 17 (DPDA by DFA Simulation). *Let A be a deterministic pushdown automaton with n states, t stack symbols, and h is the length of the longest word pushed in a single transition. If $L(A)$ is regular then $2^{2^{O(n^2 \log n + \log t + \log h)}}$ states are sufficient for a DFA to accept the language $L(A)$.*

In the levels of exponentiation this bound is tight, since the following double exponential lower bound has been obtained in [51]. It is open whether the precise lower bound or the precise upper bound can be improved in order to obtain matching bounds.

Theorem 18 (DPDA by DFA Simulation). *Let $n \geq 1$. Then there is a language L_n accepted by a deterministic pushdown automaton of size $O(n^3)$, and each equivalent DFA has at least 2^{2^n} states.*

It is clear that these bounds on the simulation by DFAs implicitly imply also bounds for NFAs. While we deal with finite automata simulations of NPDAs in the next subsection, to our knowledge the remaining simulation of UPDAs accepting regular languages by finite automata is an open problem in the sense that (1) it is not known whether regularity for UPDAs is decidable and (2) whether the trade-off between UPDAs and finite automata is non-recursive or not. Note, that the succinctness result for UPDAs and finite automata corresponds to the decidability result of regularity for UPDAs as follows: assume that $f(n)$ is an upper bound on the number of states for the simulation of an n-size UPDA by a finite automaton. To decide whether a UPDA A accepts a regular language, just enumerate all finite automata with fewer states than $f(n)$ and check equivalence with A, which is decidable by [58].

Finally let us mention that the situation on simulations involving pushdown automata is different again, to the general case, when pushdown automata accepting unary languages are considered. This is somehow comparable to the case of finite automata. It is well known that every unary context-free language is regular [9]. From the viewpoint of descriptional complexity, unary DPDAs and NPDAs have been investigated in, e.g., [54,55]. For further results concerning simulations involving pushdown automata we refer to the comprehensive survey [26].

5.2 Non-recursive Trade-Offs

Now we present some pushdown automata simulations that cause non-recursive trade-offs. To keep the presentation simple, we introduce only the necessary terminology, a more general and elaborately treatment is given in [26]. Assume that we have two classes of automata C_1 and C_2 which induce a non-empty intersection on the corresponding languages accepted by these types of devices. Then a *non-recursive trade-off* between C_1 and C_2, means that there is an infinite family of languages accepted by both device types, such that when changing from the C_1-descriptors to equivalent minimal C_2-descriptors, the blow-up in *size* cannot be bounded by any recursive function. A cornerstone of descriptional complexity is the result of Meyer and Fischer [51] who showed for the first time a non-recursive trade-off. It appears between context-free grammars or equivalently NPDAs and finite automata. In Theorem 17 we have seen that the trade-off between DPDAs and finite automata is recursive, where the proof relies on the fact that regularity is decidable for DPDAs. This goes hand in hand with the undecidability of regularity for NPDAs

Theorem 19 (NPDA by FA Simulation). *The trade-off between NPDAs and finite automata is non-recursive.*

Even the computational power of DPDAs is not enough, similarly, the non-recursive trade-off between NPDAs and DPDAs follows (cf. [61]):

Theorem 20 (NPDA by DPDA Simulation). *The trade-off between NPDAs and DPDAs is non-recursive.*

Most proofs of non-recursive trade-offs that appear in the literature basically rely on one of two different proof schemes. One fundamental technique is due to Hartmanis [21]. In [22] a generalization is developed that relates semi-decidability to trade-offs and a slightly generalized and unified form of this technique can be found in [40]. When applying these techniques very often non-semi-decidable properties of Turing machines are utilized by encoding complex Turing machine computations in small automata [20]. To this end encodings of *(in)valid computations of Turing machines* and variants thereof are considered. Nevertheless, even simpler proof schemes only using (full) TRIO-closure properties of the underlying formal language families and semi-decidability of certain decision problems were recently developed and applied in [18]. Recall that a formal language family is called a *TRIO* (*full TRIO*, respectively) if it is closed under λ-free morphism (general morphism, respectively), inverse morphism, and intersection with regular languages [29].

Here we are particularly interested in the remaining trade-offs caused by the devices "in between" NPDAs and FAs, that is in the trade-offs between NPDAs and UPDAs as well as between UPDAs and DPDAs. The next result from [67] compares DPDAs and unambiguous context-free grammars or equivalently UPDAs. It exploits the following crucial result on the size of DPDAs. If for some DPDA A with state set Q and set of stack symbols Γ the string w is the shortest string such that wa and wb are accepted, then there is a positive constant k such that $|Q| \cdot |\Gamma| \geq (\log |w|)^k$. This can be used to show the next non-recursive trade-off:

Theorem 21 (UPDA by DPDA Simulation). *The trade-off between UPDAs and DPDAs is non-recursive.*

The remaining trade-off between NPDAs and UPDAs has been shown in [62].

Theorem 22 (NPDA by UPDA Simulation). *The trade-off between NPDAs and UPDAs is non-recursive.*

5.3   Bounded Ambiguity and Bounded Nondeterminism

The quantitative study of nondeterminism in context-free languages originates from [69], where two measures for the amount of nondeterminism in pushdown automata are proposed. By bounding the number of nondeterministic steps dependent on the length of the input, a hierarchy of three classes is obtained. A modification of the measure can be found in [59]. The second measure depends on the depth of the directed acyclic graph that represents a given pushdown automaton. The corresponding proof of an infinite nondeterministic hierarchy of properly included classes is completed in [60]. The so-called *branching* as measure of nondeterminism in connection with pushdown automata, introduced for finite automata [12], is studied in [14,23]. In [14] lower bounds for the minimum amount of nondeterminism to accept certain context-free languages are established. Pushdown automata with limited nondeterminism are investigated in [41] from the viewpoint of context-dependent nondeterminism, and in [42] from the viewpoint of regulated nondeterminism.

Considering a computation of a pushdown automaton we call a single step nondeterministic if the automaton has more than one choice for its move. The *branching* of the step is defined to be the number of choices. The branching of a computation is the product of the branchings of all steps of the computation. In order to be more precise, let A be a NPDA, then we define the branching branch_A as follows:

1. The *branching of a configuration* c is $\text{branch}_A(c) = |\{\, c' \mid c \vdash c' \,\}|$.
2. A sequence of configurations (computation) $C = c_0 \vdash c_1 \vdash \cdots \vdash c_k$ has branching
$$\prod_{i=0}^{k-1} \text{branch}_A(c_i).$$
3. For words $w \in L(A)$ we define the branching as
$$\text{branch}_A(w) = \min\{\, \text{branch}_A(C) \mid C \text{ is an accepting computation on } w \,\}.$$
4. Finally, let the *branching of A* be $\text{branch}_A = \sup\{\, \text{branch}_A(w) \mid w \in L(A) \,\}$.

In an NPDA A whose branching is bounded by a constant k all computations can be cut off when the branching exceeds k without changing the accepted language. So, the branching of an NPDA tells us up to which width the computation tree of some input word has to be examined until an accepting computation is found. The branching of a word is not necessarily equal to the number of computations on this word. Moreover, there is no relation between the ambiguity and the branching of an NPDA, since there are NPDAs A with $\text{amb}_A = 1$ and $\text{branch}_A = \infty$ as well as with $\text{amb}_A = \infty$ and $\text{branch}_A = 1$.

In [3] and [23] a two-dimensional infinite hierarchy dependent on the finite degree of ambiguity and the finite branching in between the deterministic and nondeterministic context-free languages is obtained. Denote the classes of pushdown automata with ambiguity and branching bounded by a constant k by $\text{NPDA}(\text{amb} \leq k)$ and $\text{NPDA}(\text{branch} \leq k)$. If both resources are bounded at the same time, we write $\text{NPDA}(\text{amb} \leq k, \text{branch} \leq k')$. Clearly, for every k, we have the inclusions[2]
$$\text{NPDA}(\text{amb} \leq k) \subseteq \text{NPDA}(\text{amb} \leq k + 1)$$
and
$$\text{NPDA}(\text{branch} \leq k) \subseteq \text{NPDA}(\text{branch} \leq k + 1).$$

In [23] it is proven that $\text{NPDA}(\text{branch} \leq k) \subseteq \text{NPDA}(\text{amb} \leq k)$. Moreover, it is shown that all of these inclusions are proper. This means that every time the

---

[2] In abuse of notation the three inclusions yet to come are meant w.r.t. the languages generated by the corresponding pushdown automata with limited ambiguity and/or branching.

allowed amount of ambiguity or the allowed amount of nondeterminism in an NPDA is increased by just one, a more powerful device is obtained. Intuitively, the corresponding language families are close together. Nevertheless, there are non-recursive trade-offs between levels of the hierarchy. In [3] the next theorem has been shown.

Theorem 23 (NPDA with Bounded Ambiguity Simulation). *Let* $k \geq 1$. *Then the trade-off between* NPDA($amb \leq k + 1$) *and* NPDA($amb \leq k$) *is non-recursive.*

The result has been generalized in [23]:

Theorem 24 (NPDA with Bounded Ambiguity and Bounded Branching by NPDA with Bounded Ambiguity Simulation). *Let* $k \geq 1$. *Then the trade-offs between*

1. NPDA($amb \leq k + 1, branch \leq k + 1$) *and* NPDA($amb \leq k$), *and*
2. NPDA($amb \leq 1, branch \leq k + 1$) *and* NPDA($branch \leq k$)

are non-recursive.

Finally, in addition to the non-recursive trade-offs a nontrivial recursive trade-off is shown in [23].

Theorem 25 (NPDA with Bounded Branching by NPDA with Bounded Ambiguity and Branching Simulation). *Let* $k \geq 1$ *and* A *be an* n-*size* NPDA *belonging to* NPDA($branch \leq k$). *Then* $2^{O(n)}$ *states are sufficient for an* NPDA *from* NPDA($amb \leq k, branch \leq k$) *to accept* $L(A)$.

References

1. Birget, J.C.: Intersection and union of regular languages and state complexity. Inform. Process. Lett. 43, 185–190 (1992)
2. Björklund, H., Martens, W.: The tractability frontier for NFA minimization. In: Aceto, L., Damgård, I., Goldberg, L.A., Halldórsson, M.M., Ingólfsdóttir, A., Walukiewicz, I. (eds.) ICALP 2008, Part II. LNCS, vol. 5126, pp. 27–38. Springer, Heidelberg (2008)
3. Borchardt, I.: Nonrecursive tradeoffs between context-free grammars with different constant ambiguity. Diploma thesis, Universität Frankfurt (1992) (in German)
4. Cho, S., Huynh, D.T.: The parallel complexity of finite-state automata problems. Inform. Comput. 97, 1–22 (1992)
5. Chrobak, M.: Finite automata and unary languages. Theoret. Comput. Sci. 47, 149–158 (1986)
6. Chrobak, M.: Errata to "finite automata and unary languages". Theoret. Comput. Sci. 302, 497–498 (2003)
7. Fischer, P.C., Kintala, C.M.R.: Real-time computations with restricted nondeterminism. Math. Systems Theory 12, 219–231 (1979)
8. Gill, A., Kou, L.T.: Multiple-entry finite automata. J. Comput. System Sci. 9, 1–19 (1974)

9. Ginsburg, S., Rice, H.G.: Two families of languages related to ALGOL. J. ACM 9(3), 350–371 (1962)
10. Glaister, I., Shallit, J.: A lower bound technique for the size of nondeterministic finite automata. Inform. Process. Lett. 59, 75–77 (1996)
11. Gold, E.M.: Complexity of automaton identification from given data. Inform. Control 37, 302–320 (1978)
12. Goldstine, J., Kintala, C.M.R., Wotschke, D.: On measuring nondeterminism in regular languages. Inform. Comput. 86, 179–194 (1990)
13. Goldstine, J., Leung, H., Wotschke, D.: On the relation between ambiguity and nondeterminism in finite automata. Inform. Comput. 100, 261–270 (1992)
14. Goldstine, J., Leung, H., Wotschke, D.: Measuring nondeterminism in pushdown automata. J. Comput. System Sci. 71, 440–466 (2005)
15. Goldstine, J., Price, J.K., Wotschke, D.: On reducing the number of states in a PDA. Math. Systems Theory 15, 315–321 (1982)
16. Goldstine, J., Price, J.K., Wotschke, D.: On reducing the number of stack symbols in a PDA. Math. Systems Theory 26, 313–326 (1993)
17. Gruber, H., Holzer, M.: Finding lower bounds for nondeterministic state complexity is hard (extended abstract). In: Ibarra, O.H., Dang, Z. (eds.) DLT 2006. LNCS, vol. 4036, pp. 363–374. Springer, Heidelberg (2006)
18. Gruber, H., Holzer, M., Kutrib, M.: On measuring non-recursive trade-offs. In: Descriptional Complexity of Formal Systems (DCFS 2009), pp. 187–198. Otto-von-Guericke-Universität Magdeburg (2009)
19. Harrison, M.A.: Introduction to Formal Language Theory. Addison-Wesley, Reading (1978)
20. Hartmanis, J.: Context-free languages and Turing machine computations. In: Proc. Symposia in Applied Mathematics, vol. 19, pp. 42–51 (1967)
21. Hartmanis, J.: On the succinctness of different representations of languages. SIAM J. Comput. 9, 114–120 (1980)
22. Hartmanis, J.: On Gödel speed-up and succinctness of language representations. Theoret. Comput. Sci. 26, 335–342 (1983)
23. Herzog, C.: Pushdown automata with bounded nondeterminism and bounded ambiguity. Theoret. Comput. Sci. 181, 141–157 (1997)
24. Holzer, M., Kutrib, M.: Descriptional and computational complexity of finite automata. In: Dediu, A.H., Ionescu, A.M., Martín-Vide, C. (eds.) LATA 2009. LNCS, vol. 5457, pp. 23–42. Springer, Heidelberg (2009)
25. Holzer, M., Kutrib, M.: Nondeterministic finite automata - Recent results on the descriptional and computational complexity. Int. J. Found. Comput. Sci. 20, 563–580 (2009)
26. Holzer, M., Kutrib, M.: Descriptional complexity – An introductory survey. In: Scientific Applications of Language Methods. Imperial College Press, London (to appear, 2010)
27. Holzer, M., Salomaa, K., Yu, S.: On the state complexity of k-entry deterministic finite automata. J. Autom., Lang. Comb. 6, 453–466 (2001)
28. Hopcroft, J.E.: An $n \log n$ algorithm for minimizing the state in a finite automaton. In: The Theory of Machines and Computations, pp. 189–196. Academic Press, London (1971)
29. Hopcroft, J.E., Ullman, J.D.: Introduction to Automata Theory, Languages, and Computation. Addison-Wesley, Reading (1979)
30. Hromkovič, J., Schnitger, G.: Ambiguity and communication. In: Theoretical Aspects of Computer Science (STACS 2009), Dagstuhl, Germany. LIPICS, vol. 3, pp. 107–118 (2009)

31. Hromkovič, J.: Communication Complexity and Parallel Computing. Springer, Heidelberg (1997)
32. Hromkovič, J., Seibert, S., Karhumäki, J., Klauck, H., Schnitger, G.: Communication complexity method for measuring nondeterminism in finite automata. Inform. Comput. 172, 202–217 (2002)
33. Ibarra, O.H., Ravikumar, B.: On sparseness, ambiguity and other decision problems for acceptors and transducers. In: Monien, B., Vidal-Naquet, G. (eds.) STACS 1986. LNCS, vol. 210, pp. 171–179. Springer, Heidelberg (1986)
34. Jiang, T., McDowell, E., Ravikumar, B.: The structure and complexity of minimal NFA's over a unary alphabet. Int. J. Found. Comput. Sci. 2, 163–182 (1991)
35. Jiang, T., Ravikumar, B.: Minimal NFA problems are hard. SIAM J. Comput. 22, 1117–1141 (1993)
36. Kappes, M.: Descriptional complexity of deterministic finite automata with multiple initial states. J. Autom., Lang. Comb. 5, 269–278 (2000)
37. Kintala, C.M.R.: Computations with a Restricted Number of Nondeterministic Steps. PhD thesis, Pennsylvania State University (1977)
38. Kintala, C.M.R., Wotschke, D.: Amounts of nondeterminism in finite automata. Acta Inform. 13, 199–204 (1980)
39. Kuich, W.: Finite automata and ambiguity. Report 253 of the IIG, Technische Universität Graz (1988)
40. Kutrib, M.: The phenomenon of non-recursive trade-offs. Int. J. Found. Comput. Sci. 16, 957–973 (2005)
41. Kutrib, M., Malcher, A.: Context-dependent nondeterminism for pushdown automata. Theoret. Comput. Sci. 376, 101–111 (2007)
42. Kutrib, M., Malcher, A., Werlein, L.: Regulated nondeterminism in pushdown automata. Theoret. Comput. Sci. 410, 3447–3460 (2009)
43. Landau, E.: Über die Maximalordnung der Permutationen gegebenen Grades. Archiv der Math. und Phys. 3, 92–103 (1903)
44. Landau, E.: Handbuch der Lehre von der Verteilung der Primzahlen. Teubner (1900)
45. Leiss, E.L.: Succinct representation of regular languages by Boolean automata. Theoret. Comput. Sci. 13, 323–330 (1981)
46. Leung, H.: Structurally unambiguous finite automata. In: Ibarra, O.H., Yen, H.-C. (eds.) CIAA 2006. LNCS, vol. 4094, pp. 198–207. Springer, Heidelberg (2006)
47. Leung, H.: Separating exponentially ambiguous finite automata from polynomially ambiguous finite automata. SIAM J. Comput. 27, 1073–1082 (1998)
48. Leung, H.: Descriptional complexity of NFA of different ambiguity. Int. J. Found. Comput. Sci. 16, 975–984 (2005)
49. Lupanov, O.B.: A comparison of two types of finite sources. Problemy Kybernetiki 9, 321–326 (1963) (in Russian); German translation: Über den Vergleich zweier Typen endlicher Quellen. Probleme der Kybernetik 6, 328–335 (1966)
50. Malcher, A.: Minimizing finite automata is computationally hard. Theoret. Comput. Sci. 327, 375–390 (2004)
51. Meyer, A.R., Fischer, M.J.: Economy of description by automata, grammars, and formal systems. In: Symposium on Switching and Automata Theory (SWAT 1971), pp. 188–191. IEEE, Los Alamitos (1971)
52. Moore, F.R.: On the bounds for state-set size in the proofs of equivalence between deterministic, nondeterministic, and two-way finite automata. IEEE Trans. Comput. 20, 1211–1214 (1971)
53. Okhotin, A.: A study of unambiguous finite automata over a one-letter alphabet. TUCS Technical Report No 951, Turku Centre for Computer Science (2009)

54. Pighizzini, G.: Deterministic pushdown automata and unary languages. In: Ibarra, O.H., Ravikumar, B. (eds.) CIAA 2008. LNCS, vol. 5148, pp. 232–241. Springer, Heidelberg (2008)
55. Pighizzini, G., Shallit, J., Wang, M.W.: Unary context-free grammars and pushdown automata, descriptional complexity and auxiliary space lower bounds. J. Comput. System Sci. 65, 393–414 (2002)
56. Rabin, M.O., Scott, D.: Finite automata and their decision problems. IBM J. Res. Dev. 3, 114–125 (1959)
57. Ravikumar, B., Ibarra, O.H.: Relating the type of ambiguity of finite automata to the succinctness of their representation. SIAM J. Comput. 18, 1263–1282 (1989)
58. Salomaa, A., Soittola, M.: Automata-theoretic Aspects of Formal Power Series. Springer, Heidelberg (1978)
59. Salomaa, K., Yu, S.: Limited nondeterminism for pushdown automata. Bull. EATCS 50, 186–193 (1993)
60. Salomaa, K., Yu, S.: Measures of nondeterminism for pushdown automata. J. Comput. System Sci. 49, 362–374 (1994)
61. Schmidt, E.M.: Succinctness of Dscriptions of Context-Free, Regular and Finite Languages. PhD thesis, Cornell University, Ithaca, NY (1978)
62. Schmidt, E.M., Szymanski, T.G.: Succinctness of descriptions of unambiguous context-free languages. SIAM J. Comput. 6, 547–553 (1977)
63. Sipser, M.: Lower bounds on the size of sweeping automata. J. Comput. System Sci. 21, 195–202 (1980)
64. Stearns, R.E.: A regularity test for pushdown machines. Inform. Control 11, 323–340 (1967)
65. Stearns, R.E., Hunt III, H.B.: On the equivalence and containment problems for unambiguous regular expressions, regular grammars, and finite automata. SIAM J. Comput. 14, 598–611 (1985)
66. Valiant, L.G.: Regularity and related problems for deterministic pushdown automata. J. ACM 22, 1–10 (1975)
67. Valiant, L.G.: A note on the succinctness of descriptions of deterministic languages. Inform. Control 32, 139–145 (1976)
68. Veloso, P.A.S., Gill, A.: Some remarks on multiple-entry finite automata. J. Comput. System Sci. 18, 304–306 (1979)
69. Vermeir, D., Savitch, W.: On the amount of nondeterminism in pushdown automata. Fund. Inform. 4, 401–418 (1981)
70. Weber, A.: Über die Mehrdeutigkeit und Wertigkeit von endlichen Automaten und Transducern. Dissertation, Institut für Informatik, Johann Wolfgang Goethe-Universität Frankfurt am Main (1987) (in German)
71. Weber, A., Seidl, H.: On the degree of ambiguity of finite automata. Theoret. Comput. Sci. 88, 325–349 (1991)

Symbolic and Compositional Reachability for Timed Automata

Kim Guldstrand Larsen

Department of Computer Science, Aalborg University, Denmark
kgl@cs.aau.dk

Extended Abstract

The model-checker UPPAAL [LPY97] is based on the theory of timed automata [AD90] and its modeling language offers additional features such as networks of timed automata, clocks and stop-watches, synchronizing over synchronous and broadcast channels, discrete variables ranging over bounded integers or structured types (arrays and records) as well as user-defined types and functions.

The first version of UPPAAL was released in 1995 and since then there has been a continuous and still on-going development of datastructures and algorithms for its verification engine with particular emphasis on efficient methods for reachability and nested reachability problems [BDL+10]. Over the years, the tool has consistently gained in performance and has by now been applied to the verification of numerous industrial case-studies[1]. More recently the branch CORA [ALTP01, BFH+01] has emerged supporting cost-minimal reachability for priced timed automata, thus allowing for the optimization of several planning and scheduling problems to be solving using reachability checking [IKY+08, HvdNV06, AM01].

In the following we give an overview of the development of the datastuctures and algorithms underlying the verification engines of UPPAAL and CORA as well as indicate on-going research directions.

Symbolic Exploration of Timed Automata. In UPPAAL the basic reachability algorithm is based on a forward, *on*-the-fly symbolic exploration of the state-space of the given timed automaton. In contrast to a classical (backwards) fixpoint computation, the principle of on-the-fly exploration allows to settle (nested) reachability properties without considering unreachable states, and – depending on the search order – possibly to terminate after having only explored a small portion of the reachable state-space.

Various datastructures are used for the symbolic exploration including Difference Bounded Matrices [Dil89, Bel58], Minimal Constraint Representation [LLPY97] and Clock Difference Diagrams [BLP+99]. These datastructures allow a tradeoff between the compactness in the representation of state-spaces and the efficiency by which symbolic successors may be computed during exploration. For (early) termination of exploration it is crucial that the chosen datastructure allow for the efficient checking of inclusion between state-sets.

---

[1] See www.uppaal.com for a detailed list.

A. Kučera and I. Potapov (Eds.): RP 2010, LNCS 6227, pp. 24–28, 2010.

Most recently the above datastructures have been used to implement the over approximate analysis of [CL00] for so-called *stop*-watch automata – i.e. timed automata where each location may stop a given sub-set of the clocks. Given its over-approximate nature, reachability problems may only be partially (negatively) answered by the method. However, several applications of this recent feature of UPPAAL to the schedulability analysis of preemptive tasks executing on a single CPU under a given scheduling principle – e.g. Fixed-Priority or Earliest-Deadline-First – indicate that the over-approximation is sufficiently accurate in practice [DKJS09, BHM08, HMB07].

Symbolic Exploration of Priced Timed Automata. The cost-optimal reachability algorithm of CORA is similarly based on an *on*-the-fly algorithm, but applies suitable extensions of the datastructures used in UPPAAL in order to represent not only state-sets, but also the *cost* by which states may be reached. Such cost-information may be represented in a finitary manner by an affine function describing the cost of all the states in a given state-set, and may be dealt with by extended versions of the computation of symbolic successors as well as inclusion between state-sets *with* cost-functions.

Abstractions. Crucial for the termination of the *f*orward symbolic exploration of UPPAAL is the *e*xtrapolation of computed symbolic successors. In extrapolation a state-set is widened taking into account the maximum constants that clocks are compared to: for a given timed automaton, two states only differing with respect to the value of clocks exceeding the corresponding maximum constant are indistinguishable with respect to (location) reachability (in fact the two states are time-abstracted bisimilar [TY96]).

In [BBFL03] a notion of *l*ocation-based extrapolation is introduced allowing the maximum constants used for the widening to be dependent on the location of the timed automaton. This notion is shown to generalize the so-called *a*ctive-clock reduction and has a potential exponential speedup compared with the classical extrapolation.

In [BBLP06, BBLP04] an even coarser extrapolation is introduced and implemented in UPPAAL by distinguishing the maximum constants used in lower and upper bounds. In fact this extrapolation – though exact with respect to (location) reachability – demonstrate performance comparable with the over-approximate *c*onvex-hull abstraction [TY96].

The modeling formalism of UPPAAL allows a very rich set of expressions – involving variables and function-calls – all allowed in comparisons with clocks. In obtaining (location-dependent, lower/upper bound) maximum constants for clocks the possible values of these expressions must be determined. Currently this is done on the basis of the declared type (hence value-range) of the involved variables. However, more exact estimates of maximum constants – and hence coarser extrapolation yielding better performance – could be obtained from a static value-analysis of expressions in the UPPAAL models.

Compositional Reachability Analysis. As all model-checking, timed automata model-checking suffer the so-called *s*tate-space-explosion problem, which refers to the fact that the size of the (symbolic) state-spaces may grow exponentially in the number of components (and clocks) of the (timed automaton) model to be analysed. Several heuristics have been proposed to overcome this problem for timed automaton, including partial order reduction, symmetry reduction, sweep-line method, bounded model-checking and distributed model-checking, several of which are implemented in UPPAAL. An alternative approach for overcoming the problem of state-space explosion is to apply compositional model checking.

One such approach is based on the notion of *quotienting* for parallel composition: given a property ϕ and a parallel system $A \mid B$, the quotient property $\phi \backslash A$ (if it exists) should satsify the following equivalence:

$$A \mid B \models \phi \text{ if and only if } B \models \phi \backslash A$$

Now consider the following typical model checking problem $(P_1 \mid \ldots \mid P_n) \models \phi$, involving a network of n timed automata components. This problem may be settled without having to construct or explore the state-space of the network $(P_1 \mid \ldots \mid P_n)$ simply by quotienting the components P_i one by one into ϕ. To make sure that the intermediate quotient formula are not much larger than the original formula, it is crucial that each quotienting is followed by a *minimization* of the formula. The timed extension of the modal μ-calculus L_ν [LLW95] has been shown to be closed under quotienting with timed automata and the quotient construction and minimization rules been implemented in the tool CMC [LL98a, LL98b], which allows for compositional model checking of network of timed automata.

Another compositional model checking approach is that of *compositional backwards reachability* [LNAB+98, BLA+99]. Again a network $(P_1 \mid \ldots \mid P_n)$ of components (finite state automata, timed automata, etc.) is assumed given. However, here the property to be settled is restricted to that of reachability of a given set of goal states g. The compositional backwards reachability method now consist in computing an increasing sequence of state-sets

$$B_{I_0}(g) \subseteq B_{I_1}(g) \subseteq \cdots \subset B_{I_i}(g) \subseteq \quad \subseteq B(g),$$

until either eventually the full set of states backwards reachable from g is obtained ($B(g)$) or the initial state is found to be included. In the approximations, I_i is a (growing sequence of) subsets of $\{1 \ldots n\}$ and $B_{I_i}(g)$ is the set of states backwards reachable from g only using transitions available from the components $\{P_j$ where $j \in I_i$. Two factor make this approach efficient. Firstly, the set $B_{I_i}(g)$ only constraints the state of the components in I_i and may thus (symbolically) be efficiently represented. Secondly, the set $B_{I_i}(g)$ may be obtained as $B_{I_i}(B_{I_{i-1}}(g))$, thus reusing the previously computed approximation. For finite state systems the method is applied in the commercial tool VISUALSTATE, and for timed systems [Nym02] has made a first promising investigation to be completed.

Discrete Semantics & Concrete Traces. Though the symbolic approaches to verification of timed automata has proven successful on several realistic examples, the computation time for manipulating the corresponding datastructures (e.g. DBMs) may sometimes appear exorbitant. We are currently looking into new ways of performing an explicit state-space exploration of timed automata under discrete-time semantics, which for reachability questions gives identical answers to that of a dens-time semantics for timed automata models with only non-strict bounds on clocks.

Also, the diagnostic (cyclic) traces provided by UPPAAL for (nested) reachability questions are symbolic, and thus requires deep understanding of the symbolic successor computation. To be of better use for the average user in debugging it would be useful to provide concrete traces. A thorough experimental investigation of this has recently been made in [PvV10].

References

[AD90]   Alur, R., Dill, D.: Automata for modeling real-time systems. In: Paterson, M. (ed.) ICALP 1990. LNCS, vol. 443, pp. 322–335. Springer, Heidelberg (1990)

[ALTP01]   Alur, R., La Torre, S., Pappas, G.J.: Optimal Paths in Weighted Timed Automata. In: Di Benedetto, M.D., Sangiovanni-Vincentelli, A.L. (eds.) HSCC 2001. LNCS, vol. 2034, pp. 49–62. Springer, Heidelberg (2001)

[AM01]   Abdeddaïm, Y., Maler, O.: Job-shop scheduling using timed automata. In: Berry, G., Comon, H., Finkel, A. (eds.) CAV 2001. LNCS, vol. 2102, pp. 478–492. Springer, Heidelberg (2001)

[BBFL03]   Behrmann, G., Bouyer, P., Fleury, E., Larsen, K.G.: Static guard analysis in timed automata verification. In: Garavel, H., Hatcliff, J. (eds.) TACAS 2003. LNCS, vol. 2619, pp. 254–277. Springer, Heidelberg (2003)

[BBLP04]   Behrmann, G., Bouyer, P., Larsen, K.G., Pelánek, R.: Lower and upper bounds in zone based abstractions of timed automata. In: Jensen, K., Podelski, A. (eds.) TACAS 2004. LNCS, vol. 2988, pp. 312–326. Springer, Heidelberg (2004)

[BBLP06]   Behrmann, G., Bouyer, P., Larsen, K.G., Pelánek, R.: Lower and upper bounds in zone-based abstractions of timed automata. STTT 8(3), 204–215 (2006)

[BDL$^+$10]   Behrmann, G., David, A., Larsen, K.G., Pettersson, P., Yi, W.: Developing uppaal over 15 years. Software – Practice and Experience (to appear, 2010)

[Bel58]   Bellman, R.: Dynamic programming and stochastic control processes. Information and Control 1(3), 228–239 (1958)

[BFH$^+$01]   Behrmann, G., Fehnker, A., Hune, T., Larsen, K.G., Pettersson, P., Romijn, J., Vaandrager, F.: Minimum-cost reachability for priced timed automata. In: Di Benedetto, M.D., Sangiovanni-Vincentelli, A.L. (eds.) HSCC 2001. LNCS, vol. 2034, pp. 147–161. Springer, Heidelberg (2001)

[BHM08]   Brekling, A.W., Hansen, M.R., Madsen, J.: Models and formal verification of multiprocessor system-on-chips. J. Log. Algebr. Program. 77(1-2), 1–19 (2008)

[BLA$^+$99]   Behrmann, G., Larsen, K.G., Andersen, H.R., Hulgaard, H., Lind-Nielsen, J.: Verification of hierarchical state/event systems using reusability and compositionality. In: Cleaveland, W.R. (ed.) TACAS 1999. LNCS, vol. 1579, pp. 163–177. Springer, Heidelberg (1999)

[BLP$^+$99]   Behrmann, G., Larsen, K.G., Pearson, J., Weise, C., Yi, W.: Efficient timed reachability analysis using clock difference diagrams. In: Halbwachs, N., Peled, D.A. (eds.) CAV 1999. LNCS, vol. 1633, pp. 341–353. Springer, Heidelberg (1999)

[CL00]   Cassez, F., Larsen, K.G.: The impressive power of stopwatches. In: Palamidessi, C. (ed.) CONCUR 2000. LNCS, vol. 1877, pp. 138–152. Springer, Heidelberg (2000)

[Dil89]   Dill, D.L.: Timing assumptions and verification of finite-state concurrent systems. In: Sifakis, J. (ed.) CAV 1989. LNCS, vol. 407, pp. 197–212. Springer, Heidelberg (1990)

[DKJS09]   David, A., Larsen, K.G., Illum, J., Skou, A.: Model-Based Framework for Schedulability Analysis Using UPPAAL 4.1. In: Model-Based Design for Embedded Systems. Computational Analysis, Synthesis, and Design of Dynamic Systems. CRC Press, Boca Raton (2009)

28   K.G. Larsen

[HMB07]   Hansen, M.R., Madsen, J., Brekling, A.W.: Semantics and verification of a lan-
             guage for modelling hardware architectures. In: Jones, C.B., Liu, Z., Woodcock,
             J. (eds.) Formal Methods and Hybrid Real-Time Systems. LNCS, vol. 4700, pp.
             300–319. Springer, Heidelberg (2007)
[HvdNV06]   Hendriks, M., van den Nieuwelaar, B., Vaandrager, F.W.: Model checker aided de-
             sign of a controller for a wafer scanner. STTT 8(6), 633–647 (2006)
[IKY⁺08]   Igna, G., Kannan, V., Yang, Y., Basten, T., Geilen, M., Vaandrager, F.W., Voorho-
             eve, M., de Smet, S., Somers, L.J.: Formal modeling and scheduling of datapaths of
             digital document printers. In: Cassez, F., Jard, C. (eds.) FORMATS 2008. LNCS,
             vol. 5215, pp. 170–187. Springer, Heidelberg (2008)
[LL98a]   Laroussinie, F., Larsen, K.G.: CMC: A tool for compositional model-checking of
             real-time systems. In: Proc. IFIP Joint Int. Conf. on Formal Description Techniques
             & Protocol Specification, Testing, and Verification (FORTE-PSTV'98), pp. 439–
             456. Kluwer Academic Publishers, Dordrecht (1998)
[LL98b]   Laroussinie, F., Larsen, K.G.: Cmc: A tool for compositional model-checking of
             real-time systems. In: Budkowski, S., Cavalli, A.R., Najm, E. (eds.) FORTE, IFIP
             Conference Proceedings, vol. 135, pp. 439–456. Kluwer, Dordrecht (1998)
[LLPY97]   Larsen, K.G., Larsson, F., Pettersson, P., Yi, W.: Efficient verification of real-time
             systems: compact data structure and state-space reduction. In: IEEE Real-Time
             Systems Symposium, pp. 14–24. IEEE Computer Society, Los Alamitos (1997)
[LLW95]   Laroussinie, F., Larsen, K.G., Weise, C.: From timed automata to logic – and back.
             In: Hájek, P., Wiedermann, J. (eds.) MFCS 1995. LNCS, vol. 969, pp. 529–539.
             Springer, Heidelberg (1995)
[LNAB⁺98]   Lind-Nielsen, J., Andersen, H.R., Behrmann, G., Hulgaard, H., Kristoffersen, K.
             J., Larsen, K.G.: Verification of large state/event systems using compositionality
             and dependency analysis. In: Steffen, B. (ed.) TACAS 1998. LNCS, vol. 1384, pp.
             201–216. Springer, Heidelberg (1998)
[LPY97]   Larsen, K.G., Pettersson, P., Yi, W.: Uppaal in a nutshell. STTT 1(1-2), 134–152
             (1997)
[Nym02]   Nyman, U.: Compositional bachwards reachability of timed automata. Master's
             thesis, Department of Computer Science, Aalborg University (2002)
[PvV10]   Poulsen, D.B., van Vliet, J.W.B.P.T.: Concrete traces for uppaal. Master's thesis,
             Department of Computer Science. Aalborg University (2010)
[TY96]   Tripakis, S., Yovine, S.: Analysis of timed systems based on time-abstracting bisim-
             ulation. In: Alur, R., Henzinger, T.A. (eds.) CAV 1996. LNCS, vol. 1102, pp. 232–
             243. Springer, Heidelberg (1996)

Temporal Logics over Linear Time Domains Are in PSPACE

Alexander Rabinovich

The Blavatnik School of Computer Science
Tel Aviv University, Tel Aviv, Israel 69978
rabinoa@post.tau.ac.il

Abstract. We investigate the complexity of the satisfiability problem of temporal logics with a finite set of modalities definable in the existential fragment of monadic second-order logic. We show that the problem is in PSPACE over the class of all linear orders. The same techniques show that the problem is in PSPACE over many interesting classes of linear orders.

1 Introduction

A major result concerning linear-time temporal logics is Kamp's theorem [12,9] which says that $TL(\text{Until}, \text{Since})$, the temporal logic having Until and Since as the only modalities, is expressively complete for first-order monadic logic of order over the class of Dedekind complete linear orders.

The order of natural numbers $\omega = (\mathbb{N}, <)$ and the order of the real numbers $(\mathbb{R}, <)$ are both Dedekind-complete. Another important class of Dedekind-complete orders is the class of ordinals. However, the order of the rationals is not Dedekind-complete. Stavi introduced two modalities Until_{Stavi} and Since_{Stavi} and proved that the temporal logic having the four modalities Until, Since, Until_{Stavi} and Since_{Stavi} is expressively complete for first-order monadic logic of order over the class of all linear orders [9].

Our concern in this paper will be with the complexity of the satisfiability problem for temporal logics over various classes of linear orders.

Sistla and Clarke [21] proved that the satisfiability problem for $TL(\text{Until}, \text{Since})$ over ω-models is PSPACE-complete. In [7], it was proven that the satisfiability problem for $TL(\text{Until}, \text{Since})$ over the class of all ordinals is PSPACE-complete. Cristau [6] provided a double exponential space algorithm for the satisfiability of the temporal logic having the four modalities Until, Since, Until_{Stavi} and Since_{Stavi} over the class of all linear orders. These proofs are based on automata theoretical techniques.

Burgess and Gurevich [5] proved that $TL(\text{Until}, \text{Since})$ is decidable over the reals. They provided two proofs. The first involves an indirect reduction to Rabin's theorem on the decidability of the monadic second-order logic over the full binary tree [14]. The second one is based on the model-theoretical composition method. Both proofs provide algorithms of non-elementary complexity.

Reynolds [17,16] proved that the satisfiability problem for $TL(\text{Until}, \text{Since})$ over the reals is PSPACE-complete and that the temporal logic with only the

A. Kučera and I. Potapov (Eds.): RP 2010, LNCS 6227, pp. 29–50, 2010.

Until modality is PSPACE-complete over the class of all linear orders. The proofs in [17,16] use temporal mosaics and are very non-trivial and difficult to grasp. Reynolds conjectured [16] that the satisfiability problem for the logic with Stavi's modalities over the class of all linear orders is in PSPACE. Our results imply this conjecture.

Let TL be a temporal logic with a finite set of modalities definable in the existential fragment of monadic second-order logic. We prove in a uniform manner that the satisfiability problem for TL is in PSPACE over the following classes of time domains: (1) all linear orders, (2) ordinals, (3) scattered linear orders, (4) Dedekind-complete linear orders, (5) continuous orders, (6) rationals, (7) reals. The proofs are based both on the composition method and on automata theoretical techniques and are easily adapted to various classes of structures and temporal and modal logics.

Our first reduction uses the following notion. Let $\varphi(X_1, \ldots, X_k)$ be a formula with free set variables among $X_1, \ldots, X_k$. An instance of φ is a formula obtained by replacing $X_1, \ldots, X_k$ by monadic predicate names. Let Φ be a set of formulas. A Φ-conjunctive formula is a conjunction of instances of formulas from Φ.

Our first reduction shows that for every temporal logic $\mathcal{L}$ with a finite set of modalities definable in the existential fragment of monadic second-order logic there is a finite set Φ of first-order formulas and a linear time algorithm that reduces the satisfiability problem for $\mathcal{L}$ to the satisfiability problem for Φ-conjunctive formulas. This algorithm is based on a simple unnesting procedure and works as it is for a much broader class of modal logics.

Next, we introduce recursively definable classes of structures. Our second reduction shows that for every finite set Φ of first-order formulas and every recursively definable class of structures $\mathcal{C}$ the satisfiability problem for the Φ-conjunctive formulas over $\mathcal{C}$ is in EXPTIME. Like the first reduction, this reduction is quite general; it relies on the composition method and is sound not only for linear orders. The first two reductions give an almost free EXPTIME algorithm for many temporal and modal logics with finite sets of modalities.

To obtain PSPACE upper bound we need more subtle arguments. We assign a rank to every structure in a recursively definable class. An algorithm similar to the algorithm in the second reduction shows that for every polynomial p the problem whether a Φ-conjunctive formula φ is satisfiable over the structures of rank $p(|\varphi|)$ is in PSPACE. The main effort to show that the satisfiability problem for a recursively definable class is in PSPACE is to establish that a formula is satisfiable if it is satisfiable over the structures of a polynomial rank in the size of the formula. We prove such a bound for many interesting classes of linear orders. Our proof uses an automata-theoretical characterization of the temporal logic with Stavi's modalities over the linear orders found by Cristau [6].

The paper is organized as follows. The next section recalls basic definitions about monadic second-order logic, its fragments and temporal logics. Sect. 3 states a linear reduction from temporal logics to conjunctive formulas. Sect. 4 reviews basic notions about the compositional method. Sect. 5 introduces recursively defined classes of structures and Sect. 6 presents an exponential algorithm

for the satisfiability of conjunctive formulas over these classes. Sect. 7 presents a
PSPACE algorithm for the satisfiability of conjunctive formulas over the class of
all linear orders and states a key lemma needed for its complexity analysis. Sect.
8 introduces finite base automata over arbitrary linear orders. Sect. 9 proves the
main lemma about runs of automata which is needed for the proof of PSPACE
bound of our algorithm. Sect. 10 proves in a "plug-and-play" manner PSPACE
bound over several interesting classes of linear orders and discusses related works.

Detailed proofs can be found in [15].

2 Monadic Logics and Temporal Logics

2.1 Monadic Second-Order Logic

Monadic second-order logic (MSO) is the fragment of the full second-order logic
allowing quantification only over elements and monadic predicates. One way to
define the monadic second-order language for a signature Δ (notation MSO(Δ))
is to augment the first-order language for Δ by quantifiable monadic predicate
variables (set variables) and by new atomic formulas $X(t)$, where t is a first-order
variable and X is a monadic predicate variable. The monadic predicate variables
range over all subsets of a structure for Δ.

The *quantifier depth* of a formula φ is defined as usual and is denoted by
$\mathrm{qd}(\varphi)$.

We will use lower case letters t, t' for the first-order variables and upper case
letters X, Y, Z for the monadic variables.

An MSO formula is existential if it is of the form $\exists X_1 \ldots \exists X_n \varphi$, where φ does
not contain second-order quantifiers. The existential fragment of MSO consists
of existential MSO formula and is denoted by $\exists$-MSO.

The first-order fragment of MSO contains formulas without the second-order
quantifiers. These formulas might contain free second-order variables which play
the same role as monadic predicate names. Hence, a formula in this fragment
is interpreted over an expansion of Δ structures by predicates which provide
meaning for the monadic variables. Sometimes, these free variables will serve as
metavariables. If $\varphi(X_1, X_2)$ is a formula and P, Q are monadic predicate names,
we will say that the formula obtained from φ by replacing X_1 by P and X_2 by
Q is an *instance* of φ.

2.2 Temporal Logics and Truth Tables

Temporal logics use logical constructs called *"modalities"* to create a language
free from quantifiers. Below is the general logical framework to define temporal
logics:

The syntax of the Temporal Logic $TL(O_1^{(k_1)}, \ldots, O_n^{(k_n)})$ has in its vocab-
ulary *monadic predicate variables* $X_1, X_2, \ldots$ and a sequence of *modality names*
with a prescribed arity, $O_1^{(k_1)}, \ldots, O_n^{(k_n)}$ (the arity notation is usually omitted).
The formulas of this temporal logic are given by the grammar:

$$\varphi ::= X \mid \neg\varphi \mid \varphi \wedge \varphi \mid O^{(k)}(\varphi_1, \cdots, \varphi_k)$$

When particular modality names are unimportant or are clear from the context, we omit them and write TL instead of $TL(O_1^{(k_1)}, \ldots, O_n^{(k_n)})$.

Structures for TL are partial orders with monadic predicates $\mathcal{M} = \langle A, <, P_1, P_2, \ldots, P_n, \ldots \rangle$, where the predicate P_i is assigned to a predicate variable X_i. Every modality $O^{(k)}$ is interpreted in every structure $\mathcal{M}$ as an operator $O_{\mathcal{M}}^{(k)} : [\mathcal{P}(A)]^k \to \mathcal{P}(A)$ which assigns "the set of points where $O^{(k)}[S_1 \ldots S_k]$ holds" to the k-tuple $\langle S_1 \ldots S_k \rangle \in \mathcal{P}(A)^k$. (Here, $\mathcal{P}$ is the power set notation, and $\mathcal{P}(A)$ denotes the set of all subsets of the domain A of $\mathcal{M}$.) Once every modality corresponds to an operator, the relation "φ holds in $\mathcal{M}$ at an element a" (notations $\langle \mathcal{M}, a \rangle \models \varphi$) is defined as follows:

- for atomic formulas $\langle \mathcal{M}, a \rangle \models X$ iff $a \in P$, where the monadic predicate P is assigned to X.
- for Boolean combinations the definition is the usual one.
- for modalities: $\langle \mathcal{M}, a \rangle \models O^{(k)}(\varphi_1, \cdots, \varphi_k)$ iff $a \in O_{\mathcal{M}}^{(k)}(P_{\varphi_1}, \cdots, P_{\varphi_k})$, where $P_\varphi = \{ b \mid \langle \mathcal{M}, b \rangle \models \varphi \}$.

Usually, we are interested in a more restricted case; for the modality to be of interest the operator $O^{(k)}$ should reflect some intended connection between the sets A_{φ_i} of points satisfying φ_i and the set of points $O[A_{\varphi_1}, \ldots, A_{\varphi_k}]$. The intended meaning is usually given by a formula in an appropriate predicate logic.

Truth Tables: A formula $\overline{O}(t_0, X_1, \ldots X_k)$ in the predicate logic L is a *Truth Table* for the modality O if for every structure $\mathcal{M}$ and subsets $P_1, \ldots, P_k$ of $\mathcal{M}$

$$O_{\mathcal{M}}(P_1, \ldots, P_k) = \{a : \mathcal{M} \models \overline{O}[a, P_1, \ldots, P_k]\} .$$

Thus, the modality $\Diamond X$, "*eventually X*", is defined by

$$\varphi(t_0, X) \equiv \exists t > t_0 (t \in X).$$

The modality $X \textrm{Until} Y$, "*X strict until Y*", is defined by

$$\exists t_1 (t_0 < t_1 \wedge t_1 \in Y \wedge \forall t (t_0 < t < t_1 \to t \in X)).$$

A truth table $\varphi(t, Y_1, \cdots, Y_k)$ defines in every structure a function from k-tuples of subsets. It associates with the tuple $Y_1, \cdots, Y_k$ of subsets of a structure $\mathcal{M}$, the set of elements t in $\mathcal{M}$ that satisfy $\varphi(t, Y_1, \cdots, Y_k)$ in $\mathcal{M}$. This is a special case of a more general way to define a function on all the structures in a given class of structures. Here is the formal notion of a definable functional.

Definition 2.1

1. *Let L be a first-order or monadic second-order logic language, and let $\mathcal{M}$ be a structure. Let $\varphi(X, Y_1, \cdots, Y_k)$ be a formula in L with no free first-order variables, and with no set variables except for those specified. φ is an* implicit *definition of the functional $X = f_\varphi^{\mathcal{M}}(Y_1, \cdots, Y_k)$ if for any k subsets $Y_1, \cdots, Y_k$ of $\mathcal{M}$, X is the only subset of $\mathcal{M}$ for which $\mathcal{M} \models \varphi(X, Y_1, \cdots, Y_k)$.*

2. *A modality $\mathcal{O}(Y_1, \cdots, Y_k)$ of a temporal logic has a generalized truth table $\varphi(X, Y_1, \cdots, Y_k)$ in a structure $\mathcal{M}$ if φ implicitly defines the operator of $\mathcal{O}$; i.e., given subsets $Y_1, \cdots, Y_k$ of a structure $\mathcal{M}$,*

$$\langle \mathcal{M}, a \rangle \models \mathcal{O}(Y_1, \cdots, Y_k) \quad \text{iff} \quad a \in f_\varphi^{\mathcal{M}}(Y_1, \cdots, Y_k).$$

φ is a generalized truth table for $\mathcal{O}$ in a class $\mathcal{C}$ of structures if φ is a generalized truth table for $\mathcal{O}$ in every $\mathcal{M} \in \mathcal{C}$.

If the logic is a second-order logic, then this definition is a special case of the classical definition of a function defined by a formula. Note that if $\theta(t_0, Y_1, \cdots, Y_k)$ is a truth table for a modality $\mathcal{O}$, then $\forall t[X(t) \leftrightarrow \theta(t, Y_1, \cdots, Y_k)]$ is a generalized truth table for $\mathcal{O}$. Therefore, the notion of a generalized truth table is more general than that of a truth table. It is strictly more general. For example, it is well-known that there is no first-order formula $\varphi(t, X)$ which defines over the naturals the set of points preceded by an even number of points in X; however, it is easy to write a first-order formula $\psi(Y, X)$ which defines this modality over $(\mathbb{N}, <)$.

If a modality O has a generalized truth table $\varphi(X, Y_1, \cdots, Y_k)$, where φ is an existential monadic second-order formula, then $\exists X\big((X(t_0)) \wedge \varphi\big)$ is an $\exists$-MSO truth table for O. Hence, a modality has an $\exists$-MSO truth table iff it has an $\exists$-MSO generalized truth table and we will say that it is $\exists$-MSO definable.

There are $\exists$-MSO definable modalities which are not definable even by generalized truth tables of the first-order logic. For example, there is an $\exists$-MSO formula $\varphi(Y, X)$ that expresses "Y holds at t if $\neg X(t)$ and t precedes by a block of X of length $3m$ some $m > 0$", i.e., $X(t-1)$, $X(t-2)$, ... $X(t-3m)$ and $\neg X(t-3m-1)$. However, there is no first-order formula equivalent to φ over $(\mathbb{N}, <)$.

Modal logics. Temporal logics are examples of modal logics. The syntax of modal logics is defined exactly like the syntax of temporal logics. However, modal logics can be interpreted not only over linear or partial orders, but over structures of a more general signature Δ. Every modality $O^{(k)}$ is interpreted in every Δ-structure $\mathcal{M}$ as an operator $O_{\mathcal{M}}^{(k)} : [\mathcal{P}(\mathcal{M})]^k \to \mathcal{P}(\mathcal{M})$. Generalized truth tables are defined by formulas over Δ. We state our results for temporal logics; however, they hold for more general modal logics as well.

3   From Temporal Logic to Conjunctive Formulas

Let $\varphi(X_1, \ldots, X_k)$ be a formula with free set variables among $X_1, \ldots, X_k$. An *instance* of φ is a formula obtained by replacing $X_1, \ldots, X_k$ by monadic predicate names or monadic variables. Let Φ be a set of formulas. A *Φ-conjunctive* formula is a conjunction of instances of formulas from Φ.

Our first reduction shows that for every temporal logic $\mathcal{L}$ with a finite set of $\exists$-MSO definable modalities there is a finite set Φ of first-order formulas and a linear time algorithm that reduces the satisfiability problem for $\mathcal{L}$ to the satisfiability problem for Φ-conjunctive formulas.

Proposition 3.1. *Let TL be a temporal logic with a finite set of modalities. Assume that every modality of TL is $\exists$-MSO definable. Then there is a finite set Φ of first-order formulas, and a linear time algorithm which for every formula $\varphi(P_1, \ldots, P_m) \in TL$ computes a Φ-conjunctive formula $\psi(P_1, \ldots, P_m, Q_1, \ldots, Q_s)$ such that for every structure $\mathcal{M}$ in the signature $\{<, P_1, \ldots, P_m\}$, φ is satisfiable in $\mathcal{M}$ iff ψ is satisfiable in an expansion of $\mathcal{M}$ by monadic predicates (which are the interpretations of $Q_1, \ldots, Q_s$).*

The proof of this proposition is based on a simple unnesting procedure. A similar proposition holds for modal logics.

4   Elements of the Composition Method

Our proofs make use of a technique known as the composition method [8,20,11,22]. To fix notations and to aid a reader unfamiliar with this technique, we briefly review the required definitions and results.

4.1   Hintikka Formulas and n-Types

Let $\mathcal{M}$ and $\mathcal{M}'$ be structures over a relational signature Σ. For $n \in \mathbb{N}$, the structures $\mathcal{M}$ and $\mathcal{M}'$ are said to be $\equiv^n$-equivalent if no first-order sentence of quantifier depth $\leq n$ distinguishes between $\mathcal{M}$ and $\mathcal{M}'$; i.e., for every φ of quantifier depth $\leq n$:
$$\mathcal{M} \models \varphi \text{ iff } \mathcal{M}' \models \varphi.$$

Lemma 4.1 (Hintikka Lemma). *For $n \in \mathbb{N}$ and a finite relational signature Σ we can compute a finite set $Hin^n := Hin^n(\Sigma)$ of sentences of quantifier depth $\leq n$ such that:*

1. *For every $\equiv^n$-equivalence class E there is a unique $\tau \in Hin^n$ such that for every Σ-structure $\mathcal{M}$: $\mathcal{M}, \in E$ if and only if $\mathcal{M} \models \tau$.*
2. *Every sentence with $\mathrm{qd}(\varphi) \leq n$ is equivalent to a (finite) disjunction of sentences from Hin^n. There is an algorithm which for every sentence φ computes a finite set $G_\varphi \subseteq Hin^{\mathrm{qd}(\varphi)}$ such that φ is equivalent to the disjunction of all the sentences from G_φ. Moreover, $\tau \in G_\varphi$ iff $\tau \to \varphi$.*

(Note that this general method to deal with sentences is not efficient in the sense of complexity theory, and that the algorithm is non-elementary.)

We call any member of Hin^n a n-Hintikka sentence. We use τ, τ_i, τ' to range over the Hintikka sentences.

Definition 4.2 (n-Type). *For $n \in \mathbb{N}$ and a Σ-structure $\mathcal{M}$, we denote by $type^n(\mathcal{M})$ the unique member of Hin^n satisfied in $\mathcal{M}$.*

4.2   The Ordered Sum of Chains and of n-Types

A (labeled) chain $\mathcal{M}$ is a linear order expanded by monadic predicates; if $\overline{P}$ is a set of monadic predicate names, and the signature of $\mathcal{M}$ is $\{<, \overline{P}\}$, we say $\mathcal{M}$ is a $\overline{P}$-chain. The *concatenation* or *ordered sum* of chains is defined as follows:

Definition 4.3 (Sum of Chains). *Let* $\mathcal{I} := (I, <^{\mathcal{I}})$ *be a linear order,* $l \in \mathbb{N}$, *and* $\mathfrak{S} := (\mathcal{M}_\alpha \mid \alpha \in I)$ *be a sequence of chains, where* $\mathcal{M}_\alpha := (A_\alpha, <^\alpha, P_1{}^\alpha, \dots, P_l{}^\alpha)$. *Assume that* $A_\alpha \cap A_\beta = \emptyset$ *whenever* $\alpha \neq \beta$ *are in* I. *The ordered sum of* $\mathfrak{S}$ *is the chain*

$$\sum_{\alpha \in \mathcal{I}} \mathcal{M}_\alpha := (\bigcup_{\alpha \in I} A_\alpha, <^{\mathcal{I},\mathfrak{S}}, \bigcup_{\alpha \in I} P_1{}^\alpha, \dots, \bigcup_{\alpha \in I} P_l{}^\alpha),$$

where:

   If $\alpha, \beta \in I$, $a \in A_\alpha$, $b \in A_\beta$, *then* $b <^{\mathcal{I},\mathfrak{S}} a$ *iff* $\beta <^{\mathcal{I}} \alpha$ *or* $\beta = \alpha$ *and* $b <^\alpha a$.

   If the domains of the $\mathcal{M}_\alpha$'s *are not disjoint, replace them with isomorphic chains that have disjoint domains, and proceed as before.*

   If $\mathcal{I} = (\{0,1\}, <)$ *and* $\mathfrak{S} = (\mathcal{M}_0, \mathcal{M}_1)$, *we denote* $\sum_{\alpha \in \mathcal{I}} \mathcal{M}_\alpha$ *by* $\mathcal{M}_0 + \mathcal{M}_1$.

   If $\mathcal{M}_\alpha$ *is isomorphic to* $\mathcal{M}$ *for every* $\alpha \in I$, *we denote* $\sum_{\alpha \in \mathcal{I}} \mathcal{M}_\alpha$ *by* $\mathcal{M} \times \mathcal{I}$.

The next proposition states that taking ordered sums preserves $\equiv^n$-equivalence.

Lemma 4.4. *Let* $n \in \mathbb{N}$. *Assume:*

1. $(I, <^{\mathcal{I}})$ *is a linear order,*
2. $(\mathcal{M}_\alpha^0 \mid \alpha \in I)$ *and* $(\mathcal{M}_\alpha^1 \mid \alpha \in I)$ *are sequences of chains (in the same signature), and*
3. *for every* $\alpha \in I$, $\mathcal{M}_\alpha^0 \equiv^n \mathcal{M}_\alpha^1$.

Then, $\sum_{\alpha \in I} \mathcal{M}_\alpha^0 \equiv^n \sum_{\alpha \in I} \mathcal{M}_\alpha^1$.

This allows us to define the sum of formulas in $Hin^n(<, P_1, \dots P_l)$ with respect to any linear order.

   In particular, this theorem justifies the notation $\tau_0 + \tau_1$ for the n-type of a chain which is the ordered sum of two chains of n-types τ_0 and τ_1, respectively. Similarly, we write $\tau \times \omega$ for the n-type of a sum $\Sigma_{i \in \omega} \mathcal{M}_i$ where all $\mathcal{M}_i$ are of n-type τ; the n-type $\tau \times \omega^{-1}$ is defined similarly, where ω^{-1} is the order type of negative integers.

   Another important operation on chains and on n-types is **shuffle**.

   Let $\mathfrak{S} := (\mathcal{M}_\alpha \mid \alpha \in \mathbb{Q})$ be a sequence of chains indexed by the rationals. Let $Q_1, \dots, Q_k \subseteq \mathbb{Q}$ be a partition of $\mathbb{Q}$ into k everywhere dense sets. Let $\mathcal{N}_1, \dots, \mathcal{N}_k$ be chains. If for $i = 1, \dots, k$ and $q \in Q_i$, $\mathcal{M}_q$ is isomorphic to $\mathcal{N}_i$, we denote $\sum_{\alpha \in \mathbb{Q}} \mathcal{M}_\alpha$ by $shuffle(\mathcal{N}_1, \dots \mathcal{N}_k)$. Note that different partitions of $\mathbb{Q}$ into k everywhere dense sets are isomorphic; hence, the shuffle is well defined. The corresponding operation on n-types will be also denoted by *shuffle*.

5 Recursively Defined Classes of Structures

Let Δ be a signature and $k \in \mathbb{N}$. A k-ary Δ-*operator* is a function F which assigns to every k-tuple of Δ-structures a Δ structure. A *finite-set Δ-operator* is a function F which assigns to every finite set of Δ-structures a Δ structure. A Δ-*operator* is a k-ary ($k \in \mathbb{N}$) or a finite-set Δ-operator.

Let $\mathcal{C}$ be a set of Δ-structures. $\mathcal{C}$ is closed under a Δ-operator F if the result of application of F to structures from $\mathcal{C}$ is in $\mathcal{C}$.

Let $\mathcal{C}$ be a set of Δ-structures and $\mathfrak{F}$ be a family of Δ-operators. The *closure* of $\mathcal{C}$ under $\mathfrak{F}$ is the minimal class $\mathcal{C}'$ of Δ-structure which contains $\mathcal{C}$ and is closed under $\mathfrak{F}$. We denote this class by $Cl(\mathcal{C}, \mathfrak{F})$. It is said to be *recursively defined* from $\mathcal{C}$ by $\mathfrak{F}$.

Let $Cl^0(\mathcal{C}, \mathfrak{F}) := \mathcal{C}$ and for $i \in \mathbb{N}$ define $Cl^{i+1}(\mathcal{C}, \mathfrak{F}) := Cl^i(\mathcal{C}, \mathfrak{F}) \cup \{ \mathcal{M} \mid \mathcal{M} = F(\mathcal{M}_1, \ldots, \mathcal{M}_k)$ for k-ary $F \in \mathfrak{F}$ and $\mathcal{M}_j \in Cl^i(\mathcal{C}, \mathfrak{F}) \} \cup \{ \mathcal{M} \mid \mathcal{M} = F(\mathcal{A})$ for finite-set operator $F \in \mathfrak{F}$ and $\mathcal{A} \subseteq Cl^i(\mathcal{C}, \mathfrak{F}) \}$. Define $Cl^*(\mathcal{C}, \mathfrak{F}) := \cup_{i \in \mathbb{N}} Cl^i(\mathcal{C}, \mathfrak{F})$. Note that $Cl^*(\mathcal{C}, \mathfrak{F}) = Cl(\mathcal{C}, \mathfrak{F})$.

Let $\sim$ be an equivalence on Δ-structures. The *index* of $\sim$ is the cardinality of the set of $\sim$-equivalence classes; $\sim$ has a *finite index* if there are only finitely many $\sim$-equivalence classes.

A k-ary Δ operator F *respects* $\sim$ if for Δ-structures $\mathcal{M}_1, \ldots, \mathcal{M}_k, \mathcal{N}_1, \ldots, \mathcal{N}_k$

$$F(\mathcal{M}_1, \ldots, \mathcal{M}_k) \sim F(\mathcal{N}_1, \ldots, \mathcal{N}_k)$$

whenever $\mathcal{M}_i \sim \mathcal{N}_i$ ($i = 1, \ldots, k$).

If F respects $\sim$, then it induces a k-ary operation on the $\sim$-equivalence classes. We denote this operation by F as it will always be clear from the context whether we use an operator on Δ-structures or the corresponding operation on the $\sim$-equivalence classes.

If $\mathcal{A}$ and $\mathcal{B}$ are sets of Δ-structures, we say that $\mathcal{A}$ is $\sim$-equivalent to $\mathcal{B}$ if $\forall \mathcal{M} \in \mathcal{A} \exists \mathcal{N} \in \mathcal{B}(\mathcal{M} \sim \mathcal{N})$ and $\forall \mathcal{M} \in \mathcal{B} \exists \mathcal{N} \in \mathcal{A}(\mathcal{M} \sim \mathcal{N})$.

A finite-set Δ-operator *respects* $\sim$ if $F(\mathcal{A}) \sim F(\mathcal{B})$ whenever $\mathcal{A} \sim \mathcal{B}$.

If a finite-set operator F respects $\sim$, then it induces an operation which assigns a $\sim$-equivalence class to every finite subset of $\sim$-equivalence classes.

A family $\mathfrak{F}$ of Δ-operators *respects* $\sim$ if every operator in $\mathfrak{F}$ respects $\sim$.

Lemma 5.1. *Assume that $\sim$ is an equivalence of finite index l, and $\mathfrak{F}$ respects $\sim$. Then for every $\mathcal{M} \in Cl(\mathcal{C}, \mathfrak{F})$ there is $\mathcal{N} \in Cl^l(\mathcal{C}, \mathfrak{F})$ such that $\mathcal{M} \sim \mathcal{N}$.*

Proof. Let E_n be the set of $\sim$-equivalence classes of structures from $Cl^n(\mathcal{C}, \mathfrak{F})$. Then, $\forall n E_n \subseteq E_{n+1}$. Hence, there is $i \leq l$ such that $E_i = E_{i+1}$. This implies that $\forall j E_i = E_{i+j}$. In particular, $\forall j E_l \supseteq E_j$, therefore, the lemma holds. $\square$

For every n the set of operators $\{+, \times\omega, \times\omega^{-1}, shuffle\}$ respects $\equiv^n$.

Strictly speaking, these are polymorphic operators. For every set $\overline{P}$ of monadic predicate names, there is a corresponding binary operator $+$ on $\overline{P}$-labeled chains.

Recall that for a Δ-structure $\mathcal{M}$ and $\Delta' \subseteq \Delta$ the Δ' reduct of $\mathcal{M}$ on Δ' is a Δ'-structure which has the same domain as $\mathcal{M}$ and the same interpretation of symbols from Δ'. We denote by $\mathcal{M}|\Delta'$ the reduct of $\mathcal{M}$ on Δ'.

The reduct distributes over the sum in the following sense:

The reduct distributes over $+$

Let $\overline{P'} \subseteq \overline{P}$ be sets of monadic predicate names, let $\mathcal{M}$ and $\mathcal{N}$ be $\overline{P}$-chains. Then $(\mathcal{M} + \mathcal{N})|\{<, \overline{P'}\}$ and $(\mathcal{M}|\{<, \overline{P'}\}) + (\mathcal{N}|\{<, \overline{P'}\})$ are isomorphic.

The reduct also distributes over $\{\times \omega, \times \omega^{-1}, shuffle\}$.

Let $\overline{P}$ be a set of monadic predicate names, let $\overline{P}_1, \ldots, \overline{P}_k \subseteq \overline{P}$ be a sequence of subsets of $\overline{P}$, and let $\mathcal{M}$ be a $\overline{P}$-chain. Define $ptype^n(\mathcal{M}; (\overline{P}_1, \ldots, \overline{P}_k))$, the *product n-type* of $\mathcal{M}$ with respect to $\overline{P}_1, \ldots, \overline{P}_k$, as

$$ptype^n(\mathcal{M}; (\overline{P}_1, \ldots, \overline{P}_k)) := (\tau_1, \ldots, \tau_k),$$

where $\tau_i = type^n(\mathcal{M}|\{<, \overline{P}_i\})$ be the n-types of the reduct.

For a class $\mathcal{C}$ of $\overline{P}$-chain,

$$ptype^n(\mathcal{C}; (\overline{P}_1, \ldots, \overline{P}_k)) := \{ptype^n(\mathcal{M}; (\overline{P}_1, \ldots, \overline{P}_k)) \mid \mathcal{M} \in \mathcal{C}\}.$$

Lemma 5.2

1. If $ptype^n(\mathcal{M}^i; (\overline{P}_1, \ldots, \overline{P}_k)) = (\tau_1^i, \ldots, \tau_k^i)$ for $i \in \{0, 1\}$, then

$$ptype^n(\mathcal{M}^0 + \mathcal{M}^1; (\overline{P}_1, \ldots, \overline{P}_k)) = (\tau_1^0 + \tau_1^1, \ldots, \tau_k^0 + \tau_k^1)$$

2. If $ptype^n(\mathcal{M}; (\overline{P}_1, \ldots, \overline{P}_k)) = (\tau_1, \ldots, \tau_k)$, then

$$ptype^n(\mathcal{M} \times \omega; (\overline{P}_1, \ldots, \overline{P}_k)) = (\tau_1 \times \omega, \ldots, \tau_k \times \omega)$$

$$ptype^n(\mathcal{M} \times \omega^{-1}; (\overline{P}_1, \ldots, \overline{P}_k)) = (\tau_1 \times \omega^{-1}, \ldots, \tau_k \times \omega^{-1})$$

3. if $\mathcal{A}$ is a finite set of structures and for $j = 1, \ldots k$, and
   $U_j = \{\tau_j \mid ptype^n(\mathcal{M}; (\overline{P}_1, \ldots, \overline{P}_k)) = (\tau_1, \ldots, \tau_j, \ldots, \tau_k) \land \mathcal{M} \in \mathcal{A}\}$, then
   $ptype^n(shuffle(\mathcal{A}); (\overline{P}_1, \ldots, \overline{P}_k)) = (shuffle(U_1), \ldots, shuffle(U_k))$.

6   EXPTIME Algorithm

In this section we present an EXPTIME algorithm for the satisfiability of conjunctive formulas.

Let Φ be a finite set of formulas of quantifier depth $\leq n$ in the first-order monadic logic over $\{<\}$ with free variables among $X_1, \ldots, X_m$.

Let $\psi = \varphi_1(\overline{P_1}) \land \cdots \land \varphi_k(\overline{P_k})$ be a Φ-conjunctive formula. Let $\mathfrak{F} := \{+, \times \omega, \times \omega^{-1}, shuffle\}$. Let $\mathcal{C}$ be a set of structures over signature $\{<, \cup_{i=1}^k \overline{P_i}\}$. Recall that $\mathfrak{F}$ respects $\equiv^n$, therefore, by Lemma 5.1, ψ is satisfiable over $Cl(\mathcal{C}, \mathfrak{F})$ if it is satisfiable over $Cl^l(\mathcal{C}, \mathfrak{F})$, where $l := |Hin^n(<, \cup_{i=1}^k \overline{P_i})|$ is the cardinality of the set $Hin^n(<, \cup_{i=1}^k \overline{P_i})$ of Hintikka formulas. This l grows like the n-time iterated exponential function $\exp(n, k)$ ($\exp(1, x) := 2^x$ and $\exp(i + 1, x) := 2^{\exp(i,x)}$). We replace this bound by a bound exponential in k and derive an exponential time algorithm for the satisfiability of Φ-conjunctive formulas over $Cl(\mathcal{C}, \mathfrak{F})$. Our arguments are valid not only for this recursively defined class, but for any recursive class which is definable by a finite set of operators that respect $\equiv^n$-equivalence and satisfy an analog of Lemma 5.2.

Lemma 6.1. *Let Φ be a finite set of formulas of the quantifier depth $\leq n$ in the first-order monadic logic over $\{<\}$ with free variables among $X_1, \ldots, X_m$. A Φ-conjunctive formula $\varphi_1(\overline{P_1}) \wedge \cdots \wedge \varphi_k(\overline{P_k})$ is satisfiable in $\mathcal{M}$ if and only if $ptype^n(\mathcal{M}; (\overline{P_1}, \ldots, \overline{P_k})) = (\tau_1, \ldots, \tau_k)$ and $\tau_i(\overline{P_i}) \to \varphi_i(\overline{P_i})$ for $i = 1, \ldots, k$.*

Define the equivalence $\sim^n_{(\overline{P_1}, \ldots, \overline{P_k})}$ on chains over the signature $\{<, \cup_{i=1}^k \overline{P_i}\}$ as

$$\mathcal{M} \sim^n_{(\overline{P_1}, \ldots, \overline{P_k})} \mathcal{N} \quad \text{iff} \quad ptype^n(\mathcal{M}; (\overline{P_1}, \ldots, \overline{P_k})) = ptype^n(\mathcal{N}; (\overline{P_1}, \ldots, \overline{P_k})).$$

The number of $\sim^n_{(\overline{P_1}, \ldots, \overline{P_k})}$ equivalence classes is $\leq |Hin^n(<, P_1, \ldots, P_m)|^k$; hence, it is at most exponential in k. $\mathfrak{F}$ respects $\sim^n_{(\overline{P_1}, \ldots, \overline{P_k})}$. Therefore, by Lemma 5.1, we obtain:

Lemma 6.2. *For every finite set Φ of first-order formulas there is c_Φ such that a Φ-conjunctive formula $\psi = \varphi_1(\overline{P_1}) \wedge \cdots \wedge \varphi_k(\overline{P_k})$ is satisfiable in $Cl(\mathcal{C}, \mathfrak{F})$ iff it is satisfiable in $Cl^{c_\Phi^k}(\mathcal{C}, \mathfrak{F})$.*

Consider the following problem.

Membership Problem for fixed $n, m \in \mathbb{N}$; all tuples $\overline{P_i}$ are of length $\leq m$.

Input: $\overline{\tau} = (\tau_1 \ldots \tau_k) \in Hin^n(<, \overline{P_1}) \times \cdots \times Hin^n(<, \overline{P_k})$ and an oracle I for membership in $ptype^n(\mathcal{C}; (\overline{P_1}, \ldots, \overline{P_k}))$.
Question: Is $\overline{\tau}$ in $ptype^n(Cl(\mathcal{C}, \mathfrak{F}); (\overline{P_1}, \ldots, \overline{P_k}))$?

Lemma 6.3. *The membership problem is in $EXPTIME^I$.*

Proof. Our algorithm is presented below.

Algorithm 1. Membership Problem is in $EXPTIME^I$

$R \leftarrow I$ { i.e., for every $\overline{\tau}$ if $\overline{\tau} \in I$ then add $\overline{\tau}$ to R.}
Updated $\leftarrow$ True.
while Updated **do**
   1. Updated $\leftarrow$ False;
   2. Compute $R' = Cl^1((R, +)$; **If** $R' \neq R$ **then** Updated $\leftarrow$ True;
   3. $R \leftarrow R'$; Compute $R' = Cl^1(R, \times\omega)$; **If** $R' \neq R$ **then** Updated $\leftarrow$ True;
   4. $R \leftarrow R'$; Compute $R' = Cl^1(R, \times\omega^{-1})$; **If** $R' \neq R$ **then** Updated $\leftarrow$ True;
   5. $R \leftarrow R'$; Compute $R' = Cl^1(R, shuffle)$; **If** $R' \neq R$ **then** Updated $\leftarrow$ True;
end while
if $\overline{\tau} \in R$ **return** True.

Let $N_0 = |Hin^n(<, X_1, \ldots, X_m)|$. The number of iterations of the loop is bounded by N_0^k.

$R' = Cl^1((R, +)$ can be computed in time $O(N_0^{2k})$ as follows. Let $R' \leftarrow R$. For each pair $\overline{\tau} = (\tau_1, \ldots, \tau_k), \overline{\tau'} = (\tau'_1, \ldots, \tau'_k) \in R$ add $(\tau_1 + \tau'_1, \ldots, \tau_k + \tau'_k)$ to R'. Hence, Step 2 can be implemented in time $O(N_0^{2k})$.

Steps 3 and 4 can be implemented in $O(N_0^k)$.

The computation of $R' = Cl^1(R, \textit{shuffle})$ is more subtle. Indeed, a naive approach can try to compute $\textit{shuffle}$ for every subset of R. However, the number of such subsets is $2^{N_0{}^k}$ and it is double-exponential. $R' = Cl^1(R, \textit{shuffle})$ can be computed in EXPTIME as follows:

Algorithm 2. Computation of $Cl^1(R, \textit{shuffle})$

Let $H_i := \mathcal{P}(Hin^n(<, \overline{P_i}))$ be the set of subsets of $Hin^n(<, \overline{P_i})$.
for every $U = (U_1, \ldots, U_k) \in H_1 \times \cdots \times H_k$ **do**
    { *Check if there is a sequence* $(\tau_1^1, \ldots, \tau_k^1), \ldots, (\tau_1^m, \ldots, \tau_k^m) \in R$ *such that* $U_i = \{\tau_i^j \mid j \leq m\}$ *and update* R' *as follows:* }

1. $(B_1, \ldots, B_k) \leftarrow (U_1, \ldots, U_k)$;
2.   **for** every $\overline{\tau} = (\tau_1, \ldots \tau_k) \in R$ **if** $\wedge_i \tau_i \in U_i$ **then** $B_i \leftarrow B_i \setminus \{\tau_i\}$;
3.   **If** $\wedge B_i = \emptyset$ **then**   {such a sequence exists, and we have to update R'}
      $R' \leftarrow R' \cup \{(\textit{shuffle}(U_1), \ldots, \textit{shuffle}(U_k))\}$;

end for

The number of iterations of the external loop is $2^{N_0 k}$ and the number of iterations of the internal loop is bounded by N_0^k. Hence, Step 5 can be implemented in time $O(2^{N_0 k} \times N_0^k)$.

Since every step can be implemented in EXPTIME and the number of iterations is exponential, we obtain that the membership problem is in EXPTIME with the oracle I. $\square$

Let *One* be the class of one-element chains. It is clear that we can decide in EXPTIME, whether $\tau \in ptype^n(One; (\overline{P_1}, \ldots, \overline{P_k}))$. Hence, as a consequence of Lemma 6.3, we obtain:

Proposition 6.4. *The satisfiability problem for Φ-conjunctive formulas over the class $Cl(One, \mathfrak{F})$ is in EXPTIME.*

Proof. For every $\varphi \in \Phi$ we can pre-compute the set $H_\varphi := \{\tau \in Hin^n(<, X_1, \ldots, X_m) \mid \tau \to \varphi\}$ (this depends only on Φ and is independent from the input).

Let $\psi = \varphi_1(\overline{P_1}) \wedge \cdots \wedge \varphi_k(\overline{P_k})$ be a Φ-conjunctive formula. First compute the set S of all $\overline{\tau}$ in $ptype^n(Cl(One, \mathfrak{F}); (\overline{P_1}, \ldots, \overline{P_k}))$. The cardinality of S is at most exponential. By the previous lemma, S can be computed in EXPTIME. Then, by Lemma 6.1, it is enough to check whether there is $(\tau_1, \ldots, \tau_k) \in S$ such that $\tau_i(\overline{P_i}) \to \varphi_i(\overline{P_i})$ for $i = 1, \ldots, k$. This can be done in EXPTIME using the pre-computed sets H_φ. $\square$

Läuchli and Leonard [13] proved[1] the following theorem:

---

[1] Läuchli and Leonard considered the logic with the order relation only. Their proof can be adapted easily to the first-order monadic logic over chains.

Theorem 6.5 *A first-order formula is satisfiable over a linear order if it is satisfiable over* $Cl(One, \mathfrak{F})$.

As a consequence of Theorem 6.5 and Propositions 6.4 and 3.1 we obtain:

Theorem 6.6 *Let TL be a temporal logic with a finite set of $\exists$-MSO definable modalities. The satisfiability problem for TL over the class of chains is in* EXPTIME.

In the next section we will show that EXPTIME upper bound can be replaced by PSPACE upper bound.

Let us conclude this section by a remark on optimality of our algorithm. The only properties of operators $\{+, \times\omega, \times\omega^{-1}, shuffle\}$ which were used in our EXPTIME algorithm are (1) they respect $\equiv^n$ and (2) the reduct distributes over these operators. If $\mathfrak{F}$ is any set of operators with these properties, then the membership problem for $Cl(One, \mathfrak{F})$ is in EXPTIME.

Below we will show that for such $\mathfrak{F}$ in general EXPTIME bound cannot be improved.

Let $\Delta_2 = \{<, Left, Right\}$ be a signature, where $<$ is a binary predicate and $Left, Right$ are unary predicates. We will interpret Δ_2 over the binary trees, where $<$ is the ancestor relation and $Left$ (respectively, $Right$) are interpreted as the set of left (respectively, right) children. Let $\mathcal{M}_1$ and $\mathcal{M}_2$ be binary trees expanded by unary predicates $P_1, \ldots, P_k$, and let R be a one element chain for these predicate names. We assume that the domains of $\mathcal{M}_1, \mathcal{M}_2$ and R are disjoint and define a ternary operation $\boxplus(\mathcal{M}_1, R, \mathcal{M}_2)$ as follows. $\boxplus(\mathcal{M}_1, R, \mathcal{M}_2)$ is a binary tree; its domain is the union of the domains of $\mathcal{M}_1$, R and $\mathcal{M}_2$; the unique node r of R is the root of this tree. The left and right subtrees of r are $\mathcal{M}_1$ and $\mathcal{M}_2$ respectively. Predicate name P_i is interpreted as the union of its interpretations in $\mathcal{M}_1, R$ and $\mathcal{M}_2$.

The operation $\boxplus$ has properties (1) and (2). The closure of *One* under $\boxplus$ is the set of all finite binary trees. As a consequence, we can derive that the satisfiability problem for any temporal logics with a finite set of $\exists$-MSO definable modalities over the class of finite binary trees is in EXPTIME. Note that CTL can be described as a temporal logic with a finite set of modalities definable in $\exists$-MSO and the satisfiability problem for CTL over the class of finite binary trees is EXPTIME hard. Hence, in general our EXPTIME upper bound for the satisfiability problem over recursively definable classes is optimal.

7 PSPACE Algorithm

Let $\mathfrak{F} = \{+, \times\omega, \times\omega^{-1}, shuffle\}$. To every chain in $Cl(One, \mathfrak{F})$ we assign a natural number - the rank of a chain. Define sets $\mathcal{C}^{\leq i} \subseteq Cl(One, \mathfrak{F})$ as follows:

1. $\mathcal{C}^{\leq 0}$ is the set of finite chains.
2. $\mathcal{C}^{\leq i+1}$ is the closure under $+$ of the union of $\mathcal{C}^{\leq i}$, $\{\mathcal{M} \times \omega \mid \mathcal{M} \in \mathcal{C}^{\leq i}\}$, $\{\mathcal{M} \times \omega^{-1} \mid \mathcal{M} \in \mathcal{C}^{\leq i}\}$ and $\{shuffle(\mathcal{A}) \mid \mathcal{A} \text{ is a finite subset of } \mathcal{C}^{\leq i}\}$.

A chain $\mathcal{M}$ has *rank* $i+1$ if $\mathcal{M} \in \mathcal{C}^{\leq i+1} \wedge \mathcal{M} \notin \mathcal{C}^{\leq i}$.

Every chain of a finite rank can be described by its finite construction tree. Let $\overline{P}$ be a set of monadic predicate names. A construction tree T for $\overline{P}$-chains is a labeled tree which has the following properties: the leaves of T are labeled by one-element $\overline{P}$-chains; the internal nodes are labeled by $+$, $\times \omega$, $\times \omega^{-1}$ and *shuffle*; a node labeled by $\times \omega$ or by $\times \omega^{-1}$ has one child; a node labeled by $+$ has at least two children and these children are linearly ordered; a node labeled by *shuffle* has at least one child.

Let T be a construction tree. A chain $[|T|]$, assigned to T, is defined as follows:

1. if T is a one-element tree then $[|T|]$ is the one-element chain which is the label of its only node.
2. If the root of T is labeled by $\times \omega$ (or by $\times \omega^{-1}$), then $[|T|]$ is $[|T_1|] \times \omega$ (respectively, $[|T_1|] \times \omega^{-1}$)) where T_1 is the subtree of T rooted at the child of its root.
3. If the root of T is labeled by $+$ and its children (ordered from younger to older) are trees $T_1, \ldots, T_m$ then $[|T|] := [|T_1|] + \cdots + [|T_m|]$.
4. If the root of T is labeled by *shuffle* and its children are trees $T_1, \ldots, T_m$ then $[|T|] := shuffle([|T_1|], \ldots, [|T_m|])$.

Lemma 7.1. *If a chain $\mathcal{M}$ has rank $\leq i$, then there is a chain construction tree T such that $\mathcal{M} = [|T|]$ and the height of T is bounded by $2i+1$.*

Proof. A chain $\mathcal{M}$ has rank $\leq i$ if there is a tree T such that $\mathcal{M} = [|T|]$ and the number of nodes labeled by $\times \omega$, $\times \omega^{-1}$ and *shuffle* on any path from the root to a leaf is bounded by i (we do not count nodes labeled by $+$). For every tree T there is a tree T' such that $[|T'|] = [|T|]$ and no $+$ node has a child labeled by $+$. Indeed, if a $+$ node v of T has as a child a $+$ node u we can remove u and make its children to be children of v (between the left and the right brothers of u). Hence, if a chain $\mathcal{M}$ has rank $\leq i$ then there is a tree T such that $\mathcal{M} = [|T|]$ and the height of T is bounded by $2i+1$.   □

We are going to present a PSPACE algorithm for the satisfiability problem for Φ-conjunctive formulas. Its correctness and complexity analysis are based on the following Lemma which refines Lemma 6.2 and will be proved in Sect. 9.

Lemma 7.2 (small rank property). *For every finite set Φ of first-order formulas there is r_Φ such that every Φ-conjunctive formula $\psi = \varphi_1(\overline{P_1}) \wedge \cdots \wedge \varphi_k(\overline{P_k})$ is satisfiable in $Cl(One, \mathfrak{F})$ iff it is satisfiable in a chain of rank $\leq k \times r_\Phi$.*

By Theorem 6.5, Lemma 7.1, and Lemma 7.2, $\varphi_1(\overline{P_1}) \wedge \cdots \wedge \varphi_k(\overline{P_k})$ is satisfiable iff

(A) there is a chain construction tree T of height $\leq 2k \times r_\Phi + 1$ such that $ptype^n([|T|]; (\overline{P_1}, \ldots, \overline{P_k})) = (\tau_1, \ldots, \tau_k)$ and
(B) $\tau_i \to \varphi_i$ for $i = 1, \ldots, k$.

Now, we are ready to improve our EXPTIME bound of Theorem 6.6 to PSPACE.

Theorem 7.3 *Let TL be a temporal logic with a finite set of $\exists$-MSO definable modalities. The satisfiability problem for TL over the class of chains is in* PSPACE.

By proposition 3.1 it is sufficient to provide a PSPACE algorithm for the sat-
isfiability of Φ-conjunctive formulas. Let $\psi = \varphi_1(\overline{P_1}) \wedge \cdots \wedge \varphi_k(\overline{P_k})$ be such a
formula. Our algorithm guesses $(\tau_1, \ldots, \tau_k)$ and checks in linear time condition
(B). Then the non-deterministic algorithm SAT, defined below, checks (A). SAT
works in polynomial space in k, assuming that the last argument is polynomial
in k which is the case with $N = 2k \times r_\Phi + 1$. Fig. 1 contains the definition of the
algorithm SAT (some details are omitted).

Membership Problem

Input 1. $(\tau_1, \ldots, \tau_k)$, where $\tau_i \in Hin^n(<, \overline{P_i})$ and $\overline{P_i} \subseteq \overline{P}$ are sets of l predicate names (note that n and l are fixed and are not part of the input).
2. $N \in \mathbb{N}$.
Output True, if there is a construction tree T of height $\leq N$ such that
$ptype^n([\|T\|]; (\overline{P_1}, \ldots, \overline{P_k})) = (\tau_1, \ldots, \tau_k)$.

- If $N = 0$ and there is a one element chain $\mathcal{M}$ such that
$ptype^n(\mathcal{M}; (\overline{P_1}, \ldots, \overline{P_k})) = (\tau_1, \ldots, \tau_k)$ then return True;
- Go non-deterministically to 1-5.
  (1.) Return SAT$((\tau_1, \ldots, \tau_k), N - 1)$.
  (2.) Guess $(\tau_1', \ldots, \tau_k')$ such that SAT$((\tau_1', \ldots, \tau_k'), N - 1)$ returns True and
  $\tau_i = \tau_i' \times \omega$ for $0 < i \leq k$.
  (3.) Guess $(\tau_1', \ldots, \tau_k')$ such that SAT$((\tau_1', \ldots, \tau_k'), N - 1)$ returns True and
  $\tau_i = \tau_i' \times \omega^{-1}$ for $0 < i \leq k$.
  (4.) Guess on-the-fly a sequence

$$\left(\tau_1^1, \ldots, \tau_k^1\right), \left(\tau_1^2, \ldots, \tau_k^2\right), \ldots, \left(\tau_1^m, \ldots, \tau_k^m\right)$$

such that
  (4.1) for $0 < i \leq m$, SAT$((\tau_1^i, \ldots, \tau_k^i), N - 1)$ returns True,
  (4.2) for $0 < j \leq k$, $\tau_j = \tau_j^1 + \ldots + \tau_j^m$.
  (5.) Guess $(U_1, \ldots, U_k)$, where $U_i \subseteq Hin^n(<, \overline{P_i})$ such that
  (5.1) for $0 < j \leq k$, $\tau_j = shuffle(U_j)$
  and guess on-the-fly a sequence

$$\left(\tau_1^1, \ldots, \tau_k^1\right), \left(\tau_1^2, \ldots, \tau_k^2\right), \ldots, \left(\tau_1^m, \ldots, \tau_k^m\right)$$

such that
  (5.2) for $0 < i \leq m$, SAT$((\tau_1^i, \ldots, \tau_k^i), N - 1)$ returns True,
  (5.3) for $0 < j \leq k$, $U_j = \{\tau_j^i \mid i \leq m\}$.

Fig. 1. Algorithm SAT

Since $+$ is associative, to verify condition (4.2) we need to keep in the
memory at every stage p only two tuples: the tuple of the partial sum
$\left(\sum_{s=1}^{s<p} \tau_1^s, \ldots, \sum_{s=1}^{s<p} \tau_k^s\right)$ and the current guess $(\tau_1^p, \ldots, \tau_k^p)$. The tuple of the

partial sums can be easily updated. We can assume that all partial sums are different; hence, m is bounded by the number of possible $ptype^n(\mathcal{M}; (\overline{P}_1, \ldots, \overline{P}_k))$ which is bounded by $|Hin^n(< .X_1, \ldots, X_l)|^k$ and the counter for m can be saved in space linear in k.

To verify condition (5.3) we need to keep in memory at every stage p only two tuples: the tuple $U_i^p = \{\tau_i^s \mid s < p\}$ (for $i = 1, \ldots, k$) and the current guess $(\tau_1^p, \ldots, \tau_k^p)$. We have to verify that $(\tau_1^p, \ldots, \tau_k^p)$ is in $(U_1, \ldots, U_k)$, i.e., $\tau_i^p \in U_i$ and update the tuple $(U_1^p, \ldots, U_k^p)$. In (5.) we can assume that no tuple occurs twice; hence, m is bounded by the number of possible $ptype^n(\mathcal{M}; (\overline{P}_1, \ldots, \overline{P}_k))$ and the counter for m can be saved in space linear in k.

The depth of recursion is bounded by N. Hence, SAT works in non-deterministic space $O(kN)$.

In order to check (A) we call SAT with $N = 2r_\Phi \times k + 1$. Therefore, our procedure works in non-deterministic polynomial space and by the Savitch theorem it can be implemented by a deterministic PSPACE algorithm.

The next two sections are geared towards the proof of Lemma 7.2.

8 Automata on Linear Orders

Büchi used finite automata over ω-words to prove that monadic second-order logic is decidable over ω. In order to prove the decidability of monadic second-order logic over countable ordinals, Büchi introduced finite automata on words of ordinal length [4]. Büchi's model extends traditional finite automata using limit transitions to handle positions with no predecessor. He proved that over countable ordinals these automata are equivalent to monadic second-order logic.

These automata were extended to finite automata on linear orderings by Bruyère and Carton [2]. This model further extends traditional finite automata using limit transitions to handle positions with no successor or no predecessor. In [18] it was shown that these automata can be complemented over countable scattered linear orderings and are equivalent to monadic second-order logic over the countable scattered linear orderings. However, this equivalence fails over dense orders and over uncountable orders [1].

We first recall some basic definitions about linear orders. Then, we introduce finite base automata which have the same expressive power as finite state automata of [2], but are more appropriate for our purposes.

In order to define the runs of an automaton, we use the notion of cut. A *cut* of a linear order J is a partition (L, U) of J such that $a < b$ for any $a \in L$ and $b \in U$. A cut (L, U) is a *gap* if neither L has a maximal element, nor U has a minimal element and $L \neq \emptyset \neq U$. An order is *Dedekind-complete* if it does not have gaps. We denote by $\widehat{J}$ the set of cuts of J. This set is equipped with the order defined by $(L_1, U_1) < (L_2, U_2)$ if $L_1 \subsetneq L_2$. This ordering on $\widehat{J}$ can be extended to $J \cup \widehat{J}$. in a natural way: $(L, U) < a$ if $a \in U$. The order $\widehat{J}$ is Dedekind-complete. Its minimal (maximal) element is $\widehat{J}_{\min} = (\emptyset, J)$ (respectively, $\widehat{J}_{\max} = (J, \emptyset)$). For any element a of J, there are two successive cuts: $a^- := (\{b \in J \mid b < a\}, \{b \in J \mid b \geq a\})$ and $a^+ := (\{b \in J \mid b \leq a\}, \{b \in J \mid b > a\})$. Note that if If $a < b$ are consecutive elements of J then a^+ and b^- denote the same cut.

Given an alphabet Σ, a Σ-word of length J is a sequence $(\sigma_a \mid a \in J)$ of elements of Σ indexed by J.

In [7] we introduced simple ordinal automata which work over words of ordinal length. We extend this definition to finite base automata working on words over arbitrary linear orders.

Finite base automata have the same expressive power as finite state automata over chains. An important parameter of a finite base automaton is the size of its base. An advantage of finite base automata over finite state automata is that taking the conjunction is easy and the base of an automaton for the conjunction grows linearly in the number of conjuncts.

Definition 8.1 (finite base automata) *A finite base automaton $\mathfrak{A}$ is a tuple of the form $(B, Q, \Sigma, \delta_{next}, \delta_{\lim}, Q_{init}, Q_{fin})$ such that*

- B *is a finite set (the basis of $\mathfrak{A}$),*
- $Q \subseteq \mathcal{P}(B)$ *(the set of states),*
- $Q_{init}, Q_{fin} \subseteq Q$ *(the sets of initial states and final states),*
- Σ *is a finite alphabet,*
- $\delta_{next} \subseteq Q \times \Sigma \times Q$ *is the next-step transition relation,*
- $\delta_{\lim} \subseteq \mathcal{P}(B) \times Q \cup Q \times \mathcal{P}(B)$ *is the limit transition relation.*

Let f be a function from a set I into $\mathcal{P}(B)$. Define

$$\mathrm{always}(f) := \{b \in B \mid \forall c \in I \quad b \in f(c)\}.$$

If I is a linear order, we define the left and right base-limit sets of f at $c \in I$ as the sets of base elements that appear in every state arbitrarily close to c (respectively, to its left and to its right). Formally, $Base_{\overrightarrow{\lim}}(c, f)$ is defined as

$$Base_{\overrightarrow{\lim}}(c, f) := \{b \in B \mid \forall a < c \exists d(a < d < c) \wedge b \in \mathrm{always}(f \! \restriction \! (d, c)\},$$

where $f \! \restriction \! (d, c)$ is the restriction of f to the interval (d, c).

$Base_{\overleftarrow{\lim}}(c, f)$ is defined similarly.

Given a finite base automaton $\mathfrak{A}$, a *run* of $\mathfrak{A}$ on Σ-word s over a linear order $\mathcal{I}$ is a function $\rho : \widehat{\mathcal{I}} \to Q$ such that

- For each $c \in \mathcal{I}$, $\rho(c^-) \xrightarrow{s(c)} \rho(c^+)$,
- if $c \in \widehat{\mathcal{I}} \setminus \widehat{\mathcal{I}}_{\min}$ has no predecessor, $(Base_{\overrightarrow{\lim}}(c, \rho), \rho(c)) \in \delta_{\lim}$, and
- if $c \in \widehat{\mathcal{I}} \setminus \widehat{\mathcal{I}}_{\max}$ has no successor, $(\rho(c), Base_{\overleftarrow{\lim}}(c, \rho)) \in \delta_{\lim}$.

An $\mathfrak{A}$-run ρ is *accepting* if $\rho(\widehat{\mathcal{I}}_{\min}) \in Q_{init}$ and $\rho(\widehat{\mathcal{I}}_{\max}) \in Q_{fin}$. $\mathfrak{A}$ *accepts a word s* if there is an accepting run on s.

Let $\mathfrak{A}_1, \ldots, \mathfrak{A}_m$ be finite base automata. One can easily construct an automaton $\mathfrak{A}$ that accepts the intersection of the languages accepted by these automata. The number of states in $\mathfrak{A}$ is the product of the numbers of states of $\mathfrak{A}_i$ and this grows exponentially in m; however, the base size of $\mathfrak{A}$ is the sum of the base sizes of $\mathfrak{A}_i$.

Lemma 8.2 (intersection of finite base automata). *Let $\mathfrak{A}_1$ and $\mathfrak{A}_2$ be finite base automata. Assume that the base size of $\mathfrak{A}_1$ and $\mathfrak{A}_2$ are n_1 and n_2. There is a finite base automaton $\mathfrak{A}$ such that the base size of $\mathfrak{A}$ is $n_1 + n_2$ and a word s is accepted by $\mathfrak{A}$ iff it is accepted by $\mathfrak{A}_1$ and by $\mathfrak{A}_2$.*

A word $s := (\sigma_a \mid a \in J)$ indexed by J over an alphabet $\{0,1\}^k$ can be identified with a chain $(J, <, P_1, \dots, P_k)$ over J where $P_i = \{a \in J \mid$ the i-th bit of $\sigma_a = 1\}$. This is a bijection between the $\{0,1\}^k$-words over J and the chain with k monadic predicates over J.

An automaton is said to be equivalent to a formula $\varphi(P_1, \dots, P_k)$ over a class $\mathcal{C}$ of linear orders if for every linear order $J \in \mathcal{C}$ and every word s indexed by J, $\mathfrak{A}$ accepts s if and only if the corresponding chain satisfies φ.

Cristau [6] proved that every formula of the first-order fragment of the monadic logic is equivalent (over the class of all linear orders) to a finite-state automaton. Hence,

Theorem 8.3 *For every first-order formula φ there is a finite base automaton $\mathfrak{A}_\varphi$ equivalent to φ over the class of all linear orders.*

9   Small Rank Property

Let $\mathfrak{A}$ be a finite base automaton, $\mathcal{L}$ a chain and $\rho : \widehat{\mathcal{L}} \to Q$ be a run of $\mathfrak{A}$ on $\mathcal{L}$. $type_{\mathfrak{A}}(\rho) := (q, D, q')$, where $\rho(\widehat{\mathcal{L}}_{\min}) = q$, $\rho(\widehat{\mathcal{L}}_{\max}) = q'$ and $D := \text{always}(\rho)$.

If $type_{\mathfrak{A}}(\rho) := (q, D, q')$ we sometimes write $\rho \; : \; q \xrightarrow{D} q'$; we write $\rho \; :\xrightarrow{D}$ if $type_{\mathfrak{A}}(\rho) := (q, D, q')$ for some q and q'.

Define an equivalence relation $\sim_{\mathfrak{A}}$ on $\mathfrak{A}$-runs:

$$\rho_1 \sim_{\mathfrak{A}} \rho_2 \text{ if and only if } type_{\mathfrak{A}}(\rho_1) = type_{\mathfrak{A}}(\rho_2)$$

Weight. Let D be a subset of the base B of $\mathfrak{A}$. The weight of D is defined as the cardinality of $B \setminus D$. The weight of a transition of $\mathfrak{A}$ is defined as follows. The weight of a successor transition is 0; the weight of limit transitions $(D, q) \in \delta_{\lim}$ and $(q, D) \in \delta_{\lim}$ is the weight of D. The weight of a run ρ is defined as the maximum of the weights of transitions that appears in ρ. We denote the weight of ρ by weight(ρ); the weight is always between 0 and the cardinality of the base of $\mathfrak{A}$.

Lemma 9.1 (Main). *Assume that ρ is a run of a finite base automaton $\mathfrak{A}$.*

1. *If $\rho :\xrightarrow{D}$ and* weight$(\rho) =$ weight$(D) = w$, *then there is a run on a chain of rank $\leq 2w + 1$, which is equivalent to ρ.*
2. *Any run of weight $\leq w$ is equivalent to a run on a chain of rank $\leq 2w + 2$.*

As a consequence, we obtain the following small rank property:

Proposition 9.2 (small rank property). *Let $\mathfrak{A}$ be a finite base automaton with base of size $n_{\mathfrak{A}}$. Every run of $\mathfrak{A}$ is equivalent to a run on a chain of rank $\leq 2n_{\mathfrak{A}} + 2$. In particular, if $\mathfrak{A}$ has an accepting run, then it accepts a chain of rank $\leq 2n_{\mathfrak{A}} + 2$.*

The complexity analysis of our PSPACE algorithm was based on Lemma 7.2. Now we are ready to prove it.

Proof. (of Lemma 7.2.) Let Φ be a finite set of first-order formulas. By Theorem 8.3, every formula in $\varphi \in \Phi$ is equivalent to a finite-base automaton $\mathfrak{A}_\varphi$. Let n_Φ be an upper bound on the base size of $\mathfrak{A}_\varphi$ for $\varphi \in \Phi$.

Let $\psi = \varphi_1(\overline{P_1}) \wedge \cdots \wedge \varphi_k(\overline{P_k})$ be a Φ-conjunctive formula. By Lemma 8.2, ψ is equivalent to a finite base automata with the base of size $\leq k \times n_\Phi$. By Proposition 9.2, if ψ is satisfiable then it is satisfiable on a chain of rank $\leq k(2n_\Phi + 2)$. Hence, we can define r_Φ as $(2n_\Phi + 2)$. □

It is instructive to compare small rank property of finite base automata with short run property of simple ordinal automata from [7]. A simple ordinal automaton is a finite base automaton with $\delta_{\lim} \subseteq \mathcal{P}(B) \times Q$. Hence, the domain of every run ρ of a simple ordinal automaton is order-isomorphic to an ordinal, and if ρ is a run on $\mathcal{M}$ then $\mathcal{M}$ is a chain over an ordinal. An ordinal α has rank $i \geq 1$ iff $\alpha < \omega^{i+1}$. Lemma 6 in [7] states that every run of a simple ordinal automaton $\mathfrak{A}$ is equivalent to an $\mathfrak{A}$-run on an ordinal $< \omega^{n_\mathfrak{A}+1}$, where $n_\mathfrak{A}$ is the size of the base of $\mathfrak{A}$.

10   Conclusion, Further and Related Results

We provided an EXPTIME algorithm for the satisfiability problem for any temporal or modal logic with a finite set of ∃-MSO definable modalities over a recursively defined class of structures, and proved that EXPTIME-bound is optimal in the worst case.

Let TL be any temporal logic with a finite set of ∃-MSO definable modalities. We proved that the satisfiability problem for TL over the class of all linear orders can be solved in PSPACE. This improves the Cristau result [6] that the satisfiability problem over this class for the temporal logic having the four modalities Until, Since, Until$_{Stavi}$ and Since$_{Stavi}$ is in double exponential space, and implies Reynolds's conjecture.

In the rest of this section we explain how the PSPACE bound can be extended uniformly to many interesting classes of linear orders.

Let ψ be an ∃-MSO sentence. A set $\mathcal{C}$ of chains is said to be *definable by* ψ, if $\mathcal{C} = \{\mathcal{M} \mid \mathcal{M} \models \psi\}$. A set $\mathcal{C}$ of chains is said to be *definable by* ψ *relatively to a class* $\mathcal{C}'$, if $\mathcal{C} = \{\mathcal{M} \in \mathcal{C}' \mid \mathcal{M} \models \psi\}$.

Theorem 7.3 immediately implies

Corrollary 10.1 *Let TL be a temporal logic with a finite set of ∃-MSO definable modalities, and let ψ be an ∃-MSO sentence. If the satisfiability problem for TL over $\mathcal{C}'$ is in PSPACE, then the satisfiability problem for TL over the class of chains definable by ψ relatively to $\mathcal{C}'$ is in PSPACE. In particular, the satisfiability problem for TL over the class of chains definable by ψ is in PSPACE.*

A linear order is called *unbounded* if it has neither a minimum nor a maximum; Note that an ∃-MSO formula φ is satisfiable in $\mathbb{Q}$ iff it is satisfiable in an unbounded dense order. There are first-order sentences *Unbound* and *Dense* that express that an order is unbounded, respectively, dense. Therefore, φ is satisfiable in $\mathbb{Q}$ iff *Unbound* $\wedge$ *Dense* $\wedge\,\varphi$ is satisfiable over a linear order. Hence, there is a PSPACE algorithm for satisfiability in $\mathbb{Q}$.

Recall that a cut (L,U) of a linear order $\mathcal{L}$ is a gap if neither L has a maximal element, nor U has a minimal element and $L \neq \emptyset \neq U$. A chain is Dedekind-complete if its underlining order does not have gaps. The class of non-Dedekind chain can be easily definable by an $\exists$-MSO sentence. Hence, there is a PSPACE algorithm for the satisfiability over the class of non-Dedekind complete chains. The class of Dedekind complete chains is not definable by an $\exists$-MSO sentence. However, we will show (Theorem 10.7) that there is a PSPACE algorithm for the satisfiability over the class of Dedekind complete chains.

Let OP be a subset of $\{\omega, \omega^{-1}, \textit{shuffle}\}$. Our proof can be easily modified to show the following variant of small rank property (Lemma 7.2).

Lemma 10.2. *For every finite set Φ of first-order formulas and every $OP \subseteq \{\omega, \omega^{-1}, \textit{shuffle}\}$ there is $N_{\Phi,OP} \in \mathbb{N}$ such that every Φ-conjunctive formula ψ is satisfiable in $Cl(One, OP\cup\{+\})$ iff it is satisfiable in a chain $\mathcal{M} \in Cl(One, OP\cup \{+\})$ of rank $\leq |\psi| \times N_{\Phi,OP}$.*

Hence, the satisfiability problem for any temporal logic with a finite set of $\exists$-MSO definable modalities over $Cl(One, OP \cup \{+\})$ is in PSPACE.

Recall that a linear order is scattered if it does not contain a dense suborder (i.e., a substructure order-isomorphic to $\mathbb{Q}$). An $\exists$-MSO formula is satisfiable in a chain over an ordinal (respectively, over a scattered order) iff it is satisfiable in $Cl(One, \{\omega, +\}$ (respectively, in $Cl(One, \{\omega, \omega^{-1}+\}$ [13,19]. Hence, we obtain:

Theorem 10.3 *Let TL be a temporal logic with a finite set of modalities definable in the existential fragment of MSO.*

1. *The satisfiability problem for TL in the class of chains over ordinals is in PSPACE [7].*
2. *The satisfiability problem for TL in the class of scattered chains is in PSPACE.*

A linear order is *continuous* if it is dense and Dedekind-complete; it is separable if it has a countable dense subset. Any unbounded separable continuous order is order-isomorphic to the reals.

Burgess and Gurevich [5] proved that $TL(\mathsf{Until}, \mathsf{Since})$ is decidable over the reals. They introduced the following class of chains.

Definition 10.4. *Let $\mathcal{C}$ be the minimal class of chains that contains all one-element chains and has the following properties:*

1. *If $\mathcal{M}$ and $\mathcal{N}$ are in $\mathcal{C}$ and $\mathcal{M}$ has a maximum or $\mathcal{N}$ has a minimum, then $\mathcal{M}+\mathcal{N} \in \mathcal{C}$.*
2. *If $\mathcal{M} \in \mathcal{C}$ and $\mathcal{M}$ has either a minimum or a maximum, then $\mathcal{M} \times \omega^{-1}$ and $\mathcal{M} \times \omega$ are in $\mathcal{C}$.*
3. *If $\mathcal{A} \subseteq \mathcal{C}$ is finite and each $\mathcal{M} \in \mathcal{A}$ has both a minimum and a maximum, and some $\mathcal{N} \in \mathcal{A}$ are one-element chains, then $\textit{shuffle}(\mathcal{A}) \in \mathcal{C}$.*

The next theorem was a key step in their decidability proof.

Theorem 10.5 *Let φ be an $\exists$-MSO formula. The following are equivalent:*

1. *φ is satisfiable over the class of Dedekind-complete separable chains.*
2. *φ is satisfiable over the class of Dedekind-complete chains.*
3. *φ is satisfiable in $\mathcal{C}$.*

As a consequence, they obtained a (non-elementary) algorithm for the decidability of $TL(\mathsf{Until}, \mathsf{Since})$ over the reals.

The definition of $\mathcal{C}$ is slightly more general than the definition of a recursively defined class of structures. However, our definition is easily extended to the (mutual) recursive definition of a finite number of classes.

One can easily rephrase Definition 10.4 as a mutual recursive definition of three classes: $\mathcal{C}$, $\mathcal{C}_{\max}$ and $\mathcal{C}_{\min}$, where $\mathcal{C}_{\max}$ (respectively, $\mathcal{C}_{\min}$) is the set of chains in $\mathcal{C}$ with a maximal, (respectively, minimal) element. (Note that $\mathcal{C}_{\max}$ and $\mathcal{C}_{\min}$ are $\exists$-MSO definable relatively to $\mathcal{C}$.)

Our results are easily extended to these classes. In particular, for every finite set Φ of first-order formulas there is r_Φ such that a Φ-conjunctive formula ψ is satisfiable in $\mathcal{C}$ iff it is satisfiable in $\mathcal{M} \in \mathcal{C}$ of rank $\leq r_\Phi \times |\psi|$. Hence,

Lemma 10.6. *Let TL be a temporal logic with a finite set of modalities definable in $\exists$-MSO. The satisfiability problem for TL in $\mathcal{C}$ is in* PSPACE.

As a consequence, we obtain:

Theorem 10.7 *Let TL be a temporal logic with a finite set of modalities definable in the existential fragment of MSO.*

1. *The satisfiability problem for TL over the class of Dedekind-complete separable chains is in* PSPACE.
2. *The satisfiability problem for TL over the class of Dedekind-complete chains is in* PSPACE.
3. *The satisfiability problem for TL in the class of chains over the reals is in* PSPACE.
4. *The satisfiability problem for TL over the class of continuous chains is in* PSPACE.

Proof. (1) and (2) follow from Theorem 10.5 and Lemma 10.6.

Let *Unbound* and *Dense* be first-order formulas that express that an order is unbounded and dense. By Theorem 10.5, $\varphi \in TL$ is satisfiable over the reals iff $\varphi \wedge Dense \wedge Unbound$ is satisfiable in $\mathcal{C}$. Therefore, (3) follows by Lemma 10.6.

$\varphi \in TL$ is satisfiable over the class of continuous chains iff $\varphi \wedge Dense$ is satisfiable in $\mathcal{C}$. Therefore, (4) follows by Lemma 10.6.   □

Similar arguments show that the satisfiability problem for TL over the classes of scattered Dedekind-complete chains, scattered non Dedekind-complete chains, and over many other classes is in PSPACE.

Reynolds [17] proved Theorem 10.7(3) for the temporal logic with two modalities Until and Since. Due to the Kamp theorem, this implies that the satisfiability problem over the reals for any temporal logic with a finite set of first-order definable modalities is in PSPACE. His proof relies on particular properties of Until and Since and uses temporal mosaics. The proofs in [17] are very non-trivial and difficult to grasp, probably because they have been developed from scratch.

We do not fully understand the Reynolds proof; however, there are some elements which are similar to our proof of Theorem 10.7(3). He considers operations on mosaics which correspond to sum, multiplication by ω and by ω^{-1} and shuffle of chains. He decides whether a finite set of small pieces is sufficient to be used to build a real-number model of a given formula. This is also equivalent to the existence of a winning strategy for player one in a two-player game played with mosaics. The search for a winning strategy is arranged into a search through a tree of mosaics. By establishing limits on the depth of the tree (a polynomial in terms of the length of the formula) he constructs a PSPACE algorithm. There is an analogy between such mosaic trees and construction trees for chains of finite rank.

Finally, let us note that the results of this paper hold for temporal logics with modalities having generalized truth tables definable by automata. Let $\mathfrak{A}$ be an automaton over the alphabet $\{0,1\}^{n+1}$. A modality O is said to be definable by $\mathfrak{A}$ if for every linear order $\mathcal{L} := \langle A, < \rangle$ and every $P_1, \ldots, P_n \subseteq A$ there is a unique P such that $\langle A, <, P, P_1, \ldots, P_n \rangle$ is accepted by $\mathfrak{A}$, moreover $P = O(P_1, \ldots, P_n)$.

Theorem 10.8 *Let TL be a temporal logic with a finite set of modalities such that every modality is definable by an automaton. Then, the satisfiability problem for TL over the class of all chains is in* PSPACE.

References

1. Bedon, N., Bes, A., Carton, O., Rispal, C.: Logic and Rational Languages of Words Indexed by Linear Orderings. In: Hirsch, E.A., Razborov, A.A., Semenov, A., Slissenko, A. (eds.) CSR 2008. LNCS, vol. 5010, pp. 76–85. Springer, Heidelberg (2008)
2. Bruyère, V., Carton, O.: Automata on linear orderings. In: Sgall, J., Pultr, A., Kolman, P. (eds.) MFCS 2001. LNCS, vol. 2136, pp. 236–247. Springer, Heidelberg (2001)
3. Büchi, J.R.: On a decision method in restricted second order arithmetic. In: Logic, Methodology and Philosophy of Science, pp. 1–11. Stanford University Press, Stanford (1962)
4. Büchi, J.R., Siefkes, D.: The Monadic Second-order Theory of all Countable Ordinals. Springer Lecture Notes, vol. 328 (1973)
5. Burgess, J.P., Gurevich, Y.: The decision problem for linear temporal logic. Notre Dame J. Formal Logic 26(2), 115–128 (1985)
6. Cristau, J.: Automata and temporal logic over arbitrary linear time. In: FSTTCS 2009, pp. 133–144 (2009)
7. Demri, S., Rabinovich, A.: The Complexity of Temporal Logic with Until and Since over Ordinals. In: Dershowitz, N., Voronkov, A. (eds.) LPAR 2007. LNCS (LNAI), vol. 4790, pp. 531–545. Springer, Heidelberg (2007)
8. Feferman, S., Vaught, R.L.: The first-order properties of products of algebraic systems. Fundamenta Mathematicae 47, 57–103 (1959)

9. Gabbay, D.M., Hodkinson, I., Reynolds, M.: Temporal Logics, vol. 1. Clarendon Press, Oxford (1994)
10. Gabbay, D.M., Pnueli, A., Shelah, S., Stavi, J.: On the Temporal Analysis of Fairness. In: 7th POPL, pp. 163–173 (1980)
11. Gurevich, Y.: Monadic second-order theories. In: Barwise, J., Feferman, S. (eds.) Model-Theoretic Logics, pp. 479–506. Springer, Heidelberg (1985)
12. Kamp, H.: Tense Logic and the Theory of Linear Order. Ph.D. thesis, University of California L.A (1968)
13. Läuchli, H., Leonard, J.: On the elementary theory of linear order. Fundamenta Mathematicae 59, 109–116 (1966)
14. Rabin, M.O.: Decidability of second-order theories and automata on infinite trees. Transactions of the American Mathematical Society 141, 1–35 (1969)
15. Rabinovich, A.: Temporal logics over linear time domains are in PSPACE (manuscript) (2009)
16. Reynolds, M.: The complexity of the temporal logic with until over general linear time. J. Comput. Syst. Sci. 66, 393–426 (2003)
17. Reynolds, M.: The Complexity of Temporal Logic over the Reals. The Annals of Pure and Applied Logic 161(8), 1063–1096 (2010)
18. Rispal, C., Carton, O.: Complementation of rational sets on countable scattered linear orderings. Int. J. Found. Comput. Sci. 16(4), 767–786 (2005)
19. Rosenstein, J.G.: Linear ordering. Academic Press, New York (1982)
20. Shelah, S.: The monadic theory of order. Ann. of Math. 102, 349–419 (1975)
21. Sistla, A.P., Clarke, E.M.: The Complexity of Propositional Linear Temporal Logics. J. ACM 32(3), 733–749 (1985)
22. Thomas, W.: Ehrenfeucht games, the composition method, and the monadic theory of ordinal words. In: Mycielski, J., Rozenberg, G., Salomaa, A. (eds.) Structures in Logic and Computer Science. LNCS, vol. 1261, pp. 118–143. Springer, Heidelberg (1997)

Lossy Counter Machines Decidability Cheat Sheet*

Philippe Schnoebelen

LSV, ENS Cachan, CNRS
61, av. Pdt. Wilson, F-94230 Cachan, France
www.lsv.ens-cachan.fr/~phs

Abstract. Lossy counter machines (LCM's) are a variant of Minsky counter machines based on weak (or unreliable) counters in the sense that they can decrease nondeterministically and without notification. This model, introduced by R. Mayr [TCS 297:337-354 (2003)], is not yet very well known, even though it has already proven useful for establishing hardness results.

In this paper we survey the basic theory of LCM's and their verification problems, with a focus on the decidability/undecidability divide.

1 Introduction

Lossy counter machines are a weakened version of Minsky counter machines. They were introduced by Richard Mayr [38,39] as a simpler version of lossy channel systems, using counters holding numerical values rather than channels recording sequences of messages in transit. Mayr proved that finiteness and uniform termination are undecidable for lossy counter machines and used this to derive various undecidability results, e.g. in [11].

Lossy counter machines are hard. Since then, lossy counter machines have been used in a variety of situations, sometimes under the guise of *counter automata with incrementation errors* [19]. Mostly, they have been used in reductions proving *hardness*, i.e., complexity lower bounds. This relies on two kinds of results. Firstly, some problems that are undecidable for Minsky machines remain undecidable for the weaker lossy counter machines. This can be used for undecidability proofs in situations where it is easier to encode lossy counters than reliable ones, e.g., as in [19,16]. Secondly, some problems that are decidable for lossy counters machines are still Ackermann-hard, i.e., they require nonprimitive-recursive time and space [43,44]. This can be used to show Ackermann-hardness of problems that are decidable but rich enough to encode lossy counters, see [18,19,32,24,46] for examples.

A survey for lossy counter machines. In this paper, we survey the main decidability and undecidability results on lossy counter machines. Most areas have not yet been investigated deeply, and some have only been superficially visited. As a consequence, our survey looks sometimes more like a road map for future research than as a record of past achievements.

---

* Work supported by the Agence Nationale de la Recherche, grant ANR-06-SETIN-001.

A. Kučera and I. Potapov (Eds.): RP 2010, LNCS 6227, pp. 51–75, 2010.

We strove for simplicity. Most decidability results can be proven by elementary arguments, relying only on generic properties like strong monotonicity of steps (Fact 2.1), the wqo property (Fact 2.3) and basic features of semilinear sets. These proofs are simpler and more versatile than the algorithms provided in, e.g., [5,28]. For undecidability, all our proofs share a single and very simple gadget, "putting a Minsky machine on a budget", making them conceptually simpler.

In this "survey" we do not always point to the earliest existing reference for each and every stated theorem. Mostly this is because these results are new, or presented in a new and extended form, or with a new and simplified proof. In general, the results come from [11,42,39] when they are specific to lossy counter machines. Some results have been first shown for lossy channel systems [15,7,6] or even well-structured systems [25,26,5,28,29].

Outline of the paper. We define counter machines, both reliable and lossy, in Section 2. We handle reachability properties in Section 3, termination and inevitability properties in Section 4, liveness properties in Section 5, finiteness properties in Section 6. All the decidability results given in these first sections are proven along the way, while the proof of the undecidability results are delayed until Section 7 where they are handled uniformly. Finally, we gather in Section 8 a few extra results on issues that are less central, or more recent, in the theory of lossy counter machines. Finally, and for the sake of completeness, the complexity of decidable problems is briefly discussed in Section 9.

2   Counter Machines

Counter machines are a model of computation where a finite-state control acts upon a finite number of *counters*, i.e., storage locations that hold natural numbers. The computation steps are usually restricted to simple tests and updates. For Minsky counter machines, the tests are zero-tests and the updates are incrementations and decrementations. Formally, a *(Minsky) counter machine* is a tuple $M = (Loc, C, \Delta)$ where $Loc = \{\ell_1, \ldots, \ell_m\}$ is finite set of *locations*, $C = \{c_1, \ldots, c_n\}$ is a finite set of *counters*, and $\Delta \subseteq Loc \times OP(C) \times Loc$ is a finite set of transition rules carrying operations from a set $OP(C) \stackrel{\text{def}}{=} C \times \{\texttt{++}, \texttt{--}, \texttt{=0?}\}$.

In pictorial representations, a counter machine is usually depicted as a directed graph where transition rules are $OP(C)$-labeled edges between control locations, see Fig. 1 for a simple example. An operation of the form $\texttt{c++}$ denotes the incrementation of counter c, while $\texttt{c--}$ denotes its decrementation. Decrementations are only firable when the counter at hand holds a strictly positive value, as is formally stipulated in the operational semantics. Operations of the form $\texttt{c=0?}$ are tests used to restrict transition steps.

2.1   Operational Semantics

Let $M = (Loc, C, \Delta)$ be a counter machine. A *configuration* of M is some $\sigma = \langle \ell, \boldsymbol{a} \rangle \in Conf \stackrel{\text{def}}{=} Loc \times \mathbb{N}^C$, i.e., a *current control location* ℓ and a C-indexed vector $\boldsymbol{a}$ of natural numbers (one *current value* for each counter in C). If we assume, as we shall do from now on, that $C = \{c_1, \ldots, c_n\}$, we may identify $\mathbb{N}^C$ with $\mathbb{N}^n$ and write σ under the form

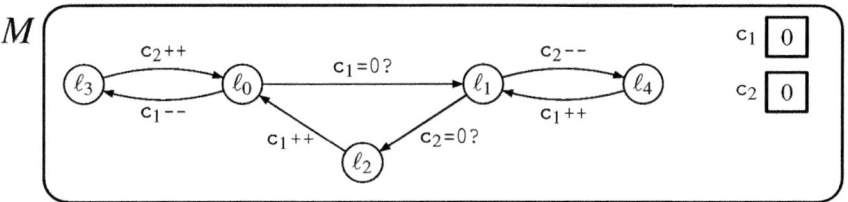

Fig. 1. M: a counter machine that enumerates all pairs $(a_1, a_2) \in \mathbb{N}^2$

$\langle \ell, a_1, \ldots, a_n \rangle$. We sometimes use counter names as positional indexes when there is a need for disambiguation, e.g., writing $\langle \mathbf{0}, c_k : 1, \mathbf{0} \rangle$ for the k-th unit vector.

The operational semantics of M is given under the form of transitions between its configurations. Formally, there is a *transition* (also called a *step*) $\sigma \xrightarrow{\delta}_{\text{std}} \sigma'$ if, and only if, σ is some $\langle \ell, a_1, \ldots, a_n \rangle$, σ' is some $\langle \ell', a_1', \ldots, a_n' \rangle$, $\delta = (\ell, op, \ell')$ and either:

- op is c_k=0? (zero test): $a_k = 0$, and $a_i' = a_i$ for all $i = 1, \ldots, n$, or
- op is c_k-- (decrementation): $a_k' = a_k - 1$, and $a_i' = a_i$ for all $i \neq k$, or
- op is c_k++ (incrementation): $a_k' = a_k + 1$, and $a_i' = a_i$ for all $i \neq k$.

As usual, we write $\sigma \rightarrow_{\text{std}} \sigma'$ when $\sigma \xrightarrow{\delta}_{\text{std}} \sigma'$ for some $\delta \in \Delta$. Chains $\sigma_0 \rightarrow_{\text{std}} \sigma_1 \rightarrow_{\text{std}} \cdots \rightarrow_{\text{std}} \sigma_k$ of consecutive steps, also called *runs*, are denoted $\sigma_0 \xrightarrow{*}_{\text{std}} \sigma_k$, and also $\sigma_0 \xrightarrow{+}_{\text{std}} \sigma_k$ when $k > 0$. For example, M from Fig. 1 has a run:

$$\langle \ell_0, 0, 0 \rangle \rightarrow_{\text{std}} \langle \ell_1, 0, 0 \rangle \rightarrow_{\text{std}} \langle \ell_2, 0, 0 \rangle \rightarrow_{\text{std}} \langle \ell_0, 1, 0 \rangle \rightarrow_{\text{std}} \langle \ell_3, 0, 0 \rangle \rightarrow_{\text{std}} \langle \ell_0, 0, 1 \rangle$$
$$\rightarrow_{\text{std}} \langle \ell_1, 0, 1 \rangle \rightarrow_{\text{std}} \langle \ell_4, 0, 0 \rangle \rightarrow_{\text{std}} \langle \ell_1, 1, 0 \rangle \rightarrow_{\text{std}} \langle \ell_2, 1, 0 \rangle \rightarrow_{\text{std}} \langle \ell_0, 2, 0 \rangle \rightarrow_{\text{std}} \langle \ell_3, 1, 0 \rangle$$

For a vector $\mathbf{a} = (a_1, \ldots, a_n)$, or a configuration $\sigma = \langle \ell, \mathbf{a} \rangle$, we let $|\mathbf{a}| = |\sigma| \overset{\text{def}}{=} \sum_{i=1}^{n} a_i$ denote its *size*. For $N \in \mathbb{N}$, we say that a run $\sigma_0 \rightarrow_{\text{std}} \sigma_1 \rightarrow_{\text{std}} \cdots \rightarrow_{\text{std}} \sigma_k$ is *N-bounded* if $|\sigma_i| \leq N$ for all $i = 0, \ldots, k$.

The above definitions use a "std" subscript when writing steps to emphasize that they rely on the usual, standard, operational semantics of counter machines, where the behavior is *reliable*. We now introduce lossy counter machines as counter machines with a different semantics.

2.2   Lossy Counter Machines

In lossy counter machines, the contents of the counters may decrease non-deterministically (the machine can "leak", or "lose data"). This behavior is not under the control of the machine, i.e., it can be seen as some inherent non-determinism. Furthermore, the lossy machine does not have any direct way of noticing if/when a loss occurs. Hence lossy counter machines are less powerful than standard, reliable, counter machines.

Technically, it is more convenient to see lossy machines as counter machines with a different operational semantics (and not as a special class of machines): thus it is possible to use simultaneously the two semantics and to relate them.

Formally, this is defined via the introduction of a partial ordering between the configurations of M:

$$\langle \ell, a_1, ..., a_n \rangle \leq \langle \ell', a_1', ..., a_n' \rangle \stackrel{\text{def}}{\Leftrightarrow} \ell = \ell' \wedge a_1 \leq a_1' \wedge \cdots \wedge a_n \leq a_n'.$$

One way to read $\sigma \leq \sigma'$ is to see σ as the result of some losses (possibly none) in σ'.

Now "lossy" steps, denoted $\sigma \stackrel{\delta}{\rightarrow}_{\text{lossy}} \sigma'$, are given by the following definition:

$$\sigma \stackrel{\delta}{\rightarrow}_{\text{lossy}} \sigma' \stackrel{\text{def}}{\Leftrightarrow} \exists \theta, \theta' : (\sigma \geq \theta \wedge \theta \stackrel{\delta}{\rightarrow}_{\text{std}} \theta' \wedge \theta' \geq \sigma'). \qquad (\dagger)$$

Note that reliable steps are a special case of lossy steps:

$$\sigma \rightarrow_{\text{std}} \sigma' \text{ implies } \sigma \rightarrow_{\text{lossy}} \sigma'. \qquad (\ddagger)$$

An immediate corollary of ($\dagger$) is the so-called "monotonicity of steps" property:

Fact 2.1 ((Strong) Monotonicity)
1. Assume $\sigma \rightarrow_{\text{lossy}} \tau$. Then $\sigma' \rightarrow_{\text{lossy}} \tau'$ for all $\sigma' \geq \sigma$ and all $\tau' \leq \tau$.
2. Assume $\sigma \stackrel{+}{\rightarrow}_{\text{lossy}} \tau$. Then $\sigma' \stackrel{+}{\rightarrow}_{\text{lossy}} \tau'$ for all $\sigma' \geq \sigma$ and all $\tau' \leq \tau$.

Remark 2.2. Here the adjective "strong" emphasizes the fact that the existence of some step $\sigma \rightarrow_{\text{lossy}} \tau$ implies the existence of $\sigma' \rightarrow_{\text{lossy}} \tau$ for all $\sigma' \geq \sigma$, (rather than *some* $\sigma' \rightarrow_{\text{lossy}} \tau'$) and, symmetrically, the existence of $\sigma \rightarrow_{\text{lossy}} \tau'$ for all $\tau' \leq \tau$. □

2.3 Dickson's Lemma

The configuration ordering enjoys the following key property:

Fact 2.3 (Wqo). $(Conf, \leq)$ *is a well-quasi-ordering.*

This is otherwise known as Dickson's Lemma. It means that any infinite sequence $\sigma_0, \sigma_1, \sigma_2, \ldots$ of configurations contains an infinite increasing subsequence $\sigma_{i_0} \leq \sigma_{i_1} \leq \sigma_{i_2} \leq \cdots$. Equivalently, not only is the ordering well-founded (there is no infinite decreasing sequence $\sigma_0 > \sigma_1 > \sigma_2 > \cdots$) but every linearisation is well-founded. In particular, there is no infinite set of pairwise incomparable configurations. See [34] for more information.

It is the combination of monotonicity of steps with the wqo-property that turns lossy counter machines into what are called *well-structured transition systems* [28,5].

2.4 Semilinear Sets of Configurations

A set of configurations $R \subseteq Conf$ is *linear* if it can be written under the form

$$R = \{ \langle \ell, \boldsymbol{a} + k_1.\boldsymbol{b}_1 + \cdots + k_m.\boldsymbol{b}_m \rangle \mid k_1, \ldots, k_m \in \mathbb{N} \}$$

for some *base configuration* $\langle \ell, \boldsymbol{a} \rangle$ and some finite set of increments $\boldsymbol{b}_1, \ldots, \boldsymbol{b}_m \in \mathbb{N}^n$. For example the upward-closure $\uparrow\sigma \stackrel{\text{def}}{=} \{ \theta \in Conf \mid \theta \geq \sigma \}$ of a single configuration is linear, with σ itself as the base, and n unit vectors, one per counter, as increments. A second example is the singleton set $\{\sigma\}$, linear too, with same base but no increments.

A set $R \subseteq Conf$ is *semilinear* if it is a finite union $R = L_1 \cup \cdots \cup L_k$ of linear sets. In particular, the empty set is semilinear (take $k = 0$) and $Conf$ itself is semilinear as $\bigcup_{\ell \in Loc} \uparrow\langle \ell, \mathbf{0} \rangle$.

It is well-known that semilinear sets are exactly the sets that can be denoted by Presburger formulae (effective translations between the two representations exist) and that they are closed under complement, intersection, projection, etc., all this in an effective way [33,37]. Slightly abusing notations, we shall use letters like $X, Y, \ldots$ to denote semilinear sets of configurations and, at the same time, to denote their finitary descriptions (e.g., Presburger formulae, or bases *cum* increments) that can be given as input to algorithms.

Not all sets of configurations are semilinear but many interesting sets can be denoted by Presburger formulae (e.g., the set of all configurations whose size satisfy a Presburger constraint) and thus are semilinear.

The following is even more important for our purposes:

Fact 2.4 (Order-closed sets are semilinear). *If $R \subseteq Conf$ is upward-closed or downward-closed, it is semilinear.*

Indeed, by the wqo-property, an upward-closed R has *finitely many* minimal elements, hence can be written $R = \bigcup_{\sigma \in \min(R)} \uparrow\sigma$ which is semilinear. For a downward-closed R, we observe that its complement is upward-closed, hence semilinear, and rely on the fact that the complement of a semilinear set is semilinear.

3 Reachability and Safety

From now on, we omit the "lossy" subscript and write $\sigma \to \sigma'$ instead of $\sigma \to_{\text{lossy}} \sigma'$. This is because the lossy steps are our main objects. We only revert to the fully explicit notation when it is necessary to consider both reliable and lossy steps at the same time (for example in Section 7).

3.1 Post-sets and Pre-sets

For $R \subseteq Conf$, we let $Post(R) \stackrel{\text{def}}{=} \{\sigma' \mid \exists \sigma \in R : \sigma \to \sigma'\}$ denote the set of *immediate successors* of configurations in R. Similarly, we let $Post^*(R)$ and $Post^+(R)$ denote the set of configurations reachable from R through an arbitrary number (resp. strictly positive number) of steps. Similarly, $Pre(R)$, $Pre^*(R)$, and $Pre^+(R)$ denote sets of *predecessors* configurations, from which a configuration in R can be reached.

A consequence of monotonicity (Fact 2.1) is the following order-closure property:

Fact 3.1. *For any $R \subseteq Conf$, $Post(R)$ and $Post^+(R)$ are downward-closed sets, while $Pre(R)$ and $Pre^+(R)$ are upward-closed sets.*

Corollary 3.2. *For any $R \subseteq Conf$, $Pre(R)$, $Pre^+(R)$, $Post(R)$ and $Post^+(R)$ are semilinear.*

Furthermore, if R itself is semilinear, then $Post^*(R)$ and $Pre^*(R)$ too are semilinear.

Here the first point is just an applications of Fact 2.4 while the second point stems from $Post^*(R) = R \cup Post^+(R)$ and symmetrically for $Pre^*(R)$.

Note that, if R is semilinear, one can compute $Post(R)$ and $Pre(R)$ uniformly from R (and M). This has little to do with lossiness: counter machines is a low-level computational model with simple operational semantics for single steps. For counter machines, the one-step relations $\to_{std}$ and $\to_{lossy}$, seen a subsets of $Conf \times Conf$, are semilinear (and easily read out of M).

3.2   Reachability Problems

The main question is the decidability of a general form of reachability questions, that we call *general reachability* in order to distinguish it from its less general variants.

General_Reachability:
>   Given: a LCM M, two semilinear sets of configurations X and Y.
>   Question: does there exist $\sigma_1 \in X$ and $\sigma_2 \in Y$ such that $\sigma_1 \xrightarrow{*} \sigma_2$? In such a case, we write $X \xrightarrow{*} Y$.
>   Equivalently: Does $Post^*(X) \cap Y \neq \varnothing$? Does $Pre^*(Y) \cap X \neq \varnothing$?

In the literature, reachability problems often appear in other forms:

Configuration_Reachability: does $\sigma_0 \xrightarrow{*} \sigma_t$ for given starting configuration σ_0 and target configuration σ_t?
Location_Reachability: is there some $\boldsymbol{a} \in \mathbb{N}^n$ such that $\sigma_0 \xrightarrow{*} (\ell, \boldsymbol{a})$ for given σ_0 and target location $\ell \in Loc$?
Coverability: is there some $\sigma \geq \sigma_t$ such that $\sigma_0 \xrightarrow{*} \sigma$ for given σ_0 and target configuration to be covered σ_t?
Safety: does $Post^*(X_0) \subseteq X_s$ for given semilinear set of starting configurations X_0 and semilinear set of "safe" configurations X_s?

Obviously, all these problems are special cases of General_Reachability (or of its complement in the case of Safety), hence are easier. We observe that location reachability is a special case of coverability, and that coverability and single-configuration reachability almost coincide since, thanks to Fact 2.1, one can cover σ_g from σ_0 if, and only if, σ_g is reachable from σ_0 or is already covered by it (i.e., $\sigma_0 \geq \sigma_g$).

3.3   Decidability of Reachability

Theorem 3.3. General_Reachability *is decidable for lossy counter machines.*

First observe that general reachability is r.e. (it is enough to guess a run and check it, which amounts to simulating M) so that there only remains to show that non-reachability is r.e. too.

For this, we rely on semilinear invariants. An *inductive invariant*, or just "an invariant", is a set of configurations I such that $Post(I) \subseteq I$ or, equivalently, $Pre(J) \subseteq J$ letting $J \stackrel{def}{=} Conf \setminus I$.

Classically, invariants are used to prove safety properties, relying on the following fact: if $R \subseteq I$ for some invariant I, then $Post^*(R) \subseteq I$. They can be used as negative witnesses for general reachability: finding an invariant I that contains X and does not intersect Y proves that one cannot reach Y from X, written $\neg(X \xrightarrow{*} Y)$ for short.

This method is *complete* since, if $\neg(X \xrightarrow{*} Y)$, this is certainly witnessed by invariants, the smallest one being $Post^*(X)$ and the largest being $Conf \smallsetminus Pre^*(Y)$ [45]. The method can be made *effective* by restricting to semilinear invariants. Only considering semilinear invariants allows enumerating candidates sets I and it allows checking that a candidate I is indeed an invariant, that it contains X, and does not intersect Y. Restricting to semilinear invariant does not hinder completeness since, e.g., $Post^*(X)$ and $Conf \smallsetminus Pre^*(Y)$ are semilinear (by Coro. 3.2).

Finally, general reachability is co-r.e., and being r.e. too, is decidable.

Remark 3.4. We observe that the key ingredient for the above proof is simply that the reachability sets $Post^*(X)$ are "regular" in some sense (for LCM's, they are semilinear) and that the one-step image $Post(X)$, or the pre-image $Pre(X)$, is semilinear too and can be computed effectively from X. This proof technique is quite general and applies to many different situations. For example, the same argument was used for reversible Petri nets in [14], or for 3-dim VASS's in [36].   □

Corollary 3.5. Configuration_Reachability, Location_Reachability, Coverability, *and* Safety *are decidable for lossy counter machines.*

3.4 Reachability Logic

The reachability problems we just proved decidable can all be stated in a first-order logic of reachability, where the basic predicates are $s \to t$, $s \xrightarrow{*} t$, and $s \in X$ for X a semilinear set.

For example, Safety is written

$$\forall s \in X_0 : \forall t \in X_s : \neg(s \xrightarrow{*} t), \qquad (\varphi_{\mathrm{Saf}})$$

while configuration reachability and coverability are written, respectively,

$$\exists s \in \{\sigma_0\} : \exists t \in \{\sigma_t\} : s \xrightarrow{*} t, \qquad (\varphi_{\mathrm{CR}})$$

$$\exists s \in \{\sigma_0\} : \exists t \in {\uparrow}\sigma_t : s \xrightarrow{*} t. \qquad (\varphi_{\mathrm{Cov}})$$

These examples show that it is convenient to allow a simple language of terms denoting semilinear sets, like singletons "$\{\sigma\}$" or upward-closure "${\uparrow}X$". Below we also use Boolean operations, e.g., "$X \smallsetminus Y$", and order-theoretic constructions e.g., writing "$\min(X)$" to denote the set of minimal configurations in X. In any case we only use Presburger-definable operations: they always denote semilinear sets that can be computed effectively from their semilinear operands.

The model-checking problem for reachability logic is a natural generalization of the reachability problems we considered in Section 3.2. This problem is undecidable in general but identifying the decidable fragment is certainly an interesting question that is still very open. The question is even more interesting since there is ample room for refining and extending the logic in meaningful ways (see Section 8.1 for related questions).

Regarding some of the simplest non-trivial formulae, we can already provide a few results:

$$\exists s \in X : \exists t \in Y : s \xrightarrow{*} t \quad \text{decidable} \qquad \text{(one-to-one)}$$

$$\forall s \in X : \exists t \in Y : s \xrightarrow{*} t \quad \text{decidable} \qquad \text{(from-all)}$$

$$\exists s \in X : \forall t \in Y : s \xrightarrow{*} t \quad \text{undecidable, } \Sigma_2^0\text{-complete} \qquad \text{(one-to-all)}$$

$$\forall s \in X : \forall t \in Y : s \xrightarrow{*} t \quad \text{undecidable, } \Pi_1^0\text{-complete} \qquad \text{(all-to-all)}$$

$$\forall t \in Y : \exists s \in X : s \xrightarrow{*} t \quad \text{undecidable, } \Pi_1^0\text{-complete} \qquad \text{(to-all)}$$

$$\exists t \in Y : \forall s \in X : s \xrightarrow{*} t \quad \text{decidable} \qquad \text{(all-to-same)}$$

The undecidability results in the above list will be proven later, in Section 7. We mention them now because they are an indication that we should find the decidability results a bit surprising.

Regarding the decidability results, one-to-one formulae are just general reachability and have been shown decidable above. Observe that this entails the decidability of

$$\exists s \in X : \exists t \in Y : s \xrightarrow{+} t. \qquad \text{(one-to-one')}$$

Indeed this formula, also written $X \xrightarrow{+} Y$, is equivalent to both $Post(X) \xrightarrow{*} Y$ and $X \xrightarrow{*} Pre(Y)$, and $Post(X)$ and $Pre(Y)$ are semilinear sets that can be computed effectively from X and Y (and M), see Coro. 3.2.

Regarding from-all formulae, they reduce to conjunctions of simple reachability questions with the following reasoning:

$$\forall s \in X : \exists t \in Y : s \xrightarrow{*} t \qquad \text{(from-all)}$$

$$\Leftrightarrow \forall s \in (X \smallsetminus Y) : \exists t \in Y : s \xrightarrow{+} t$$

$$\Leftrightarrow \forall s \in \min(X \smallsetminus Y) : \exists t \in Y : s \xrightarrow{+} t$$

where the last step of the reduction relies on monotonicity of lossy steps (Fact 2.1). Now, $\min(X \smallsetminus Y)$ is some finite set $\{\sigma_1, \ldots, \sigma_k\}$ (Fact 2.3) that can be computed effectively from X and Y. Thus we have reduced a from-all formula to a finite conjunction of one-to-one' formulae.

We now turn to all-to-same formulae. The main idea is easier to understand if we consider a version where $\xrightarrow{+}$ is used:

$$\exists t \in Y : \forall s \in X : s \xrightarrow{+} t. \qquad \text{(all-to-same')}$$

One can simplify this by using monotonicity *on both sides of the steps:*[1]

$$\exists t \in Y : \forall s \in X : s \xrightarrow{+} t \quad \Leftrightarrow \quad \exists t \in \min(Y) : \forall s \in \min(X) : s \xrightarrow{+} t.$$

---

[1] Here it is crucial that the source is universally quantified upon and the destination is existentially quantified upon. It would not work the other way around.

Hence, letting $\min(X) = \{\sigma_1, \ldots, \sigma_k\}$ and $\min(Y) = \{\sigma_1', \ldots, \sigma_m'\}$, we have reduced all-to-same' to $\bigvee_{j=1}^{m} \bigwedge_{i=1}^{k} \sigma_i \xrightarrow{+} \sigma_j'$, a finite disjunction of conjunctions of decidable questions.

One can now show the decidability of all-to-same formulae by adapting the above idea. One possible way is to rely on, e.g.,

$$\exists t \in Y : \forall s \in X : s \xrightarrow{*} t \;\;\Leftrightarrow\;\; \left(\begin{array}{c} \exists t \in \min(Y) : \forall s \in \min(X) : s \xrightarrow{+} t \\ \vee\; \exists t \in \min(X) \cap Y : \forall s \in \min(X) : s \xrightarrow{*} t \end{array} \right).$$

Again, we end up with a finite combination of decidable reachability questions.

3.5   Computing Co-reachability Sets

One can go beyond Theorem 3.3 and compute the co-reachability sets.

Theorem 3.6 (Pre^* is effective). *For semilinear $X \subseteq Conf$, $Pre^*(X)$ can be computed effectively as a function of X and M.*

Indeed, we know that $Pre^*(X)$ is a semilinear set X_0 that satisfies both

$$X_0 \subseteq Pre^*(X), \quad \text{i.e., } \forall s \in X_0 : \exists t \in X : s \xrightarrow{*} t, \tag{1}$$

and

$$X_0 \supseteq Pre^*(X), \quad \text{i.e., } \neg\big(\exists s \notin X_0 : \exists t \in X : s \xrightarrow{*} t\big). \tag{2}$$

These two formulae are decidable for given X and X_0: (1) is a from-all formula while (2) is a negated one-to-one formula. Thus we can effectively recognize when a given X_0 coincides with $Pre^*(X)$. There only remains to enumerate all semilinear X_0 until we encounter $Pre^*(X)$, which is bound to eventually happen.

Computing $Pre^*(X)$ is useful in many situations where just deciding reachability questions would be insufficient. For example, Theo. 3.6 lets us list, or count, the number of starting configurations that do not satisfy a given safety property.

3.6   Computing Reachability Sets

Surprisingly, it is not possible to compute $Post^*(X)$ effectively. This is captured more precisely by the following statement:

Theorem 3.7 (On computing $Post^*$)
1. The question whether, for semilinear X and Y, $Post^*(X) \subseteq Y$ is decidable.
2. The question whether, for semilinear X and Y, $Post^*(X) \supseteq Y$ is Π_1^0-complete.

Indeed, Point 1 is the decidability of Safety, and Point 2 is the undecidability of to-all formulae (Section 3.4).

There is a troubling lack of symmetry here, between the computable Pre^* and the non-computable $Post^*$. We stress that this situation has little to do with the specifics of counter machines. Indeed, most of the proofs above only rely on monotonicity of steps, on Dickson's Lemma, and basic assumptions on the operational semantics (e.g.,

Presburger-definable one-step relation) that are fulfilled by many models. The bottom line is that most decidability proofs above rely on the closure properties stated in Coro. 3.2 where the asymmetry appears: upward-closed sets have a finite basis (on which one can base algorithms), while downward-closed sets do not.[2]

4   Termination and Inevitability

In this section, we consider termination and more general inevitability properties.

4.1   Termination

Consider the following problems:

Termination:
>   Given: a LCM M and an initial configuration σ_0,
>   Question: does M terminate?
>   Equivalently: are all runs starting from σ_0 finite?

Looping:
>   Given: a LCM M and an initial configuration σ_0,
>   Question: may the system loop? I.e., is there a configuration σ s.t. $\sigma_0 \xrightarrow{*} \sigma \xrightarrow{+} \sigma$?

Of course, looping is a special case of non-termination. That they coincide is less usual!

Lemma 4.1. *A lossy counter machine is looping if, and only if, it does not terminate.*

Indeed, assume there is an infinite run $\sigma_0 \to \sigma_1 \to \sigma_2 \to \dots$. The wqo property entails that there must be positions $k < l$ along this run with $\sigma_k \leq \sigma_l$. Since $\sigma_k \xrightarrow{+} \sigma_l$, monotonicity (Fact 2.1) entails $\sigma_k \xrightarrow{+} \sigma_k$ and we have a loop.

Theorem 4.2. *Termination and looping are decidable for lossy counter machines.*

The proof of Theorem 4.2 is much simpler than one would expect.
     First, we observe that termination is r.e.: since the transition relation is finitely branching, we know (Kőnig's Lemma) that if all runs from σ_0 are finite, then the tree of all runs is finite and an exhaustive simulation algorithm will terminate after examining finitely many runs.
     On the other hand, looping too is r.e.: one just has to guess a looping run $\sigma_0 \xrightarrow{*} \sigma_k \xrightarrow{+} \sigma_k$, which can be represented finitely and checked in finite time.
     Now since looping and non-termination coincide, the two problems are r.e. and co-r.e., hence decidable.

---

[2] Finite representations of upward-closed sets exist but they use some kind of "limits points" [27]. For lossy counter machines, the limit points are extended configurations where some counters contain ω. These behave like directed sets of configurations, not like real individual configurations.

Remark 4.3. The beauty of this proof is that termination and looping are r.e. *very generally*. That is to say, termination is r.e. for most sensible computation models, e.g., Turing machines or Minsky counter machines, and the same is true of looping. Thus that part of the proof is totally generic. What is *specific to lossy counter machines* is that non-termination and looping coincide. Indeed, they do not usually coincide for other models where a system may have infinite runs but no looping ones.   □

4.2 Inevitability

Inevitability means that all runs will eventually stumble into something. We consider a slightly more general form:

Strong_Inevitability:
>   Given: a LCM M, an initial configuration σ_0, and two semilinear sets $X_1, X_2 \subseteq Conf$
>   of configurations,
>   Question: do all runs from σ_0 stay within X_1 until they eventually visit X_2?
>   Equivalently: does the *CTL* formula $\mathsf{A}[X_1 \, \mathcal{U} X_2]$ hold in σ_0?

Observe that termination is a special case of strong inevitability (by letting $X_2 = Halt \overset{\text{def}}{=} Conf \smallsetminus Pre(Conf)$ be the set of all "dead" configurations, from which no move is possible).

Theorem 4.4. *Strong inevitability is decidable for lossy counter machines.*

The reasoning is similar to what we did for termination: First, strong inevitability is r.e. There remains to see that it is also co-r.e., i.e. that there are finite witnesses for non-inevitability. So assume that there is a run that violates strong inevitability, that run is either finite or infinite. If it is finite, it is a finite witness. If it is infinite, then the LCM has an infinite run that remains inside $X_1 \smallsetminus X_2$. By the wqo property, there are two configurations $\sigma_i \leq \sigma_j$ along this run. By the monotonicity property, there is a looping run $\sigma_0 \xrightarrow{*} \sigma_i \xrightarrow{+} \sigma_i$. This looping run remains inside $X_1 \smallsetminus X_2$ and is the finite witness we need.

4.3 Undecidability

The decidability of termination and inevitability is very fragile. We only give two examples:

Uniform_Termination:
>   Given: a LCM M,
>   Question: does M terminate from all starting configurations $\sigma \in Conf$?

Repeated_Inevitability:
>   Given: a LCM M, an initial configuration σ_0, and a semilinear set $X \subseteq Conf$ of
>   configurations,
>   Question: do all runs from σ_0 visit X infinitely many times?
>   Equivalently: does the *ECTL* formula $\mathsf{AF}^\infty X$ hold in σ_0?

Theorem 4.5. Uniform_Termination *and* Repeated_Inevitability *are* Π_1^0-*complete for lossy counter machines.*

For these two problems, membership in Π_1^0 is a consequence of the results we already saw. Indeed, the complement of Uniform_Termination can be written $\exists \sigma, \sigma' \in Conf :$ $\sigma \xrightarrow{*} \sigma' \xrightarrow{+} \sigma'$, or even $\exists \sigma \in Conf : \sigma \xrightarrow{+} \sigma$, which is in Σ_1^0, while the complement of Repeated_Inevitability is $\exists$ a run $\sigma_0 \xrightarrow{*} \sigma \xrightarrow{+} \sigma$ such that X is not visited along the $\sigma \xrightarrow{+} \sigma$ loop. Π_1^0-hardness is shown as Coro. 7.2 in Section 7.

Corollary 4.6. *The set Halt of configurations from which M must terminate cannot be computed.*

Note that, for lossy counter machines, *Halt* is both downward-closed and an invariant, and it has a decidable membership problem (Theorem 4.2).

5   Büchi and Liveness

Here we consider the following problems:

Buchi:
>   Given: a LCM M, a configuration σ_0, and a location $\ell \in Loc$,
>   **Question:** is there a run starting from σ_0 that visits ℓ infinitely many times?

Looping_on_location:
>   Given: a LCM M, a configuration σ_0, and a location $\ell \in Loc$,
>   **Question:** is there a looping run on ℓ, i.e., does $\sigma_0 \xrightarrow{*} \langle \ell, \boldsymbol{a} \rangle \xrightarrow{+} \langle \ell, \boldsymbol{a} \rangle$ for some $\boldsymbol{a}$?

At first glance, the situation with Buchi and Looping_on_location appears very similar to what we encountered in Section 4. Now, instead of just considering the existence of infinite runs, we ask for infinite runs that visit a given ℓ infinitely many times. Still, we can adapt Lemma 4.1:

Lemma 5.1. Buchi *and* Looping_on_location *coincide.*

Proof. Obviously, Looping_on_location entails Buchi. For the reverse direction, assume there exists an infinite run visiting ℓ infinitely often:

$$\sigma_0 \xrightarrow{*} \langle \ell, \boldsymbol{a}_1 \rangle \xrightarrow{+} \langle \ell, \boldsymbol{a}_2 \rangle \xrightarrow{+} \langle \ell, \boldsymbol{a}_3 \rangle \xrightarrow{+} \cdots$$

By the wqo property, there exists some $\boldsymbol{a}_i \leq \boldsymbol{a}_j$ for some $i < j$. Hence $\langle \ell, \boldsymbol{a}_j \rangle \xrightarrow{+} \langle \ell, \boldsymbol{a}_j \rangle$ by the monotonicity property. Finally, we have proven the existence of a run looping on ℓ. □

From there, we cannot prove decidability by claiming that Buchi is both r.e. and co-r.e., as we did for non-termination, It is r.e. since looping on ℓ is. But the absence of Büchi runs does not have finite witnesses, as the absence of infinite runs has. (For Minsky machines, non-termination is Σ_1^0-complete while Buchi is Σ_1^1-complete).

Finally Buchi is undecidable:

Theorem 5.2. Buchi *and* Looping_on_location *are* Σ_1^0-*complete for lossy counter machines.*

For these two equivalent problems, membership in Σ_1^0 is clear. Σ_1^0-hardness is shown as Coro. 7.4 in Section 7.

6   Finiteness of the Reachability Sets

Here we consider the following problems:

Finiteness**:**
>   Given: a LCM M and an initial configuration σ_0,
>   Question: is the reachability set $Post^*(\sigma_0)$ finite?
>   Equivalently: (Boundedness) is there a *bound* $B \in \mathbb{N}$ such that $|\sigma| \leq B$ for all reachable σ?

Unbounded_Run**:**
>   Given: a LCM M and a configuration σ_0,
>   Question: is there an infinite run from σ_0 that visits ever larger configurations?
>   Equivalently: is there a run that visits infinitely many different configurations?

The two problems are complementary since a system is unbounded if, and only if, it has an unbounded run. To see this, which is not specific to lossy counter machines, assume that $Post^*(\sigma_0)$ is infinite. Since every reachable configuration is reachable via a *pure* run, i.e., a run that does not visit any configuration twice, we conclude that there are infinitely many pure runs. By arranging them in a tree and invoking Kőnig's lemma, we conclude that there exists an infinite pure run (since all its finite prefixes are pure). Hence M has an unbounded run.

6.1   Undecidability

Finiteness is undecidable for LCM's:

Theorem 6.1. Finiteness *is* Σ_1^0-*complete and* Unbounded_Run *is* Π_1^0-*complete for lossy counter machines.*

When it first surfaced (in [39]), undecidability of Finiteness was a bit surprising in a way that is difficult to explain in retrospect. The result is now well-known and we give a direct proof in Section 7. Before undecidability was known, there were two lines of reasoning pointing to a conjecture of decidability: firstly, the fact that $Post^*(\sigma_0)$ is regular suggested that one could compute it, and secondly, one expected Karp and Miller's procedure to extend to all monotonic systems, inferring an unbounded run from an increasing prefix $\sigma_0 \xrightarrow{*} \sigma_1 \xrightarrow{+} \sigma_2$ with $\sigma_1 < \sigma_2$.

6.2   Uniform Finiteness

Uniform finiteness is to finiteness what uniform termination is to termination:

Uniform_Finiteness:
    Given: a LCM M,
    Question: are all the reachability sets $Post^*(\sigma)$ finite?
    Equivalently: does every run in M visit only finitely many different configurations?

Mayr showed that uniform finiteness is undecidable for lossy counter machines. This result is perhaps not surprising in view of the undecidability of finiteness. However the proof is still delicate since, in the encoding showing hardness, one cannot easily anchor the considered behaviors on some given natural starting configuration.

Theorem 6.2. Uniform_Finiteness *is* Π_2^0-*complete for lossy counter machines.*

Here, membership in Π_2^0 is obvious since finiteness is in Σ_1^0. For Π_2^0-hardness, we refer to Section 7.

7   Proving Undecidability

Undecidability, and more generally hardness, results are almost always established by reductions. This means taking some hard computational problems and encoding it in LCM's. This encoding can be tricky since, as we noted, LCM's are hard to control because of the possibly adversarial losses. Early undecidability proofs for lossy systems (e.g. [6,39,1]) are sometimes hard to understand and then to adapt to related problems.

In this section we want to explain how the idea of "*putting a counter machine on a budget*" can be used as a simple, yet versatile and powerful, gadget allowing easy-to-understand hardness proofs.

7.1   Putting Counter Machines on a Budget

With a Minsky counter machine $M = (Loc, C, \Delta)$ we associate a derived Minsky machine denoted $M^{\text{on\_budget}}$, or M^b for short.

In essence, $M^{\text{on\_budget}}$ is obtained by adding to M an extra "budget" counter B and by adapting the rules of Δ so that any incrementation (resp. decrementation) in the original counters is balanced by a corresponding decrementation (resp. incrementation) on the new counter B. Thus, *the sum of the counters remains constant* in M^b. This is a classic idea in Petri nets and counter machines. The construction is described on a schematic example (Fig. 2) that is more explicit that a formal definition. Observe that extra intermediary locations (in gray) are used, and that a step in M that increments some c_i will be forbidden in M^b when the budget is exhausted (instead, M^b may reach a new, terminal, bankrupt location).

This construction enjoys a few obvious properties that we now state informally (formal statements are given in [44]).

M^b **simulate** M: Any reliable run $\langle \ell, \boldsymbol{a} \rangle \xrightarrow{*}_{\text{std}} \langle \ell', \boldsymbol{a}' \rangle$ of M can be simulated as some $\langle \ell, B, \boldsymbol{a} \rangle \xrightarrow{*}_{\text{std}} \langle \ell', B', \boldsymbol{a}' \rangle$ in M^b provided with some large enough budget $B \in \mathbb{N}$.

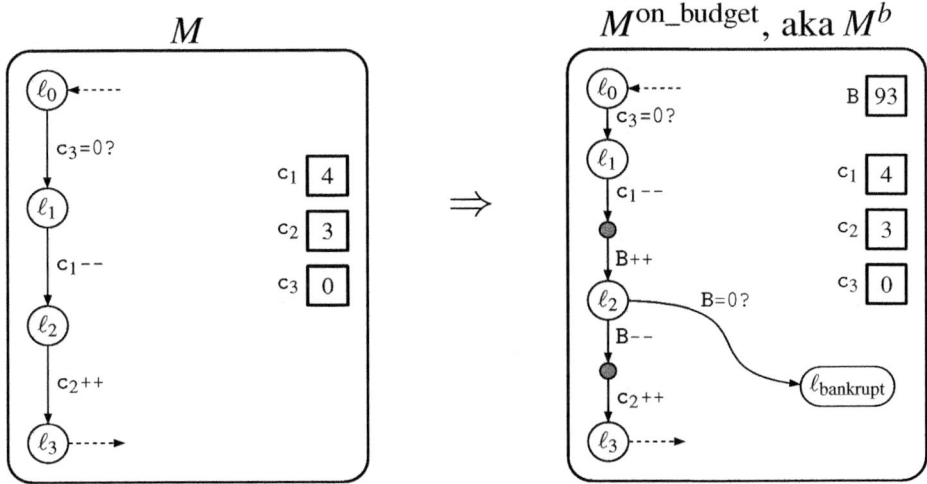

Fig. 2. From M to M^b (schematically)

M^b can only simulate M: Any reliable run in M^b can be seen as a run in M if we forget about the extra budget counter.

Counters are bounded: A lossy run $\langle \ell, \boldsymbol{a} \rangle \xrightarrow{*}_{\text{lossy}} \langle \ell', \boldsymbol{a}' \rangle$ in M^b has $|\boldsymbol{a}'| \leq |\boldsymbol{a}|$, i.e., the total sum of the counters can not increase.

Losses are visible: A lossy run $\langle \ell, \boldsymbol{a} \rangle \xrightarrow{*}_{\text{lossy}} \langle \ell', \boldsymbol{a}' \rangle$ in M^b is also a reliable run if, and only if, $|\boldsymbol{a}| = |\boldsymbol{a}'|$, i.e., if the total sum of the counters is unchanged (and the run does not bankrupt).

7.2 Undecidability of Uniform Termination

The above properties can be put to use immediately. Let M be some Minsky machine and $\sigma = \langle \ell, \boldsymbol{a} \rangle$ one of its configurations.

Proposition 7.1. *There is a loop $\langle \ell, \boldsymbol{a} \rangle \xrightarrow{+}_{\text{std}} \langle \ell, \boldsymbol{a} \rangle$ in M if, and only if, there is a $B \in \mathbb{N}$ and a loop $\langle \ell, B, \boldsymbol{a} \rangle \xrightarrow{+}_{\text{lossy}} \langle \ell, B, \boldsymbol{a} \rangle$ in M^b.*

Indeed, the loop in M is simulated in M^b by taking a large enough budget. And the loop in M^b must be a reliable run since the total sum of the counters is unchanged, hence it can be simulated in M.

Now recall that the question whether a Minsky machine has a loop $\sigma \xrightarrow{+}_{\text{std}} \sigma$ (where σ is existentially quantified upon) is undecidable, more precisely Σ^0_1-complete[3].

Corollary 7.2 (Undecidability). Uniform_Termination *is Π^0_1-hard for lossy counter machines.*

Indeed, M^b has an infinite run (starting from somewhere) if, and only if, it has a loop (from somewhere). Hence Π^0_1-hardness.

---

[3] This applies even if we do not restrict to configurations that are reachable from a given starting σ_0. I do not have a reference at hand but it is an easy exercise in computability theory.

7.3   Undecidability of Büchi Acceptance

We now show the undecidability of Buchi, or equivalently, of Looping_on_location, for lossy counter machines. This can be obtained by elaborating on the proof used for Coro. 7.2 above, but we find it more instructive to present another reduction that can be adapted for the next section.

Let M be a Minsky machine with a starting location ℓ_{init} and an accepting location ℓ_{end}. With M we associate a new machine M' obtained as follows (see schematics in Fig. 3): First we put M on a budget. Then we add two extra locations: ℓ_0 where B can be given any value, and ℓ_1 from which we can start M (on a budget). Finally, from ℓ_{end} it is possible to reset all counters to zero and go back to ℓ_1. This resetting uses the B (budget) counter to store the total sum the other counters had, using perhaps a few extra intermediary locations that are of no interest.

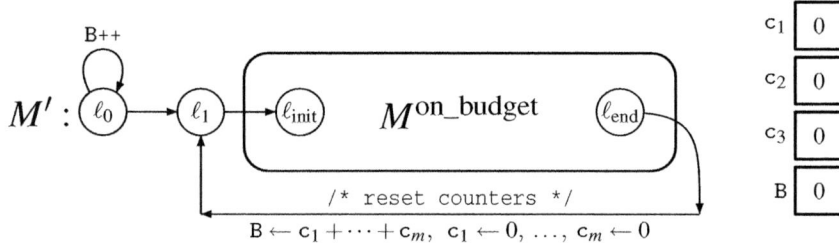

Fig. 3. Reduction for undecidability of Buchi

Proposition 7.3. *M has an accepting run* $\langle \ell_{\text{init}}, \mathbf{0} \rangle \xrightarrow{*}_{std} \langle \ell_{\text{end}}, \mathbf{a} \rangle$ *if, and only if, M' has a lossy run starting from* $\langle \ell_0, \mathbf{0} \rangle$ *and visiting ℓ_1 infinitely many times.*

Here, the left-to-right implication is clear: if M has an accepting run, this can be simulated by M' after it looped in ℓ_0 to start with a large enough budget. Once the accepting run has been completely simulated, M' can reset the counters, go back to ℓ_1 and repeat the simulation infinitely many times.

Reciprocally, if M' has a run that visits ℓ_1 infinitely many times, this run cannot increase the total sum of the counters once it has left ℓ_0. Hence this total sum can only decrease or stay constant. If the run is infinite, the total sum will eventually stay constant. Thus, after some time, the lossy run only has reliable steps. Since it visits ℓ_1 (and thus also ℓ_{init} and ℓ_{end}) infinitely many times, after some time its reliable steps will witness an accepting run of M.

Since the existence of an accepting run is Σ_1^0-complete for Minsky machines, we deduce:

Corollary 7.4 (Undecidability). Buchi *is Σ_1^0-hard for lossy counter machines.*

7.4   Undecidability of Finiteness

Our next reduction is a simple adaptation of the previous one (see schematics in Fig. 4). The modifications are as follows: (1) the resetting of the counters is not reached from ℓ_{end} but from the bankrupt location $\ell_{bankrupt}$ that M^b reaches when its budget appears to be too small (recall Fig. 2), and (2) the initial value of B cannot be chosen as large as one wants via a loop on ℓ_0: instead, B can only be incremented in the step from ℓ_1 to ℓ_{init}.

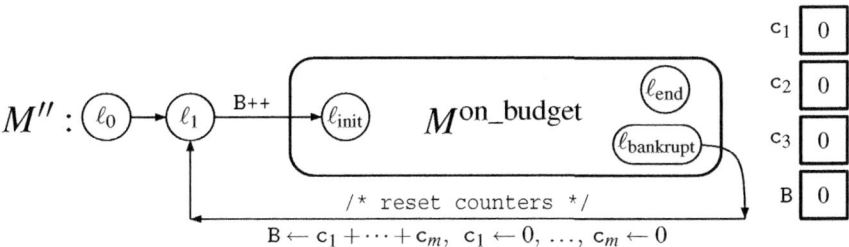

Fig. 4. Reduction for undecidability of Finiteness

Proposition 7.5. *M has an unbounded (reliable) run starting from* $\langle \ell_{init}, \mathbf{0} \rangle$ *if, and only if, M'' has an unbounded (lossy) run starting from* $\langle \ell_0, \mathbf{0} \rangle$.

Here again the left-to-right implication is clear. The unbounded run of M can be simulated by M''. This simulation is done in incremental stages. First M'' reaches ℓ_{init} with a low budget $B = 1$. The simulation proceeds until the budget is too low for continuing. M'' is then in the bankrupt location, resets its counters and goes back to ℓ_1. There B is incremented and the simulation can be started from scratch, this time with $B = 2$. It will now take more steps before bankrupting, resetting the counters, and starting again with a larger budget. This simulation will reenact longer and longer prefixes of the unbounded run of M, leading to a run of M'' that is itself unbounded.

The right-to-left implication is more subtle. Assume M'' has an unbounded run. Necessarily, this run visits ℓ_1 infinitely many times since this is the only way to increase the total sum of the counters. Let us write this unbounded run in the following way, isolating the places where ℓ_1 is visited:

$$\langle \ell_0, \mathbf{0} \rangle \xrightarrow{+} \langle \ell_1, \mathbf{a}_1 \rangle \xrightarrow{+} \langle \ell_1, \mathbf{a}_2 \rangle \xrightarrow{+} \langle \ell_1, \mathbf{a}_3 \rangle \xrightarrow{+} \cdots$$

Zooming in a little bit on the part between two consecutive visits to ℓ_1, we see it must be some subrun π_i of the form

$$\langle \ell_1, \mathbf{a}_i \rangle \equiv \langle \ell_1, B_i, \mathbf{0} \rangle \rightarrow \langle \ell_{init}, 1 + B_i, \mathbf{0} \rangle \xrightarrow{*} \langle \ell_{bankrupt}, B, \mathbf{c} \rangle \xrightarrow{+} \langle \ell_1, B_{i+1}, \mathbf{0} \rangle \equiv \langle \ell_1, \mathbf{a}_{i+1} \rangle.$$

Now, $B_{i+1} \leq 1 + B_i$ since "Counters are bounded" and the sequence $B_1, B_2, \ldots$ can only increase by 1 at a time. It can also decrease (by losses) but, since the run is unbounded, it must eventually increase and for every $k \in \mathbb{N}$, there is an index i such that $B_i = k$. If now we assume that i_k is the first such index, we deduce $B_{i_k} = 1 + B_{i_k-1}$, hence the run π_{i_k-1} only uses reliable steps (indeed, "Losses are visible"). Reliable steps simulate M, hence π_{i_k-1} witnesses a run $\pi'_k \equiv \langle \ell_{\text{init}}, \mathbf{0} \rangle \xrightarrow{+} \langle \ell, \mathbf{c} \rangle$ for some ℓ and some $\mathbf{c}$ of size k. If we assume that M is deterministic, these runs are longer and longer prefixes of the infinite unbounded run of M. If M is non-deterministic, we use Kőnig's Lemma to extract an unbounded run from these ever larger finite runs.

Since the existence of an unbounded run is Π^0_1-complete for Minsky machines, we deduce:

Corollary 7.6 (Undecidability). Finiteness *is* Σ^0_1*-hard for lossy counter machines.*

The reduction also shows undecidability for the to-all and all-to-all formulae of the reachability logic (Section 3.4). For to-all formulae, i.e., formulae of the form $\forall t \in Y :$ $\exists s \in X : s \xrightarrow{*} t$, we observe that by taking $X = \{\sigma_0\}$ and $Y = \{\langle \ell_1, k, \mathbf{0} \rangle \mid k \in \mathbb{N}\}$, the formula expresses the existence of an unbounded run in M''. Since in this reduction X is a singleton, the reduction also works for all-to-all formulae, of the form $\forall s \in X : \forall t \in Y : s \xrightarrow{*} t$.

7.5 Undecidability of Uniform Finiteness

We further adapt the previous reduction (see schematics in Fig. 5). Now M''' has an extra counter K that is never modified and that is used to store a value with which to reinitialize c_1 when looping back to ℓ_1.

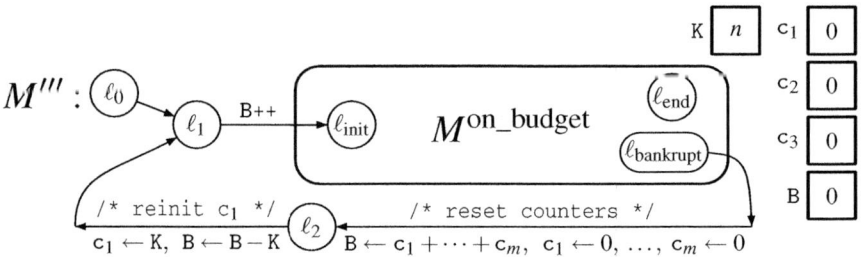

Fig. 5. Reduction for undecidability of Uniform_Finiteness

Proposition 7.7. *M has an unbounded (reliable) run starting from some $\langle \ell_{\text{init}}, c_1 : n, \mathbf{0} \rangle$ if, and only if, M''' has an unbounded (lossy) run starting from some σ.*

We reason as for the proof of Prop. 7.5, with very minor adaptations.

Again, the left-to-right implication is the easier one. Assume M has an unbounded run from $\langle \ell_{\text{init}}, n, \mathbf{0} \rangle$. This can be simulated by M''' starting from $\langle \ell_{\text{init}}, B, K : n, c_1 : n, \mathbf{0} \rangle$, i.e., after we make sure that the extra counter K contains exactly n. As with Proposition 7.5, the simulation proceeds until the budget bankrupts. Then, M''' loops back to ℓ_1, where the budget is incremented. and the simulation starts anew. This loop back to ℓ_1 resets the counters with $c_1 = n$, using the memory K to find the value (truly, a Minsky machine needs an auxiliary storage for this copy, but c_2 can do the job). By visiting ℓ_1 infinitely many times, this simulation manages to produce an unbounded run of M'''.

For the right-to-left implication, we assume that M''' has an unbounded run from some arbitrary σ. Since the only way to increase the total sum of the counters is to go through ℓ_1, the run must visit ℓ_1 infinitely many times, and increase the total sum of the counters by at most one between such visits. Also, since K can only decrease (by losses) it will eventually stays constant. Once K is constant (say $= n$), we have, for any $k \in \mathbb{N}$, a run like π_{i_k-1} above that increments B from $k-1$ to k, going from $\langle \ell_{\text{init}}, B : k-1, K : n, c_1 : n, \mathbf{0} \rangle$ to $\langle \ell_{\text{init}}, k, n, n, \mathbf{0} \rangle$. This run only uses reliable steps and witnesses, inside the Minsky machine, a path $\langle \ell_{\text{init}}, n, \mathbf{0} \rangle \xrightarrow{*} \langle \ell, \boldsymbol{a} \rangle$ for some $\boldsymbol{a}$ of size k. Hence M has an unbounded run from $\langle \ell_{\text{init}}, n, \mathbf{0} \rangle$.

Since the question whether there exists some $n \in \mathbb{N}$ such that a Minsky machine has an unbounded run starting from $\langle \ell_{\text{init}}, n, \mathbf{0} \rangle$ is Σ_2^0-complete, we deduce:

Corollary 7.8 (Undecidability). Uniform_Finiteness *is Π_2^0-hard for lossy counter machines.*

The reduction also shows Σ_2^0-hardness of the one-to-all formulae of the reachability logic. These have the form $\exists s \in X : \forall t \in Y : s \xrightarrow{*} t$. By taking $X = Conf$ and $Y = \{\langle \ell_2, B : k, \mathbf{0} \rangle \mid k \in \mathbb{N}\}$, the formula expresses the existence of an unbounded run in M''', i.e., the negation of uniform finiteness.

8 Further Developments

We gather in this section a few results, remarks, and pointers to the literature, regarding problems that are less central in the theory of lossy counter machines as it exists today.

8.1 Temporal Logic Model-Checking

Temporal logics [22] can express behavioral properties of systems in general, and of lossy counter machines in particular. It has been observed in the literature on lossy systems that temporal logic model-checking is generally undecidable (e.g., [6] shows the undecidability of both *CTL* model-checking and *LTL* model-checking for lossy channel systems). However, as with the reachability logic we considered in Section 3.4, the picture can be more interesting if we focus on relevant fragments of general logics.

For lossy counter machines, the $\exists CTL$ fragment of *CTL* has a decidable model-checking problem. This fragment, also denoted $B(\mathsf{E}\,\mathcal{U}, \mathsf{EX})$, is the branching-time logic built on two *CTL* modalities $\mathsf{E}\,\mathcal{U}$ and EX. Arbitrary nesting and Boolean combinations are allowed, and we take all the semilinear sets as basic propositions.

Theorem 8.1 (Decidability of $\exists CTL$ model-checking)
1. The problem, given a LCM M, a configuration σ, and an $\exists CTL$ formula φ, whether $M, \sigma \models \varphi$, is decidable.

2. Moreover, the set $\mathsf{Mod}(\varphi) \overset{def}{=} \{\sigma \in Conf \mid M, \sigma \models \varphi\}$ is a semilinear set that can be computed effectively from M and φ.

Computing $\text{Mod}(\varphi)$ is done by induction over the structure of φ. This uses standard techniques like

$$\text{Mod}(\neg\varphi) = \textit{Conf} \smallsetminus \text{Mod}(\varphi),$$
$$\text{Mod}(\varphi \vee \psi) = \text{Mod}(\varphi) \cup \text{Mod}(\psi),$$
$$\text{Mod}(\text{EX}\varphi) = \textit{Pre}(\text{Mod}(\varphi)),$$

and relies on the fact that semilinear sets are closed under complementation, union and the *Pre* operator, all this in an effective way.

For $\text{Mod}(E\varphi\,\mathcal{U}\psi)$, semilinearity is seen after one unfolding of the Until:

$$\text{Mod}(E\varphi\,\mathcal{U}\psi) = \text{Mod}(\psi \vee \varphi \wedge \text{EXE}\varphi\,\mathcal{U}\psi)$$
$$= \text{Mod}(\psi) \cup \text{Mod}(\varphi) \cap \textit{Pre}(\text{Mod}(E\varphi\,\mathcal{U}\psi)).$$

The last expression denotes a semilinear set since $\textit{Pre}(\cdots)$ is always semilinear.

The computability of $\text{Mod}(E\varphi\,\mathcal{U}\psi)$ can be shown with the same technique we used, in Section 3.5, for the computability of $\textit{Pre}^*(X)$. Alternatively, one can use backward-chaining algorithms whose termination is guaranteed by Dickson's Lemma (see [9]).

Remark 8.2. The same techniques can be used to enlarge decidability from $\exists CTL$ to some existential fragment of the branching-time mu-calculus, where regular properties like *"there exists a run along which every even-numbered configuration is in X"* can be stated. See [11,9]. ☐

Regarding other temporal modalities, we know that model checking one $A\varphi\,\mathcal{U}\psi$ formula is decidable when $\text{Mod}(\varphi)$ and $\text{Mod}(\psi)$ are effectively given semilinear sets (this is the decidability of Strong_Inevitability from Section 4.2) but it is *not possible* to compute $\text{Mod}(A\varphi\,\mathcal{U}\psi)$, nor even (by Coro. 4.6) $\text{Mod}(\text{AF}\neg\text{EX}\top)$.

As a consequence, nested $A\mathcal{U}$ modalities give undecidable model-checking problems (e.g., they can easily encode uniform termination).

Model-checking is also undecidable for *ECTL* modalities like EF^∞ (this is the Buchi problem from Section 5) and AF^∞ (this is repeated inevitability from Section 4.3).

8.2   Games People Play on Lossy Counter Machines

Sections 3 to 5 focused on classical reachability, inevitability, or liveness properties, but one is also interested in more general game-theoretical problems where several opponents have conflicting goals. Branching-time temporal logic is only a first step toward these new issues.

The question of checking game-theoretical properties of lossy counter machines has barely been scratched. Obviously, one could expect that undecidability is everywhere since the properties are more general. One could be wrong.

Let us illustrate this on an example. We consider a reachability game played in turn by two opponents on a single LCM. Starting from σ_0, Alice tries to reach ℓ_{end} by picking the odd-numbered lossy steps of a growing run, while Bob tries to frustrate her by choosing adversarially the even-numbered lossy steps. The decision problem is:

Reachability_Game:
  Given: a LCM M, an initial configuration σ_0, and a goal location ℓ_{end}.
  Question: does Alice have a winning strategy?

Surprisingly, this problem is very easy.

Theorem 8.3. Reachability_Game *is* PTIME-*complete for lossy counter machines.*

The paradox is explained when we realize that an optimal strategy for both players can choose to always lose all the contents of the counters at every step. Indeed, losing everything can only reduce our opponent's options (because of strong monotonicity). It also reduces our later options, but anyway the opponent will have the possibility to lose everything if it hurts us.

Finally, it is possible to solve the game by restricting to the finite graph of all configurations $\langle \ell, \mathbf{0} \rangle$ for $\ell \in Loc$, which is PTIME-complete.

Games on LCM's can be more interesting. We could decide that Bob can only play reliable steps. Or that Alice and Bob choose reliable steps while losses in the counters are chosen probabilistically by the environment, leading to games with $2\,1/2$ players. Or that the objective is more complex than just reachability. Many variations are possible, motivated by different situations. We refer to [3,41,9,10,2,4] for results on such games.

8.3 Equivalence Checking

Comparing two systems is a classic decision problem. In the simplest situations, the comparison criterion is an equivalence relation, sometimes a preorder.

When dealing with systems (like LCM's) that give rise to infinite-state transition systems, the behavioral equivalences one could use for verification purposes are often undecidable. The main exception is *strong bisimilarity* that has been shown decidable in many cases (and undecidable in many other cases) [13].

For lossy counter machines, equivalences are hard. One way to put it is to say that all interesting relations between lossy counter machines are undecidable, even if we only consider lossy VAS's (i.e., lossy counter machines without zero-tests). A proof for all relations between bisimilarity and trace containment can be obtained (see [42]) by adapting Jančar's classic proof for Petri nets [30]. The proof certainly extends, e.g., to all equivalences between equality of the reachability set and trace containment modulo invisibility of internal steps.

On the other hand, comparison between a lossy counter machine and a *finite transition system* is very often decidable.

This line of positive results was started by Abdulla and Kindahl [8] with the simulation preorder and the bisimulation equivalence.

It turns out that there is a generic approach to these problems: the question whether $S \preceq F$ or $S \approx F$ for some finite F can often be translated as a temporal question, whether $S \models \varphi$ for some formula $\varphi = \varphi_F^{\preceq}$ or $\varphi = \varphi_F^{\approx}$, called a *characteristic formula for F*, that states exactly what is required to be $\preceq F$ or $\approx F$. We refer to [12,31,35] for more details.

In the special case of lossy counter machines, comparison with finite systems is decidable for all the equivalences and preorders that admit characteristic formulae in $\exists CTL$. This is a direct corollary of Theorem 8.1. The equivalences and preorders thus covered are numerous and include, e.g., weak bisimulation and branching bisimulation.

9   Decidable but Hard

Problems that are decidable for lossy counter machines are usually very hard.

9.1   Lower Bounds for Complexity

Reachability and termination are Ackermann-hard for LCM's. We refer to [44] for a recent and simplified proof that uses the same "counter machine on a budget" gadget that we used in Section 7. Hardness extends, via obvious reductions, to most decidable problems we listed in the previous sections (one major exception is the reachability game from Section 8.2).

A finer analysis of the lower bounds shows that the most important parameter here is the *number of counters* in a lossy counter machine. The hardness proof uses a number of counters that cannot be bounded *a priori*. For a fixed number of counters, one only obtains lower bounds at a finite, primitive-recursive, level in the Fast Growing Hierarchy, see [44]. This is in accordance with what is known on upper bounds.

9.2   Upper Bounds

All along this paper, we deliberately avoided giving explicit algorithms for our decidability proofs. However, algorithms exist in the literature. Their termination arguments usually rely on the wqo property, and more precisely Dickson's Lemma. From these, upper bounds can be deduced, based on the length of bad sequences for the $(\mathbb{N}^n, \leq)$ wqo [40,17].

These upper bounds lie in the Fast Growing Hierarchy. The good news is that they closely match the known lower bounds. In particular, an Ackermann upper bound holds for most decidable problems on lossy counter machines, and this can be refined to primitive-recursive upper bounds at various levels when one restricts attention to machines with a fixed number of counters. We refer to our upcoming paper for more details [23].

10   Concluding Remarks

Lossy counter machines are a paradoxical computational model where unreliability brings decidability. At the moment, they have mostly been used as a tool for hardness results (undecidability or Ackermann-hardness). They have sometimes been used under the symmetrical guise of counters with incrementation errors [19].

In a leisurely way, we surveyed the main known results on both sides of the decidability frontier. From this, two main conclusions emerge:

1. Most decidability results rely only superficially on specific features of lossy counter machines. They can be obtained by a combination of very general properties enjoyed by most models (e.g., finitely branching non-determinism, effective one-step relation, ...) and the combination of strong monotonicity of steps with the wqo property of configurations. As a consequence, most of our decidability proofs can be easily adapted to other classes of well-structured transition systems. For example, they hold *mutatis mutandis* for lossy channel systems [7] or Reset Petri nets [20].

2. Most hardness results can be proved with the "machine on a budget" gadget. For counter systems, this gadget is used in two different ways (pioneered by [21]). It can bound the total sum of the counters, so that this sum must eventually stabilize along an infinite behavior, or can only grow in controlled ways. Then, when the sum is stabilized, the behavior must be reliable and hardness can be inherited from the Turing-powerful Minsky machines.

Acknowledgements. We thank Pierre Chambart, Jérôme Leroux and Sylvain Schmitz who greatly helped by proof-reading this paper at various stages.

References

1. Abdulla, P.A., Baier, C., Purushothaman Iyer, S., Jonsson, B.: Simulating perfect channels with probabilistic lossy channels. Information and Computation 197(1–2), 22–40 (2005)
2. Abdulla, P.A., Ben Henda, N., de Alfaro, L., Mayr, R., Sandberg, S.: Stochastic games with lossy channels. In: Amadio, R.M. (ed.) FOSSACS 2008. LNCS, vol. 4962, pp. 35–49. Springer, Heidelberg (2008)
3. Abdulla, P.A., Bertrand, N., Rabinovich, A., Schnoebelen, P.: Verification of probabilistic systems with faulty communication. Information and Computation 202(2), 141–165 (2005)
4. Abdulla, P.A., Bouajjani, A., d'Orso, J.: Monotonic and downward closed games. Journal of Logic and Computation 18(1), 153–169 (2008)
5. Abdulla, P.A., Čerāns, K., Jonsson, B., Tsay, Y.-K.: Algorithmic analysis of programs with well quasi-ordered domains. Information and Computation 160(1/2), 109–127 (2000)
6. Abdulla, P.A., Jonsson, B.: Undecidable verification problems for programs with unreliable channels. Information and Computation 130(1), 71–90 (1996)
7. Abdulla, P.A., Jonsson, B.: Verifying programs with unreliable channels. Information and Computation 127(2), 91–101 (1996)
8. Abdulla, P.A., Kindahl, M.: Decidability of simulation and bisimulation between lossy channel systems and finite state systems. In: Lee, I., Smolka, S.A. (eds.) CONCUR 1995. LNCS, vol. 962, pp. 333–347. Springer, Heidelberg (1995)
9. Baier, C., Bertrand, N., Schnoebelen, P.: On computing fixpoints in well-structured regular model checking, with applications to lossy channel systems. In: Hermann, M., Voronkov, A. (eds.) LPAR 2006. LNCS (LNAI), vol. 4246, pp. 347–361. Springer, Heidelberg (2006)
10. Baier, C., Bertrand, N., Schnoebelen, P.: Verifying nondeterministic probabilistic channel systems against ω-regular linear-time properties. ACM Trans. Computational Logic 9(1) (2007)
11. Bouajjani, A., Mayr, R.: Model checking lossy vector addition systems. In: Meinel, C., Tison, S. (eds.) STACS 1999. LNCS, vol. 1563, pp. 323–333. Springer, Heidelberg (1999)

12. Browne, M.C., Clarke, E.M., Grumberg, O.: Characterizing finite Kripke structures in propositional temporal logic. Theoretical Computer Science 59(1–2), 115–131 (1988)
13. Bukart, O., Caucal, D., Moller, F., Steffen, B.: Verification on infinite structures. In: Bergstra, J.A., Ponse, A., Smolka, S.A. (eds.) Handbook of Process Algebra, ch. 9, pp. 545–623. Elsevier, Amsterdam (2001)
14. Cardoza, E., Lipton, R., Meyer, A.R.: Exponential space complete problems for Petri nets and commutative subgroups. In: Proc. STOC '76, pp. 50–54. ACM Press, New York (1976)
15. Cécé, G., Finkel, A., Purushothaman Iyer, S.: Unreliable channels are easier to verify than perfect channels. Information and Computation 124(1), 20–31 (1996)
16. Chambart, P., Schnoebelen, P.: Computing blocker sets for the Regular Post Embedding Problem. In: Proc. DLT 2010. LNCS. Springer, Heidelberg (to appear, 2010)
17. Clote, P.: On the finite containment problem for Petri nets. Theoretical Computer Science 43(1), 99–105 (1986)
18. Demri, S.: Linear-time temporal logics with Presburger constraints: An overview. J. Applied Non-Classical Logics 16(3-4), 311–347 (2006)
19. Demri, S., Lazić, R.: LTL with the freeze quantifier and register automata. In: Proc. LICS 2006, pp. 17–26. IEEE Computer Society Press, Los Alamitos (2006)
20. Dufourd, C., Finkel, A., Schnoebelen, P.: Reset nets between decidability and undecidability. In: Larsen, K.G., Skyum, S., Winskel, G. (eds.) ICALP 1998. LNCS, vol. 1443, pp. 103–115. Springer, Heidelberg (1998)
21. Dufourd, C., Jančar, P., Schnoebelen, P.: Boundedness of reset P/T nets. In: Wiedermann, J., Van Emde Boas, P., Nielsen, M. (eds.) ICALP 1999. LNCS, vol. 1644, pp. 301–310. Springer, Heidelberg (1999)
22. Emerson, E.A.: Temporal and modal logic. In: van Leeuwen, J. (ed.) Handbook of Theoretical Computer Science, ch. 16, vol. B, pp. 995–1072. Elsevier, Amsterdam (1990)
23. Figueira, D., Figueira, S., Schmitz, S., Schnoebelen, P.: Ackermann and primitive-recursive upper bounds with Dickson's lemma (2010) (in preparation)
24. Figueira, D., Segoufin, L.: Future-looking logics on data words and trees. In: Královič, R., Niwiński, D. (eds.) MFCS 2009. LNCS, vol. 5734, pp. 331–343. Springer, Heidelberg (2009)
25. Finkel, A.: A generalization of the procedure of Karp and Miller to well structured transition systems. In: Ottmann, T. (ed.) ICALP 1987. LNCS, vol. 267, pp. 499–508. Springer, Heidelberg (1987)
26. Finkel, A.: Reduction and covering of infinite reachability trees. Information and Computation 89(2), 144–179 (1990)
27. Finkel, A., Goubault-Larrecq, J.: Forward analysis for WSTS, part I: Completions. In: Proc. STACS 2009. Leibniz International Proceedings in Informatics, vol. 3, pp. 433–444. Leibniz-Zentrum für Informatik (2009)
28. Finkel, A., Schnoebelen, P.: Well-structured transition systems everywhere! Theoretical Computer Science 256(1–2), 63–92 (2001)
29. Henzinger, T.A., Majumdar, R., Raskin, J.-F.: A classification of symbolic transition systems. ACM Trans. Computational Logic 6(1), 1–32 (2005)
30. Jančar, P.: Undecidability of bisimilarity for Petri nets and some related problems. Theoretical Computer Science 148(2), 281–301 (1995)
31. Jančar, P., Kučera, A., Mayr, R.: Deciding bisimulation-like equivalences with finite-state processes. Theoretical Computer Science 258(1–2), 409–433 (2001)
32. Jurdziński, M., Lazić, R.: Alternation-free modal mu-calculus for data trees. In: Proc. LICS 2007, pp. 131–140. IEEE Comp. Soc. Press, Los Alamitos (2007)
33. Kracht, M.: A new proof of a theorem by Ginsburg and Spanier. Dept. Linguistics, UCLA (December 2002) (manuscript)
34. Kruskal, J.B.: The theory of well-quasi-ordering: A frequently discovered concept. Journal of Combinatorial Theory, Series A 13(3), 297–305 (1972)

35. Kučera, A., Schnoebelen, P.: A general approach to comparing infinite-state systems with their finite-state specifications. Theoretical Computer Science 358(2–3), 315–333 (2006)
36. van Leeuwen, J.: A partial solution to the reachability-problem for vector-addition systems. In: Proc. STOC '74, pp. 303–309. ACM Press, New York (1974)
37. Leroux, J., Point, G.: TaPAS: The Talence Presburger Arithmetic Suite. In: Kowalewski, S., Philippou, A. (eds.) Proc. TACAS 2009. LNCS, vol. 5505, pp. 182–185. Springer, Heidelberg (2009)
38. Mayr, R.: Undecidable problems in unreliable computations. In: Gonnet, G.H., Viola, A. (eds.) LATIN 2000. LNCS, vol. 1776, pp. 377–386. Springer, Heidelberg (2000)
39. Mayr, R.: Undecidable problems in unreliable computations. Theoretical Computer Science 297(1–3), 337–354 (2003)
40. McAloon, K.: Petri nets and large finite sets. Theoretical Computer Science 32(1–2), 173–183 (1984)
41. Raskin, J.-F., Samuelides, M., Van Begin, L.: Games for counting abstractions. In: Proc. AVoCS 2004. Electronic Notes in Theor. Comp. Sci, vol. 128(6), pp. 69–85. Elsevier Science, Amsterdam (2005)
42. Schnoebelen, P.: Bisimulation and other undecidable equivalences for lossy channel systems. In: Kobayashi, N., Pierce, B.C. (eds.) TACS 2001. LNCS, vol. 2215, pp. 385–399. Springer, Heidelberg (2001)
43. Schnoebelen, P.: Verifying lossy channel systems has nonprimitive recursive complexity. Information Processing Letters 83(5), 251–261 (2002)
44. Schnoebelen, P.: Revisiting Ackermann-Hardness for Lossy Counter Machines and Reset Petri Nets. In: Hliněny, P., Kučera, A. (eds.) MFCS 2010. LNCS, vol. 6281, pp. 616–628. Springer, Heidelberg (2010)
45. Sifakis, J.: A unified approach for studying the properties of transitions systems. Theoretical Computer Science 18, 227–258 (1982)
46. Tan, T.: On pebble automata for data languages with decidable emptiness problem. In: Královič, R., Niwiński, D. (eds.) MFCS 2009. LNCS, vol. 5734, pp. 712–723. Springer, Heidelberg (2009)

Behavioral Cartography of Timed Automata[*]

Étienne André and Laurent Fribourg

LSV – ENS de Cachan & CNRS, France

Abstract. We aim at finding a set of timing parameters for which a given timed automaton has a "good" behavior. We present here a novel approach based on the decomposition of the parametric space into *behavioral tiles*, i.e., sets of parameter valuations for which the behavior of the system is uniform. This gives us a *behavioral cartography* according to the values of the parameters. It is then straightforward to partition the space into a "good" and a "bad" subspace, according to the behavior of the tiles. We extend this method to probabilistic systems, allowing to decompose the parametric space into tiles for which the minimal (resp. maximal) probability of reaching a given location is uniform. An implementation has been made, and experiments successfully conducted.

1 Introduction

The admissible behaviors of timed automata are determined by sets of linear constraints over timing parameters. The parameters in these constraints represent constants or values chosen by the designer. The behavior is very sensitive to the values of these parameters, and it is rather difficult to find their correct values. The *good parameters problem* is the following (see [14]): Given a parametrized timed automaton $\mathcal{A}$ and a rectangular real-valued parameter domain, what is the largest set of parameters values for which $\mathcal{A}$ behaves well? We say that $\mathcal{A}$ behaves well if it satisfies a certain set of properties. We are interested here in properties that are invariant for automata having the same set of *traces* (alternating sequences of locations and actions, i.e., time-abstract runs) [3]. This is in particular the case of linear-time properties [7].

Related Work. The parameter design problem for timed automata was formulated in [15], where a straightforward solution is given, based on the generation of the whole parametric state space until a fixpoint is reached. Unfortunately, in all but the most simple cases, this is is prohibitively expensive due, in particular, to the brute exploration of the whole parametric state space.

The problem of parameter synthesis for timed automata has been applied to two main domains: telecommunication protocols and asynchronous circuits. For example, concerning telecommunication protocols, the Bounded Retransmission Protocol has been verified in [24] using UPPAAL [22] and Spin [17], and the Root

[*] This work is partially supported by the Agence Nationale de la Recherche, grant ANR-06-ARFU-005.

A. Kučera and I. Potapov (Eds.): RP 2010, LNCS 6227, pp. 76–90, 2010.
© Springer-Verlag Berlin Heidelberg 2010

Contention Protocol in [13] using TREX [6]. Concerning asynchronous circuits, Clarisó and Cortadella have proposed methods with approximations [11].

In [14], the authors propose an extension based on the *counterexample guided abstraction refinement* (CEGAR) [12]. When finding a counterexample, the system obtains constraints on the parameters that *make* the counterexample infeasible. When all the counterexamples have been eliminated, the resulting constraints describe a set of parameters for which the system is safe.

We propose here an alternative approach. We generate a constraint on the parameters ("tile") for each integer point located within a given rectangle V_0. Such a tile is called "behavioral tile" because $\mathcal{A}$ behaves similarly under any parameter valuation corresponding to a point of the tile: the sets of traces coincide [3]. This allows us to decompose the parametric space into behavioral tiles. Then, it is easy to partition the parametric space into a subset of "good" tiles (which correspond to "good behaviors") and a subset of "bad" ones. Often in practice, what is covered is not the *bounded* and *integer* subspace of the parameter rectangle, but two major extensions: first, not only the integer points but all the *real-valued* points of the rectangle is covered by the tiles; second, the tiles are often unbounded and cover most of the parametric space beyond V_0.

Plan of the Paper. We first recall Parametric Timed Automata in Section 2. We then state the good parameters problem in Section 3 using an example of flip-flop circuit. We then present the behavioral cartography algorithm in Section 4, apply it to the example, and give a sufficient condition to get a full coverage of the parametric space. We present an extension to probabilistic systems in Section 5, summarize experiments in Section 6, and conclude in Section 7.

2   Parametric Timed Automata

Throughout this paper, we assume a fixed set $X = \{x_1, \ldots, x_H\}$ of *clocks*. A *clock* is a variable x_i with value in $\mathbb{R}_{\geq 0}$. All clocks evolve linearly at the same rate. We define a *clock valuation* as a function $w : X \to \mathbb{R}_{\geq 0}$ assigning a non-negative real value to each clock.

Throughout this paper, we assume a fixed set $P = \{p_1, \ldots, p_M\}$ of *parameters*. A *parameter valuation* π is a function $\pi : P \to \mathbb{R}_{\geq 0}$ assigning a nonnegative real value to each parameter. There is a one-to-one correspondence between valuations and points in $(\mathbb{R}_{\geq 0})^M$. We will often identify a valuation π with the point $(\pi(p_1), \ldots, \pi(p_M))$.

Definition 1 (Constraint). *A* linear inequality on the parameters P *(resp. linear inequality on the clocks X and parameters P) is an inequality $e \prec e'$, where $\prec \in \{<, \leq\}$, and e, e' are two linear terms of the form*

$$\Sigma_i \alpha_i p_i + c, \qquad (resp. \ \Sigma_i \alpha_i p_i + \Sigma_j \beta_j x_j + c)$$

where $1 \leq i \leq M, 1 \leq j \leq H$ and $\alpha_i, \beta_j, c \in \mathbb{N}$. A constraint on the parameters *(resp. constraint on the clocks and parameters) is a conjunction of inequalities on P (resp. on X and P).*

Given a parameter valuation π and a constraint C, $C[\pi]$ denotes the constraint obtained by replacing each parameter p in C with $\pi(p)$. Likewise, given a clock valuation w, $C[\pi][w]$ denotes the expression obtained by replacing each clock x in $C[\pi]$ with $w(x)$. A clock valuation w *satisfies* constraint $C[\pi]$ (denoted by $w \models C[\pi]$) if $C[\pi][w]$ evaluates to true. We say that a parameter valuation π *satisfies* a constraint C, denoted by $\pi \models C$, if the set of clock valuations that satisfy $C[\pi]$ is nonempty.

Likewise, we say that a parameter valuation π *satisfies* a constraint K on the parameters, denoted by $\pi \models K$, if the expression obtained by replacing each parameter p in K with $\pi(p)$ evaluates to true. We consider *True* as a constraint on the parameters, corresponding to the set of all possible values for P.

We assume familiarity with timed automata [1]. The following definition is an extension of timed automata to the parametric case. Parametric timed automata allow within guards and invariants the use of parameters in place of constants [2].

Definition 2 (PTA). *Given a set of clocks X and a set of parameters P, a parametric timed automaton (PTA) $\mathcal{A}$ is a 6-tuple of the form $\mathcal{A} = (\Sigma, Q, q_0, K, I, \rightarrow)$, where Σ is a finite set of actions, Q is a finite set of locations, $q_0 \in Q$ is the initial location, K is a constraint on the parameters, I is the invariant assigning to every $q \in Q$ a constraint I_q on the clocks and the parameters, and $\rightarrow$ is a step relation consisting in elements of the form (q, g, a, ρ, q') where $q, q' \in Q$, $a \in \Sigma$, $\rho \subseteq X$ is a set of clocks to be reset by the step, and g (the step guard) is a constraint on the clocks and the parameters.*

In the sequel, we consider the PTA $\mathcal{A} = (\Sigma, Q, q_0, K, I, \rightarrow)$. We simply denote this PTA by $\mathcal{A}(K)$, in order to emphasize the fact that only K will change in $\mathcal{A}$.

For every parameter valuation $\pi = (\pi_1, \ldots, \pi_M)$, $\mathcal{A}[\pi]$ denotes the PTA $\mathcal{A}(K)$, where K is $\bigwedge_{i=1}^{M} p_i = \pi_i$. This corresponds to the PTA obtained from $\mathcal{A}$ by substituting every occurrence of a parameter p_i by constant π_i in the guards and invariants. We say that p_i is *instantiated* with π_i. Note that, as all parameters are instantiated, $\mathcal{A}[\pi]$ is a standard timed automaton. (Strictly speaking, $\mathcal{A}[\pi]$ is only a timed automaton if π assigns an integer to each parameter.)

Also recall that the composition of several PTAs (Network of Parametric Timed Automata, or NPTA) results in a PTA (see, e.g., [3]).

Definition 3 (State). *A (symbolic) state s of $\mathcal{A}(K)$ is a couple (q, C) where q is a location, and C a constraint on the clocks and the parameters.*

For each valuation π of the parameters P, we may view a state s as the set of pairs (q, w) where w is a clock valuation such that $w \models C[\pi]$. The *initial state* of $\mathcal{A}(K)$ is a state s_0 of the form (q_0, C_0), where $C_0 = K \wedge I_{q_0} \wedge \bigwedge_{i=1}^{H-1} x_i = x_{i+1}$. K is the initial constraint, I_{q_0} is the invariant of the initial state, and the rest of the expression lets clocks evolve from the same initial value.

The symbolic semantics of a PTA is given in the following. Given a constant $d \in \mathbb{R}_{\geq 0}$, we use $X + d$ to denote the set $\{x_1 + d, \ldots, x_H + d\}$. Given a constraint C, we rename the set of variables $X = \{x_1, \ldots, x_H\}$ as $X' = \{x'_1, \ldots, x'_H\}$. We use the notation $C(X)$ (resp. $C(X')$) to indicate that X (resp. X') is the set of clocks occurring in C. We use $X' = \rho(X)$, where X' is a renaming of X, to denote the conjunction of equalities $x'_i = 0$ for all $x_i \in \rho$, and $x'_i = x_i$ otherwise. Given a state $s = (q, C)$, a step of the automaton from s is defined below:

- $(q, C) \xrightarrow{a} (q', C')$ if $(q, g, a, \rho, q') \in \rightarrow$, and C' is a constraint on the clocks and parameters defined, using the set of (renamed) clocks X', by:
  $C'(X') = (\exists X : (C(X) \wedge g(X) \wedge X' = \rho(X) \wedge I_{q'}(X')))$.
- $(q, C) \xrightarrow{d} (q, C')$, where d is a new parameter with values in $\mathbb{R}_{\geq 0}$, which means that C' is given by: $C'(X') = (\exists X : (C(X) \wedge X' = X + d \wedge I_q(X')))$.
- $(q, C) \xRightarrow{a} (q', C')$ if $\exists C''$ such that $(q, C) \xrightarrow{a} (q', C'')$ and $(q', C'') \xrightarrow{d} (q', C')$, i.e., C' is a constraint on the clocks and the parameters obtained by removing X and d from the following expression:
  $C'(X') = (\exists X, d : (C(X) \wedge g(X) \wedge X' = \rho(X) + d \wedge I_{q'}(X' - d) \wedge I_{q'}(X')))$.
  It can be shown that C' can be put under the form of a constraint on the clocks and the parameters.

Definition 4 (Run). *A run of $\mathcal{A}(K)$ is a finite alternating sequence of states and actions of the form $s_0 \xRightarrow{a_0} s_1 \xRightarrow{a_1} \cdots \xRightarrow{a_{m-1}} s_m$, such that for all $i = 0, \ldots, m-1$, $a_i \in \Sigma$ and $s_i \xRightarrow{a_i} s_{i+1}$ is a step of $\mathcal{A}(K)$.*

Definition 5 (Trace associated to a run). *Given a PTA $\mathcal{A}$ and a run R of $\mathcal{A}$ of the form $(q_0, C_0) \xRightarrow{a_0} \cdots \xRightarrow{a_{m-1}} (q_m, C_m)$, the trace associated to R is the alternating sequence of locations and actions $q_0 \xRightarrow{a_0} \cdots \xRightarrow{a_{m-1}} q_m$.*

The *trace set of $\mathcal{A}$* refers to the set of traces associated to the runs of $\mathcal{A}$.

In the following, we are interested in verifying properties on the trace set of $\mathcal{A}$. For example, given a predefined set of "bad locations", a reachability property is satisfied by a trace if this trace never contains a bad location; such a trace is "good" w.r.t. this reachability property. A trace can also be said to be "good" if a given action always occurs before another one within the trace (see example in Section 3). Actually, the good behaviors that can be captured with trace sets are relevant to *linear-time properties* [7], which can express properties more general than reachability properties.

Formally, given a property on traces, we say that a trace is *good* if it satisfies the property, and *bad* otherwise. Likewise, we say that a trace set is *good* if all its traces are good, and bad otherwise.

3   The Good Parameters Problem

We consider an example of asynchronous "D flip-flop" circuit described in [11] and depicted in Figure 1 left. It is composed of 4 gates (G_1, G_2, G_3 and G_4) interconnected in a cyclic way, and an environment involving two input signals D and CK. The global output signal is Q. Each gate G_i has a delay in the parametric interval $[\delta_i^-, \delta_i^+]$, with $\delta_i^- \leq \delta_i^+$. There are 4 other parameters (viz., $T_{HI}, T_{LO}, T_{setup}$, and T_{Hold}) used to model the environment. The output signal

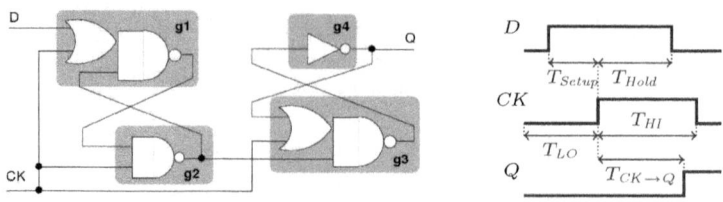

Fig. 1. Flip-flop circuit (left) and its environment (right)

of a gate G_i is named g_i (note that $g_4 = Q$). The rising (resp. falling) edge of signal D is denoted by $D^\uparrow$ (resp. $D^\downarrow$) and similarly for signals $CK, Q, g_1, \ldots, g_4$.

We consider an environment starting from $D = CK = Q = 0$ and $g_1 = g_2 = g_3 = 1$, with the following ordered sequence of actions for inputs D and CK: $D^\uparrow$, $CK^\uparrow$, $D^\downarrow$, $CK^\downarrow$, as depicted in Figure 1 right. Therefore, we have the implicit constraint $T_{setup} \leq T_{LO} \wedge T_{Hold} \leq T_{HI}$. Each gate is modeled by a PTA, as well as the environment. We consider a bi-bounded inertial model for gates (see [8,23]), where any change of the input may lead to a change of the output (after some delay). The PTA $\mathcal{A}$ modeling the system results from the composition of those 5 PTAs. The initial location q_0 corresponds to the initial levels of the signals according to the environment. The initial constraint C_0 (regardless of the equality between the clock variables, see Section 2) is:

$$T_{setup} \leq T_{LO} \wedge T_{Hold} \leq T_{HI} \wedge \bigwedge_{i=1,..,4} \delta_i^- \leq \delta_i^+$$

We consider that the circuit has a *good behavior* if it verifies the following property $Prop_1$: "every trace contains both $Q^\uparrow$ and $CK^\downarrow$, and $Q^\uparrow$ occurs before $CK^\downarrow$". We are now interested in identifying parameter valuations for which the system has such a good behavior.

More generally, the *good parameters problem* can be stated as follows [14]:

> Given a PTA $\mathcal{A}$ and a rectangular real-valued parameter domain V_0, what is the largest set of parameters values within V_0 for which $\mathcal{A}$ behaves well?

4   The Behavioral Cartography Algorithm

4.1   The Inverse Method

We first recall the inverse method algorithm, as defined in [3]. Given a PTA $\mathcal{A}$ and a valuation π of the parameters, the inverse method $IM(\mathcal{A}, \pi)$ generates a constraint K on the parameters, such that:

1. $\pi \models K$, and
2. For all $\pi_1, \pi_2 \models K$, the trace sets of $\mathcal{A}[\pi_1]$ and $\mathcal{A}[\pi_2]$ are equal.

We informally describe the algorithm IM in the following. Starting with $K = True$, we iteratively compute a growing set of reachable states. When a π-*incompatible* state (q, C) is encountered (i.e., when $\pi \not\models C$), K is refined as follows: a π-incompatible inequality J (i.e., such that $\pi \not\models J$) is selected within the projection of C onto the parameters and $\neg J$ is added to K. The procedure is then started again with this new K, and so on, until no new state is computed. We finally return the intersection of the projection onto the parameters of all the constraints associated to the reachable states.

A more detailed version of the inverse method is given in Algorithm 1. Given a linear inequality J of the form $e < e'$ (resp. $e \leq e'$), the expression $\neg J$ denotes the negation of J and corresponds to the linear inequality $e' \leq e$ (resp. $e' < e$). Given a constraint C on the clocks and the parameters, the expression $\exists X : C$ denotes the constraint on the parameters obtained from C after elimination of the clocks, i.e., $\{\pi \mid \pi \models C\}$. We define $Post^i_{\mathcal{A}(K)}(S)$ as the set of states reachable from S in exactly i steps, and $Post^*_{\mathcal{A}(K)}(S)$ as the set of all states reachable from S in $\mathcal{A}(K)$ (i.e., $Post^*_{\mathcal{A}(K)}(S) = \bigcup_{i \geq 0} Post^i_{\mathcal{A}(K)}(S)$). Given two sets of states S and S', we write $S \sqsubseteq S'$ iff $\forall s \in S, \exists s' \in S'$ s.t. $s = s'$.

Algorithm 1. $IM(\mathcal{A}, \pi)$

> **input** : A PTA $\mathcal{A}$ of initial state $s_0 = (q_0, C_0)$
> **input** : Valuation π of the parameters
> **output**: Constraint K on the parameters

1. $i \leftarrow 0$; $K \leftarrow \textit{True}$; $S \leftarrow \{s_0\}$
2. **while** *True* **do**
3.   **while** *there are π-incompatible states in S* **do**
4.   Select a π-incompatible state (q, C) of S (i.e., s.t. $\pi \not\models C$) ;
5.   Select a π-incompatible J in $(\exists X : C)$ (i.e., s.t. $\pi \not\models J$) ;
6. $K \leftarrow K \wedge \neg J$;
7. $S \leftarrow \bigcup_{j=0}^{i} Post^j_{\mathcal{A}(K)}(\{s_0\})$;
8.   **if** $Post_{\mathcal{A}(K)}(S) \sqsubseteq S$ **then return** $K \leftarrow \bigcap_{(q,C) \in S} (\exists X : C)$
9. $i \leftarrow i + 1$;
10. $S \leftarrow S \cup Post_{\mathcal{A}(K)}(S)$;   // $S = \bigcup_{j=0}^{i} Post^j_{\mathcal{A}(K)}(\{s_0\})$

The termination of *IM* is not guaranteed in general. However, we provide in [3] sufficient condition for termination; in particular, *IM* is guaranteed to terminate for a form of acyclic automata.

The output K of *IM* is a *behavioral tile* in the following sense: A constraint K is said to be a *behavioral tile* (or more simply a *tile*), if for all $\pi_1, \pi_2 \in K$, the trace sets of $\mathcal{A}[\pi_1]$ and $\mathcal{A}[\pi_2]$ are equal. Note that a tile corresponds to a convex and dense set of real-valued points. Given a tile K, the trace set of $\mathcal{A}(K)$ will be simply referred to as "the trace set of K". Note that such a trace set is a (possibly infinite) set of finite traces.

Given a tile K and a trace property *Prop*, we say that K is *good* if its trace set is good. From the inverse method [3], in order to decide whether K is good or bad, it is sufficient to select any $\pi \models K$ and check the truth of *Prop* for $\mathcal{A}[\pi]$.

4.2   The Behavioral Cartography Algorithm

Principle. By iterating the above inverse method *IM* over all the *integer* points of a rectangle[1] V_0 (of which there are a finite number), one is able to decompose (most of) the parametric space included into V_0 into behavioral tiles. Formally:

Algorithm 2. Behavioral Cartography Algorithm $BC(\mathcal{A}, V_0)$

---

    input   : A PTA $\mathcal{A}$, a finite rectangle $V_0 \subseteq \mathbb{R}_{\geq 0}^M$
    output: *Tiling*: list of tiles (initially empty)

1 **repeat**
2   select an integer point $\pi \in V_0$;
3   **if** π *does not belong to any tile of Tiling* **then**
4   ⌊ Add $IM(\mathcal{A}, \pi)$ to *Tiling*;
5 **until** *Tiling contains all the integer points of V_0*;

Note that two tiles with distinct trace sets are necessarily disjoint. On the other hand, two tiles with the same trace sets may overlap.

In many cases, all the real-valued space of V_0 is covered by *Tiling* (see Section 6). Besides, the space covered by *Tiling* often largely exceeds the limits of V_0 (see Section 4.4 for a sufficient condition of full coverage of the parametric space).

Partition Between Good and Bad Tiles. If now a decidable trace property is given then one can check which tiles are good (i.e., the tiles whose trace set satisfies the property), and which ones are bad. One can thus partition the rectangle V_0 into a good (resp. bad) subspace, i.e., a union of good (resp. bad) tiles.

Advantages. First, the cartography itself does not depend on the property one wants to check. Only the partition between good and bad tiles involves the considered property. Moreover, the algorithm is interesting because one does not need to compute the set of all the reachable states. On the contrary, each call to the inverse method algorithm quickly reduces the state space by removing the incompatible states. This allows us to overcome the state space explosion problem, which prevents other methods, such as the computation of the whole set of reachable states (and then the intersection with the bad states) [15], to terminate in practice. Finally note that the algorithm could easily be parallelized, e.g., by performing different calls to the inverse method in parallel, which is not possible in general when computing the set of all reachable states.

4.3   Application to the Flip-Flop Example

We are interested in studying the correctness of the flip-flop described in Section 3. For the sake of simplicity, we consider a model with only 2 parameters,

---
[1] Actually, V_0 can be a convex set containing a finite number of integer points.

with the following V_0: $\delta_3^+ \in [8, 30]$ and $\delta_4^+ \in [3, 30]$. The other parameters are instantiated as follows:

$$T_{HI} = 24 \qquad T_{LO} = 15 \qquad T_{Setup} = 10 \qquad T_{Hold} = 17 \qquad \delta_1^- = 7$$
$$\delta_1^+ = 7 \qquad \delta_2^- = 5 \qquad \delta_2^+ = 6 \qquad \delta_3^- = 8 \qquad \delta_4^- = 3$$

We compute the cartography of the flip-flop circuit according to δ_3^+ and δ_4^+, depicted in Figure 2. The dashed rectangle corresponds to V_0.

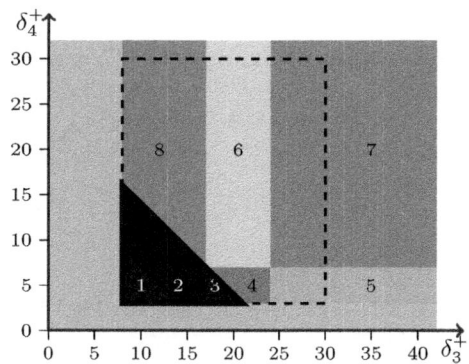

Fig. 2. Behavioral cartography of the flip-flop according to δ_3^+ and δ_4^+

First note that the whole (real-valued) V_0 is covered. Note also that tiles 5 to 8 are unbounded. Actually, this cartography covers the whole[2] real-valued parametric space $\mathbb{R}_{\geq 0} \times \mathbb{R}_{\geq 0}$. According to the nature of the trace sets, we can easily partition the tiles into good and bad tiles w.r.t. property $Prop_1$ (see Section 3).

For example, the trace set of tile 3 (corresponding to the constraint $\delta_3^+ + \delta_4^+ < 24 \wedge \delta_3^+ \geq 17 \wedge \delta_4^+ \geq 3$) is given in Figure 3. This tile is a *good* tile because $Q^\uparrow$ occurs before $CK^\downarrow$ for all traces.

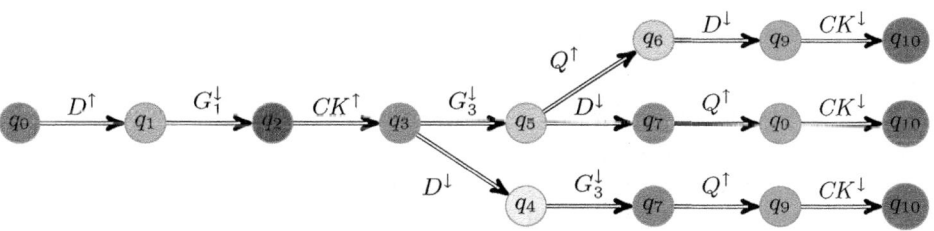

Fig. 3. Trace set of tile 3 for the flip-flop case study

---

[2] Apart from the irrelevant zone originating from the model ($\delta_3^+ < 8$ or $\delta_4^+ < 3$).

Likewise, the trace set of tile 7 (corresponding to the constraint $\delta_3^+ \geq 24 \wedge \delta_4^+ \geq 7$) is given in Figure 4. This is a *bad* tile because there exist traces where $Q^\uparrow$ occurs after $CK^\downarrow$.

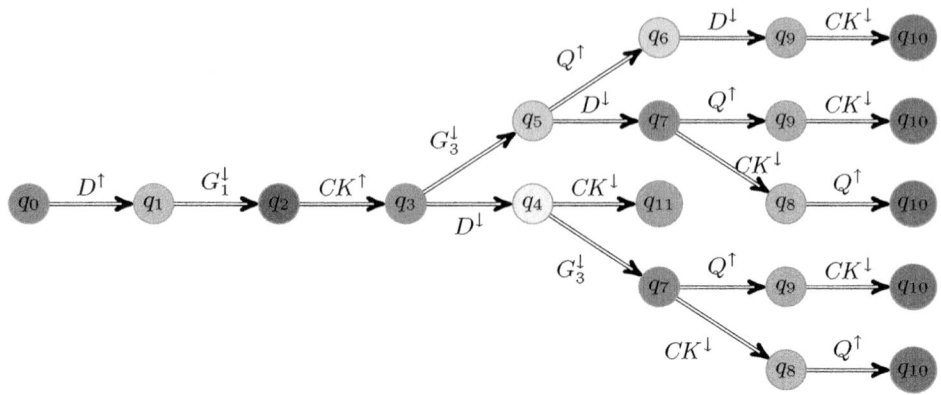

Fig. 4. Trace set of tile 7 for the flip-flop case study

One sees more generally that tiles 1 to 3 are good while tiles 4 to 8 are bad. From this partition into good and bad tiles, we infer the following constraint:

$$\delta_3^+ + \delta_4^+ \leq 24 \quad \wedge \quad \delta_3^+ \geq 8 \quad \wedge \quad \delta_4^+ \geq 3$$

which gives the *maximal* set of good parameters, thus solving the good parameters problem for this example.

Comparison with other methods. By computing in a brute manner the whole set of reachable states for all possible valuations of the parameters, and performing the intersection with the set of bad locations, we get the same constraint ensuring the good behavior of the system. Note that this comparison is possible because this example is rather simple; for bigger examples, such a computation would be impossible because of the state space explosion problem (see the Root Contention Protocol in Section 5.3). In [11], a constraint guaranteeing a good behavior is given. The projection of this constraint onto δ_3^+ and δ_4^+ gives $\delta_3^+ < 11 \wedge \delta_3^+ + \delta_4^+ < 18 \wedge \delta_3^+ \geq 8 \wedge \delta_4^+ \geq 3$, which is strictly included in our constraint[3].

4.4 A Sufficient Condition for Full Coverage

In this section, we show that for "acyclic" automata, a variant of the cartography algorithm allows us to cover the whole real-valued space of parameters within V_0.

The graphical representation of a PTA $\mathcal{A}$ is an oriented graph where vertices correspond to locations, and edges correspond to actions of $\mathcal{A}$. We say that a PTA is *graphically acyclic* (or, more simply, *acyclic*) if its graph is acyclic.

---

[3] Actually, the comparison is not completely fair, because the two models are slightly different.

Lemma 1 (Termination). *Given an acyclic PTA $\mathcal{A}$ and a rectangle V_0, the algorithm $BC(\mathcal{A}, V_0)$ always terminates.*

Proof. Based on the termination of the inverse method (see Proposition 23 in [3]) and the finite number of integer points in V_0.

Note that the acyclicity of the PTA is a sufficient, but non-necessary, termination condition of BC. See Section 5.3 for an example of non acyclic PTA for which the cartography algorithm terminates.

The algorithm BC guarantees to cover the *integer* points within V_0. However, there may exist a finite number of "small holes" within V_0 (containing no integer point) that are not covered by any tile of *Tiling*. In order to fill these holes, one can refine the algorithm in a simple way. This variant, say BC', is obtained from BC by repeatedly generating at the end of BC new tiles of the form $IM(\mathcal{A}, \pi)$, where π is a *rational* (instead of integer) point selected within the holes. In the case of acyclic PTAs, the termination of BC' is guaranteed. This is due to the *finiteness* of the number of different tiles which can be output by $IM(\mathcal{A}, \pi)$, for any *rational* point π of V_0. Formally:

Proposition 1. *Let $\mathcal{A}$ be an acyclic PTA. The set of tiles $\{IM(\mathcal{A}, \pi) \mid \pi \in V_0 \cap \mathbb{Q}_{\geq 0}\}$ is finite.*

Moreover, one can show that BC covers the whole parametric space beyond V_0, for a "sufficiently large" V_0. Formally:

Proposition 2. *Let $\mathcal{A}$ be an acyclic PTA. Then there exists a rectangle V_0 such that $BC(\mathcal{A}, V_0)$ covers the whole real-valued parametric space outside V_0.*

5   Application to the Probabilistic Framework

5.1   Extending the Inverse Method to Probabilistic Systems

Probabilistic Timed Automata are an extension of Timed Automata to the probabilistic case [19]. Parametric Probabilistic Timed Automata (PPTAs) are an extension of those Probabilistic Timed Automata to the parametric case [4]. In this framework, the discrete actions are *distributions* of actions. Roughly speaking, instead of going from a location to another location, one goes from a location to a distributions of locations. A *scheduler* is a mapping which associates to every state *one* output distribution. For each scheduler σ, one can define a probability space for a given probabilistic timed automaton $\mathcal{A}[\pi]$. In particular, one can define the *probability of reaching a given location* for $\mathcal{A}[\pi]$ under a given σ. Such probabilities can be computed using the PRISM model-checker [16].

Given a PPTA $\mathcal{A}$, one considers the non-probabilistic version $\mathcal{A}^*$ of $\mathcal{A}$ [4]: this is done roughly speaking by replacing each distribution of actions by a set of standard non-deterministic actions. We have shown in [4] that the minimum (resp. maximum) probability *prob* of reaching a given location in $\mathcal{A}[\pi]$ is uniquely determined by the trace set of $\mathcal{A}^*[\pi]$. Hence, in order to determine *prob* for $\mathcal{A}[\pi]$, it is sufficient to proceed as follows:

1. Compute $K = IM(\mathcal{A}^*, \pi)$;
2. Compute *prob* (using, e.g., PRISM) for $\mathcal{A}[\pi']$, for some $\pi' \in K$.

One advantage of this method is that one can take π' small enough in order to make the computation of PRISM easier, because the performance of PRISM depends on the size of the state space of the model used as input, which in turn depends on the size of the constants used in the probabilistic timed automata.

5.2 Extending the Cartography to the Probabilistic Framework

Using the cartography described in Section 4 and the result of [4], we can construct a cartography of a probabilistic system. We get a set of tiles such that, for any point in a given tile, the minimum (resp. maximum) probability of reaching a given location is the same. Formally, given a PPTA $\mathcal{A}$, a rectangle V_0 and a reachability property rp:

1. Compute $Tiling = BC(\mathcal{A}^*, V_0)$;
2. For each tile $K \in Tiling$, select $\pi \models K$, and compute the minimum (resp. maximum) probability of satisfying rp in $\mathcal{A}[\pi]$ (using, e.g., PRISM).

Note that, if one wants to consider another reachability property rp', one can keep $Tiling$ as computed in step 1, and only needs to redo step 2.

This cartography method is useful for finding appropriate timing parameters, e.g., in randomized protocols. To our knowledge, no other method allows the synthesis of constraints on the parameters within which the values of reachability probabilities are preserved.

5.3 Example: Root Contention Protocol

This case study concerns the Root Contention Protocol of the IEEE 1394 ("FireWire") High Performance Serial Bus, considered in the parametric framework in [20]. We consider the following valuation π_0 of the parameters given in [20]: $rc\_fast\_min = 76$, $rc\_fast\_max = 85$, $rc\_slow\_min = 159$, $rc\_slow\_max = 167$, and $delay = 30$. We are interested in computing the minimum probability $prob_1$ of satisfying the following property rp_1: "a leader is elected after three rounds or less". Using PRISM, it is possible to determine that $prob_1 = 0.75$ for π_0. To study this probability for other points around π_0, we compute a cartography with the following V_0: $rc\_slow\_min \in [140, 200]$, $rc\_slow\_max \in [140, 200]$ and $delay \in [1, 50]$. The two other parameters remain constant, as in π_0.

The cartography is given in Figure 5. For the sake of clarity, we project onto $delay$ and rc_slow_min. In each tile, the parameter rc_slow_max is only bound by the implicit constraint $rc\_slow\_min \leq rc\_slow\_max$.

Note that tiles 1 and 6 are infinite towards dimension rc_slow_min, and all tiles are infinite towards dimension rc_slow_max. Moreover, although all the integer points within V_0 are covered (from the algorithm), note that the real-valued part of V_0 is not fully covered, because there are some "holes" (real-valued zones without integer points) in the lower right corner. It would not be

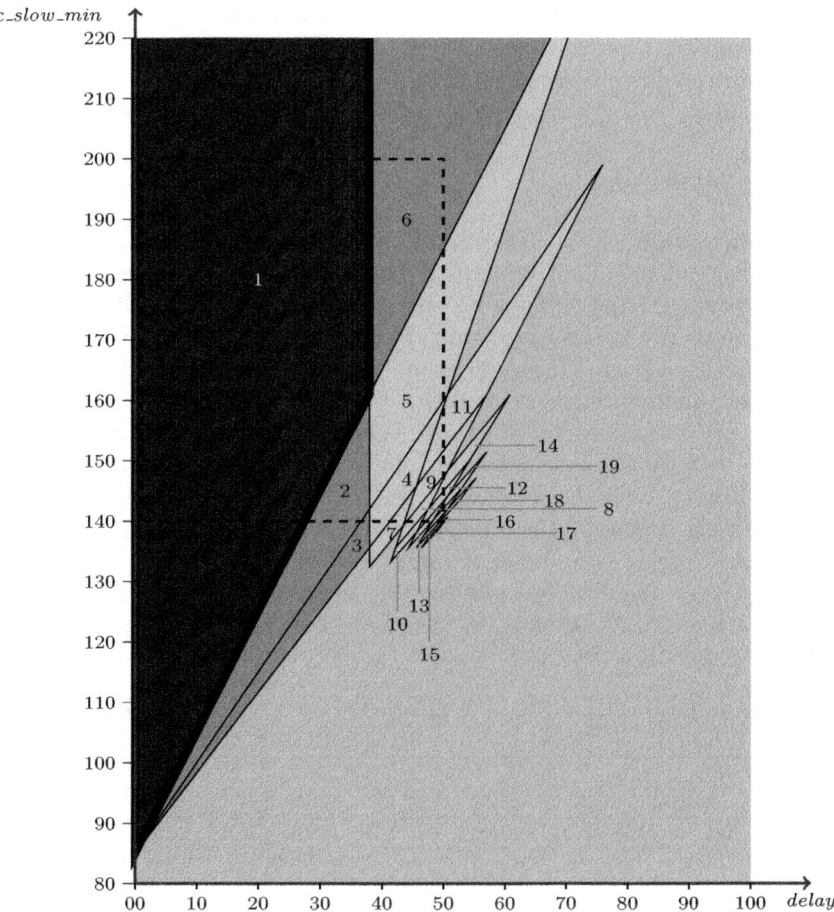

Fig. 5. Behavioral cartography of the Root Contention Protocol according to *delay* and *rc_slow_min*

possible to fill completely those holes, using the refinement of the algorithm *BC* given in Section 4.4, because Proposition 1 does not hold any longer here. Note that, nevertheless, our method is still capable of giving valuable information by partitioning most of the parametric space within V_0 into good and bad tiles. Finally note that the computation of the whole set of reachable states (see, e.g., [15]) does not terminate in this example, due to the infinite number of generated traces (with incomparable constraints).

Partition into good and bad subspaces. Applying PRISM to one point of each tile, we find $prob_1 = 0.75$ for tile 1. For tiles 2, 3 and 6, we have $prob_1 = 0.625$. For the other tiles, $prob_1 = 0.5$. Let us suppose that a tile is good when the probability $prob_1$ is greater than 0.7, and bad otherwise. In this case, only tile 1 is a good tile, and the others are bad tiles.

An advantage of the cartography algorithm is that, if one considers another property than rp_1, there is no need to re-compute the cartography again. Various other properties have been considered (e.g., the election of a leader after *five* rounds or less), leading to different partitions into good and bad subspaces.

6   Case Studies

An implementation of the behavioral cartography algorithm has been made, called IMITATOR II. This program is a complete new version, written in OCaml, of the prototype IMITATOR [5]. The execution of IMITATOR II is fully automated, from the source file to the generation of the behavioral tiles and the corresponding trace sets under a graphical form. IMITATOR II makes use of the library APRON for the manipulation of constraints [18].

Results are presented in the table below. The input rectangle V_0 in each case study was chosen for containing the reference valuation π_0 of the model, corresponding to a reference behavior (see, e.g., [3]). We give from left to right the name of the example, the number of PTAs composing the global system $\mathcal{A}$, the lower and upper bounds on the number of locations per PTA, the number of clocks, of non-instantiated parameters, of integer points within V_0, of tiles computed, the average number per tile of states and transitions of the trace set, and the computation time in seconds.

Example	PTAs	loc./PTA	$|X|$	$|P|$	$|V_0|$	tiles	states	trans.	Time
SR-latch	3	$[3,8]$	3	3	1331	6	5	4	0.3
Flip-flop [11]	5	$[4,16]$	5	2	644	8	15	14	3
SPSMALL [9]	10	$[3,8]$	10	2	3149	259	60	61	1194
CSMA/CD [21]	3	$[3,8]$	3	3	2000	140	349	545	269
RCP [20]	5	$[6,11]$	6	3	186050	19	5688	9312	7018

Note that the version of the algorithm that we used in IMITATOR II is the classical algorithm (viz., BC, and not BC'). Also note that only the SR-latch case study is modeled with an acyclic PTA (see Section 4.4).

For all those examples, the cartography covers 100 % of the real-valued space of V_0, except for the Root Contention Protocol, where "only" 99,99 % of V_0 is covered (see Section 5.3). Moreover, a significant part of the real-valued space outside V_0 is also covered. Those examples, as well as other case studies, can be found on IMITATOR II's Web page[4].

Finally note that it is possible to find examples (such as the "And–Or" circuit considered in [10,3]) for which the algorithm BC does not terminate for some V_0, because the algorithm IM does not terminate for some $\pi \in V_0$.

7   Final Remarks

In this paper, we presented a cartography algorithm, which covers most of the parametric space with *tiles*, for which the behavior is uniform. This gives a

---

[4] http://www.lsv.ens-cachan.fr/~andre/IMITATOR2/

new approach for solving the *good parameters problem*. Our algorithm has been successfully applied to various examples of asynchronous circuits and protocols. Our cartography algorithm often covers the whole real-valued space of V_0 as well as a significant part of the space beyond V_0.

This method extends naturally to probabilistic systems. This allows us to decompose the parametric space into tiles which are uniform w.r.t. probabilistic reachability properties. The tiles generated by the cartography are always the same, whatever the considered probabilistic property is. Only the partition into good and bad subspaces changes.

Our approach has the following limitation: the equivalence relation on parameters that leads to "tiles" as equivalence classes is strong (because of the equality of trace sets). This may lead to a big (even infinite) number of small equivalence classes (as shown in Section 5.3). It would be interesting to consider a more general inverse method in order to weaken the equivalence relation.

As suggested in Section 4.4, it is interesting to consider variants of BC with a strategy of dynamic point selection for IM: instead of starting from the set of all integer points of V_0, one starts from a sparse subset of points, and fill incrementally the uncovered zones by selecting (non-necessarily integer) points in the "holes".

Finally, it would be interesting to extend the method to hybrid systems, where clocks evolve at different rates.

Acknowledgment. We thank the anonymous referees for their helpful comments.

References

1. Alur, R., Dill, D.L.: A theory of timed automata. TCS 126(2), 183–235 (1994)
2. Alur, R., Henzinger, T.A., Vardi, M.Y.: Parametric real-time reasoning. In: STOC '93, pp. 592–601. ACM, New York (1993)
3. André, É., Chatain, T., Encrenaz, E., Fribourg, L.: An inverse method for parametric timed automata. International Journal of Foundations of Computer Science 20(5), 819–836 (2009)
4. André, É., Fribourg, L., Sproston, J.: An extension of the inverse method to probabilistic timed automata. In: AVoCS'09. Electronic Communications of the EASST, vol. 23 (2009)
5. André, É.: IMITATOR: A tool for synthesizing constraints on timing bounds of timed automata. In: Leucker, M., Morgan, C. (eds.) Theoretical Aspects of Computing - ICTAC 2009. LNCS, vol. 5684, pp. 336–342. Springer, Heidelberg (2009)
6. Annichini, A., Bouajjani, A., Sighireanu, M.: Trex: A tool for reachability analysis of complex systems. In: Berry, G., Comon, H., Finkel, A. (eds.) CAV 2001. LNCS, vol. 2102, pp. 368–372. Springer, Heidelberg (2001)
7. Baier, C., Katoen, J.-P.: Principles of Model Checking. The MIT Press, Cambridge (2008)
8. Brzozowski, J.A., Seger, C.J.: Asynchronous Circuits. Springer, Heidelberg (1995)
9. Chevallier, R., Encrenaz, E., Fribourg, L., Xu, W.: Timed verification of the generic architecture of a memory circuit using parametric timed automata. Formal Methods in System Design 34(1), 59–81 (2009)

10. Clarisó, R., Cortadella, J.: Verification of concurrent systems with parametric delays using octahedra. In: ACSD '05. IEEE Computer Society, Los Alamitos (2005)
11. Clarisó, R., Cortadella, J.: The octahedron abstract domain. Sci. Comput. Program. 64(1), 115–139 (2007)
12. Clarke, E.M., Grumberg, O., Jha, S., Lu, Y., Veith, H.: Counterexample-guided abstraction refinement. In: Emerson, E.A., Sistla, A.P. (eds.) CAV 2000. LNCS, vol. 1855, pp. 154–169. Springer, Heidelberg (2000)
13. Collomb–Annichini, A., Sighireanu, M.: Parameterized reachability analysis of the IEEE 1394 Root Contention Protocol using TReX. In: RT-TOOLS '01 (2001)
14. Frehse, G., Jha, S.K., Krogh, B.H.: A counterexample-guided approach to parameter synthesis for linear hybrid automata. In: Egerstedt, M., Mishra, B. (eds.) HSCC 2008. LNCS, vol. 4981, pp. 187–200. Springer, Heidelberg (2008)
15. Henzinger, T.A., Wong-Toi, H.: Using HyTech to synthesize control parameters for a steam boiler. In: Abrial, J.-R., Börger, E., Langmaack, H. (eds.) Dagstuhl Seminar 1995. LNCS, vol. 1165, Springer, Heidelberg (1996)
16. Hinton, A., Kwiatkowska, M., Norman, G., Parker, D.: PRISM: A tool for automatic verification of probabilistic systems. In: Hermanns, H., Palsberg, J. (eds.) TACAS 2006. LNCS, vol. 3920, pp. 441–444. Springer, Heidelberg (2006)
17. Holzmann, G.: Spin model checker, the: primer and reference manual. Addison-Wesley, Reading (2003)
18. Jeannet, B., Miné, A.: Apron: A library of numerical abstract domains for static analysis. In: Bouajjani, A., Maler, O. (eds.) Computer Aided Verification. LNCS, vol. 5643, pp. 661–667. Springer, Heidelberg (2009)
19. Kwiatkowska, M., Norman, G., Segala, R., Sproston, J.: Automatic verification of real-time systems with discrete probability distributions. TCS 282, 101–150 (2002)
20. Kwiatkowska, M., Norman, G., Sproston, J.: Probabilistic model checking of deadline properties in the IEEE 1394 FireWire root contention protocol. Formal Aspects of Computing 14(3), 295–318 (2003)
21. Kwiatkowska, M., Norman, G., Sproston, J., Wang, F.: Symbolic model checking for probabilistic timed automata. Information and Computation 205(7), 1027–1077 (2007)
22. Larsen, K.G., Pettersson, P., Yi, W.: UPPAAL in a nutshell. International Journal on Software Tools for Technology Transfer 1(1-2), 134–152 (1997)
23. Maler, O., Pnueli, A.: Timing analysis of asynchronous circuits using timed automata. In: Camurati, P.E., Eveking, H. (eds.) CHARME 1995. LNCS, vol. 987, pp. 189–205. Springer, Heidelberg (1995)
24. D'Argenio, P.R., Katoen, J.P., Ruys, T.C., Tretmans, G.J.: The bounded retransmission protocol must be on time! In: Brinksma, E. (ed.) TACAS 1997. LNCS, vol. 1217. Springer, Heidelberg (1997)

On the Joint Spectral Radius for Bounded Matrix Languages

Paul C. Bell[1], Vesa Halava[2], and Mika Hirvensalo[2]

[1] Department of Computer Science, University of Liverpool, Ashton Building,
Ashton St, Liverpool, L69 3BX, U.K.
p.c.bell@liverpool.ac.uk
[2] TUCS-Turku Centre for Computer Science, Department of Mathematics,
University of Turku, FIN-20014, Turku, Finland
vehalava@utu.fi, mikhirve@utu.fi

Abstract. We show several problems concerning probabilistic finite automata with fixed numbers of letters and of fixed dimensions for bounded cut-point and strict cut-point languages are algorithmically undecidable by a reduction of Hilbert's tenth problem using formal power series.

For a finite set of matrices $\{M_1, M_2, \ldots, M_k\} \subseteq \mathbb{Q}^{t \times t}$, we then consider the decidability of computing the joint spectral radius (which characterises the maximal asymptotic growth rate of a set of matrices) of the set $X = \{M_1^{j_1} M_2^{j_2} \cdots M_k^{j_k} | j_1, j_2, \ldots, j_k \geq 0\}$, which we term a bounded matrix language. Using an encoding of a probabilistic finite automaton shown in the paper, we prove the surprising result that determining whether the joint spectral radius of a bounded matrix language is less than or equal to one is undecidable, but determining if it is strictly less than one is in fact decidable (which is similar to a result recently shown for quantum automata).

This has an interpretation in terms of a control problem for a switched linear system with a fixed and finite number of switching operations; if we fix the maximum number of switching operations in advance, then determining convergence to the origin for all initial points is decidable whereas determining boundedness of all initial points is undecidable.

1 Introduction

Most decision problems on (non-)deterministic finite automata are known to be decidable, however if we extend the model to *probabilistic finite automata* (PFA), their computational power increases dramatically (PFA may be interpreted as having a probability distribution of possible states).

A typical question we may ask on a PFA is the decidability of emptiness for cut-point languages, that is, given a PFA R acting on alphabet A and a cut-point $\lambda \in \mathbb{Q}$, does there exist any word $w \in A^*$ such that R has probability greater than or equal to λ of being in a final state upon input w. The emptiness problem for strict cut-point languages may be defined analogously, see Section 2 for formal definitions. The emptiness problem for cut-point and strict cut-point languages on PFA was shown to be undecidable, even with just two letters and

A. Kučera and I. Potapov (Eds.): RP 2010, LNCS 6227, pp. 91–103, 2010.
© Springer-Verlag Berlin Heidelberg 2010

47 states (corresponding to two rational matrices of dimension 47, see Section 2 for details) in [3] and this was recently improved to two letters and 25 states in [10] by using "Claus instances" of Post's correspondence problem.

The emptiness problem was shown to be undecidable for 2-counter deterministic finite automata with reversal bounded counters in [12]. However, the emptiness problem for two-way nondeterministic finite automata with one reversal-bounded counter on bounded languages was shown to be *decidable* in [7]. We investigate decision questions for probabilistic finite automata whose inputs come from a bounded language (see Section 2.1 for definitions).

In this paper, we also show the undecidability of a set of problems denoted F-problems, following [12], for *bounded strict and non-strict cut-point languages* in PFA. The PFA are defined on all words from A^*, but only words from a bounded language L are possible solutions. We mainly concentrate on bounded languages of the form $L = x_1^* \cdots x_k^* \subseteq A^*$ where $A = \{x_1, \ldots, x_k\}$. We show the undecidability via a reduction of Hilbert's tenth problem into a PFA by using formal power series and a result from [1].

We then consider the *joint spectral radius* (see Sec. 5 for definitions) of a set of matrices $X = \{M_1^{j_1} M_2^{j_2} \cdots M_k^{j_k} | j_1, j_2, \ldots, j_k \geq 0\}$, where each $M_i \in \mathbb{Q}^{t \times t}$, which we term a *bounded matrix language*. Following a technique used in [5] and an encoding of a PFA given in this paper, we prove the surprising result that determining whether the joint spectral radius of a bounded matrix language is less than or equal to 1 is undecidable, but determining if it is strictly less than 1 is in fact decidable. This is similar to a result in the field of *quantum automata* where it was shown that for *non-strict* cut point languages, the emptiness problem is decidable, whereas for *strict* cut point languages it is undecidable, see [6], [10].

The joint spectral radius characterises the maximal asymptotic growth rate of a set of matrices and can be considered as a stability condition for a discrete-time switched linear system. In such a system, we are given a set of matrices $M = \{M_1, M_2, \ldots, M_n\}$ and we update an initial vector x_0 by:

$$x_{i+1} = M_{\sigma(i)} x_i$$

where $\sigma : \mathbb{N} \to \{1, \ldots, n\}$ is a switching signal (we can think of this signal as changing the matrix being applied at each step according to some criteria). If all trajectories for any initial vector x_0 and any switching signal σ converge to zero, then we say the switched linear system is stable. This is characterised by the value of the joint spectral radius of M written $\overline{\rho}(M)$. A stable switched linear system satisfies $\hat{\rho}(M) < 1$. Determining if there exists an algorithm to calculate if $\hat{\rho}(M) < 1$ for a finite matrix set M is a well-known and important open problem [5].

In this paper we study the joint spectral radius for *bounded matrix languages*. We may think of this as characterising the stability of a switched linear system where we are allowed to apply the switching signal to change from one matrix to another a *fixed number of times*. This is a natural question to ask as pointed out in [8], since in many applications it is desirable to minimize the number of switches between different modes and this is a measure of cost used in hybrid control applications. In [8], the authors show that it is NP-hard to determine whether there exists some switching signal σ which changes matrix a fixed number of times and which drives an initial point x_0 to the origin.

We shall consider instead whether all such switching signals with a fixed maximum number of switches cause *any* x_0 to *converge* to the origin (this is equivalent to determining if the JSR of a bounded matrix language is < 1). We show that this problem is decidable. However, to determine whether the switched linear system has a *bounded trajectory* for any initial point x_0 (this is equivalent to determining if the JSR of a bounded matrix language is ≤ 1) we show is actually *undecidable*. For the system we use in our proofs, we show that the only possible trajectories that do not converge towards zero have a very specific form and the order of changes of matrices one must check can be fixed in advance. For products not using such a form, they will always converge towards zero.

2 Preliminaries

2.1 Probabilistic Finite Automata

Let $A = \{x_1, x_2, \ldots, x_k\}$ be a finite set of *letters* called an *alphabet*. A word w is a finite sequence of letters from A, the set of all words over A is denoted A^* and the set of nonempty words is denoted A^+. The *empty word* is denoted by ε. For two words $u = u_1 u_2 \cdots u_i$ and $v = v_1 v_2 \cdots v_j$, where $u, v \in A^*$, the concatenation of u and v is denoted by $u \cdot v$ (or by uv for brevity) such that $u \cdot v = u_1 u_2 \cdots u_i v_1 v_2 \cdots v_j$. A subset L of A^* is called a *language*. Language $L \subseteq A^*$ is called a *bounded language* if and only if there exist words $w_1, w_2 \ldots, w_m \in A^+$ such that $L \subseteq w_1^* w_2^* \cdots w_m^*$.

A vector $y \in \mathbb{Q}^n$ is called a *probability distribution* if its elements are nonnegative and sum to 1 (we say y has an L_1 norm of 1). A matrix M is called a *column stochastic matrix* if each column is a probability distribution, a *row stochastic matrix* if each row is a probability distribution and it is called a *doubly stochastic matrix* if it is both row and column stochastic. For any row stochastic matrix M, if y is a probability distribution, then so is $y^T M$, since M preserves the L_1 norm on vectors and has no negative elements. The product of two row/column/doubly stochastic matrices is also row/column/doubly stochastic (respectively) as is not difficult to verify.

A *probabilistic finite automaton* (PFA, see [14] for further details) over an alphabet A is a triplet (u, φ, v), where $u \subset \mathbb{Q}^n$ ($n - |A|$) is the *initial probability distribution*, $\varphi : A^* \to \mathbb{Q}^{n \times n}$ is a monoid homomorphism whose range is the set of n-dimensional row stochastic matrices and $v \in \mathbb{Q}^n$ is the *final state vector* whose ith coordinate is 1, if state i is final, and 0 otherwise.[1]

---

[1] The definition of a PFA in the literature often interchanges the roles of u and v from our definition and requires column stochastic matrices, but the two can easily be seen to be equivalent by transposing all matrices and interchanging u and v. Our definition makes the proof of Theorem 3 easier to read.

For a given PFA denoted $R = (u, \varphi, v)$ and a word $w \in A^*$, we shall also use the notation $f_R : A^* \to [0, 1]$, where:

$$f_R(w) = u^T \varphi(w) v \in [0, 1]; \quad w \in A^*.$$

This is the probability of R being in a final state after reading word $w \in A^*$.

Let $L \subseteq A^*$ be a given language over an alphabet A, R be a probabilistic finite automaton and $\lambda \in [0, 1]$. We define the cut-point languages by:

$$\Psi_{\Delta\lambda}(R, L) = \{w \in L \mid f_R(w) \Delta \lambda\}; \quad \Delta \in \{\leq, <, >, \geq\} \tag{1}$$

It is known that testing the emptiness of the language $\Psi_{\Delta\lambda}(R, A^*)$ for any $\Delta \in \{\leq, <, >, \geq\}$, i.e., when the language the words are taken over is unrestricted, is undecidable. We will show that it is undecidable to determine whether:

$$\Psi_{\Delta\lambda}(R, L) \overset{?}{=} \emptyset; \quad \Delta \in \{\leq, <, >, \geq\} \tag{2}$$

for a bounded input language $L = x_1^* x_2^* \cdots x_k^* \subseteq A^*$. Note that our automata will be defined on any input word $w \in A^*$, but due to the construction, any possible solution must be a member of L, thus we may restrict to testing words in L.

2.2   Formal Power Series

We use the definitions and terminology for *formal power series* as in [2]. Let K be a semiring and A a finite alphabet generating a free monoid denoted by A^*. A formal power series S is defined to be a function $S : A^* \to K$, and the image of a word $w \in A^*$ under S is denoted (S, w) and is called the coefficient of w in S. The set of formal power series (FPS) over A with coefficients in K is denoted by $K\langle\langle A \rangle\rangle$. If there are only finitely many nonzero coefficients in a FPS, then it is called a *polynomial* and denoted by $K\langle A \rangle$. We can use the following standard notation to define a FPS $S \in K\langle\langle A \rangle\rangle$:

$$S = \sum_{w \in A^*} (S, w) w.$$

The operations of sum, product, external products and star product can all be defined in a natural and precise way, see [2] for definitions. These make up the *rational operations* of a FPS.

A subset of $K\langle\langle A \rangle\rangle$ is *rationally closed* if it is closed under the rational operations. The smallest rationally closed subset of $K\langle\langle A \rangle\rangle$ containing a subset E, is called the rational closure of E. A formal power series is called K-*rational* if it is contained within the rational closure of $K\langle A \rangle$.

A formal power series $S \in K\langle\langle A \rangle\rangle$ is called *recognizable* if there exists an integer $n \geq 1$, two vectors $\rho, \tau \in K^n$ and a monoid homomorphism $\mu : A^* \to K^{n \times n}$, such that for all words $w \in A^*$,

$$(S, w) = \rho^T \mu(w) \tau$$

and then (ρ, μ, τ) is called a *linear representation* of S.

The following fundamental theorem was shown by Kleene and Schützenberger, see [2] for details.

Theorem 1 (Schützenberger, 1961 [17]). *A formal power series is rational if and only if it is recognizable.*

2.3 Hilbert's Tenth Problem

The following problem was posed in 1900 by David Hilbert:

Hilbert's Tenth Problem - Given a Diophantine equation with any number of unknown quantities and with rational integral numerical coefficients: To devise a process according to which it can be determined by a finite number of operations whether the equation is solvable in rational integers.

A "negative solution" to the problem was shown in 1970 by Y. Matiyasevich building upon earlier work of many mathematicians, including M. Davis, H. Putman and J. Robinson. For more details of the history of the problem as well as the full proof of the undecidability of this problem, see [13]. We may, without loss of generality, restrict the variables to be natural numbers, see [13, p.6].

Let $P(n_1, n_2, \ldots, n_k)$ be an integer polynomial with k variables. Hilbert's tenth problem can be rephrased to instead determine if there exists a procedure to find if there exist $x_1, x_2, \ldots, x_k \in \mathbb{N}$ such that: $P(x_1, x_2, \ldots, x_k) = 0$. It is well known that this may be reduced to a problem in formal power series. It was shown in [16, p.73] that the above problem can be reduced to that of determining for a $\mathbb{Z}$-rational formal power series $S \in \mathbb{Z}\langle\langle A \rangle\rangle$, whether there exists any word $w \in A^*$ such that $(S, w) = 0$. The following theorem was proven in [1]:

Theorem 2. *[1] Given integral matrices $M_1, M_2, \ldots, M_k$ of dimension $n \times n$, it is algorithmically undecidable to determine whether there exists a solution to the equation:*

$$M_1^{i_1} M_2^{i_2} \cdots M_k^{i_k} = Z,$$

where Z denotes the zero matrix and $i_1, i_2, \ldots, i_k \in \mathbb{N}$ are variables.

From the construction shown in [1], the following corollary is immediate:

Corollary 1. *Given an integer polynomial $P(n_1, n_2, \ldots, n_k)$, one can construct two vectors $\rho = (1, 0, \ldots, 0)^T \in \mathbb{N}^n$ and $\tau = (0, 0, \ldots, 1)^T \in \mathbb{N}^n$, an alphabet $A = \{x_1, x_2, \ldots, x_k\}$ and a homomorphism $\mu : A^* \to \mathbb{Z}^{n \times n}$, such that for words of the form $w = x_1^{n_1} x_2^{n_2} \cdots x_k^{n_k} \in A^+$:*

$$\rho^T \mu(w) \tau = P(n_1, n_2, \ldots, n_k)^2, \tag{3}$$

for any word $w' \in A^+$ not of this form, $\rho^T \mu(w') \tau = 1$ and for the empty word ε we have that $\rho^T \mu(\varepsilon) \tau = 0$. The triple (ρ, μ, τ) is a linear representation of a $\mathbb{Z}$-regular formal power series $S \in \mathbb{N}\langle\langle A \rangle\rangle$.

Thus, determining if there exists any word $w \in A^+$ such that $\rho^T \mu(w) \tau = 0$ is undecidable. Note that Eqn. (3) only holds for *nonempty* words w since in fact $\rho^T \mu(\varepsilon) \tau = 0$. We shall require Corollary 1 in the proof of Theorem 3 where the pathological case of empty words will be specifically dealt with in Step 2.

3 Probabilistic Encoding

In this section we shall show an encoding of Hilbert's tenth problem into a probabilistic finite automaton by using Corollary 1 in order to show that the (strict) emptiness problems for PFA are undecidable even over bounded languages. This is an important theorem for several later results since it shows the possible solutions of the problems must be from the given bounded language and any words not in this language cannot be solutions.

Theorem 3. *Given a probabilistic finite automaton $R = (u, \varphi, v)$ over an alphabet $A = \{x_1, x_2, \ldots, x_k\}$, a bounded language $L \subseteq A^*$ and a rational cut-point $\lambda \in [0, 1]$. Determining if $\Psi_{\Delta\lambda}(P, L) = \emptyset$ where $\Delta \in \{\le, <, >, \ge,\}$ is undecidable. Moreover, this result holds even when we know $\Psi_{\Delta\lambda}(P, \overline{L}) = \emptyset$ and thus we only need test words from language L.*

Proof. Let us first give an intuitive notion of the theorem for the equality $\le$ as an example. Given the probabilistic finite automata R, cut-point $\lambda \in [0, 1]$ and the bounded language L, we would like to determine if there exists any word $w \in L$ such that $f_R(w) \le \lambda$. In our construction, if $w' \notin L$, then $f_R(w') > \lambda$ and so we may restrict to testing words in L.

We shall reduce an instance of Hilbert's tenth problem into the emptiness problem for the cut-point language of a PFA. Let $P(n_1, n_2, \ldots, n_k)$ be an integer coefficient polynomial. According to Corollary 1, there exists a $\mathbb{Z}$-rational formal power series S with linear representation (ρ, μ, τ) over an alphabet $A = \{x_1, x_2, \ldots, x_k\}$ such that

$$(S, w) = \rho^T \mu(w)\tau = \begin{cases} P(n_1, \ldots, n_k)^2; \text{ if } w \in L \setminus \{\varepsilon\} \\ 1; \text{ if } w \in A^* \setminus L, \\ 0; \text{ if } w = \varepsilon, \end{cases} \qquad (4)$$

where L is the bounded language $L = x_1^* x_2^* \cdots x_k^* \subseteq A^*$. Let $(t - 2)$ be the dimension of the vectors and matrices of the linear representation, i.e., $\rho, \tau \in \mathbb{Z}^{(t-2)}, \mu : A^* \to \mathbb{Z}^{(t-2) \times (t-2)}$. It can thus be seen that it is undecidable to determine if there exists a *nonempty* word $w \in A^+$ such that $\rho^T \mu(w)\tau = 0$ by the undecidability of Hilbert's tenth problem.

Step 1. Our first step is to convert the set $\mathcal{G} = \{\mu(x_i) : 1 \le i \le k\} \subseteq \mathbb{Z}^{(t-2) \times (t-2)}$ of matrices into a set of strictly positive doubly stochastic matrices[2]. Let $\mu_1 : A^+ \to \mathbb{Z}^{t \times t}$ be defined by:

$$\mu_1(x_i) = \begin{pmatrix} 0 & 0 & 0 \\ t_i & \mu(x_i) & 0 \\ s & r_i^T & 0 \end{pmatrix} ; \quad 1 \le i \le k,$$

where $t_i, r_i \in \mathbb{Z}^{(t-2)}$ and $s \in \mathbb{Z}$ are chosen so that the row and column sums of each $\mu_1(x_i)$ are 0 (note that these values are well defined and unique). It is not

---

[2] This step follows the construction of P. Turakainen [19], see also [10].

difficult to verify that the product of two such matrices retains the given form and still has zero row and column sums.

Now define the matrix $\Omega \in \mathbb{Z}^{t \times t}$ to be a matrix such that all elements equal 1. Clearly $\Omega^2 = t\Omega$, thus $\Omega^i = t^{i-1}\Omega$ for $i \geq 1$. Let $Z \in \mathbb{Z}^{t \times t}$ denote the zero matrix and by the definition of μ_1, for all $1 \leq i \leq k$, it holds that

$$\mu_1(x_i) \cdot \Omega = \Omega \cdot \mu_1(x_i) = Z. \tag{5}$$

Let $c \in \mathbb{Z}^+$ be chosen so that $\mu_1(x_i) + c\Omega$ is a strictly positive matrix for each $1 \leq i \leq k$ (i.e., each element is > 0). Next, define $\mu_2 : A^+ \to (\mathbb{Q}^+)^{t \times t}$ by:

$$\mu_2(x_i) = \left(\frac{1}{ct}\right)\left(\mu_1(x_i) + c\Omega\right) \quad ; 1 \leq i \leq k,$$

where $\mathbb{Q}^+$ is the set of positive rationals. For a word $w \in A^+$, it thus holds that:

$$\mu_2(w) = \left(\frac{1}{ct}\right)^{|w|}\left(\mu_1(w) + c^{|w|}t^{|w|-1}\Omega\right) \quad ; 1 \leq i \leq k,$$

by using the fact that μ_1 is a homomorphism, Eqn. (5) to cancel the central summands and the property that $\Omega^i = t^{i-1}\Omega$. By the choice of c, we see that $\mu_2 : A^+ \to [0,1]^{t \times t}$. Each $\mu_2(x_i)$ for $1 \leq i \leq k$ is doubly stochastic since the row and column sums of $\mu_1(x_i) + c\Omega$ for each $x_i \in A$ equal ct.

Finally, we define the vectors $\rho_2 = (0, \rho^T, 0)^T = (0, 1, 0, \ldots, 0)^T \in \mathbb{N}^t$ and $\tau_2 = (0, \tau^T, 0)^T = (0, \ldots, 0, 1, 0)^T \in \mathbb{N}^t$. The converted linear representation is given by (ρ_2, μ_2, τ_2) which is the linear representation of a $\mathbb{Q}^+$-rational formal power series $S' \in \mathbb{Q}^+\langle\langle A \rangle\rangle$. It is clear that for a word $w \in A^+$,

$$\rho_2^T \mu_2(w)\tau_2 = \left(\frac{1}{ct}\right)^{|w|}\rho_2^T\left(\mu_1(w) + c^{|w|}t^{|w|-1}\Omega\right)\tau_2 \tag{6}$$

$$= \left(\frac{1}{ct}\right)^{|w|}\left(\rho^T\mu(w)\tau\right) + \frac{1}{t} \geq \frac{1}{t}, \tag{7}$$

with equality if and only if $\rho^T\mu(w)\tau = 0$. Testing whether this value equals zero is undecidable by Corollary 1, thus testing whether there exists any word $w \in A^+$ such that $\rho_2^T \mu_2(w)\tau_2 = 1/t$ is also undecidable. However, we have to take account of the case that $w = \varepsilon$ since $\rho_2^T I \tau_2 = 0$ where I is the identity matrix. Our next step will avoid this situation.

Step 2. Let us define $\rho_3 = (0, 0, \frac{1}{2}, 0, \ldots, 0, \frac{1}{2})^T$ and $\tau_3 = (0, \ldots, 0, 1, 0, 1)^T$ where $\rho_3, \tau_3 \in (\mathbb{Q}^+)^{t+2}$. Note that ρ_3 is $\frac{1}{2}\rho_2$ with a 0 appended to the start and $\frac{1}{2}$ appended to the end of the vector and τ_3 is τ_2 with a 0 appended at the start and a 1 at the end. Now, define the homomorphism $\mu_3 : A^* \to (\mathbb{Q}^+)^{(t+2) \times (t+2)}$:

$$\mu_3(x_i) = \begin{pmatrix} \frac{1}{2} & 0 & \frac{1}{2} \\ 0 & \mu_2(x_i) & 0 \\ \frac{1}{2} & 0 & \frac{1}{2} \end{pmatrix} \quad ; 1 \leq i \leq k$$

and note that this is still a doubly stochastic matrix and retains the given form under multiplication. Note also that $\rho_3^T \mu_3(\varepsilon)\tau_3 = \rho_3^T \tau_3 = \frac{1}{2}$, so the empty word now maps to $\frac{1}{2}$. For a word $w \in A^*$, we can compute that:

$$\rho_3^T \mu_3(w)\tau_3 = \frac{1}{2}\left(\rho_2^T \mu_2(w)\tau_2\right) + \frac{1}{4} \geq \left(\frac{1}{2t} + \frac{1}{4}\right)$$

which follows from Eqn. (6) and Eqn. (7), with equality if and only if $\rho^T \mu(w)\tau = 0$ as required. Since $(t-2)$ is the dimension of the initial linear representation, we may assume $t > 2$. We thus set the cut-point to be $\lambda = \frac{1}{2t} + \frac{1}{4}$. For the empty word we have: $\rho_3^T \mu_3(\varepsilon)\tau_3 = \frac{1}{2}$ which is greater than λ when $t > 2$, thus determining if there exists any $w \in A^*$ such that $\rho_3^T \mu_3(w)\tau_3 \leq \lambda$ is undecidable. In fact, by Corollary 1, we now see the only possible solutions to the problem come from L, proving the last statement of the Theorem. Let $u = \rho_3$, $v = \tau_3$, $\varphi = \mu_3$ and $\lambda = \frac{1}{2t} + \frac{1}{4}$ and we get the undecidability for the bounded cut-point language '$\leq$'.

Step 3. We may modify the formal power series to obtain the undecidability for the inequalities $<, >$ and $\geq$. Let $(S_2, w) = -(S, w)$ for all $w \in A^*$. We may avoid Step 2, since the empty word mapping to 0 will be less than the (nonzero) bound we shall set. Following this proof, we create a PFA such that it is undecidable to determine if there exists any $w \in A^*$ such that $u^T \varphi(w)v \geq \lambda$ for the same bounded language L for $\lambda \in (0, 1]$.

Let us define two formal power series, $(S_3, w) = 1 - (S, w)$ and $(S_4, w) = (S, w) - 1$, for all $w \in A^*$. Both S_3 and S_4 are still rational and thus by Theorem 1, they are recognizable. Using these FPS in Eqn. (4) and following the above proof (setting an appropriate threshold), it is not difficult to obtain the undecidability of the bounded *strict* cut-point languages, thus proving the theorem.   □

4   F-Problems

We may now show that the other "F-Problems" studied in [12] are also undecidable by using the probabilistic finite automata constructions from the proof of Theorem 3. Given two PFA R_1 and R_2 with respective cut-points λ_1, λ_2, we use the definition of $\Psi_{\Delta\lambda}(R, L)$ from the preliminaries. The *emptiness problem* has already been defined, i.e., is $\Psi_{\Delta\lambda_1}(R_1, L) = \emptyset$? The *infiniteness problem* asks whether $\Psi_{\Delta\lambda_1}(R_1, L)$ is an infinite set. The *disjointedness problem* asks whether the intersection $\Psi_{\Delta\lambda_1}(R_1, L) \cap \Psi_{\Delta\lambda_2}(R_2, L)$ is empty. The *containment problem* asks if the following containment holds: $\Psi_{\Delta\lambda_1}(R_1, L) \subseteq \Psi_{\Delta\lambda_2}(R_2, L)$. The *universe problem* asks if $\Psi_{\Delta\lambda_1}(R_1, L)$ is the set of all strings in L. The *equivalence problem* asks if $\Psi_{\Delta\lambda_1}(R_1, L) = \Psi_{\Delta\lambda_2}(R_2, L)$.

Corollary 2. *The "F-Problems" are undecidable for bounded cut-point languages on probabilistic finite automata.*

Proof. Let R_1 be a PFA over an alphabet $A = \{x_1, x_2, \ldots, x_k\}$ as in Theorem 3 and λ_1 the corresponding cut-point. Then we know that determining if

$\Psi_{\Delta\lambda_1}(R_1, L) = \emptyset$ where $\Delta \in \{\leq, <, >, \geq, \}$ is undecidable for the bounded language $L = x_1^* x_2^* \cdots x_k^* \subseteq A^*$.

Let $S \in \mathbb{Z}\langle\langle A \rangle\rangle$ be such that $S = \text{char}(L)$ where we recall that $\text{char}(L)$ denotes the characteristic series of language L. Since this power series is rational, it is recognizable by Theorem 1, thus it has a linear representation and we can convert it to a PFA, R_2, as we did in Theorem 3. A cut-point $\lambda_2 \in [0, 1]$ can then easily be computed such that

$$\Psi_{\Delta\lambda_2}(R_2, A^*) = L; \quad \Delta \in \{\leq, <, >, \geq, \}$$

in other words, this PFA accepts any word $w \in A^*$ with probability $\Delta\lambda_2$ if and only $w \in L$ (we shall use several Δ for different problems below).

For the disjointedness problem, we may consider the language intersection: $\Psi_{\leq\lambda_1}(R_1, L) \cap \Psi_{\leq\lambda_2}(R_2, A^*)$ which is empty if and only if for all $w \in A^*$, $f_R(w) > \lambda_1$ which is undecidable. For the containment problem, we consider the problem $\Psi_{\leq\lambda_2}(R_2, A^*) \subseteq \Psi_{>\lambda_1}(R_1, L)$ which holds if and only if $w \in A^*$, $f_{R_1}(w) > \lambda_1$ using the same PFA as for disjointedness but with $\leq$ replaced by $>$. Showing the equivalence problem's undecidability is also straightforward, simply consider $\Psi_{\leq\lambda_2}(R_2, A^*) = \Psi_{>\lambda_1}(R_1, L)$ as in containment but with $\subseteq$ replaced by $=$. For the universe problem, we need a slight modification by removing the characteristic series for the language L in the defining formal power series for R_1, but we shall not give the details. Once this is done, we consider $\Psi_{>\lambda_1}(R_1, L)$ which equals L if and only if $\neg\exists w \in A^* : f_{R_1}(w) \leq \lambda_1$.

Finally we show the infiniteness problem is undecidable. We define a PFA R_3 as in Theorem 3, but extend the alphabet to $A' = A \cup \{x_0\}$ and construct R_3 using polynomial $(n_0 + 1)(P(n_1, n_2, \ldots, n_k)^2)$. Recall that all variables are natural numbers, thus if this polynomial equals 0, then $P(n_1, n_2, \ldots, n_k)^2 = 0$. In this case, the polynomial has an infinite number of solutions for all $n_0 \in \mathbb{N}$. Thus for bounded language $L' = x_0^* x_1^* \cdots x_k^* \subseteq (A')^*$, we see that:

$$|\Psi_{\leq\lambda_1}(R_3, L')| = \infty \text{ if and only if } \Psi_{\leq\lambda_1}(R_1, L) \neq \emptyset. \qquad \square$$

5   The Joint Spectral Radius

We now define the joint spectral radius of a set of matrices and our interpretation of it for bounded matrix languages. We shall show a dichotomy result concerning the decidability of computing the joint spectral radius for bounded matrix languages, dependent upon whether we use a non-strict (Theorem 4) or strict (Theorem 5) cut point in the problem.

Given a set of matrices S, a measure of the largest possible growth rate of a product of matrices from S is given by the *joint spectral radius* (JSR):

$$\hat{\rho}(S) = \limsup_{r \to \infty} \left(\max_{M \in S^r} (||M||^{1/r}) \right),$$

where $|| \cdot ||$ is a matrix norm (the JSR can be shown not to depend upon the chosen norm). Analogously the *generalized spectral radius* of S is defined by:

$$\overline{\rho}(S) = \limsup_{r \to \infty} \left(\max_{M \in S^r} \left(\rho(M)^{1/r} \right) \right),$$

where ρ is the standard spectral radius of a single matrix. It is known that for a finite set of matrices S, $\hat{\rho}(S) = \overline{\rho}(S)$ and as r increases, the limiting sequence defining $\hat{\rho}(S)$ approaches this value from above whilst the sequence defining $\overline{\rho}(S)$ approaches it from below. The joint spectral radius can thus be approximated to any desired accuracy, although this is known to be NP-hard in general, see [4].

It was shown in [5] that deciding whether the joint spectral radius of a given set of matrices is ≤ 1 is undecidable. We shall show that determining the joint spectral radius remains undecidable even over a matrix equation corresponding to a bounded language. For a given set of matrices $S = \{M_1, M_2, \ldots, M_k\} \subseteq \mathbb{Q}^{t \times t}$, we define a *bounded matrix language* as $X = \{M_1^{j_1} M_2^{j_2} \cdots M_k^{j_k}\}$ where $j_1, j_2, \ldots, j_k \geq 0$ are variables. Define by $X_r \subseteq X$ the subset of X formed by a product of length $r \geq 0$, i.e., $X_r = \{M_1^{j_1} M_2^{j_2} \cdots M_k^{j_k} | j_1 + j_2 + \ldots + j_k = r\}$. We now formalize the definition of the JSR of such a bounded matrix language:

$$\hat{\rho}(X) = \limsup_{r \to \infty} \left(\max_{M \in X_r} \left(||M||^{1/r} \right) \right),$$

where the generalized spectral radius for X is defined analogously. Clearly equality $\overline{\rho}(X) = \hat{\rho}(X)$ still holds. We now show that determining if the joint spectral radius of a bounded matrix language is ≤ 1 is undecidable. This also has the interpretation that determining if all trajectories of a switched linear system with a fixed, finite number of switching signals are bounded, is undecidable.

Theorem 4. *Computing whether the joint (or equivalently generalized) spectral radius of a bounded matrix language is less than or equal to 1 is undecidable.*

Proof. The proof is essentially the same as in [5] but using the PFA described in Theorem 3 with the inequality $>$ as described in Step 3 of the proof.

In [5], the authors show a clever encoding of a probabilistic finite automata into a set of matrices which allow them to obtain a similar result to that denoted in our theorem but over arbitrary products of matrices. If one instead encodes the PFA described in Theorem 3 with the inequality $>$ as described in Step 3 of the proof, then we may obtain the undecidability result for products over a bounded matrix language.

We must add a matrix $M_{k+1} = \tau_2 \rho_2^T \in \mathbb{Q}^{t \times t}$ which is zero except for a single element which is 1. Thus we are essentially determining if there exists $j_1, j_2, \ldots, j_{k-1} \geq 0$ such that

$$\rho(M_1^{j_1} M_2^{j_2} \cdots M_k^{j_k} M_{k+1}) > 1.$$

Each of the matrices $M_1, \ldots, M_k \in \mathbb{Q}^{t \times t}$ tends towards Ω/t as we take higher powers by the Perron-Frobenius theorem. Note that any matrix in the semigroup generated by M not of this form has spectral radius ≤ 1, as is not difficult to see from the encoding used in [5]. $\qquad\square$

The following corollary may be derived from the above proof. Blondel and Tsitsiklis also derived such a result, but for arbitrary matrix products, in [5].

Corollary 3. *Given a set of matrices $S = \{M_1, M_2, \ldots, M_k\} \subseteq \mathbb{Q}^{t \times t}$, determining the boundedness of $M_1^{j_1} M_2^{j_2} \cdots M_k^{j_k}$ where each $j_i \geq 0$, is undecidable.*

Proof. The corollary follows in a similar way as in [5]. For the matrices one constructs by their encoding but using the modified PFA as above, we have that $\hat{\rho}(\{M_1^{j_1} M_2^{j_2} \cdots M_{k+1}^{j_{k+1}}\}) \leq 1$ (here we denote the JSR of a bounded matrix language) if and only if the matrix product $M_1^{j_1} M_2^{j_2} \cdots M_{k+1}^{j_{k+1}}$ is bounded. The reason is that if $\rho(M_1^{j_1} M_2^{j_2} \cdots M_{k+1}^{j_{k+1}}) > 1$, then clearly this product is unbounded. If $\rho(M_1^{j_1} M_2^{j_2} \cdots M_{k+1}^{j_{k+1}}) \leq 1$ however, then the encoding technique used in the proof is such that a particular matrix norm defined on this product is less than or equal to 1. □

For an arbitrary finite set of matrices S, an important open problem is whether it is decidable to determine if the joint spectral radius of S is strictly less than 1. If $\hat{\rho}(S) < 1$ then this means *any* product of matrices from S will converge to the zero matrix. We now prove that an analogous problem to that defined in Theorem 4 but for a *strict inequality* is actually *decidable*.

Theorem 5. *Computing whether the joint (or equivalently generalized) spectral radius of a bounded matrix language is strictly less than 1 is decidable.*

Proof. Given a set of matrices $S = \{M_1, M_2, \ldots, M_k\} \subseteq \mathbb{Q}^{t \times t}$ defining a bounded matrix language $X = \{M_1^{j_1} M_2^{j_2} \cdots M_k^{j_k} | j_1, j_2, \ldots, j_k \geq 0\} \subseteq \mathbb{Q}^{t \times t}$. If $\rho(M_i) \geq 1$ for some $M_i \in S$ then clearly $\overline{\rho}(X) \geq 1$ by the definition of $\overline{\rho}$, thus we may assume that $\rho(M_i) < 1$ for all $M_i \in S$. Note that computing inequalities of the spectral radius of a single matrix (with algebraic entries) is known from the literature to be decidable by Tarski-Seidenberg elimination (see [15] for details of the Tarski-Seidenberg theorem) and thus determining if $\rho(M_i) < 1$ is decidable.

In the Jordan normal form J_i of any matrix M_i, it is well known that the entries of J_i^j are given by an expression of the form $p(j)\lambda^j$ (where $p(\cdot)$ is a polynomial and λ is an eigenvalue of M_i). Since for each eigenvalue λ, we have $|\lambda| < 1$, then for any $\epsilon > 0$, after some computable x (found by considering the derivatives of $p(\cdot)$), $p(j)\lambda^j$ is always smaller than ϵ for $j \geq x$. Applying this property entrywise to all elements of M_i, we see that for higher powers than x, all entries of the matrix will be strictly less than ϵ and monotonically decreasing, since λ^j is exponentially decreasing to zero whereas $p(j)$ only has at most polynomial growth.

The following equality (know as Gelfand's formula, see [9] for a proof) states that for any matrix norm $|| \cdot ||$ and matrix $A \subseteq \mathbb{C}^{n \times n}$:

$$\rho(A) = \lim_{j \to \infty} ||A^j||^{1/j} \tag{8}$$

Since eventually the individual entries of powers of any M_i are exponentially and monotonically decreasing towards zero, then, for some computable y_i, the value $||M_i^{j_i}||^{1/j_i}$ will *always* be strictly less than 1 for any $j_i > y_i$ since this value tends towards $\rho(M_i)$ by (8) and $\rho(M_i) < 1$ by the above assumption. We can find such a value y_i for each matrix M_i. Since $||\cdot||$ is submultiplicative, for each M_i and $j_i > y_i$ then

$$||M_1^{j_1} M_2^{j_2} \cdots M_k^{j_k}|| \le \prod_{r=1}^{k} ||M_r^{j_r}|| < \prod_{r=1,\, r\neq i}^{k} ||M_r^{j_r}||$$

with $j_1, j_2 \cdots j_k \ge 0$ (in other words, the norm is larger by removing the element $M_i^{j_i}$ from the product).

In the definition of $\hat{\rho}(S)$, since we know the form of a product is from a bounded matrix language and $\hat{\rho}(S)$ is defined by a supremum limit, some matrix must occur an infinite number of times. This will, in the limit, contribute $\lim_{j\to\infty} ||M_i^j||^{1/j} = \rho(M_i) < 1$ to the matrix norm that we are trying to maximize. There should thus be exactly one matrix used an infinite number of times, otherwise the norm would strictly increase by removing that matrix from the product completely (i.e. setting its exponent to 0 in the product).

Finally then, it is not difficult to see there is a finite number of matrix products to check to determine $\hat{\rho}(S)$ exactly and since $\hat{\rho}(S) = \overline{\rho}(S)$, we are done. To see this, we individually consider each M_i being used an infinite number of times giving a multiplicative factor of $\rho(M_i)$ and for the other matrices M_j (with $j \neq i$), we know that it only makes sense to consider powers up to y_j, since for higher powers, the resulting matrix norm would start to decrease.   □

6   Conclusion

In this paper, we considered several computational problems for bounded languages, most notably Theorem 3 dealing with emptiness problems for probabilistic finite automata and Theorems 4 and 5 giving a dichotomy result for the decidability of the joint spectral radius (JSR) on bounded matrix languages when considering either strict or non-strict cut points.

The main motivation for considering the joint spectral radius for bounded matrix languages was that is characterises the maximal asymptotic growth rate of a system where we may change the matrix being applied to some initial vector only a fixed, finite number of times. It is perhaps surprising and interesting that undecidability results can be obtained from such restricted systems and this comes directly from encoding Hilbert's tenth problem rather than the more widespread tool of Post's correspondence problem for example where such a restriction does not seem possible. For the case that the number of changes of matrix is unbounded, we get the standard JSR of a set of matrices Σ and the important and long standing problem of whether $\hat{\rho}(\Sigma) < 1$ remains open.

It is worth noting that the undecidability results hold for a finite number of matrices related to the number of unknowns in the polynomials for which Hilbert's tenth problem is undecidable (currently 9, see [11]).

References

1. Bell, P., Halava, V., Harju, T., Karhumäki, J., Potapov, I.: Matrix Equations and Hilbert's Tenth Problem. International Journal of Algebra and Computation 18(8), 1231–1241 (2008)
2. Berstel, J., Reutenauer, C.: Rational Series and Their Languages. Springer, Heidelberg (1988)
3. Blondel, V., Canterini, V.: Undecidable Problems for Probabilistic Automata of Fixed Dimension. Theory of Comp. Sys. 36, 231–245 (2003)
4. Blondel, V., Tsitsiklis, J.: The Lyapunov Exponent and Joint Spectral Radius of Pairs of Matrices are Hard - when not Impossible – to Compute and to Approximate. Math. of Control, Signals, and Sys. 10, 31–40 (1997)
5. Blondel, V., Tsitsiklis, J.: The Boundedness of all Products of a Pair of Matrices is Undecidable. Sys. and Control Letters 41(2), 135–140 (2000)
6. Blondel, V., Jeandel, E., Koiran, P., Portier, N.: Decidable and Undecidable Problems about Quantum Automata. SIAM Journal on Computing 34(6), 1464–1473 (2005)
7. Dang, Z., Ibarra, O., Sun, Z.: On the emptiness problem for two-way NFA with one reversal-bounded counter. In: Bose, P., Morin, P. (eds.) ISAAC 2002. LNCS, vol. 2518, pp. 103–114. Springer, Heidelberg (2002)
8. Egerstedt, M., Blondel, V.: How Hard Is It to Control Switched Systems? In: Proc. of the American Control Conference, Anchorage (2002)
9. Horn, R., Johnson, C.: Matrix Analysis. Cambridge University Press, Cambridge (1990)
10. Hirvensalo, M.: Improved Undecidability Results on the Emptiness Problem of Probabilistic and Quantum Cut-Point Languages. In: van Leeuwen, J., Italiano, G.F., van der Hoek, W., Meinel, C., Sack, H., Plášil, F. (eds.) SOFSEM 2007. LNCS, vol. 4362, pp. 309–319. Springer, Heidelberg (2007)
11. Jones, J.P.: Universal Diophantine Equation. The Journal of Symbolic Logic 47(3), 549–571 (1982)
12. Ibarra, O.: Reversal-Bounded Multicounter Machines and their Decision Problems. Journal of the ACM 25(1), 116–133 (1978)
13. Matiyasevich, Y.: Hilbert's Tenth Problem. MIT Press, Cambridge (1993)
14. Paz, A.: Introduction to Probabilistic Automata. Academic Press, London (1971)
15. Renegar, J.: On the Complexity and Geometry of the First-order Theory of the Reals. Parts I, II, and III. Journal of Symbolic Computation 13(3), 255–352 (1992)
16. Salomaa, A., Soittola, M.: Automata-Theoretic Aspects of Formal Power Series. Springer, Heidelberg (1978)
17. Schützenberger, M.P.: On the Definition of a Family of Automata. Information and Control 4, 245–270 (1961)
18. Schützenberger, M.P.: On a Theorem of R. Jungen. Proc. Amer. Math. Soc. 13, 885–890 (1962) ISSN 0002-9939
19. Turakainen, P.: Generalized automata and stochastic languages. Proceedings of American Mathematical Society 21, 303–309 (1969)

Z-Reachability Problem for Games on 2-Dimensional Vector Addition Systems with States Is in P[*]

Jakub Chaloupka

Faculty of Informatics, Masaryk University,
Botanická 68a, 60200 Brno, Czech Republic
xchalou1@fi.muni.cz

Abstract. We consider a two-player infinite game with zero-reachability objectives played on a 2-dimensional vector addition system with states (VASS), the states of which are divided between the two players. Brázdil, Jančar, and Kučera (2010) have shown that for $k > 0$, deciding the winner in a game on k-dimensional VASS is in $(k - 1)$-EXPTIME. In this paper, we show that, for $k = 2$, the problem is in P, and thus improve the EXPTIME upper bound.

1 Introduction

Vector addition systems with states (VASS) are an abstract computational model equivalent to Petri nets [6] which is well suited for modelling and analysis of distributed concurrent systems. Roughly speaking, a *k-dimensional VASS*, where $k > 0$ is an automaton with a finite control and k unbounded counters which can store non-negative integers. It can be represented as a finite k-weighted directed graph $G = (V, E, w)$. For simplicity, the weights of the edges are restricted to vectors from the set $\{-1, 0, 1\}^k$. At the beginning of the computation, a token is placed on one of the vertices. In each step of the computation, a VASS can move the token to one of the destination vertices of the edges emanating from the current vertex with the token. This also updates the vector of current counter values by adding the weight of the traversed edge. Since the counters cannot become negative, transitions which attempt to decrease a zero counter are disabled. Configurations of a given VASS are written as pairs $(v, \overrightarrow{n})$, where v is the current vertex and $\overrightarrow{n} \in \mathbb{N}_0^k$ is a vector of the current counter values.

Brázdil, Jančar, and Kučera [1] extended VASS in two respects. First, the set of vertices is divided between two players, named $\square$ and $\lozenge$, and so we get a turn-based two-player game where the choice of an outgoing edge is upon the player who owns the current vertex with the token. Second, the weights of edges may contain symbolic components (denoted by ω) whose intuitive meaning is "add an arbitrarily large non-negative integer to the appropriate counter". Edges

---

[*] This work has been partially supported by the Grant Agency of the Czech Republic grants No. 201/09/1389, 102/09/H042.

A. Kučera and I. Potapov (Eds.): RP 2010, LNCS 6227, pp. 104–119, 2010.

with symbolic components represent infinite number of transitions. This two-fold extension of a VASS is called a *game on k-dim VASS* and it has been shown in [1] to be capable of modelling interesting systems.

Various problems on games on k-dim VASS have been considered in [1]. In particular, the Z-reachability problem is the problem of deciding whether for a given starting configuration $(v, \overrightarrow{n})$, the player $\square$ has a strategy that ensures that not one of the k counters is ever equal zero, which is the complement of the problem of deciding whether the player $\lozenge$ has a strategy that ensures that eventually at least one of the counters is zero, i.e., a configuration $(v', (n'_1, \ldots, n'_k))$ such that $(\exists i \in \{1, \ldots, k\})(n'_i = 0)$ is reached. This problem was shown in [1] to belong to the complexity class $(k-1)$-EXPTIME. In particular, for $k = 1$ and $k = 2$, the problem is in P and EXPTIME, respectively.

Our Contribution. In this paper, we show that 2-dimensional VASS games with Z-reachability objectives are solvable in polynomial time, and thus improve the EXPTIME upper bound given in [1]. More precisely, we show that the winner in 2-dim VASS games can be decided in polynomial time, and a finite description of winning starting configurations of both players is also computable in polynomial time. This contrasts sharply with the previous results about VASS (or, equivalently, Petri nets) where the undecidability/intractability border usually lies between one and two counters. For example, k-dim VASS are equivalent to Petri nets with k unbounded places, and it has been shown that the bisimilarity problem is decidable for Petri nets with one unbounded place and undecidable for Petri nets with two or more unbounded places [4,5]. The Z-reachability problem for games on 2-dim VASS also seems to be harder than the 1-dim case, because unlike for the games on 1-dim VASS, in games on 2-dim VASS, if we add an arbitrarily small rational number to some element of some edge-weight, then the set of vertices of G which are part of some winning configuration for $\square$ may change.

An interesting open question is whether the techniques presented in this paper can be extended to three- (or even more-) dimensional VASS games. Since the presented results about 2-dimensional VASS are relatively complicated (despite investing some effort, we did not manage to find any substantial simplifications), we suspect this problem as difficult.

The Z-reachability problem for games on k-dim VASS can be also thought of as a problem of deciding the winner in an ordinary two-player reachability game with infinite arena. The arena consists of all possible configurations $(v, \overrightarrow{n}) \in V \times \mathbb{N}_0^k$ and it is divided between $\square$ and $\lozenge$ according to the first component of the configurations. The set of target configurations is the set $Z = \{(v, (n_1, \ldots, n_k)) \mid (\exists i \in \{1, \ldots, k\})(n_i = 0)\}$. $\square$ wants to avoid the set Z while $\lozenge$ wants to reach it. We note that the game is upward-closed in the sense that if $\square$ has a strategy to win from a configuration $(v, \overrightarrow{n}) \in V \times \mathbb{N}_0^k$, then the same strategy also wins each play starting from $(v, \overrightarrow{n}') \in V \times \mathbb{N}_0^k$ such that $\overrightarrow{n}' \geq \overrightarrow{n}$. Therefore, there is a finite set of minimal winning starting configurations.

2 Preliminaries

For technical convenience, we will define the game in a slightly different way than in Section 1, and then we will show how the properties of the modified game imply existence of a polynomial algorithm for solving the original game. The properties of the modified game are proved in Section 3, the main part of this paper.

A *game on 2-dim vector addition system with states (VASS)* is a tuple $\Gamma = (G, V_\square, V_\diamond)$, where $G = (V, E, w)$ is a finite two-weighted directed graph such that V is a disjoint union of the sets $V_\square$ and $V_\diamond$, $E \subseteq V^2$, $w : E \to \{-1, 0, 1\}^2$, and each vertex has at least one outgoing edge. The graph G can also be thought of as a 2-dim VASS [3]. The game is played by two opposing players, named $\square$ and $\diamond$. A play starts by placing a token on some given vertex and the players move the token along the edges of G ad infinitum. If the token is on vertex $v \in V_\square$, $\square$ moves it. If the token is on vertex $v \in V_\diamond$, $\diamond$ moves it. This way an infinite path $p_\infty = (v_0, v_1, v_2, \dots)$ is formed. The path p_∞ is also called a *play*. The play is winning for $\square$, if both components of the sum of the weights of the traversed edges are above some constant $K \in \mathbb{Z}$ during the whole play, i.e., $(\exists K \in \mathbb{Z})(\forall k \in \mathbb{N}_0)(\sum_{i=0}^{k-1} w(v_i, v_{i+1}) \geq (K, K))$ where the sum and the inequality are element-wise. The play is winning for $\diamond$, if for any constant $K \in \mathbb{Z}$, there is a point in the play where at least one of the components of the sum of the traversed edges is below K, i.e., $(\forall K \in \mathbb{Z})(\exists k \in \mathbb{N}_0)(\sum_{i=0}^{k-1} w_1(v_i, v_{i+1}) < K \vee \sum_{i=0}^{k-1} w_2(v_i, v_{i+1}) < K)$. Please note that the initial vector of counter values is $(0, 0)$ and the counters are allowed to go negative.

A *strategy* of $\square$ is a function $\sigma : V^* \cdot V_\square \to V$ such that for each finite path $p = (v_0, \dots, v_k)$ with $v_k \in V_\square$, it holds that $(v_k, \sigma(p)) \in E$. Recall that each vertex has out-degree at least one, and so the definition of a strategy is correct. The set of all strategies of $\square$ in Γ is denoted by Σ^Γ. We say that an infinite path $p_\infty = (v_0, v_1, v_2, \dots)$ agrees with the strategy $\sigma \in \Sigma^\Gamma$ if for each $v_i \in V_\square$, $\sigma(v_0, \dots, v_i) = v_{i+1}$. A strategy π of Min is defined analogously. The set of all strategies of Min in Γ is denoted by Π^Γ. Given an initial vertex $v \in V$, the *outcome* of two strategies $\sigma \in \Sigma^\Gamma$ and $\pi \in \Pi^\Gamma$ is the (unique) infinite path $\text{outcome}^\Gamma(v, \sigma, \pi) = (v = v_0, v_1, v_2, \dots)$ that agrees with both σ and π.

The set V can be partitioned into two sets, $W_\square$ and $W_\diamond$, so that if the play starts at some vertex $v \in W_\square$, then $\square$ has a strategy that ensures that he will win, and if the play starts at some vertex $v \in W_\diamond$, then $\diamond$ has a strategy that ensures that she will win [1]. Formally:

$$v \in W_\square \Leftrightarrow (\exists \sigma \in \Sigma^\Gamma)(\forall \pi \in \Pi^\Gamma) \tag{1}$$
$$(\text{outcome}^\Gamma(v, \sigma, \pi) = (v = v_0, v_1, v_2, \dots) \wedge$$
$$(\exists K \in \mathbb{Z})(\forall k \in \mathbb{N}_0)(\sum_{i=0}^{k-1} w(v_i, v_{i+1}) \geq (K, K)))$$

To solve the game is to determine the sets $W_\square$ and $W_\diamond$. In this paper, we will show that there is a constant $K_{\min} \in \mathbb{Z}$ of *polynomial size* with respect to $|V|$ such that for each $v \in W_\square$, the constant K in (1) can always be chosen so that $K \geq K_{\min}$. By the statement that $K_{\min} \in \mathbb{Z}$ is of polynomial size with respect to $|V|$, we mean that $|K_{\min}| \leq l \cdot |V|^k$ for some fixed constants $k, l \in \mathbb{N}$.

The polynomial size of $K_{\min}$ implies that the values of both counters in all minimal winning configurations of $\square$ in the original reachability game with infinite arena is of polynomial size with respect to $|V|$ (cf. the full version of this paper [2]). It follows that we can obtain the solution of the original game by solving only a restricted game, where the values of both counters are bounded by a number of polynomial size with respect to $|V|$. Since a reachability game can be solved in polynomial time with respect to the number of its configurations, we have a polynomial-time algorithm for solving the original reachability game with infinite arena. Our definition of the game on 2-dim VASS does not consider edge-weights with the symbolic component ω. We outline how to extend the proofs to games with symbolic components in edge-weights in the full version of this paper [2].

If $e \in E$, then $w_1(e)$ is the first component of $w(e)$ and $w_2(e)$ is the second component of $w(e)$, i.e., $w(e) = (w_1(e), w_2(e))$. Simple cycle in G is a cycle with no repeated vertex. In this paper, we will work only with simple cycles, and so we will often omit the adjective "simple". If $c = (v_0, \ldots, v_{k-1}, v_k = v_0)$ is a cycle, then $w(c)$ is the sum of the weights of its edges, element-wise, i.e., $w(c) = (\sum_{i=0}^{k-1} w_1(v_i, v_{i+1}), \sum_{i=0}^{k-1} w_2(v_i, v_{i+1}))$. The terms $w_1(c)$ and $w_2(c)$ have the intuitive meaning. Because of the limitations on the weights of the edges, it always holds that $|w_1(c)|, |w_2(c)| \leq |V|$, for each cycle c in G. The weight of a path $(v_0, \ldots, v_k)$ is defined analogically.

The cycles of G can be partitioned into four sets. The first set, P, is the set of cycles c such that $w_1(c) \geq 0 \wedge w_2(c) \geq 0$. The second set, N, is the set of cycles c such that $(w_1(c) \leq 0 \wedge w_2(c) < 0) \vee (w_1(c) < 0 \wedge w_2(c) \leq 0)$. The third set, A, is the set of cycles c such that $w_1(c) > 0 \wedge w_2(c) < 0$. Finally, the fourth set, B, is the set of cycles such that $w_1(c) < 0 \wedge w_2(c) > 0$.

The ratio of the weights of a cycle c is the fraction $\frac{w_1(c)}{w_2(c)}$. We will use $\mathcal{R}$ to denote the set of all possible ratios of weights of the cycles from $A \cup B$, i.e., $\mathcal{R} = \{\frac{a}{b} \mid a \in \{-|V|, \ldots, -1\} \wedge b \in \{1, \ldots, |V|\}\}$. For each $X \in \{A, B\}$, $\sim \in \{<, \leq, =, \geq, >\}$, and $R \in \mathcal{R}$, we will use $X_{\sim R}$ to denote the set of cycles $\{c \in X \mid \frac{w_1(c)}{w_2(c)} \sim R\}$.

Let $\Gamma = (G = (V, E, w), V_\square, V_\Diamond)$ be a game on 2-dim VASS such that $W_\square \neq \emptyset$, and let $v \in W_\square$. We can define the following finite directed tree rooted at v. $T^{\Gamma,v} = (T_V^{\Gamma,v}, T_E^{\Gamma,v})$, where

$$T_V^{\Gamma,v} = \{p = (v = v_0, v_1, \ldots, v_k) \mid p \text{ is a path in } G \wedge$$
$$(\forall 0 \leq i < j < k)(v_i \neq v_j) \wedge$$
$$(\forall 0 \leq i < k)(v_i \in W_\square) \wedge$$
$$(v_k \in W_\Diamond \vee (\exists 0 \leq i < k)(v_i = v_k)) \}$$

That is, the set of nodes of the tree is the set of paths in G starting from v and ending either at the first repeated vertex or at the first vertex from $\Diamond$'s winning region. If $p = (v_0, \ldots, v_k) \in T_V^{\Gamma,v}$, then $\text{last}(p) = v_k$. We define depth of a node $p = (v_0, \ldots, v_k) \in T_V^{\Gamma,v}$ as $\mathsf{h}(p) = k$.

There is an edge $((v_0, \ldots, v_k), (u_0, \ldots, u_l)) \in T_E^{\Gamma,v}$ if and only if $l = k+1$, for each $i \in \{0, \ldots, k\}$, $v_i = u_i$, and $(v_k, u_l) \in E$. If the game Γ is clear from the context, then the tree is denoted simply T^v. The set of nodes, T^v_V, is divided into inner nodes and leaves. The leaves of the tree are the nodes with no successors. Let $q = (v_0, \dots, v_k)$ be a leaf. If $\mathsf{last}(q) \notin W_\Diamond$, then $\mathsf{ce}(q) = (v_i, \dots, v_k)$, $\mathsf{rh}(q) = i$, and $\mathsf{ph}(q) = (v_0, \dots, v_i)$, where $i < k$ such that $v_i = v_k$. That is, $\mathsf{ce}(q)$ is the cycle closed at v_k, $\mathsf{rh}(q)$ is the depth of the node at which the closed cycle starts, and $\mathsf{ph}(q)$ is the path from the root to the starting vertex of the cycle. It holds that $\mathsf{rh}(q) = \mathsf{h}(\mathsf{ph}(q))$.

For the whole paper, let $\Gamma = (G = (V, E, w), V_\Box, V_\Diamond)$ be a game on 2-dim VASS. The elements of V will be called vertices. For each $v \in W_\Box$, the elements of T^v_V will be called nodes, inner nodes, leaves, or, when it is convenient, paths, because they are paths in G. We suppose that $|V| > 1$. For $|V| = 1$ the game is very simple to solve: There is only one vertex v with a self-loop, and so $v \in W_\Box$ if and only if the self-loop is in the set P.

3   The Proof

We prove that if $v \in W_\Box$, then $\Box$ has a strategy σ such that for each play $(v_0, v_1, v_2, \dots)$ agreeing with σ, it holds that $(\forall k \in \mathbb{N}_0)(\sum_{i=0}^{k-1} w(v_i, v_{i+1}) \geq (K_{\min}, K_{\min}))$, where $K_{\min}$ is of polynomial size with respect to $|V|$. Therefore, we can reduce the problem of solving a game on 2-dim VASS to solving a reachability game with finite arena of polynomial size with respect to $|V|$, as described in the full version of this paper [2]. For reachability games there are polynomial-time algorithms. We first give an outline of the proof and then prove it formally.

3.1   Proof Outline

Each prefix $p^k_\infty = (v_0, \dots, v_k)$ of an infinite path $p_\infty = (v_0, v_1, v_2, \dots)$ in G can be partitioned using the following procedure: Start at v_0 and go along the path until an already visited vertex is encountered, then remove the closed cycle, leaving only the first vertex of the cycle, and continue in the same fashion. This way, p^k_∞ is partitioned into a set of cycles $c_1, \dots, c_l$ and remaining path with no repeated vertex. If for each $i \in \{0, \dots, k\}$, it holds that $v_i \in W_\Box$, then the partitioning corresponds to a traversal of the tree T^{v_0} in the following sense. The traversal starts at $(v_0) \in T^{v_0}_V$. When a leaf q is reached, $\mathsf{ce}(q)$ is added to the set of traversed cycles and the traversal continues at $\mathsf{ph}(q)$ until a node $p \in T^{v_0}_V$ such that $\mathsf{last}(p) = v_k$ is reached. The path p is the remaining path. The partitioning of paths into simple cycles plays a crucial role in our proof.

It is easy to see that if $\Box$ can ensure that only simple cycles from P are traversed, then he can win. However, this is not the only way he can win. $\Box$ can also win if he is able to balance the cycles from A and B. The cycles from A increase the first counter and decrease the second counter, and the cycles from B decrease the first counter and increase the the second counter. What is important are the ratios of the first and the second weights of the simple cycles. If $c_1 \in A$ and $c_2 \in B$ are the only simple cycles that can be traversed, and $\Box$ is able to alternate them arbitrarily, then he can win if and only if $\frac{w_1(c_1)}{w_2(c_1)} \leq \frac{w_1(c_2)}{w_2(c_2)}$, or, equivalently $w_1(c_1)w_2(c_2) \geq w_1(c_2)w_2(c_1)$. Moreover, he can alternate the cycles in such a way that both counters are always greater or equal to $-|V|$. Please note, that the set of all possible ratios of cycles in G from A and B is a subset of $\mathcal{R}$, and so it has at most $|V|^2$ elements.

If $v \in W_\square$, then for each $R \in \mathcal{R}$, for a play starting at v, $\square$ can ensure that only cycles from $A_{\leq R} \cup B_{\geq R} \cup P$ are traversed. This does not mean that $\square$ can ensure that all these three types of cycles are traversed, we only claim that $\square$ can ensure that each traversed cycle is from $A_{\leq R}$ or $B_{\geq R}$ or P. For example, consider the following situation winning for $\square$. In this situation, $\square$ can force only two cycles c_1 and c_2 such that $w(c_1) = (1, -1)$, $w(c_2) = (-1, 1)$, and these cycles have a common vertex so that $\square$ is able to alternate between them. In this example, $\square$ is not able to force a cycle from P and the ratio of both $c_1 \in A$ and $c_2 \in B$ is -1. Now, consider three cases: $R = -1$, $R < -1$, and $R > -1$. If $R = -1$, then $\square$ is able to force a cycle from $A_{\leq R}$, namely, the cycle c_1, and he is also able to force a cycle from $B_{\geq R}$, namely, the cycle c_2. If $R < -1$, he is able to force a cycle only from $B_{\geq R}$, and if $R > -1$, then he is able to force a cycle only from $A_{\leq R}$. To sum up, in all the three cases, $\square$ can ensure that only cycles from $A_{\leq R} \cup B_{\geq R} \cup P$ are traversed. To see why the claim holds in general, recall that each play in Γ starting at v corresponds to a traversal of the tree T^v.

Let $v \in W_\square$ and $R \in \mathcal{R}$, then $\square$ can ensure that all reached leaves in T^v correspond to cycles from $A_{\leq R} \cup B_{\geq R} \cup P$, because if $\Diamond$ could ensure that a leaf q such that $\mathsf{ce}(q) \in A_{>R} \cup B_{<R} \cup N$ is reached, then she would be able to ensure that all reached leaves correspond to a cycle from $\mathsf{ce}(q) \in A_{>R} \cup B_{<R} \cup N$ (Recall that if a leaf q is reached, then the play continues at $\mathsf{ph}(q)$). Therefore, if the play is long enough, then at least one of the counters goes below arbitrary constant. We omitted the possibility that a leaf q such that $\mathsf{last}(q) \in W_\Diamond$ is reached, because if such a leaf is reached, then $\Diamond$ can also win.

Unfortunately, the strategy of $\square$, σ_R^v, that ensures that all traversed cycles are from $A_{\leq R} \cup B_{\geq R} \cup P$ may not be the sought strategy, because it may not be winning for $\square$. The reason is that he may not be able to alternate the cycles from $A_{\leq R}$ and $B_{\geq R}$ so that both counters are always above some constant. For example, $\Diamond$ may be able to ensure that out of the cycles from $A_{\leq R} \cup B_{\geq R} \cup P$, only cycles from $A_{\leq R}$ are traversed, and so the second counter goes to $-\infty$. However, the sought strategy for $\square$ can be assembled from the strategies σ_R^v for all $v \in W_\square$ and $R \in \mathcal{R}$, albeit we may have to select much less number than $-|V|$ as the constant $K_{\min}$, but still polynomial with respect to $|V|$. The sought strategy is assembled in the following way.

Let $v \in W_\square$ be the starting vertex. We select $R \in \mathcal{R}$ arbitrarily, and start using the strategy σ_R^v. We are using the strategy σ_R^v until there is a certain "disbalance" between the cycles from $A_{\leq R}$ and the cycles from $B_{\geq R}$. Let u be the current vertex when the disbalance occurs. If too many cycles from $A_{\leq R}$ were traversed, then we change the current strategy to $\sigma_{R'}^u$ such that the disbalance was caused by cycles from $A_{=R'}$ where $R' < R$, and if too many cycles from $B_{\geq R}$ were traversed, then we change the current strategy to $\sigma_{R''}^u$ such that the disbalance was caused by cycles from $B_{=R''}$ where $R'' > R$. The precise definition of the disbalance (it must be polynomial somehow) and the precise rules for selecting the new ratio will be given later. Before we get to the formal proof, one additional point has to be discussed.

From the previous paragraph, it follows that it is not enough that the strategy σ_R^v traverses only cycles from $A_{<R} \cup B_{>R} \cup P$. It must also be able to balance the cycles from $A_{=R}$ and $B_{=R}$, so that a disbalance between $A_{<R}$ and $B_{>R}$ is never caused by the cycles from $A_{=R}$ or $B_{=R}$. Therefore, the strategy σ_R^v we will define guarantees that only cycles from $A_{<R} \cup B_{>R} \cup P$ are traversed and the traversed cycles from $A_{=R}$ or $B_{=R}$ are kept in balance. The balance will not be the best possible as if we were able to alternate the cycles arbitrarily, but it will be such that the sum of the weights of the traversed cycles from $A_{=R} \cup B_{=R}$ is always greater or equal to $(-2 \cdot |V|^2, -2 \cdot |V|^2)$. This "balancing property" also ensures that if $R = \min \mathcal{R}$, then only the cycles from $B_{>R}$ can cause a disbalance, and if $R = \max \mathcal{R}$, then only the cycles from $A_{<R}$ can cause a disbalance.

3.2 Formal Proof

We will first define the "local" strategies for each $v \in W_\square$ and $R \in \mathcal{R}$, and then we will assemble the "global" strategy from the local strategies. So let $v \in W_\square$, $R \in \mathcal{R}$, and consider the tree T^v.

We define values of the nodes of the tree T^v: $\mathsf{value} : T_V^v \to \{-1, 0, \ldots, |V|\}^2 \cup \{0, 1\}$.

The values are defined recursively. The values of leaves are defined as follows. Let $q = (v_0, \ldots, v_k) \in T_V^v$ be a leaf.

$$
\mathsf{value}(p) = \begin{cases} 0 & \text{if } \mathsf{last}(q) \in W_\diamond \\ 0 & \text{if } \mathsf{last}(q) \in W_\square \wedge \mathsf{ce}(q) \in N \cup A_{>R} \cup B_{<R} \\ 1 & \text{if } \mathsf{last}(q) \in W_\square \wedge \mathsf{ce}(q) \in P \cup A_{<R} \cup B_{>R} \\ (\mathsf{rh}(q), -1) & \text{if } \mathsf{last}(q) \in W_\square \wedge \mathsf{ce}(q) \in A_{=R} \\ (-1, \mathsf{rh}(q)) & \text{if } \mathsf{last}(q) \in W_\square \wedge \mathsf{ce}(q) \in B_{=R} \end{cases} \quad (2)
$$

To define the value of an inner node $p = (v_0, \ldots, v_k) \in T_V^v$, we introduce some notation:

$$\mathsf{amin}(p) = \min\{a \mid (\exists (p, q) \in T_E^v)(\mathsf{value}(q) = (a, b))\}$$

$$\mathsf{bmin}(p) = \min\{b \mid (\exists (p, q) \in T_E^v)(\mathsf{value}(q) = (a, b))\}$$

$$\mathsf{amax}(p) = \max\{a \mid (\exists (p, q) \in T_E^v)(\mathsf{value}(q) = (a, b))\}$$

$$\mathsf{bmax}(p) = \max\{b \mid (\exists (p, q) \in T_E^v)(\mathsf{value}(q) = (a, b))\}$$

If there is no successor of p with value from $\{-1, 0, \ldots, |V|\}^2$, i.e., all successors have the value 0 or 1, then $\mathsf{amin}(p) = \mathsf{bmin}(p) = \infty$ and $\mathsf{amax}(p) = \mathsf{bmax}(p) = -\infty$. If $\mathsf{last}(p) \in V_\square$, then $\mathsf{value}(p)$ is defined as follows.

$$\mathsf{value}(p) = \begin{cases} \mathbf{0} & \text{if } (\forall (p,q) \in T_E^v)(\mathsf{value}(q) \neq \mathbf{1}) \wedge \\ & \quad (\mathsf{amin}(p) \geq \mathsf{h}(p) \vee \mathsf{bmin}(p) \geq \mathsf{h}(p)) \\ (\mathsf{amin}(p), \mathsf{bmin}(p)) & \text{if } (\forall (p,q) \in T_E^v)(\mathsf{value}(q) \neq \mathbf{1}) \wedge \\ & \quad \mathsf{amin}(p) < \mathsf{h}(p) \wedge \mathsf{bmin}(p) < \mathsf{h}(p) \\ \mathbf{1} & \text{if } (\exists (p,q) \in T_E^v)(\mathsf{value}(q) = \mathbf{1}) \end{cases} \quad (3)$$

If $\mathsf{last}(p) \in V_\Diamond$, then $\mathsf{value}(p)$ is defined as follows.

$$\mathsf{value}(p) = \begin{cases} \mathbf{1} & \text{if } (\forall (p,q) \in T_E^v)(\mathsf{value}(q) = \mathbf{1}) \\ (\mathsf{amax}(p), \mathsf{bmax}(p)) & \text{if } (\forall (p,q) \in T_E^v)(\mathsf{value}(q) \neq \mathbf{0}) \wedge \\ & \quad -\infty < \mathsf{amax}(p), \mathsf{bmax}(p) < \mathsf{h}(p) \\ \mathbf{0} & \text{if } (\exists (p,q) \in T_E^v)(\mathsf{value}(q) = \mathbf{0}) \vee \\ & \quad \mathsf{amax}(p) \geq \mathsf{h}(p) \vee \mathsf{bmax}(p) \geq \mathsf{h}(p) \end{cases} \quad (4)$$

The cycles from $N \cup A_{>R} \cup B_{<R}$ are called *bad cycles*. The cycles from $P \cup A_{<R} \cup B_{>R}$ are called *good cycles*. The cycles from $A_{=R} \cup B_{=R}$ are not given any special name.

We will show that the value of the root $(v) \in T_V^v$ is either $\mathbf{1}$ or $(-1, -1)$ (Please note that if $\mathsf{value}((v)) = (a, b)$, then the condition $a, b < \mathsf{h}((v)) = 0$ implies $a = b = -1$). We will show this by proving that if $\mathsf{value}((v)) = \mathbf{0}$, then $\Diamond$ has a winning strategy, which is in contradiction with $v \in W_\Box$. From the fact that the root has value $\mathbf{1}$ or $(-1, -1)$, we will infer a strategy for $\Box$ that ensures that only cycles from $A_{<R} \cup B_{>R} \cup P$ are traversed, and the cycles from $A_{=R}$ and $B_{=R}$ are kept in balance. So, let's first prove that the value of the root cannot be $\mathbf{0}$. We will only give a sketch of the proof, the whole formal proof is in the full version of this paper [2].

We will use a proof by contradiction. We will suppose that $\mathsf{value}((v)) = \mathbf{0}$ and show that $\Diamond$ has a strategy that ensures that for each $K \in \mathbb{Z}$, the first counter or the second counter will eventually go below K. The strategy is outlined below.

If $\mathsf{value}((v)) = \mathbf{0}$, then $\Diamond$ has a strategy that ensures that only cycles from $A_{\geq R} \cup B_{<R} \cup N$ are traversed or a leaf $q \in T_V^v$ such that $\mathsf{last}(q) \in W_\Diamond$ is reached. Moreover, she can choose the strategy in such a way that whenever a node p such that $\mathsf{value}(p) = \mathbf{0}$ is visited, then either the strategy ensures that if the next reached leaf r has $\mathsf{ce}(r) \in A_{=R} \cup B_{=R}$, then $\mathsf{ce}(r) \in A_{=R} \wedge \mathsf{rh}(r) \geq \mathsf{h}(p)$, or the strategy ensures that if the next reached leaf r has $\mathsf{ce}(r) \in A_{=R} \cup B_{=R}$, then $\mathsf{ce}(r) \in B_{=R} \wedge \mathsf{rh}(r) \geq \mathsf{h}(p)$. This allows $\Diamond$ to prevent $\Box$ from alternating cycles from $A_{=R}$ and $B_{=R}$. We note that $\Box$ may be able to perform a few alternations, because he can sometimes prevent $\Diamond$ from forcing the chosen kind of cycle, but only at the cost of visiting another node with value $\mathbf{0}$ that is deeper, and since the maximal depth is $|V|$, this cannot be repeated infinitely many times. Actually, $\Box$ may be able to perform infinite number of alternations, but at the cost of traversing a bad cycle infinitely many times.

To sum up, $\Diamond$ has a strategy that ensures that exactly one of the following four things happens. First, a leaf q such that $\mathsf{last}(q) \in W_\Diamond$ is reached. Second, only leaves q corresponding to bad cycles or cycles from $A_{=R} \cup B_{=R}$ are reached, and a bad cycle is traversed infinitely many times. Third, there is a point from which onwards all reached leaves q have $\mathsf{ce}(q) \in A_{=R}$. Fourth, there is a point

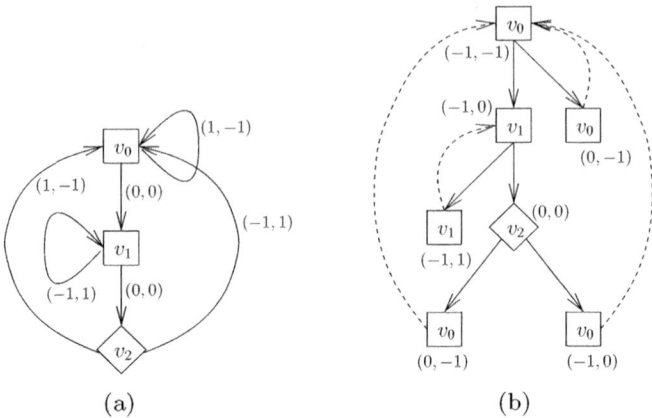

Fig. 1. Example tree valuation: (a) example game, (b) tree T^{v_0}

from which onwards all reached leaves q have $ce(q) \in B_{=R}$. For the last three possibilities, at least one of the counters goes below arbitrary constant. For the first possibility, $\Diamond$ can apply her winning strategy from $last(q) \in W_\Diamond$, and so at least one of the counters goes below arbitrary constant too. The whole formal proof is in the full version of this paper [2]. Therefore, there are only two possibilities for the value of the root: $\mathbf{1}$ and $(-1, -1)$. Let's now define the strategy for $\Box$ and show that it has the desired properties. We will start with some intuition.

The intuitive meaning of the node value $\mathbf{1}$ is that $\Box$ has a strategy to reach a leaf corresponding to a good cycle. The meaning of the node value (a, b) is more complex.

If a node p has the value (a, b), then $\Box$ has a strategy to reach a leaf corresponding to a good cycle or a cycle from $A_{=R} \cup B_{=R}$. Moreover, the strategy can be chosen in such a way that if the reached leaf q has $ce(q) \in A_{=R}$, then $rh(q) \leq a$, or the strategy can be chosen in such a way that if the reached leaf q has $ce(q) \in B_{=R}$, then $rh(q) \leq b$. In particular, if $a = -1$, then $\Box$ can force a good cycle or a cycle from $B_{=R}$ (albeit nothing can be said about the depth the play returns to), and if $b = -1$, then $\Box$ can force a good cycle or a cycle from $A_{=R}$ (albeit nothing can be said about the depth the play returns to). The rules for assigning values to nodes stipulate that $a < h(p)$ and $b < h(p)$. This is important for balancing the cycles from $A_{=R}$ and $B_{=R}$.

The player $\Box$ may not be able to alternate the cycles from $A_{=R}$ and $B_{=R}$ arbitrarily, as Figure 1 shows. In Figure 1 (a), there is a game on 2-dim VASS. Squares are $\Box$'s vertices and the diamond is a $\Diamond$'s vertex. The pairs of numbers are weights of the edges depicted as arrows. In this game, $\Box$ can win from all vertices. Let $R = -1$, then all cycles in the figure are from $A_{=R} \cup B_{=R}$. In Figure 1 (b), there is the tree T^{v_0}. The pairs of numbers are values of the nodes and the dashed arrows emanating from leaves show, for each leaf, where the game (projected on the tree) continues when it reaches the leaf.

If the play starts from v_0, then at the beginning, $\square$ is able to traverse a cycle from $A_{=R}$ arbitrary number of times (the cycle (v_0, v_0)), after that he is able to traverse a cycle from $B_{=R}$ arbitrary number of times (the cycle (v_1, v_1)). However, after that he is not able to start traversing cycles from $A_{=R}$ immediately. The value of the node $(v_0, v_1) \in T_V^{v_0}$ at depth 1 is $(-1, 0)$, which indicates that $\square$ is able to force a cycle from $B_{=R}$, but not from $A_{=R}$. However, $\square$ has a strategy that ensures that if $\lozenge$ forces a cycle from $B_{=R}$, then the play returns to a node at smaller depth, namely the depth 0. At the depth 0, $\square$ is, again, able to force a cycle from $A_{=R}$.

In general, we claim that $\square$ has a strategy that ensures that only good cycles and cycles from $A_{=R} \cup B_{=R}$ are traversed. Moreover, the strategy also ensures that both the sum of the first weights of the cycles from $A_{=R} \cup B_{=R}$ and the sum of the second weights of the cycles from $A_{=R} \cup B_{=R}$ is always greater or equal to $-2 \cdot |V|^2$.

In the case where $\mathsf{value}((v)) = 1$, $\square$ has a strategy to traverse only the good cycles and the claim obviously holds.

The second case is that $\mathsf{value}((v)) = (-1, -1)$. In this case, $\square$ has a strategy that ensures that only nodes p with value $\mathbf{1}$ or value $(a, b) \in \{-1, \ldots, |V|\}^2$ are visited. This alone implies that only good cycles and cycles from $A_{=R} \cup B_{=R}$ are traversed. Moreover, he is able to choose the strategy in such a way that it balances the cycles from $A_{=R}$ and $B_{=R}$. When a disbalance between the cycles from $A_{=R}$ and $B_{=R}$ occurs, let's say that too many cycles from $A_{=R}$ have been traversed, then $\square$ aims to traverse cycles from $B_{=R}$ or good cycles. If the current node p has the value $\mathbf{1}$, then $\square$ can ensure that the next traversed cycle is a good cycle, which does not worsen the disbalance. If p has the value (a, b) and $a \neq -1$, $\lozenge$ can force a cycle from $A_{=R}$, but if she does, $\square$ can ensure that the play returns to the depth a or smaller, and since $a < \mathsf{h}(p)$, we return to a smaller depth than the depth of p. We can continue using the same reasoning and conclude that after traversing at most $|V| - 1$ (maximal depth of an inner tree node) "unwanted" cycles from $A_{=R}$, we get to the root, where $\square$ can force cycles from $B_{=R}$ or good cycles. Therefore, he can alleviate the disbalance caused by the cycles from $A_{=R}$. Of course, the case when a disbalance is caused by cycles from $B_{=R}$ is symmetric. Formal definition of this "balancing" strategy of $\square$ is as follows.

A general strategy of $\square$ is a function $\sigma : V^* \cdot V \to V$, i.e., it decides based on the whole history of the play. However, the strategy we define now will decide only based on the current node of the tree T_V^v (which consists of fragments of the whole history) and some additional memory which could be computed from the complete history of the play.

Apart from the current node, the player $\square$ keeps a triple $(x, y, z) \in \{-2 \cdot |V|^2, \ldots, 0, \ldots, 2 \cdot |V|^2\}^2 \times \{0, 1\}$, where x is the sum of the first weights of the traversed cycles from $A_{=R} \cup B_{=R}$, y is the sum of the second weights of the traversed cycles from $A_{=R} \cup B_{=R}$, and z is the mode of the strategy: $z = 0$ means that the strategy aims to traverse cycles from $A_{=R}$, and $z = 1$ means that the strategy aims to traverse cycles from $B_{=R}$. The memory plays a crucial role in keeping the traversed cycles from $A_{=R}$ and $B_{=R}$ in balance.

The strategy of $\square$ visits only nodes p of the tree T^v with $\mathsf{value}(p) = \mathbf{1}$ or $\mathsf{value}(p) = (a, b)$ (recall that $a, b < \mathsf{h}(p)$). The play starts at the root (v). It holds that $\mathsf{h}((v)) = 0$, and $\mathsf{value}((v)) = \mathbf{1}$ or $\mathsf{value}((v)) = (-1, -1)$. Initial state of the memory is $(0, 0, 0)$. Let's consider a general situation where we are at the inner node p such that $\mathsf{last}(p) \in V_{\square}$, $\mathsf{value}(p) = \mathbf{1}$ or $\mathsf{value}(p) = (a, b)$ such that $a, b < \mathsf{h}(p)$, and the current state of memory is (x, y, z), then the strategy of $\square$, denoted by σ, works as follows. Please note that the strategy does not have to consider leaves, because at each leaf q, the play automatically returns to the inner node $\mathsf{ph}(q)$. First, how a successor is chosen:

$$\sigma(p, (x, y, z)) = \begin{cases} q \text{ if } (p, q) \in T_E \wedge \mathsf{value}(p) = \mathbf{1} \wedge \mathsf{value}(q) = \mathbf{1} \\ q \text{ if } (p, q) \in T_E \wedge \mathsf{value}(p) = (a, b) \wedge z = 0 \wedge \mathsf{value}(q) = (a', b) \\ q \text{ if } (p, q) \in T_E \wedge \mathsf{value}(p) = (a, b) \wedge z = 1 \wedge \mathsf{value}(q) = (a, b') \end{cases}$$
$$(5)$$

Please note that for a node p with $\mathsf{value}(p) = (a, b)$, the existence of a successor with value (a', b) and the existence of a successor with value (a, b') follows from (3). It is also possible that these are not two distinct successors but only one with value (a, b).

Second, how the memory is updated. The memory is updated only when a leaf is reached, so let's suppose that we have reached the leaf q. Then the memory (x, y, z) is updated to:

$$
\begin{aligned}
&(x, y, z) && \text{if } \mathsf{ce}(q) \text{ is a good cycle} \\
&(x + w_1(\mathsf{ce}(q)), y + w_2(\mathsf{ce}(q)), z) && \text{if } \mathsf{ce}(q) \in A_{=R} \cup B_{=R} \wedge \\
& && z = 0 \wedge \\
& && (\, x + w_1(\mathsf{ce}(q)) < 0 \vee \\
& && (\, x + w_1(\mathsf{ce}(q)) \in [-|V|^2, |V|^2] \wedge \\
& && y + w_2(\mathsf{ce}(q)) \in [-|V|^2, |V|^2] \,)\,) \\
&(x + w_1(\mathsf{ce}(q)), y + w_2(\mathsf{ce}(q)), z) && \text{if } \mathsf{ce}(q) \in A_{=R} \cup B_{=R} \wedge \\
& && z = 1 \wedge \\
& && (\, y + w_2(\mathsf{ce}(q)) < 0 \vee \\
& && (\, x + w_1(\mathsf{ce}(q)) \in [-|V|^2, |V|^2] \wedge \\
& && y + w_2(\mathsf{ce}(q)) \in [-|V|^2, |V|^2] \,)\,) && (6) \\
&(x + w_1(\mathsf{ce}(q)), y + w_2(\mathsf{ce}(q)), 1) && \text{if } \mathsf{ce}(q) \in A_{=R} \cup B_{=R} \wedge \\
& && z = 0 \wedge \\
& && x + w_1(\mathsf{ce}(q)) \geq 0 \wedge \\
& && (\, |x + w_1(\mathsf{ce}(q))| > |V|^2 \vee \\
& && |y + w_2(\mathsf{ce}(q))| > |V|^2 \,) \\
&(x + w_1(\mathsf{ce}(q)), y + w_2(\mathsf{ce}(q)), 0) && \text{if } \mathsf{ce}(q) \in A_{=R} \cup B_{=R} \wedge \\
& && z = 1 \wedge \\
& && y + w_2(\mathsf{ce}(q)) \geq 0 \wedge \\
& && (\, |x + w_1(\mathsf{ce}(q))| > |V|^2 \vee \\
& && |y + w_2(\mathsf{ce}(q))| > |V|^2 \,)
\end{aligned}
$$

We note again that if a leaf q is reached, then the play automatically continues at node $\mathsf{ph}(q)$, and so the play is infinite. Let's now take a closer look at the memory updates.

While $x, y \in [-|V|^2, |V|^2]$, the strategy does not change the type of cycles it aims for, z is not changed (first 3 items in (6)). When $|x|$ or $|y|$ exceeds $|V|^2$, $z = 0$, and $x \geq 0$, it means that too many cycles from $A_{=R}$ have been traversed. Therefore z is changed to 1, and so the strategy aims for cycles from $B_{=R}$ (4th item in (6)). As described before, even after this action, some cycles from $A_{=R}$ may be traversed before cycles from $B_{=R}$, but there can be at most $|V| - 1$ of these unwanted cycles, therefore x and y do not leave the interval $[-2 \cdot |V|^2, 2 \cdot |V|^2]$. The situation where too many cycles from $B_{=R}$ have been traversed is dealt with analogously (5th item in (6)).

The following two lemmas show that the strategy σ satisfies the desired properties. An intuition why they hold was already given. Their formal proofs are in the full version of this paper [2].

Lemma 1. *Let $\Gamma = (G = (V, E, w), V_\square, V\Diamond)$ be a game on 2-dim VASS. Let further $v \in W_\square$ be the starting vertex, $R \in \mathcal{R}$, and let the strategy σ be defined as in (5). Then the following holds. If the value of the root (v) of the tree T^v is* value$((v)) = 1$*, then the strategy σ ensures that only nodes p with* value$(p) = 1$ *are visited. If the value of the root (v) of the tree T^v is* value$((v)) = (-1, -1)$*, then the strategy σ ensures that only nodes p with* value$(p) = 1$ *or* value$(p) = (a, b)$ *such that $a, b < h(p)$ are visited.* ∎

Lemma 1 implies that only good cycles and cycles from $A_{=R} \cup B_{=R}$ are traversed. The next lemma states that the cycles from $A_{=R}$ and $B_{=R}$ are kept in balance.

Lemma 2. *Let $\Gamma = (G = (V, E, w), V_\square, V\Diamond)$ be a game on 2-dim VASS. Let further $v \in W_\square$ be the starting vertex, $R \in \mathcal{R}$, let the root (v) of the tree T^v have the value 1 or $(-1, -1)$, and let the strategy σ be defined as in (5). Let $\square$ use the strategy σ, let $\Diamond$ use arbitrary strategy. The outcome of these two strategies corresponds to a sequence of nodes $(p_0, p_1, p_2, \ldots)$. Let $(q_0, q_1, q_2, \ldots)$ be the subsequence of the sequence containing all reached leaves corresponding to cycles from $A_{=R} \cup B_{=R}$. In particular, for each $i \in \mathbb{N}_0$, ce$(q_i) \in A_{=R} \cup B_{=R}$. Then for each $k \in \mathbb{N}_0$, it holds that $|\sum_{i=0}^{k} w_j(ce(q_i))| \leq 2 \cdot |V|^2$ where $j = 0, 1$.* ∎

For technical convenience, let's number the elements of the set of the cycle ratios, namely, let $\mathcal{R} = \{R_1, \ldots, R_{|\mathcal{R}|}\}$ where $R_1 < \cdots < R_{|\mathcal{R}|}$. It holds that $|\mathcal{R}| \leq |V|^2$. By Lemma 2, for each $v \in W_\square$ and R_k such that $k \in \{1, \ldots, |\mathcal{R}|\}$, the player $\square$ has the strategy σ_k^v that ensures that only cycles from $P \cup A_{<R_k} \cup B_{>R_k}$ are traversed. Moreover, the cycles from $A_{=R_k}$ and $B_{=R_k}$ are balanced in the sense that the absolute value of both components of the sum of their weights never exceeds $2 \cdot |V|^2$. Also, when using the strategy σ_k^v, the play never leaves the set $W_\square$.

Using the above facts, we will now assemble a global strategy σ of $\square$ such that there is a constant $K_{min} \in \mathbb{Z}$ of polynomial size with respect to $|V|$ such that whatever strategy π the opponent $\Diamond$ uses, the resulting infinite play outcome$^\Gamma(v_0, \sigma, \pi) = (v_0, v_1, v_2, \ldots)$ satisfies the following. For each $k \in \mathbb{N}_0$, $\sum_{i=0}^{k-1} w_1(v_i, v_{i+1}) \geq K_{min}$ and $\sum_{i=0}^{k-1} w_2(v_i, v_{i+1}) \geq K_{min}$. The strategy σ will be assembled from the strategies σ_k^v where $v \in W_\square$ and $k \in \{1, \ldots, |\mathcal{R}|\}$. So, let's describe how this is done.

Each strategy σ_k^v has the three-component memory as described before. Let $k \in \{1, \ldots, |\mathcal{R}|\}$. For each $v \in W_\square$, the strategy σ_k^v balances the cycles from $A_{=R_k}$ and $B_{=R_k}$. We will let all the strategies with the same k use the same three-component memory. Therefore, the global strategy σ will have $|\mathcal{R}|$ three-component memories, one for each k. For a specific $k \in \{1, \ldots, |\mathcal{R}|\}$, the tree-component memory will be denoted by (x_k, y_k, z_k). Apart from that, σ will have additional memory that consists of two $|\mathcal{R}|$-tuples. The first $|\mathcal{R}|$-tuple will be $(a_1, \ldots, a_{|\mathcal{R}|}) \in \{0, \ldots, 4 \cdot |V|^4 + 3 \cdot |V|\}^{|\mathcal{R}|}$ and it will store the sums of the first weights of the traversed cycles from A, separately for each ratio. The second $|\mathcal{R}|$-tuple will be $(a_1', \ldots, a_{|\mathcal{R}|}') \in \{-4 \cdot |V|^4 - |V|, \ldots, 0\}^{|\mathcal{R}|}$ and it will store the sums of the first weights of the traversed cycles from B, separately for each ratio. However, when using the strategy σ_k^v, only traversed cycles from A and B with ratios R_i such that $i \neq k$ will be recorded in the additional memory. The traversed cycles with the ratio R_k will be recorded only in the three-component memory (x_k, y_k, z_k). The global strategy σ will also remember which strategy σ_k^v it is currently using by remembering the vertex v and the integer k. The strategy σ is defined as follows.

We will not describe (again) how the three-component memories are used and updated, we will only describe how the two additional $|\mathcal{R}|$-tuples are handled. The current tree that the strategy is working with is denoted by $T^v = (T_V^v, T_E^v)$ where (v) is the root of the tree. Let v, k, $(a_1, \ldots, a_{|\mathcal{R}|})$, $(a_1', \ldots, a_{|\mathcal{R}|}')$ be the current state of the additional memory, and let p be the current inner node in the current tree T^v. We will first describe how the strategy decides and then how the memory is updated. The strategy decides as follows:

$$\sigma(p, v, k, (a_1, \ldots, a_{|\mathcal{R}|}), (a_1', \ldots, a_{|\mathcal{R}|}')) = \sigma_k^v(p) \tag{7}$$

Now, let us describe how the memory is updated. The initial state of the memory is $(v, 1, (0, \ldots, 0), (0, \ldots, 0))$ where v is the vertex the play starts from, and so the first tree the strategy σ works with is the tree T^v rooted at v, and the first used substrategy is σ_1^v. The two $|\mathcal{R}|$-tuples in the memory play a crucial role in keeping the traversed cycles from A and B in balance. As was already mentioned, the first $|\mathcal{R}|$-tuple records the sums of the first weights of the traversed cycles from A. There are two bounds that bound the elements of the tuple from above: a soft bound and a hard bound. The soft bound is equal to $4 \cdot |V|^4 + 2 \cdot |V|$ and we denote it by C_A. If some element a_i exceeds the soft bound, then the strategy takes some actions so that a_i is not increased further and it never exceeds the hard bound $\bar{C}_A$ which is equal to $4 \cdot |V|^4 + 3 \cdot |V|$. Similarly, there is a soft bound and a hard bound for the second $|\mathcal{R}|$-tuple. The second $|\mathcal{R}|$-tuple records the sums of the first weights of the traversed cycles from B. Unlike for the first tuple, the bounds for the second tuple bound the elements of the tuple from below. The soft bound is $C_B = -4 \cdot |V|^4$, and the hard bound is $\bar{C}_B = -4 \cdot |V|^4 - |V|$. Before explaining the actions the strategy takes to ensure that the hard bounds are never exceeded, we describe precisely how the memory is updated. It is updated only when a leaf in the current tree is reached, so let's suppose that we have reached the leaf q. Then the memory $(v, k, (a_1, \ldots, a_{|\mathcal{R}|}), (a'_1, \ldots, a'_{|\mathcal{R}|}))$ is updated to:

$$
\begin{array}{ll}
(v, k, (a_1, \ldots, a_{|\mathcal{R}|}), & \text{if } \mathsf{ce}(q) \in P \cup A_{=R_k} \cup B_{=R_k} \\
\quad (a'_1, \ldots, a'_{|\mathcal{R}|})) & \\[4pt]
(v, k, (a_1, \ldots, a_i + w_1(\mathsf{ce}(q)), \ldots, a_{|\mathcal{R}|}), & \text{if } \mathsf{ce}(q) \in A_{=R_i} \wedge \\
\quad (a'_1, \ldots, a'_{|\mathcal{R}|})) & \quad i < k \wedge \\
& \quad a_i + w_1(\mathsf{ce}(q)) \leq C_A \\[4pt]
(v, k, (a_1, \ldots, a_{|\mathcal{R}|}), & \text{if } \mathsf{ce}(q) \in B_{=R_j} \wedge \\
\quad (a'_1, \ldots, a'_j + w_1(\mathsf{ce}(q)), \ldots, a'_{|\mathcal{R}|})) & \quad j > k \wedge \\
& \quad a'_j + w_1(\mathsf{ce}(q)) \geq C_B \\[4pt]
(v, k, (a_1, \ldots, a_i - a_i, \ldots, a_{|\mathcal{R}|}), & \text{if } \mathsf{ce}(q) \in A_{=R_i} \wedge \\
\quad (a'_1, \ldots, a'_j - a'_j, \ldots, a'_{|\mathcal{R}|}) & \quad i < k \wedge \\
& \quad a_i + w_1(\mathsf{ce}(q)) > C_A \wedge \\
& \quad j > i \wedge a'_j < C_B \\[4pt]
(v, k, (a_1, \ldots, a_i - a_i, \ldots, a_{|\mathcal{R}|}), & \text{if } \mathsf{ce}(q) \in B_{=R_j} \wedge \\
\quad (a'_1, \ldots, a'_j - a'_j, \ldots, a'_{|\mathcal{R}|}) & \quad j > k \wedge \\
& \quad a'_j + w_1(\mathsf{ce}(q)) < C_B \wedge \\
& \quad i < j \wedge a_i > C_A \\[4pt]
(\mathsf{last}(q), i, (a_1, \ldots, a_i + w_1(\mathsf{ce}(q)), \ldots, a_{|\mathcal{R}|}), & \text{if } \mathsf{ce}(q) \in A_{=R_i} \wedge \\
\quad (a'_1, \ldots, a'_{|\mathcal{R}|})) & \quad i < k \wedge \\
& \quad a_i + w_1(\mathsf{ce}(q)) > C_A \wedge \\
& \quad (\nexists j > i)(a'_j < C_B) \\[4pt]
(\mathsf{last}(q), j, (a_1, \ldots, a_{|\mathcal{R}|}), & \text{if } \mathsf{ce}(q) \in B_{=R_j} \wedge \\
\quad (a_1, \ldots, a'_j + w_1(\mathsf{ce}(q)), \ldots, a'_{|\mathcal{R}|})) & \quad j > k \wedge \\
& \quad a'_j + w_1(\mathsf{ce}(q)) < C_B \wedge \\
& \quad (\nexists i < j)(a_i > C_A)
\end{array}
\tag{8}
$$

We note that if a leaf q is reached, then there are two possibilities as to which node the play continues at. The first case is when σ does not change the substrategy σ_k^v (first 5 items in (8)). In this case the play continues at node $\mathsf{ph}(q)$. The second case is when σ does change the substrategy σ_k^v (last 2 items in (8)). In this case the play continues at the root $(\mathsf{last}(q))$ of the new tree $T^{\mathsf{last}(q)}$.

Before getting to formal proofs we will describe how the definition of the strategy σ corresponds to what was said in Section 3.1.

While using the substrategy σ_k^v, only cycles from $P \cup A_{<R_k} \cup B_{>R_k}$ are traversed. Moreover, by Lemma 2, the effects of the cycles from $A_{=R_k}$ and $B_{=R_k}$ are balanced. The additional memory of the global strategy σ is used to detect a disbalance between the cycles from $A_{<R_k}$ and $B_{>R_k}$. A disbalance is suspected when some a_i such that $i < k$ goes above $C_A = 4 \cdot |V|^4 + 2 \cdot |V|$, or some a'_j such that $j > k$ goes below $C_B = -4 \cdot |V|^4$. However, this does not necessarily imply a disbalance. We will look only at the first case, the other one is symmetric. If some a_i such that $i < k$ goes above C_A, and there is also some $j > i$ such that a'_j is below C_B, then there is no disbalance. The effects of the corresponding cycles from $A_{=R_i}$ and $B_{=R_j}$ balance each other. The bounds were selected so that the sum of the weights of these cycles is greater or equal to $(|V|, |V|)$, which justifies the zeroing of the appropriate elements of the memory (4th item in (8)) and also compensates for the possibly negative simple paths that are "lost" when switching a substrategy.

A substrategy is changed when there is no a'_j that would compensate for a_i, and so a disbalance occurs. The substrategy is changed to σ_i^u where u is the current vertex when the disbalance occurred (6th item in (8)). It holds that $u = \text{last}(q)$ where q is the appropriate leaf in the tree T^v, the visit of which caused the disbalance. The substrategy is changed to ensure that a_i is not further increased. The substrategy σ_i^u works with the tree T^u, and so the path $\text{ph}(q)$ from v to u is lost in the sense that it is reflected neither in the local nor in the global memory. However, as mentioned above this lost paths are compensated for, and so the global memory together with the local memories gives a lower bound on the first counter, and indirectly also on the second counter. Since all the components of the memories are of polynomial size, so are the lower bounds.

The following theorem makes the above arguments precise. Its formal proof is in the full version of this paper [2].

Theorem 1. *Let $\Gamma = (G = (V, E, w), V_\square, V\Diamond)$ be a game on 2-dim VASS. Let further $v \in W_\square$ be the starting vertex, and let $\square$ use the strategy σ as defined in (7). Let $\Diamond$ use an arbitrary strategy π, and let $\text{outcome}^\Gamma(v, \sigma, \pi) = (v = v_0, v_1, v_2, \ldots)$ be the resulting play. Let k be the state of the play after k steps, i.e., we are at the vertex v_k. Let $(v', l, (a_1, \ldots, a_{|\mathcal{R}|}), (a'_1, \ldots, a'_{|\mathcal{R}|}))$ be the state of the global memory, and let $(x_i, y_i, z_i)_{i \in \{1, \ldots, |\mathcal{R}|\}}$ be the state of the local memories of the substrategies. Then the following holds:*

$$\textstyle\sum_{i=0}^{k-1} w_1(v_i, v_{i+1}) \geq \sum_{i \in \{1, \ldots, |\mathcal{R}|\}} (a_i + a'_i + x_i) - |V|^3 - 2 \cdot |V|$$

$$\textstyle\sum_{i=0}^{k-1} w_2(v_i, v_{i+1}) \geq \sum_{i \in \{1, \ldots, |\mathcal{R}|\}} (-|V|a_i - \tfrac{1}{|V|}a'_i + y_i) - |V|^3 - 2 \cdot |V| \quad \blacksquare$$

For each $i \in \{1, \ldots, |\mathcal{R}|\}$, it holds that $0 \leq a_i \leq \bar{C}_A = 4 \cdot |V|^4 + 3 \cdot |V|$, and $-4 \cdot |V|^4 - |V| = \bar{C}_B \leq a'_i \leq 0$, and $x_i, y_i \in [-2 \cdot |V|^2, 2 \cdot |V|^2]$. Therefore, by Theorem 1, if we set $K_{\min}$ to, for example, $-100 \cdot |V|^7$, then for each play $(v_0, v_1, v_2, \ldots)$ with $v_0 \in W_\square$, agreeing with the strategy σ, it holds that $(\forall k \in \mathbb{N}_0)(\sum_{i=0}^{k-1} w(v_i, v_{i+1}) \geq (K_{\min}, K_{\min}))$.

Acknowledgement. I would like to thank to Tomáš Brázdil, Petr Jančar, and Antonín Kučera for fruitful consultations and advice.

References

1. Brázdil, T., Jančar, P., Kučera, A.: Reachability games on extended vector addition systems with states. In: Proc. International Colloquium on Automata, Languages and Programming. LNCS. Springer, Heidelberg (2010)
2. Chaloupka, J.: Z-reachability problem for games on 2-dimensional vector addition systems with states is in P. Technical Report FIMU-RS-2010-06, Faculty of Informatics, Masaryk University, Brno, Czech Republic (2010)

3. Hopcroft, J.E., Pansiot, J.-J.: On the reachablility problem for 5-dimensional vector addition systems. Theoretical Computer Science 8(2), 135–159 (1979)
4. Jančar, P.: Undecidability of bisimilarity for petri nets and related problems. Theoretical Computer Science 148, 281–301 (1995)
5. Jančar, P.: Decidability of bisimilarity for one-counter processes. Information and Computation 158, 1–17 (2000)
6. Reisig, W.: Petri Nets – An Introduction. Springer, Heidelberg (1985)

Towards the Frontier between Decidability and Undecidability for Hyperbolic Cellular Automata

Maurice Margenstern

Université Paul Verlaine − Metz, IUT de Metz,
LITA EA 3097, UFR MIM,
Campus du Saulcy,
57045 METZ Cédex 1, France
margens@univ-metz.fr
http://www.lita.sciences.univ-metz.fr/~margens

Abstract. In this paper, we look at two ways to implement one dimensional cellular automata into hyperbolic cellular automata in three contexts: the pentagrid, the heptagrid and the dodecagrid, these tilings being classically denoted by $\{5,4\}$, $\{7,3\}$ and $\{5,3,4\}$ respectively. As an application, this may give a hint for the boundary between decidable and undecidable problems for hyperbolic cellular automata.

Keywords: Cellular automata, weak universality, decidability, hyperbolic spaces, tilings.

1 Introduction

In this paper, we look at the possibility to embed one-dimensional cellular automata, $1D$- for short, into hyperbolic cellular automata in the pentagrid, the heptagrid or the dodecagrid which are denoted by $\{5,4\}$, $\{7,3\}$ and $\{5,3,4\}$ respectively. We consider $1D$-cellular automata which are deterministic and whose number of cells is infinite. This will have consequences on the border between a decidable and an undecidable halting problem for a large class of hyperbolic cellular automata.

First, we shall prove a general theorem, and then we shall try to strengthen it at the price of a restriction on the set of cellular automata which we wish to embed in the case of the pentagrid.

The first theorem says:

Theorem 1. *There is a uniform algorithm to transform a deterministic $1D$-cellular automaton with n states into a deterministic cellular automaton in the pentagrid, the heptagrid or the dodecagrid with, in each case, $n+1$ states. Moreover, the cellular automaton obtained by the algorithm is rotation invariant.*

Later on, as we consider deterministic cellular automata only, we drop this precision. This theorem has a lot of corollaries, in particular we get this one, about weak universality:

A. Kučera and I. Potapov (Eds.): RP 2010, LNCS 6227, pp. 120–132, 2010.
© Springer-Verlag Berlin Heidelberg 2010

Corollary 1. *There is a weakly universal cellular automaton in the pentagrid, in the heptagrid and in the dodecagrid which is weakly universal and which has three states exactly, one state being the quiescent state. Moreover, the cellular automaton is rotation invariant.*

We prove Theorem 1 and Corollary 1 in Section 2. In particular, we remind the notion of rotation invariance, especially for the $3D$ case. In Section 3, we strengthen the results, but this needs a restriction on the cellular automata under consideration in the case of the pentagrid.

2 Proof of Theorem 1 and Its Corollary

The idea of theorem 1 is very simple. Consider a one-dimensional cellular automaton A. The support of the cells of A is transported into a structure of the hyperbolic grid which we consider as a **line** of tiles. In each one of the three tilings which we shall consider, we define the line of tiles in a specific way. We examine these case, one after the other.

2.1 Pentagrid and Heptagrid

In the case of the pentagrid and of the heptagrid, it is the set of cells such that one side of the cells is supported by the same line of the hyperbolic plane. In the pentagrid, it is a line of the tiling, which is supported by a side of a cell, fixed once for all. In the heptagrid, it is what we call a mid-point line, a notion for which we refer the reader to [3]. Indeed, it was there proved that the mid-points of two contiguous sides of a heptagon define a line which cuts the other tiles of the heptagrid at the mid-points of two contiguous sides.

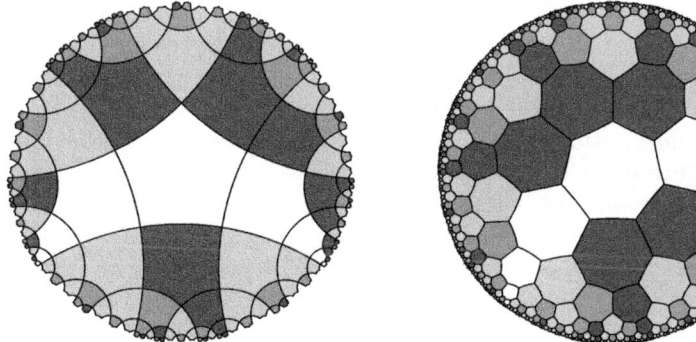

Fig. 1. Implementation of a cellular automaton in the pentagrid, left-hand side, and in the heptagrid, right-hand side. The white cells represent the line of tiles used for the $1D$-CA. The gray cells represent the cells which receive the new state.

In each case, the just defined line is called the **guideline** of the implementation. The guideline is illustrated in Figure 1. In this figure, the line on which we implement the $1D$ cellular automaton is represented by the white cells along the guideline. Note that a white cell has exactly two white neighbours. The cells are generated by the shift along the guideline which transforms one of the neighbours of the cell on the line into the cell itself.

In the figure, the white colour is assumed to represent the n states of the original automaton. The gray cells represent the additional state which is different from the n original ones. In the figure, there are three hues of gray which allow us to represent the tree structure of the tiling. These different hues represent the same state.

From the figure, it is plain that we have the following situation: white cells have exactly two white cells among their neighbours, the cell itself not being taken into account. In the pentagrid, a gray cell has at most one white cell in its neighbourhood. In the heptagrid, it has at most two white neighbours. Accordingly, this difference is enough to define the implementation of the rules in the pentagrid and in the heptagrid.

We can make this more precise as follows: denote the format of a rule by $\eta_0\eta_1...\eta_\alpha\eta_0^1$ with $\alpha \in \{5,7\}$ and where η_0 is the current state of the cell, η_i is the current state of neighbour i of the cell and η_0^1 is the new state of the cell, obtained after the rule was applied. We remind the reader that the neighbour i is the cell which shares the side i of the cell. We assume that the rules are **rotation invariant**. This means that if π is a circular permutation on $\{1..5\}$ and if $\eta_0\eta_1...\eta_\alpha\eta_0^1$ is a rule of the automaton, $\eta_0\eta_{\pi(1)}...\eta_{\pi(\alpha)}\eta_0^1$ is also a rule of the automaton. Now, as we assume the rules to be invariant, the numbering has only to be fixed according to the orientation: we consider that it increases from 1 to α as we clockwise turn around the tile. Which side is number 1 is not important. However, for the convenience of the reader, we shall fix it in a way which will be the most convenient for us.

In [4], we fixed the numbering in a rather uniform way. It consists in fixing number 1 to one side of the central cell. Then, for all other cells, number 1 is given to the side shared with the father: we remind the reader that the central cell is the father of the roots of the sectors which are displayed around itself.

Here, we keep this general setting for most cells except the white cells and those which share a side with a white cell. As the white cells are put along a linear structure defined by their guideline, we can order them. Accordingly, starting from now on, any white cell has one white left-hand side neighbour exactly and one white right-hand side neighbour exactly. Looking at Figure 1, the white left-hand side neighbour of a white cell is indeed on its left-hand side, both in the pentagrid and in the heptagrid. Now, we number the cells in such a way that the white left-hand side neighbour of a cell shares the side α of the cell. This fixes the cell with number 1 and, consequently, all the other neighbours. In the pentagrid, a gray cell c is in contact with at most one white cell. In this case, we consider that the white cell is number 5 for c. In the heptagrid, a gray cell c

is in contact with at most two white cells. We decide that they are numbered 6 and 7 for c or, in case of a unique white neighbour, that it is numbered 7 for c.

The rules for a white cell are: $\eta_0 \mathbf{b}\mathbf{b}^a \eta_{2+a} \mathbf{b}^a \eta_\alpha \eta_0^1$, with $a = 1$ or 2 for the pentagrid, the heptagrid respectively. Moreover, $\eta_{2+a} \eta_0 \eta_\alpha \rightarrow \eta_0^1$ is the unique rule of A which can be associated to the cell. For a gray cell which is in contact with a white cell, the rule is $\mathbf{b}\mathbf{b}^{2+2a} \eta_\alpha \mathbf{b}$ or, in the case of the heptagrid, it is the rule $\mathbf{b}\mathbf{b}^6 \eta_\alpha \mathbf{b}$. Now, the rule for a gray cell which is not in contact with a white cell is: $\mathbf{b}\mathbf{b}^\alpha \mathbf{b}$.

Accordingly, we proved Theorem 1 for what are the grid of the hyperbolic plane which we considered. It can easily be proved that the same result holds for all the grids of the hyperbolic plane of the form $\{p, 4\}$ and $\{p+2, 3\}$, with $p \geq 5$.

2.2   In the Dodecagrid

In the dodecagrid, we use the representation introduced in [7]. We briefly remind it the reader for his/her convenience.

In fact, we consider the projection of the dodecahedra on a plane which is defined by a fixed face of one of them: this will be the plane of reference Π_0. The trace of the tiling on Π_0 is a copy of the pentagrid. So that, using a projection of each dodecahedron which is in contact with Π_0 and on the same half-space it defines which we call the half-space **above** Π_0, we obtain a representation of

Fig. 2. Implementation of a cellular automaton in the dodecagrid. The white cells represent the line of tiles used for the one-dimensional CA. The gray cells represent the cells which receive the new state.

the line which is given by Figure 2. Indeed, the projection of each dodecahedron on this face looks like a Schlegel diagram, see [7,3] for more details on this tool dating from the 19th century. Figure 3 also illustrates this representation for one dodecahedron.

Accordingly, the guideline is simply a line of the pentagrid which lies on Π_0. On the figure, we can see that the line which implements the one-dimensional cellular automaton is represented by the white cells, the other cells which receive the new state being gray. This line of white cells will be also called the **white line**. As in Figure 1, the different hues of gray are used in order to show the spanning trees of the pentagrid, dispatched around the central cell.

To define the rules of a cellular automaton, we also introduce a numbering of the faces of a dodecahedron which will allow us to number the neighbours. This numbering is given by Figure 3.

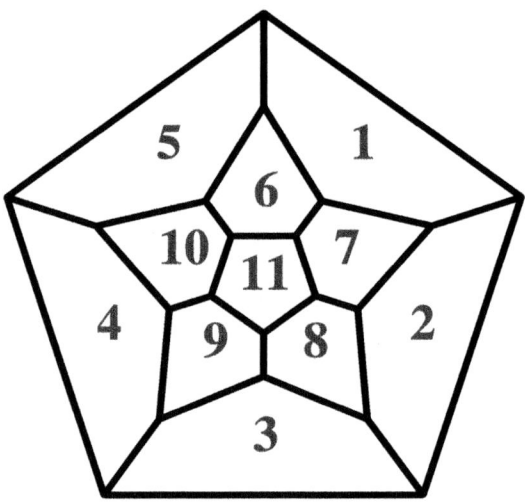

Fig. 3. The numbering of the faces of dodecahedron. Face 0 is delimited by the biggest pentagon of the figure.

Accordingly, the format of a rule is of the form $\eta_0^0 \eta_0 ... \eta_{11} \eta_0^1$. Now, as the rules are assumed to be rotation invariant, which face receives number 1 is not important. However, for the convenience of the reader, we shall adopt the following convention. For all the white cells, we consider that the face which is on Π_0 is face 0. Accordingly, the numbers should appear in Figure 2 as they appear in Figure 3. Moreover, we consider that the other face of the cell which is in contact with the guideline is face 5.

Now, we come to the notion of **rotation invariant** cellular automata on the dodecagrid. We say that a motion in the hyperbolic 3D space is a **positive invariant displacement** of the dodecahedron if it leaves the dodecahedron globally invariant and if it preserves orientation. We shall say later positive displacement. Let μ be a positive invariant displacement of the dodecahedron. We denote by $\mu(i)$ the number of the face which is the image of face i under μ. Now, let $\rho = \eta_0^0 \eta_0 ... \eta_{11} \eta_0^1$ be a rule. We say that $\eta_0^0 \eta_{\mu(0)} ... \eta_{\mu(11)} \eta_0^1$ is a **rotated form** of ρ. Say that $\eta_0^0 \eta_0 ... \eta_{11}$ is the **context** or ρ. Then, we shall say that $\eta_0^0 \eta_{\mu(0)} ... \eta_{\mu(11)}$ is a rotated image of the context of ρ. Now, a cellular automaton is called **rotation invariant** if and only if two rules having contexts which are rotated forms of each other always produce the same new state.

Now, there are 60 positive displacements of the dodecahedron. They constitute a group which is called the icosahedral rotation group and which is isomorphic to A_5, the group of permutations on 5 elements whose signature is positive. It is well known that A_5 is a simple non-abelian group. This means that representations are difficult and that there is no canonical way to do that. In [10], we provided a simple algorithm to enumerate the positive displacements of the dodecahedron which we call the **rotation algorithm**.

Using this algorithm, we can define all the rotated forms of the context of a rule. These forms are words on the alphabet of the states of the cellular automaton and we can order these words lexicographically. As this order is total, there is a smallest element which we call the **minimal form** of the context. Similarly, we can define the **minimal form** of a rule. This allows us to obtain the following result:

Lemma 1 (see [7]) *A cellular automaton on the dodecagrid is rotation invariant if and only if for any pair of rules, if their minimal forms have the same context, they have the same new state too.*

Now, checking this property can easily be performed thanks to the rotation algorithm.

As we already indicated, we decided that face 0 of the cells belonging to the line of the implementation are on Π_0 and that the other face which has a side on the guideline is face 5. As a consequence, a white cell is in contact with two white neighbours by its faces 1 and 4. We decide that the face 1 of a cell is the same as the face 4 of the next white neighbour and, accordingly, its face 4 is the same as the face 1 of the other white neighbour. This allows to define two directions on the white line. The direction from left to right on the one-dimensional cellular automaton is, by convention, the direction from face 1 to face 4 of the same cell.

For the proof of Theorem 1 in the case of the dodecagrid, the rules for a gray cell have the form $\mathbf{b}\eta_0 ... \eta_{11}\mathbf{b}$ with all states in $\eta_0 ... \eta_{11}$ being $\mathbf{b}$ except, possibly, one of them. From the just defined convention on the numbering of the faces of the white cells, the rules for a white cell are of the form $\eta_0 \mathbf{b}\eta_1 \mathbf{b}\mathbf{b}\eta_4 \mathbf{b}\mathbf{b}\mathbf{b}\mathbf{b}\mathbf{b}\mathbf{b}\eta_0^1$, where $\eta_1 \eta_0 \eta_4 \to \eta_0^1$ is the rule of the one-dimensional cellular automaton.

Now, as the gray cells have at most one white neighbour and as the white cells have two white neighbours exactly, the difference between the rules is clearly recognizable.

This completes the proof of Theorem 1.   ■

Now, the proof of Corollary 1 is very easy: it is enough to apply the theorem to the elementary cellular automaton defined by rule 110 which is now known to be weakly universal, see [1,13].

3   Refinement of Theorem 1

Now, we shall prove that, under particular hypotheses in the case of the pentagrid and no restriction in the case of the heptagrid and of the dodecagrid, a $1D$ cellular automaton with n states can be simulated by a hyperbolic cellular automaton with n states too.

In order to formulate this hypothesis, consider a one-dimensional deterministic cellular automaton A. Say that a state s of A is **fixed** in the context x, y in this order, if the rule $xsy \rightarrow s$ belongs to the table of transitions of A. As an example, a **quiescent** state for A, usually denoted by 0, is fixed in the context $0, 0$. Now, we say that A is a **fixable** cellular automaton if it has a quiescent state 0 and another state, denoted by 1, such that 0 is also fixed in the context $1, 0$ and 1 is fixed in the context $0, 0$.

We can now formulate the following results:

Theorem 2. *There is an algorithm which transforms any fixable $1D$ cellular automaton A with n states into a rotation invariant cellular automaton B in the pentagrid with n states too, such that B simulates A on a line of the pentagrid.*

Theorem 3. *There is an algorithm which transforms any deterministic $1D$ cellular automaton A with n states into a rotation invariant deterministic cellular automaton B in the heptagrid, the dodecagrid respectively, with n states too, such that B simulates A on a line of the heptagrid, the dodecagrid respectively.*

We have not the room to produce a full proof of these theorems: we refer the reader to [8] for such a proof. Here, we simply sketch the outlines of the proof of Theorem 2.

Consider the left-hand side picture of Figure 4. The white colour is still used to represent any state of the automaton A. Now, the gray colour represents the quiescent state 0, and the black one represents the state 1 which is fixed in the context $0, 0$. We also assume that 0 is fixed in the context $1, 0$.

We shall consider all the neighbours of the central cell. Its black neighbour will be numbered by 1, and the others from 2 to 5, increasing as we clockwise turn around the cell. We also consider the cells which just has one vertex in common with the central cell. All the other cells are in quiescent state or they belong to the white line or are neighbouring a cell belonging to this line. In this latter case, such a cell is obtained from one of those we consider around the central cell by a shift along the guideline.

Define B with n states represented by different letters from those used from A. We fix a bijection between the states of A and those of B in which **B** is associated to the state 1 of A and **W** is associated to the state 0 of A.

Consider the configuration around the central cell. If we write the states of the cell and then those of its neighbours according to the order of their numbers, we get the following word: $YBWZWX$, where X, Y, Z are taken among the states of B. Now, if $Z = \mathbf{B}$, we can start from this neighbour in state **B** which has number 3, and we get the word $YBWXBW$ in which we see **B** in position 4. If $X = \mathbf{B}$, then we get the word $YBBWZW$ in which we see **B** in position 2. In both case, the configuration around the cell is different from the one we obtain by starting from position 1. We can synthesise this information as follows:

		1	2	3	4	5
0	Y	B	W	Z	W	X
		B	W	X	B	W
		B	B	W	Z	W

The first line corresponds to the configuration which triggers the application of the rule of A corresponding to $XYZ \rightarrow X'$. Clearly, as already noticed with the positions of the fixed **B** and **W**, the other lines do not correspond to the application of a rule of A.

We shall do this for all the neighbours of the central cell, and in Table 1, we can see all the possible configurations for the neighbours of the central cell.

Table 1. Table of the configurations around the central cell in the pentagrid for the automaton B

		1	2	3	4	5
0	Y	B	W	Z	W	X
		B	W	X	B	W
		B	B	W	Z	W
1_1	B	Y	W	W	W	W
2_1	W	B	W	W	W	W
1_2	W	Y	W	W	W	B
		B	W	W	W	B
		B	B	W	W	B
		B	W	W	W	W
2_2	B	W	W	W	W	Z
		B	W	W	W	W
1_3	Z	Y	B	W	T	W
		B	B	W	T	W
		B	W	T	W	Y
		B	W	Y	B	W

		1	2	3	4	5
2_3	W	Z	W	W	W	W
1_4	W	Y	W	W	W	W
2_4	W	W	W	W	W	X
		B	W	W	W	W
1_5	X	Y	W	U	B	W
		B	W	U	B	W
		B	B	W	Y	W
		B	W	Y	W	U
2_5	W	X	W	W	W	B
		B	W	W	W	B
		B	B	W	W	W
		B	W	W	W	W

In Table 1, we indicate the coordinate of the cell which we represent together with its state. Then, if there are states as U, X, Y, Z, T, we also represent the case when one of this variable takes the value **B** and we represent the configuration around the cell when this **B** is put onto position 1.

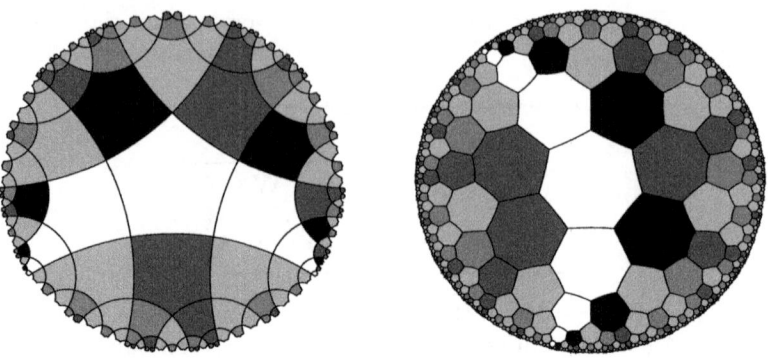

Fig. 4. Implementation of a $1D$ cellular automaton in the pentagrid, left-hand side, and in the heptagrid, right-hand side. The white cells represent the line of tiles used for the $1D$-CA. The gray cells represent the cells which receive a particular state among the states of the $1D$-CA.

The left-hand side picture of Figure 4 allows us to check the correctness of Table 1. We refer the reader to [8] for a further checking.

This completes the proof of Theorem 2.

Table 2. Table of the configurations around the central cell in the pentagrid for the automaton B

		1	2	3	4	5	6	7				1	2	3	4	5	6	7
0	Y	X	**B**	**W**	**B**	Z	**W**	**W**		1_4	**B**	Y	**W**	**W**	**W**	**W**	**W**	Z
		B	**B**	**W**	**B**	Z	**W**	**W**				**B**	**W**	**W**	**W**	**W**	**W**	Z
		B	**W**	**B**	Z	**W**	**W**	X				**B**	Y	**W**	**W**	**W**	**W**	**W**
		B	Z	**W**	**W**	X	**B**	**W**		1_5	Z	Y	**B**	**W**	**B**	T	**W**	**W**
		B	**W**	**W**	X	**B**	**W**	**B**				**B**	**B**	**W**	**B**	T	**W**	**W**
1_1	X	Y	**W**	**W**	U	**B**	**W**	**B**				**B**	**W**	**B**	T	**W**	**W**	Y
		B	**W**	**W**	U	**B**	**W**	**B**				**B**	T	**W**	**W**	Y	**B**	**W**
		B	**B**	**W**	**B**	Y	**W**	**W**				**B**	**W**	**W**	Y	**B**	**W**	**B**
		B	**W**	**B**	Y	**W**	**W**	U		1_6	**W**	Y	Z	**W**	**W**	**W**	**W**	**W**
		B	Y	**W**	**W**	U	**B**	**W**				**B**	Z	**W**	**W**	**W**	**W**	**W**
1_2	**B**	Y	X	**W**	**W**	**W**	**W**	**W**				**B**	**W**	**W**	**W**	**W**	**W**	Y
		B	X	**W**	**W**	**W**	**W**	**W**		1_7	**W**	Y	**W**	**W**	**W**	**W**	**W**	X
		B	**W**	**W**	**W**	**W**	**W**	Y				**B**	**W**	**W**	**W**	**W**	**W**	X
1_3	**W**	Y	**B**	**W**	**W**	**W**	**W**	**B**				**B**	Y	**W**	**W**	**W**	**W**	**W**
		B	**B**	**W**	**W**	**W**	**W**	**B**										
		B	**W**	**W**	**W**	**W**	**B**	Y										

Now, let us turn to the case of the heptagrid. In this case, the situation is in some sense easier as it requires no special hypothesis on the deterministic $1D$ cellular automaton. Indeed, the fact is that due to the number of neighbours, there is a way to differentiate the cells belonging to the white line from those which do not. As mentioned in Subsection 2.1, the white line is now implemented along a mid-point line of the heptagrid which is fixed, once for all. As in the case of the pentagrid, the white colour represents any state of automaton A. Now, we assume that A has at least two states, 0 and 1. In the right-hand side picture of Figure 4, these states are represented in gray and in black respectively. As in the case of the pentagrid, we use different hues of gray in order to make visible the tree structure which spans the tiling. Now, it is easy to see that the configurations allowing the application of a rule of A are reached only in the case of cells of the white line and that for these cells, among the rotated contexts, exactly one is compatible with the application of a rule of A. This can be checked on the figure and we report this examination in Table 2.

Looking at each entry of the table attached to a cell, we can see that there is at most a single configuration which is compatible with the application of a rule of A. Moreover, the admissible configuration occurs only for the cells which are on the white line and never for the others. Accordingly, the rule which consists in applying the rule of A when there is one for that and to leave the current state unchanged otherwise works more easily here. This completes the proof of Theorem 3 in the case of the heptagrid.

Let us now look at the same problem in the case of the dodecagrid. This, time, we can take advantage of a bigger number of neighbours and of their spatial display to strengthen the difference between a cell of the white line which is implemented as indicated in Subsection 2.2 and the cells which does not belong to this line. The way in which we establish this difference is illustrated by Figure 6. In this figure, the white colour represents the states of B which, by construction, are in bijection with those of A. As previously, the gray colour is associated with the state $\mathbf{W}$ which corresponds to the quiescent state 0 of A, and the black colour is associated with the state $\mathbf{B}$ which corresponds to the state 1 of A.

Now, each cell of the white line has four black neighbours. Numbering the cells as indicated in Subsection 2.2, the faces with a black neighbour are: 0, 3, 9 and 10. Figure 5 represents a cut in the plane of the face 4 of a white cell and it makes it easy to understand the configuration. Due to the fact that face 0 is on the plane Π_0, we can see only three black faces on the cells of the white line in Figure 6.

We refer the reader to [8] in order to check that the cells which do not belong to the white line have at most two black neighbours.

This completes the proof of Theorem 3.

Now, we can see that from Theorem 3 we have as an immediate corollary:

Corollary 2. *There is a weakly universal rotation invariant cellular automaton on the heptagrid, as well as in the dodecagrid with two states exactly.*

In both cases, we apply the construction defined in the proof of Theorem 3 to the elementary cellular automaton with rule 110. Now, if we look at the transitions of

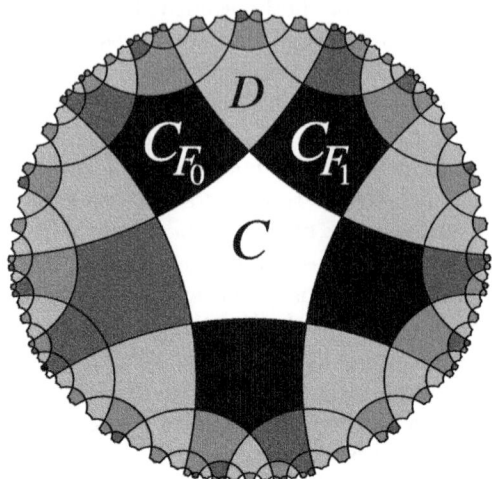

Fig. 5. Implementation of a cellular automaton in the heptagrid. The white cells represent the line of tiles used for the $1D$ CA. The gray cells represent the cells which receive a particular state among the states of the $1D$ CA.

Fig. 6. Implementation of a cellular automaton in the dodecagrid. The white cells represent the line of tiles used for the $1D$ CA. The gray cells represent the cells which receive a particular state among the states of the $1D$ CA.

rule 110, we can see that 0 is a quiescent state, that it is fixed for the context $1, 0$ and that 1 is fixed for the context $0, 0$. This proves that the elementary cellular automaton with rule 110 is fixable. Consequently, applying Theorem 2 to this $1D$-cellular automaton, we get:

Corollary 3. *There is a weakly universal rotation invariant cellular automaton on the pentagrid with two states exactly.*

4 Conclusion

With this result, we reached the frontier between decidability and weak universality for cellular automata in hyperbolic spaces: starting from 2 states there are weakly universal such cellular automata, with 1 state, there are none, which is trivial.

We can remark that the argument of Theorem 3 can be applied to all tilings of the form $\{p, 4\}$ and $\{p+2, 3\}$ with $p \geq 5$.

We can also remark that the result proved in this paper suffers the same defect as the result indicated in [7] with 3 states. The results proved in this paper can be obtained in a not too complicate manner by an appropriate implementation of rule 110 which is weakly universal, as already mentioned. In the case of the dodecagrid, the author proved a similar result with 3 states but involving a much more elementary construction which is also an actual $3D$ construction. In the case of the heptagrid, he obtained 4 states with an actual planar construction, see [5,9] and the best result known for the pentagrid is 9 states, see [12], again with elementary tools and using an actual planar construction. What can be done in this direction is also an interesting question.

Accordingly, there is some work ahead, probably the hardest as we are now so close to the goal.

References

1. Cook, M.: Universality in elementary cellular automata. Complex Systems 15(1), 1–40 (2004)
2. Lindgren, K., Nordahl, M.G.: Universal computation in simple one-dimensional cellular automata. Complex Systems 4, 299–318 (1990)
3. Margenstern, M.: Cellular Automata in Hyperbolic Spaces Theory, vol. 1, p. 422, OCP, Philadelphia (2007)
4. Margenstern, M.: Cellular Automata in Hyperbolic Spaces Implementation and computations, vol. 2, p. 360, OCP, Philadelphia (2008)
5. Margenstern, M.: A new universal cellular automaton on the ternary heptagrid, 35p (2009) arXiv:0903.2108[cs.FL]
6. Margenstern, M.: Surprising Areas in the Quest for Small Universal Devices. Electronic Notes in Theoretical Computer Science 225, 201–220 (2009)
7. Margenstern, M.: A weakly universal cellular automaton in the hyperbolic 3D space with three states, 54p. (2010) arXiv:1002.4290[cs.FL]
8. Margenstern, M.: About the embedding of one dimensional cellular automata into hyperbolic cellular automata, 19p (2010) arXiv:1004.1830[cs.FL]

9. Margenstern, M.: A universal cellular automaton on the heptagrid of the hyperbolic plane with four states. Theoretical Computer Science (2010) (accepted)
10. Margenstern, M.: A weakly universal cellular automaton in the hyperbolic 3D space with three states, Discrete Mathematics and Theoretical Computer Science (to appear)
11. Margenstern, M., Skordev, G.: Tools for devising cellular automata in the hyperbolic 3D space. Fundamenta Informaticae 58(2), 369–398 (2003)
12. Margenstern, M., Song, Y.: A new universal cellular automaton on the pentagrid. Parallel Processing Letters 19(2), 227–246 (2009)
13. Wolfram, S.: A new kind of science. Wolfram Media, Inc. (2002)

Rewriting Systems for Reachability in Vector Addition Systems with Pairs

Paulin Jacobé de Naurois and Virgile Mogbil

LIPN, UMR CNRS 7030 - Université Paris 13,
Institut Galilée, 99, avenue Jean-Baptiste Clément, 93430 Villetaneuse, France

Abstract. We adapt hypergraph rewriting system to a generalization of
Vector Addition Systems with States (VASS) that we call vector addition
systems with pairs (VASP). We give rewriting systems and strategies,
that allow us to obtain reachability equivalence results between some
classes of VASP and VASS. Reachability for the later is well known be
equivalent to reachability in Petri nets. VASP generalize also Branching Extension of VASS (BVASS) for which it is unknown if they are
more expressive than VASS. We consider here a more restricted notion
of reachability for VASP than that for BVASS. However the reachability
decision problem corresponding is already equivalent to decidability of
the provability in Multiplicative and Exponential Linear Logic (MELL),
a question left open for more than 20 years.

1 Introduction

Vector Addition Systems with Pairs (VASP) are Vector Addition Systems with
States (VASS) extended with paired arcs. A VASS is a directed graph whose
arcs are labeled by vectors in $\mathbb{Z}^m$, and nodes are used as control states. Vector
addition is done when traversing an arc, starting from a value associated to the
source state and producing a value associated to the target state. A VASP is a
VASS, together with a set of disjoint arc pairs, where two arcs of a pair share
the same source or the same target. The configurations of a VASP are multisets
of vectors (values) in $\mathbb{Z}^m$, and its operational semantics is the following: when
traversing an arc pair with shared source the value of the source state is split, and
when the target is shared the values of the two sources are added. While VASS
are well known to be equivalent to Petri Nets, VASP correspond to Petri Nets
with split and join transitions, where a multiset of markings evolves accordingly
to the transitions fired, the size of this multiset being increased or decreased
when firing a split or join transition respectively.

VASP are defined as a restriction of directed hypergraph. They inherit notions of paths in hypergraph and connectedness [5], but the chosen presentation
as paired graph allows us to keep also usual paths in underlying graphs without pairs (in other words paths using part of hyperarcs). Hypergraph rewriting
systems give rewriting systems for VASP. Yet, (hyper- and) graph rewriting termination in general is undecidable [16]. In order to obtain termination, we look

A. Kučera and I. Potapov (Eds.): RP 2010, LNCS 6227, pp. 133–145, 2010.

at rewriting strategies for VASP, which we use to rewrite some classes of VASP as VASS, and to transfer VASS reachability results to these classes of VASP.

Branching Extension of VASS (BVASS also called VATA [2]) for which Karp-Miller trees were designed [18] are by the way a particular restriction of VASP, where arcs in a pair do only share their target. A motivating result about BVASS was given by [2]: the reachability decision problem for BVASS is equivalent to the open decision problem of the provability in Multiplicative and Exponential Linear Logic (MELL [8]). The VASP operational semantic we consider is restricted, so we have not full generalization of BVASS but an essential intersection. In fact we allow to traverse pairs only under a condition called division of values, that preserves the sign component-wise. However our condition is implicit for reachability problems with positive values, like in the proof given by [2] to establish their equivalence result.

Originally VASP were designed by the first author (work in progress) to work on the provability decidability in MELL. The second author gives here a slightly different presentation with explicit paths to study them by rewriting systems. We think that VASP allow to work on an adaptation of the technical proof of the reachability problem decidability for Petri nets [11,13,17,12,4], with the goal to obtain the reachability decidability for Petri nets with split and join transitions. This is a work in progress not presented here, which may imply the decidability of the provability in MELL.

Outline. We present in the first section basic definitions of VASP and ribbons, which are paths in VASP. VASP model which generalizes VASS need to introduce new material and redefine both the notions of paths and reachability. Then we give the operational semantic. It is made through promenades which give the reachable values in a VASP. Reachability decision problem is defined in this subsection.

The second section is devoted to rewriting systems for VASP. The definitions are standard in rewriting systems for hyper-graphs. We present rewriting systems and rules as a tool for reachability study. An important subsection contains the set of rules we use and our key lemma of reachability preservation when rules are applied. We also describe a limited strategy for ribbons.

In the last section we give results of reachability relationships between VASP and VASS. There is two kind of results: lemmas about reachability preservation by rewriting strategies, and corollaries about reduction of reachability decision problem for certain classes of VASP to reachability decision problem for VASS.

2   VASP and Reachability

2.1   Basic Definitions

Given $m > 0$, values are vectors in $\mathbb{Z}^m$. If not precised, operations done on vectors are component-wise. Components of a vectors are given by the projections $(x)_j$ for $1 \leqslant j \leqslant m$. A value $x \in \mathbb{Z}^m$ is *divided into* (x_1, x_2) when $x = x_1 + x_2$ and $\forall 1 \leqslant j \leqslant m, |(x)_j| = |(x_1)_j| + |(x_2)_j|$. Remark that positive components of a value are divided into positive integers.

Lemma 1. *Given $m > 0$, let $x \geqslant y$ be values in $\mathbb{Z}^m$. If (y_1, y_2) is a division of y then there exists a division (x_1, x_2) of x such that $x_1 \geqslant y_1$ and $x_2 \geqslant y_2$.*

Definition 1 (VASP). *A* Vector Addition System with States *(VASS) (m, G, v) of dimension $m > 0$ is a directed graph $G = (Q, A)$ whose vertices are called* states, *together with a labeling function $v : A \mapsto \mathbb{Z}^m$, called* valuation, *that associates a value to each arc in A. For a given arc $a = (s, t) \in Q^2$, we call* source $S(a) = s$ *and* target $T(a) = t$ *respectively the source state and the target state of a.*

A Vector Addition System with Pairs *(VASP) (m, G, P, v) of dimension m is a vector addition system with states (m, G, v) whose graph $G = (Q, A)$ is equipped with a set $P \subseteq A \times A$ of disjoint pairs, such that the two arcs of each pair in P share the same source or the same target, called a* paired state. *A source or target sharing pair (resp. shared arc) is called a* split *or* join pair *respectively (resp.* split *or* join arc*). An arc is called* regular *if it does not occur in the pair set. A* paired graph *(G, P) is a graph G equipped with such a pair set P. A paired graph (G', P') is a* subgraph *of (G, P) if and only if $P' \subseteq P$ and G' is a subgraph of G such that no arc in $G' \backslash P'$ is paired in P. A* sub-VASP *of a VASP V is a VASP of same dimension and valuation whose paired graph is a subgraph of that of V. The* reverse *of a VASP V, denoted V^{rev}, is a VASP with same dimension, valuation, states and paired states, obtained by reversing arc orientations.*

Remark that VASS are VASP with empty pair set. Without lost of generality, we consider VASP of dimension m where all paired arcs are valued with the null vector denoted 0^m.[1]

Definition 2 (configuration). *A* single configuration *of a VASP $(m, G = (Q, A), P, v)$ is a couple $(q, x) \in Q \times \mathbb{Z}^m$. A* configuration *of (m, G, P, v) is a multiset of single configurations. A configuration of (m, G, P, v) is* positive *when the value of any of its single configurations is positive. A configuration of (m, G, P, v) is* divisible *if the set of contained values is a division of its sum.*

With the generalization to paired graphs, there are multiple kinds of paths. We keep the simplest one from graphs but the notion of cycle is generalized. E.g. $(2, 4, 3)$ is a cycle from 2 to 3 in Fig. 1(b).

Definition 3 (path). *A* path *in a VASP $(m, G = (Q, A), P, v)$ is a path in the graph G. We say that (m, G, P, v) is* weakly connected *if G is connected when orientation is removed. We say that t is* connected *to s in (m, G, P, v) if there is a path from s to t in G. Given a path p in (m, G, P, v), $\overline{p}$ is the minimal subgraph of (G, P) containing p. We say that a path p from $s = S(a) \in \overline{p}$ to $t = S(b) \in \overline{p}$ is a* cycle *if $a = b$ or $\{a, b\}$ is a pair in $\overline{p}$. In a* simple *path all arcs are distinct.*

This notion of path in graphs is extended to VASP in the following way: in our paired graphs, a path is split and joined accordingly to paired arcs. We call ribbons such paths, by analogy with a (two sides) ribbon of paper cut with scissors (and sometimes paste). In order to have good properties over reversibility, ribbons are based on the notion of B-paths for which each source state must be reachable before the arc is traversable (Fig. 1(a)).

---

[1] This will be clarified with the reachability definition.

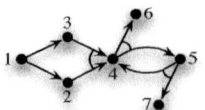   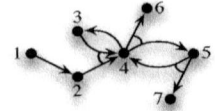   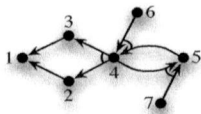

(a) A B-path   (b) Not a B-path from {1}   (c) Reverse of Fig. 1(a) VASP

Fig. 1. Examples

Definition 4 (ribbon). *Given two sets of states S and T, a* Backward-path *(or B-path) B from S to T in a VASP V is a minimal weakly connected sub-VASP of V with state set Q' such that i) $S, T \subseteq Q'$, ii) if $q \in Q'$ then q is connected in B to a state $s \in S$ by means of an acyclic simple path.*

A Forward-path *(or F-path) from S to T in a VASP is a B-path from T to S in the reversed VASP. A* ribbon *(or BF-path) from S to T in a VASP is both a B-path and a F-path from S to T. A state t is* B-connected *(respectively F-connected, BF-connected) to state s if there exists a B-path (respectively F-path, BF-path) from $\{s\}$ to $\{t\}$. A* bridge *in a ribbon ρ from S to T is a regular arc or an arc pair which disconnects ρ into two or three connected components when it is removed, such that each of them gives a partition of S or T but not of both.*

Paths in VASP subsume paths in graphs whereas B-path, F-path and BF-path are paths in hypergraph considering that paired arcs are hyperarcs. E.g. the VASP in Fig. 1(b) is not a B-path from {1} because the only path connecting 3 to 1 contains the cycle $(2, 4, 3)$. However the cycle $(4, 5, 4)$ in Fig. 1(a) is not contained in any simple path from 1 to 7. See Fig. 2 for ribbon examples.

Proposition 1 ([5]). *Given a B-path from $\{s\}$ containing an arc pair $\{a, b\}$, states $S(a)$ and $S(b)$ are B-connected to state s.*

2.2   Reachability

When starting from a positive configuration $\{(s, x_s)\}_{s \in S}$ of a VASP, values reached following a ribbon from S are given by a promenade:

Definition 5 (promenade, reachability). *Given a VASP $V = (m, G, P, v)$ with a positive configuration S, a* promenade *p on V from S is a sequence of configurations $(\mathcal{C}_i)_{i=0, \cdots, f}$ associated to a ribbon ρ in V from states of S such that the* initial configuration *of p is $\mathcal{C}_0 = S$ and,*

- *given $c = (q, x) \in \mathcal{C}_i$ and a regular arc $a = (q, q') \in \rho$, then $\mathcal{C}_{i+1} = \mathcal{C}_i - \{c\} \cup \{c'\}$ where $c' = (q', x + v(a))$,*
- *given $c_1 = (q_1, x_1) \in \mathcal{C}_i$ and $c_2 = (q_2, x_2) \in \mathcal{C}_i$ and a join pair of ρ (q_1, q') and (q_2, q'), then $\mathcal{C}_{i+1} = \mathcal{C}_i - \{c_1, c_2\} \cup \{c'\}$ where $c' = (q', x')$, and (x_1, x_2) is a division of x' $(\star)$,*
- *given $c = (q, x) \in \mathcal{C}_i$ and a split pair of ρ (q, q_1) and (q, q_2), then $\mathcal{C}_{i+1} = \mathcal{C}_i - \{c\} \cup \{c'_1, c'_2\}$ where $c'_1 = (q_1, x_1)$, $c'_2 = (q_2, x_2)$ and x is non-deterministically divided into (x_1, x_2).*

A promenade from S to the final *configuration T is a promenade associated to a ribbon from states of S to states of T such that division conditions are valid. A* positive promenade *on a VASP is a promenade whose configurations are positive. We say that the final configuration $\mathcal{C}_f$ of a positive promenade on V is reachable from the initial one $\mathcal{C}_0$. We denote it by: $\mathcal{C}_0 \rightsquigarrow_V \mathcal{C}_f$.*

Remark that our strong definition of both ribbons and division conditions for arc pairs in promenades imply that $\mathcal{C}_0 \rightsquigarrow_V \mathcal{C}_f \Leftrightarrow \mathcal{C}_f \rightsquigarrow_{V^{rev}} \mathcal{C}_0$. Remark also that ribbons in a VASS coincide with paths, and a promenade (respectively a positive promenade) on a VASS V, considering it as a VASP with empty pair set, is then a sequence of single configurations (respectively with values in $\mathbb{N}^m$) associated to a path in V. So the classical reachability decision problem for VASS coincides with the one for VASP restricted to an empty pair set:

Reachability decision problem for VASP, denoted $\mathcal{RP}_{\text{VASP}}$:
Input: Given a VASP V, two sets of single configurations S and T of V,
Question: Is there a positive promenade on V between configurations whose underlying sets are S and T respectively?

Remark that contrary to BVASS case, $\mathcal{RP}_{\text{VASP}}$ is equivalent to a simpler restriction: Given a VASP V and two configurations S and T of V, is there a positive promenade on V between S and T?

Variation. Branching VASS (BVASS) are VASP where we allow only regular arcs and join arcs. Compared to the operational semantic of BVASS, the operational semantic of VASP is restricted by the division condition for arc pairs in promenades, denoted $(\star)$ in the definition. Nevertheless the reachability decision problem for VASP without split arcs is equivalent to $\mathcal{RP}_{\text{BVASS}}$. Indeed, in both cases, promenades are positive. It turns out that $\mathcal{RP}_{\text{VASP}}$ implies $\mathcal{RP}_{\text{BVASS}}$, which is equivalent to the decidability of MELL provability [2].

3   VASP Rewriting Systems

In this section we establish results concerning VASP reachability. For this purpose, we consider different restrictions of VASP, such as the separated ribbon (Figure 2).

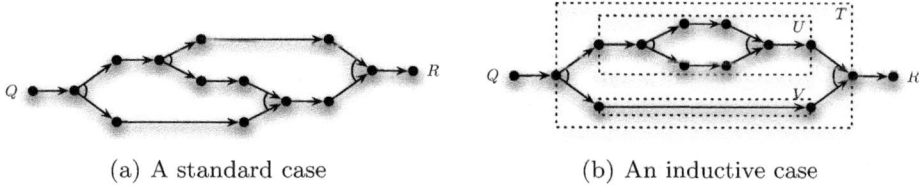

(a) A standard case   (b) An inductive case

Fig. 2. Examples of separated ribbons

Definition 6 (Separated ribbon). *A 2-tree with root s and leave set L is a ribbon from $\{s\}$ to L which contains no join arc and whose underlying graph is a rooted binary tree. A separated ribbon from $\{s\}$ to $\{t\}$ (Fig. 2) is a ribbon whose paired graph consists of a 2-tree with root s and leaves set L, and a reversed 2-tree from t to L. An inductive ribbon is a sequence of regular arcs, or is a separated ribbon that consists of 1) two disjoint inductive ribbons (like U, V in Fig. 2(b)), related by 2) a sequence of regular arcs which finishes by a split pair, and by 3) a join pair which finishes by a sequence of regular arcs.*

The separation refers to the set of arc pairs that is separated accordingly to split pairs and join pairs. In an inductive ribbon we can "glue" the sub-ribbons and then reduce reachability to VASS reachability:

Lemma 2. *Let V be a inductive ribbon from $\{s\}$ to $\{t\}$ with valuation v. Let W be a VASP of same dimension which is only a regular arc (s', t') valued by $\Sigma v(a)$ for all regular arc $a \in V$. We have:*

$$\{(s', x)\} \rightsquigarrow_W \{(t', y)\} \quad \Rightarrow \quad \{(s, x)\} \rightsquigarrow_V \{(t, y)\}.$$

Proof. Remark that by definition of inductive ribbons we have equality of the underlying binary subtree heights. Given $m > 0$, we define an inductive ribbon $S_{U,V}$ of dimension m inductively on $size(S_{U,V}) = 1 + max\{size(U), size(V)\}$, where U, V are the two disjoint inductive ribbons of the definition (like in Fig. 2(b)). The result is obtained by strong induction on this size. ∎

Corollary 1. *The reachability problem for inductive ribbon reduces to the reachability problem for VASS (via many-one reductions).*

3.1   Rewriting System Definitions

We generalize the previous approach by using rewriting systems for VASP as a tool for reachability proofs. We present rewriting systems as a restriction of hypergraph rewriting system. The goal is to give reachability results between VASP and rewritten VASP depending on rewriting systems and chosen strategies. As consequence, when we rewrite a VASP as a VASS, we have transfer reachability results from VASS to VASP.

Definition 7 (Morphism). *A morphism $f : V \to V'$ between two VASP $V = (m, G = (Q, A), P, v)$ and $V' = (m, G' = (Q', A'), P', v')$ consists of two functions $f_q : Q \to Q'$ and $f_a : A \to A'$ preserving arcs, paired states and valuations. Such a morphism is an isomorphism if the functions f_q and f_a are bijective. In this case V and V' are isomorphic, which is denoted by $V \simeq V'$.*

Definition 8 (Rule, Rewrite step). *A rule $r = (m, L \supseteq K \subseteq R)$ is a triple of VASP of dimension m such that K is a sub-VASP of both L and R. The VASP L and R are called the* left- *and* right-hand side *of r, and K is the* interface.

Given a VASP V of dimension m and a set of rules $\mathcal{R}$, there is a rewrite step from V based on $\mathcal{R}$ if there is a rule $r = (m, L \supseteq K \subseteq R)$ in $\mathcal{R}$ and a morphism

$f : L \rightarrow V$ satisfying the following conditions: No arc in $V - f(L)$ is incident to any state in $f(L) - f(K)$, and for all distincts items $x, y \in L$, $f(x) = f(y)$ only if $x, y \in K$. We called $f(L)$ a redex for the rule r. The result (or reduct) of such a rewrite step is isomorphic to the VASP W of dimension m constructed as follows: let U be the sub-VASP of V obtained by removing all arcs and states in $f(L) - f(K)$ and by restricting the valuation of V, let W be obtained from U by adding disjointly all arcs, states and valuations in $R - K$.

Rewrite steps from V to W based on $\mathcal{R}$ define the relation $\rightarrow_{\mathcal{R}}$ between V and W. We denote $\rightarrow_{\mathcal{R}}^*$ the transitive and reflexive closure of $\rightarrow_{\mathcal{R}}$, and relation sequences denote the composition. We abusively denote a rewriting rule $r = (m, L \supseteq K \subseteq R)$ as a rewrite step from the left-hand side $L \rightarrow_{\{r\}} R$ where valuation is given, since K is clear from the context.

Definition 9 (Rewriting system). Given some $n \geqslant 0$, a rewriting of length n from V to V' based on $\mathcal{R}$ is a sequence of the form $V \simeq V_0 \rightarrow_{\mathcal{R}} V_1 \rightarrow_{\mathcal{R}} \cdots \rightarrow_{\mathcal{R}} V_n = V'$. A rewriting system $(m, \mathcal{R})$ is an integer $m > 0$ and a finite set $\mathcal{R}$ of rules of dimension m. A rewriting system $(m, \mathcal{R})$ is terminating if there is not an infinite sequence of rewrite steps based on $\mathcal{R}$. Given a rewriting system $(m, \mathcal{R})$, a VASP V of dimension m is in normal form if there is not a VASP W such that $V \rightarrow_{\mathcal{R}} W$, and V has a normal form if there is a finite sequence from V to some normal form.

3.2 Our Rewriting Rules and Strategies

When a rule interface is only a set of states, we give it by states labelled with capital letters $Q, R, S, \ldots$. Given $m > 0$, we consider rules given in Fig. 3 called *Regular Sum* (RSum), *Backward Zip* (BZip), *Backward Swap* (BSwap), *Collapse* (Col), *Zed* (Zed) and *Backward Expansion* (BExp). For each rule, valuations are *divided*: that is, the valuation (of the regular arcs) of one side is a division of the valuation (of the regular arcs) of the other side. So they are set of rules. Abusively we consider rule sub-cases with the same name: BZip where one of the left-hand side regular arc is erased (and the corresponding source and target are merged), and BExp without regular arcs both side (then corresponding source and target are merged). We define rules called *Forward Zip* (FZip), *Forward Swap* (FSwap) and *Forward Expansion* (FExp) by respectively BZip, BSwap and BExp on the reversed VASP. We denote r^{-1} the reversed relation of rule r: r^{-1} goes from right-hand side of rule r to left-hand side of rule r.

Remark that Zed, Col and $RSum$ rules are their own reversed. Remark that by definition of rules and rewrite steps, there is no arc other than those indicated, to or from states which are not in a rule interface.

Lemma 3 (Key lemma). Let $m > 0$, let $r = (m, L \supseteq K \subseteq R)$ be one of the previously defined rules except Zed, but including reversed and inverted rules. Let $\mathcal{C}$ be a configuration of zero in-degree states of L (labelled Q, Q' for Backward rules in Fig.3). Let $\mathcal{C}'$ be a configuration of zero out-degree states of R. Then,

$$\mathcal{C} \rightsquigarrow_L \mathcal{C}' \quad \Leftrightarrow \quad \mathcal{C} \rightsquigarrow_R \mathcal{C}'.$$

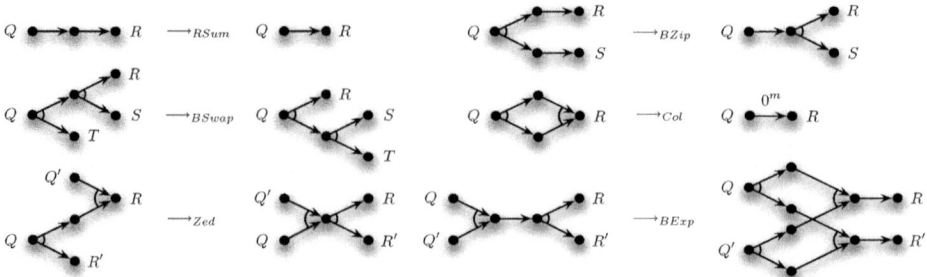

Fig. 3. Rewriting rules

Proof. Let $r \in \mathcal{R}$. Since by definition $\mathcal{C}$ and $\mathcal{C}'$ are configurations of the interface of rule r, they are configurations of R. The result is easily obtained by a case analysis because of a division of a split pair is the "reverse" of a division of a join pair, and reciprocally. Notably, the result is obvious for $BSwap, Col$ and $RSum$, for all reversed Backward rules, and for inverse rules when proved for the corresponding rule. An interesting case is for the $BZip$ rule: the right implication is clear. For the converse let us denote by c the regular arc of R, and a and b the regular arcs of L. By definition of $BZip$ we have a divided valuation: $(v(a), v(b))$ is a division of $v(c)$. Let $C = \{(Q, x)\}$, if $\mathcal{C} \rightsquigarrow_R \mathcal{C}'$ then $x \geqslant v(c)$ in R, and for any division (x_1, x_2) of $x - v(c)$ we have $C' = \{(R, x_1), (S, x_2)\}$. By lemma 1 let us take a division (x_1, x_2) of $x - v(c)$ such that $x_1 \geqslant v(a)$ and $x_2 \geqslant v(b)$. This is the requirement for reachability from C in L: we obtain $\mathcal{C} \rightsquigarrow_L \mathcal{C}' \Leftarrow \mathcal{C} \rightsquigarrow_R \mathcal{C}'$.

For $BZip$ rules, it is important to understand that only the requirement of divided valuation in VASP gives the left implication. Remark that only $\mathcal{C} \rightsquigarrow_L \mathcal{C}' \Rightarrow \mathcal{C} \rightsquigarrow_R \mathcal{C}'$ holds for rule Zed.

From a reachability point of view, we cannot use a rewriting system without knowing if it is terminating, but (hyper- and) graph rewriting termination is undecidable [16]. Here we present a notion of strategies for a rewriting system that allows us to study termination of rewriting systems in a restricted case. Other methods are certainly useful but we are just interested in reachability. A strategy for a rewriting system is a VASP transformation that defines when a rewrite step is performed and what rule it takes:

Definition 10 (Strategy). *Given a VASP rewriting system $\mathcal{S}$, a strategy is a function f_S from VASP set to itself. A strategy f_S is normalizing if whenever V has a normal form, then there is some n so that $f_S{}^n(V)$ is a normal form.*

Given a rewriting system with a singleton rule set $\{r\}$, a strategy is usually a function that maps a VASP V with a redex into $f_S(V)$, the corresponding reduct obtained by one rewrite step from V. Sharper strategies give an order on the redexes for determining which redex is rewritten. A strategy implementation is often an algorithm for VASP traversal with a decision function to choose rules to be applied. We use in what follows this set of rules:
$\mathcal{R}_2 = \{RSum, BZip^{-1}, FZip^{-1}, BSwap, FSwap, BExp\}$.

We consider the following *separation* strategy using $\mathcal{R}_2$ rules, which is a recursive function that maps a VASP V with a ribbon ρ to an isomorphic VASP where ρ is rewritten into a separated ribbon by pushing away every split arcs to the left of join arcs (or the converse, from join arcs pushed away to the right, or by mixing them). *BExp* rule allows to cross in the right direction two arc pairs with "opposite" sharing. We are interested in terminaison of the separation strategy, but the *BExp* rule may create new *BExp* redexes. However we have:

Lemma 4. *Given a rewriting system* $(m, \{BExp\})$, *there is no infinite sequence of rewrite steps in a ribbon.*

Proof. We give a sketch by generalizing VASP pairs of paired graphs to hyperarcs of hypergraphs. In this case there is a measure that decreases in every *BExp* redex context, so terminaison for this rewrite rule generalizes to hyperarcs. This give us a bound on the number of *BExp* rewrite steps in the VASP by simulating with a fixed maximal number of steps the rule for hyperarcs.

4   Reachability Relationship between VASP and VASS

We give a simple example illustrating how rewriting systems are used as a tool to obtain a reachability equivalence. With VASP rewriting system we just need to consider an ad-hoc strategy to rewrite a separated ribbon into a VASS.

Lemma 5. *Let* V *be a separated ribbon from* $\{s\}$ *to* $\{t\}$ *with valuation* v. *Let* W *be a VASP of same dimension which is only a regular arc* (s', t') *valued by* $\Sigma v(a)$ *for all regular arc* $a \in V$. *We have:*

$$\{(s, x)\} \rightsquigarrow_V \{(t, y)\} \quad \Leftrightarrow \quad \{(s', x)\} \rightsquigarrow_W \{(t', y)\}$$

Proof. Let V be a separated ribbon from $\{s\}$ to $\{t\}$ of dimension $m > 0$ and valuation v. Let W be the regular arc defined in the lemma hypothesis. Let $\mathcal{V} = (m, \{RSum, Col, BZip, FZip\})$ be a rewriting system. Let U be the normal form of V obtained by the following strategy on $\mathcal{V}$: firstly from s we apply $\overrightarrow{\mathcal{F}} = (\rightarrow^*_{RSum} \rightarrow_{BZip})^*$ on the 2-tree with root $\{s\}$, and we apply from t the same reversed strategy, that is $\overleftarrow{\mathcal{F}} = (\rightarrow^*_{RSum} \rightarrow_{FZip})^*$, on the reversed 2-tree with root $\{t\}$. Secondly we apply $\rightarrow^*_{Col}$ and we finish with $\rightarrow^*_{RSum}$.

Corollary 2. *The reachability problem for separated ribbon between states reduces to the reachability problem for VASS (via many-one reductions).*

Now we give an example using a separation strategy which preserves reachability.

Lemma 6. *Let* V *be a ribbon from* $\{s\}$ *to* $\{t\}$. *Let* $\mathcal{V} = (m, \mathcal{R}_2)$ *be a rewriting system. There is separating strategy for* $\mathcal{V}$ *rewriting* V *into a separated ribbon* W *from* $\{s'\}$ *to* $\{t'\}$ *such that:* $\quad \{(s, x)\} \rightsquigarrow_V \{(t, y)\} \quad \Leftrightarrow \quad \{(s', x)\} \rightsquigarrow_W \{(t', y)\}$

Proof. Let V be a ribbon from $\{s\}$ to $\{t\}$. Let the separation strategy be:

For each shared source of pairs, we call it d,
    if a path p from s to d is not a branch of a 2-tree from s
    then apply $BExp$, using other $\mathcal{R}_2$ rules in order to reduce
        the length of p and to reveal $BExp$ redexes.

Remark that if there is a subpath p' of p from a shared target of a pair to a d state, then its length can always be reduced to zero by applying rules of $\mathcal{R}_2 - \{BExp\}$. It follows that in a not separated ribbon, $BExp$ redexes can always be revealed. If the d states to treat are chosen with smallest distance from s then by lemma 4 the strategy terminates. Remark that $\mathcal{V}$ rewrites a ribbon into a ribbon. So $\mathcal{V}$ is rewritten into a ribbon such that every shared source paired states are in a branch of a 2-tree from s. In other words this ribbon is separated.

Remark that a ribbon is defined to be both B-path and F-path, and this is essential to ensure that the strategy terminates by building a separated ribbon: there is no Zed rule to apply to build a new $BExp$ redex, so one can continue the strategy preserving reachability, or we have already a separated ribbon.

Corollary 3. *The reachability problem for ribbon between states reduces to the reachability problem for separated ribbon between states.*

We easily extend the lemma 6 to ribbons from $\{s\}$ to an arbitrary set T: the implemented separation strategy both terminates and normalizes in a separated ribbon from $\{s\}$ to T (extended as expected) preserving the reachability.

   This is generalizable to separation for ribbons between arbitrary sets when there is a bridge between S and T (Definition 4). We are interested in bridged ribbons because they are always associated to a positive promenade in a BVASS.

Lemma 7. *Let V be a bridged ribbon from S to T. Let $\mathcal{V} = (m, \mathcal{R}_2)$ be a rewriting system. There is a separating strategy for $\mathcal{V}$ rewriting V into a separated ribbon W from S to T such that:* $S' \rightsquigarrow_V T' \quad \Leftrightarrow \quad S' \rightsquigarrow_W T'.$

Proof. Let ρ be a ribbon from S to T with a bridge such that the, at most three, simply connected components are denoted by V_i^ρ, $i \in I$. Let $i \in I$. V_i^ρ is by definition a ribbon from S_i to T_i where either S_i or T_i is a singleton, whose state is a state of the bridge. W.l.g. let $S_i = \{s_i\}$ be an arbitrary such singleton. By the previous extension of lemma 7, V_i^ρ is separable in W_i^ρ between the same sets such that reachability is preserved. Let W be the normal form by separation strategy of the ribbon which consists of the bridge of ρ added to the W_i^ρ ribbon. We have that W is the normal form of ρ and again reachability is preserved.

Remark that there is a bridge in all ribbons from S to T if at least one of these sets is a singleton. In fact one bridge is the arc or arc pair which is to or from the state of the singleton set. So bridged ribbons generalize ribbons from a singleton to a set.

   To compare bridged ribbon reachability to VASS reachability, we want to reduce reachability of arbitrary separated ribbon to VASS reachability. We have:

Lemma 8. *Let ρ be a separated ribbon between arbitrary sets S and T. Let s and t be two states not in ρ. Let $\theta_{s,S}$ (respectively $\theta_{T,t}$) be a VASP of same dimension than ρ consisting of a binary tree of split pairs (respectively of join pairs) from $\{s\}$ to S (respectively from T to $\{t\}$). Let W be the ribbon from $\{s\}$ to $\{t\}$ which consists of $\theta_{s,S}$ composed with ρ and composed with $\theta_{T,t}$ (by identity morphism on S and T). We have: if x (respectively y) is a division of $\{x_i\}_{1 \leqslant i \leqslant |S|}$ (respectively of $\{y_j\}_{1 \leqslant i \leqslant |T|}$) then*

$$\{(s_i, x_i)_{s_i \in S}\} \rightsquigarrow_\rho \{(t_j, y_j)_{t_j \in T}\} \quad \Leftrightarrow \quad \{(s,x)\} \rightsquigarrow_W \{(t,y)\}$$

Remark that the ribbon W is separable, therefore there is a reduction between reachability for bridged ribbon and VASS reachability using a separability strategy. So by lemma 7 and 8 we have:

Corollary 4. *The reachability problem for bridged ribbons reduces to the reachability problem for VASS (via many-one reductions). Then the former is decidable.*

We finish a last step further with a strategy for VASP which are not ribbons:

```
Repeat
    rewrite a ribbon between arbitrary sets by separation strategy
Until all ribbons are separated.
```

This (too strong) strategy does not always terminate, sometimes for bad reasons: rules cannot be applied because of interface restrictions, for example, when there is an arc to a node of the left-hand side of a rule, whose target or source is not in the interface. Rewriting rules with interfaces which consist of all the states of the left-hand side are quite inextricable (from a reachability point of view). Thus we are even far from semidecidability.

Lemma 9. *Given a VASP V, if the separation strategy terminates for V in a normal form W, we have: $S \rightsquigarrow_V T \quad \Rightarrow \quad S \rightsquigarrow_W T$.*

In such a normal form, all ribbons are separated. So by corollary 4 we have:

Proposition 2. *Given a VASP V, if the separation strategy terminates for V, then the reachability problem for V with divisible initial and final configurations reduces to VASS reachability problem.*

5   Conclusion

We introduce a generalization of VASS called Vector Addition Systems with Pairs (VASP) by pairing arcs with same source or with same target. These correspond to split and joint transitions with a multiset of vectors. The reachability decision problem for VASP $\mathcal{RP}_{\text{VASP}}$ subsumes the one for BVASS (as a sub-case of VASP without split pairs) which is equivalent to the open MELL provability decision problem. There is also a natural simplification of $\mathcal{RP}_{\text{VASP}}$ not valid for BVASS.

We present graph rewriting systems in order to study paths in VASP. This tool permits reduction between restricted forms of VASP and VASS, preserving reachability properties. Notably the reachability problem is decidable for VASP in which our separation strategy terminates.

Other strategies, like *zipping* one using $\{RSum, BZip, BSwap, BCol\}$ rules and reversed rules, can be used to obtain reachability for other kind of VASP. By zipping strategy we think to rewrite a ribbon starting from a source state and applying rules step-by-step on each outgoing arcs (source paired or not), making synchronization on each target paired state by reducing the remaining branch of ribbon before it.

The main other way for reachability decision is to adapt the original proof of reachability for VASS to VASP. It seems approachable to obtain decidability associated to Karp and Miller "trees" for VASP.

References

1. Brázdil, T., Jancar, P., Kucera, A.: Reachability games on extended vector addition systems with states. CoRR (2010) abs/1002.2557
2. de Groote, P., Guillaume, B., Salvati, S.: Vector addition tree automata. In: LICS, pp. 64–73. IEEE Computer Society, Los Alamitos (2004)
3. Demri, S., Jurdzinski, M., Lachish, O., Lazic, R.: The covering and boundedness problems for branching vector addition systems. In: Kannan, R., Kumar, K.N. (eds.) FSTTCS. LIPIcs, vol. 4, pp. 181–192 (2009)
4. Esparza, J., Nielsen, M.: Decidability issues for petri nets - a survey. Bulletin of the EATCS 52, 244–262 (1994)
5. Gallo, G., Longo, G., Pallottino, S.: Directed hypergraphs and applications. Discrete Applied Mathematics 42(2), 177–201 (1993)
6. Ginsburg, S., Spanier, E.H.: Semigroups, presburger formulas, and languages. Pacific Journal of Mathematic 16(2), 285–296 (1966)
7. Ginzburg, A., Yoeli, M.: Vector addition systems and regular languages. J. Comput. Syst. Sci. 20(3), 277–284 (1980)
8. Girard, J.-Y.: Linear logic. Theor. Comput. Sci. 50, 1–102 (1987)
9. Hopcroft, J.E., Pansiot, J.-J.: On the reachability problem for 5-dimensional vector addition systems. TCS 8, 135–159 (1979)
10. Karp, R.M., Miller, R.E.: Parallel program schemata. J. Comput. Syst. Sci. 3(2), 147–195 (1969)
11. Kosaraju, S.R.: Decidability of reachability in vector addition systems (preliminary version). In: STOC, pp. 267–281. ACM, New York (1982)
12. Lambert, J.-L.: A structure to decide reachability in petri nets. Theor. Comput. Sci. 99(1), 79–104 (1992)
13. Mayr, E.W.: An algorithm for the general petri net reachability problem. SIAM J. Comput. 13(3), 441–460 (1984)
14. Müller, H.: The reachability problem for vas. In: Rozenberg, G., Genrich, H.J., Roucairol, G. (eds.) APN 1984. LNCS, vol. 188, pp. 376–391. Springer, Heidelberg (1985)
15. Parikh, R.: On context-free languages. J. ACM 13(4), 570–581 (1966)
16. Plump, D.: Termination of graph rewriting is undecidable. Fundam. Inform. 33(2), 201–209 (1998)

17. Reutenauer, C.: Aspects Mathématiques des Réseaux de Pétri. Masson (1989)
18. Verma, K.N., Goubault-Larrecq, J.: Karp-miller trees for a branching extension of vass. Discrete Mathematics & Theoretical Computer Science 7(1), 217–230 (2005)
19. Verma, K.N., Goubault-Larrecq, J.: Alternating two-way ac-tree automata. Inf. Comput. 205(6), 817–869 (2007)

The Complexity of Model Checking for Intuitionistic Logics and Their Modal Companions

Martin Mundhenk and Felix Weiß

Universität Jena, Institut für Informatik, Jena, Germany
{martin.mundhenk,felix.weiss}@uni-jena.de

Abstract. We study the model checking problem for logics whose semantics are defined using transitive Kripke models. We show that the model checking problem is P-complete for the intuitionistic logic KC. Interestingly, for its modal companion S4.2 we also obtain P-completeness even if we consider formulas with one variable only. This result is optimal since model checking for S4 without variables is NC^1-complete. The strongest variable free modal logic with P-complete model checking problem is K4. On the other hand, for KC formulas with one variable only we obtain much lower complexity, namely LOGDCFL as an upper bound.

1 Introduction

We investigate the complexity of the model checking problem for intuitionistic propositional logics and for its modal companions. Intuitionistic propositional logic IPC (see e.g. [1]) is the part of classical propositional logic that goes without the use of the excluded middle $a \vee \neg a$. We will use its semantical definition by Kripke models with a partially ordered set of states and a monotone valuation function. A straightforward upper bound follows from the Gödel-Tarski translation (see e.g. [2, p.96]) that embeds intuitionistic logic into the modal logic S4. Since the model checking problem—given a formula and a model, does the model satisfy the formula (or does the formula evaluate to "true" under the model)?—for modal logic is in P [3], we obtain the same as an upper bound for the problem in intuitionistic logic. For classical propositional logic, the model checking problem can be solved in logarithmic space [4] and even better in alternating logtime [5]. Since the models for classical logic can be seen as a special case of Kripke models with one state only, we cannot expect such a low complexity for intuitionistic logic, where the models may consist of many states.

More generally, we will consider the classical propositional logic PC, the intuitionistic logics LC (Gödel-Dummet logic, see [6]), KC (Jankov's logic, see [6]), IPC, and BPL (Visser's basic propositional logic [7]), and their respective modal companions S5, S4.3, S4.2, S4, and K4 (see e.g. [2] for an overview). Remind that PC ⊃ LC ⊃ KC ⊃ IPC ⊃ BPL.

Our first hardness result (Theorem 2) is the P-hardness of the model checking problem for the superintuitionistic (or intermediate) logic KC. This hardness

A. Kučera and I. Potapov (Eds.): RP 2010, LNCS 6227, pp. 146–160, 2010.

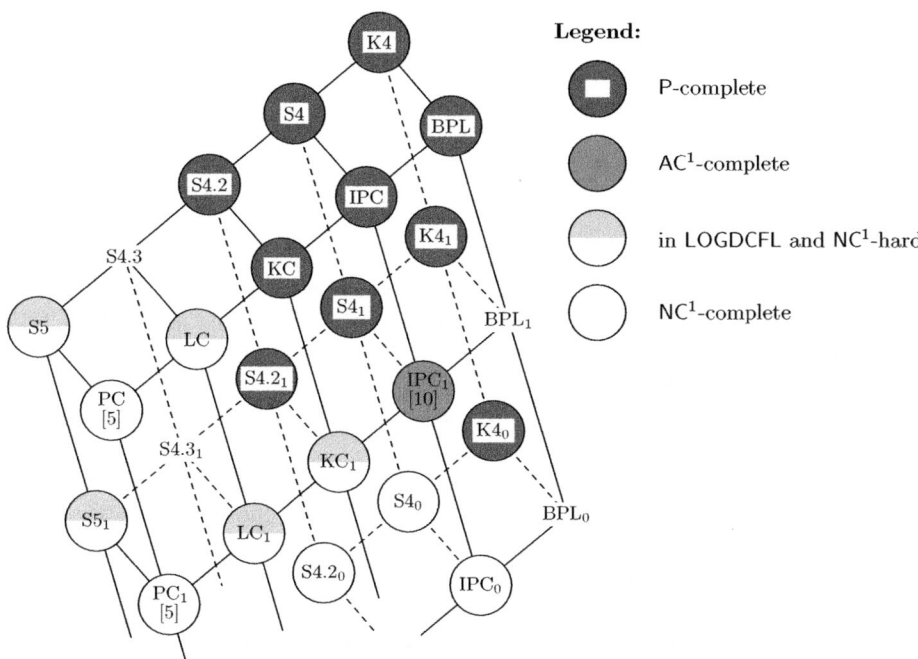

Fig. 1. Summary of results: the structure of the logics and the complexity of the model checking problem. Lower and upper bounds for the uncircled logics follow from their neighbourhoods, but non-trivial bounds are unknown.

result consequently also holds for IPC and BPL and their companions S4.2, S4, and K4. Hence, the well-known upper bound [3] turns out to be the lower bound.

Since the expressivity of intuitionistic logics seems to be much lower than that of their modal companions, it is somewhat surprising that all these logics have P-hard model checking problems. In fact, the satisfiability problem for S4.2 up to K4 are PSPACE-complete [8,9], whereas the satisfiability problem for intuitionistic logic has the same complexity as that for classical logic—both are NP-complete. We can point out some differences for the model checking problem that can be seen as a result of the greater expressivity of modal logics. This difference appears if we consider formulas with one variable only or without any variables. In Theorem 3 we show that the model checking problem remains P-hard for S4.2, even if we consider formulas with one variable only. For K4 we show P-hardness, even if we consider formulas without variables (Theorem 4). These results are in contrast to the recent result in [10] showing that the model checking problem for IPC with one variable only is AC^1-complete. For KC with one variable only we will show that the complexity of model checking is even lower, namely in LOGDCFL (Theorem 7). Regarding the number of variables for S4.2 resp. S4, Theorem 3 is optimal. We show that model checking for the variable free fragment of S4 is NC^1-complete (Theorem 8).

Figure 1 summarizes our results. There, PC denotes classical propositional logic, and subscript 1 or 0 (e.g. $S4.2_1$) denotes the fragment with one variable only resp. without variables.

Technically, our hardness results use a reduction from the alternating graph accessibility problem AGAP, being one of the standard P-complete problems [11,12]. It can straightforwardly be logspace reduced to the model checking problem for propositional modal logic by taking the alternating graph as the frame of a Kripke model (with an empty valuation function) and a formula essentially consisting of a sequence of $\Box$ and $\Diamond$ operators that simulates the search through the graph. This straightforward approach does not work anymore when we want to reduce to Kripke models with transitive frames—like for the modal logic S4 or intuitionistic propositional logic. On the one hand, making an alternating graph transitive, destroys essential properties it has, and on the other hand, a logspace reduction does not have enough computational power to calculate the transitive closure of a directed graph.

This paper is organized as follows. In Section 2 we introduce the notations for the logics under consideration, and we show P-completeness of a graph accessibility problem for a special case of alternating graphs that will be used for our P-hardness proofs. In Section 3 we give P-hardness proofs for the model checking problem for KC, $S4.2_1$, and $K4_0$. The upper bounds are presented in Section 4. The resulting completeness results and conclusions are drawn in Section 5.

2   Preliminaries

Kripke Models. We will consider different propositional logics whose formulas base on a countable set PROP of *propositional variables* (resp. atoms). A *Kripke model* is a triple $\mathcal{M} = (U, R, \xi)$, where U is a nonempty and finite set of *states*, R is a binary relation on U, and $\xi : \text{PROP} \to \mathfrak{P}(U)$ is a function—the *valuation function*. Informally spoken, for any variable it assigns the set of states in which this variable is satisfied. (U, R) can also be seen as a directed graph—it is called a *frame* in this context.

Modal Propositional Logic. The language $\mathcal{ML}$ of modal logic is the set of all formulas of the form
$$\varphi ::= \bot \mid p \mid \varphi \to \varphi \mid \Diamond \varphi,$$
where $p \in \text{PROP}$. As usual, we use the abbreviations $\neg\varphi := \varphi \to \bot$, $\top := \neg\bot$, $\varphi \lor \psi := (\neg\varphi) \to \psi$, $\varphi \land \psi := \neg(\varphi \to \neg\psi)$, and $\Box\varphi := \neg\Diamond\neg\varphi$.

The semantics is defined via Kripke models. Given a model $\mathcal{M} = (U, R, \xi)$ and a state $s \in U$, the *satisfaction relation for modal logics* $\models_M$ is defined as follows.

$$\mathcal{M}, s \not\models_M \bot$$
$$\mathcal{M}, s \models_M p \qquad \text{iff } s \in \xi(p), \ p \in \text{PROP},$$
$$\mathcal{M}, s \models_M \varphi \to \psi \ \text{ iff } \ \mathcal{M}, s \not\models_M \varphi \text{ or } \mathcal{M}, s \models_M \psi,$$
$$\mathcal{M}, s \models_M \Diamond\varphi \qquad \text{iff } \exists t \in U : sRt \text{ and } \mathcal{M}, t \models_M \varphi.$$

A formula φ is *satisfied* by model $\mathcal{M}$ in state s iff $\mathcal{M}, s \models_M \varphi$. If it is satisfied by $\mathcal{M}$ in every state s of $\mathcal{M}$, then we write $\mathcal{M} \models_M \varphi$.

The modal logic defined in this way is called K (after Saul Kripke) and it is the weakest normal modal logic. We will consider the stronger modal logics K4, S4, S4.2, S4.3, and S5. The formulas in all these logics are the same as for $\mathcal{ML}$. Since we are interested in formula evaluation, we use the semantics defined by Kripke models. They will be defined by properties of the frame (i.e. graph) (U, R) that is part of the model. A frame (U, R) is *reflexive*, if xRx for all $x \in U$, and it is *transitive*, if for all $a, b, c \in U$, it follows from aRb and bRc that aRc. A reflexive and transitive frame is called a *preorder*. If a preorder (U, R) has the additional property that for all $a, b \in U$ there exists a $c \in U$ with aRc and bRc, then (U, R) is called a *directed preorder*. If for all $a, b \in U$ holds aRb or bRa, then (U, R) is called a *linear preorder*.

The semantics of several modal logics can be defined by restricting the class of Kripke frames under consideration. The semantics of K4 is defined by transitive frames. This means, that a formula α is a theorem of K4 if and only if $\mathcal{M} \models_M \alpha$ for all models $\mathcal{M}$ whose frame is transitive. The semantics of S4 is defined by preorders, of S4.2 by directed preorders, of S4.3 by linear preorders, and of S5 by equivalence relations (symmetric preorders). For any logic L, let L_i denote its fragment with i variables only. The fragment L_0 has no variables but the constant $\bot$ only.

Intuitionistic Propositional Logic. The language $\mathcal{IPC}$ of intuitionistic propositional logic is the same as that of propositional logic $\mathcal{PC}$, i.e. it is the set of all formulas of the form

$$\varphi ::= \bot \mid p \mid \varphi \wedge \varphi \mid \varphi \vee \varphi \mid \varphi \rightarrow \varphi,$$

where $p \in \text{PROP}$. As usual, we use the abbreviations $\neg\varphi := \varphi \rightarrow \bot$ and $\top := \neg\bot$. Because of the semantics of intuitionistic logic, one cannot express $\wedge$ or $\vee$ using $\rightarrow$ and $\bot$.

The semantics is defined via Kripke models $\mathcal{M} = (U, R, \xi)$ that fulfill certain restrictions. Firstly, R is a preorder on U, and secondly, the valuation function $\xi : \text{PROP} \rightarrow \mathfrak{P}(U)$ is monotone in the sense that for every $p \in \text{PROP}$, $a, b \in U$: if $a \in \xi(p)$ and aRb, then $b \in \xi(p)$. We will call such models *intuitionistic*.

Given an intuitionistic model $\mathcal{M} = (U, \leqslant, \xi)$ and a state $s \in U$, the *satisfaction relation for intuitionistic logics* $\models_I$ is defined as follows.

$$\mathcal{M}, s \not\models_I \bot$$
$$\mathcal{M}, s \models_I p \qquad \text{iff} \quad s \in \xi(p), \ p \in \text{PROP},$$
$$\mathcal{M}, s \models_I \varphi \wedge \psi \quad \text{iff} \quad \mathcal{M}, s \models_I \varphi \text{ and } \mathcal{M}, s \models_I \psi,$$
$$\mathcal{M}, s \models_I \varphi \vee \psi \quad \text{iff} \quad \mathcal{M}, s \models_I \varphi \text{ or } \mathcal{M}, s \models_I \psi,$$
$$\mathcal{M}, s \models_I \varphi \rightarrow \psi \quad \text{iff} \quad \forall n \geqslant s : \text{ if } \mathcal{M}, n \models_I \varphi \text{ then } \mathcal{M}, n \models_I \psi$$

An important property of intuitionistic logic is the monotonicity property: if $\mathcal{M}, s \models_I \varphi$ then $\forall n \geqslant s$ holds $\mathcal{M}, n \models_I \varphi$, for all formulas φ.

int. logic	modal companion	frame properties
BPL	K4	transitive
IPC	S4	preorder
KC	S4.2	directed preorder
LC	S4.3	linear preorder
PC	S5	equivalence relation

Fig. 2. Intuitionistic logics, their modal companions, and the common frame properties

A formula φ is *satisfied* by an intuitionistic model $\mathcal{M}$ in state s iff $\mathcal{M}, s \models_I \varphi$. Intuitionistic propositional logic IPC is the set of $\mathcal{IPC}$-formulas that are satisfied by every intuitionistic model.

Notice that IPC is a proper subset of the tautologies in classical propositional logic PC.[1] The superintuitionistic (or intermediate) logics KC and LC are also subsets of the tautologies in classical propositional logic, but proper supersets of IPC. Syntactically, KC results from adding the weak law of the excluded third $\neg a \vee \neg\neg a$ to IPC. Its semantics is defined by Kripke frames that are directed preorders—similar as for S4.2. LC (also called Gödel-Dummett logic) results syntactically from adding $(a \to b) \vee (b \to a)$ to IPC. Its semantics is defined by Kripke frames that are linear preorders–similar as for S4.3. The logic BPL is Visser's basic propositional logic [7]. Its semantics is defined by transitive (not necessarily reflexive) Kripke models with monotone valuation functions. Hence it holds that BPL $\subseteq$ IPC. Finally, the classical propositional logic PC can syntactically be seen as IPC plus the law of the excluded third $a \vee \neg a$. Its semantics is defined by Kripke frames that are equivalence relations–similar as for S5. Notice that in a Kripke frame being an equivalence relation and having a monotone valuation function, all equivalent states satisfy exactly the same formulas. Therefore, evaluating a formula φ in a state w in such a model is the same as evaluating φ in the classical propositional sense under the assignment in which exactly those variables p with $w \in \xi(p)$ are set to true.

The Gödel-Tarski translation (see e.g. [2, p.96]) maps any $\mathcal{IPC}$-formula α to a modal formula by inserting a $\square$ before every implication and every atom. For a formula α, let α_{GT} be its Gödel-Tarski translation. The goal of this translation is to preserve validity. I.e., α is a theorem for IPC (resp. BPL, KC, LC, PC) iff α_{GT} is a theorem for S4 (resp. K4, S4.2, S4.3, S5). Therefore, S4 (resp. K4, S4.2, S4.3, S5) is called a *modal companion* of IPC (resp. BPL, KC, LC, PC). Figure 2 gives an overview about the intuitionistic logics and their modal companions used here. The Gödel-Tarski translation also preserves satisfaction in the different logics.

Lemma 1. *Let α be a formula from $\mathcal{IPC}$, and an intuitionistic $\mathcal{M}$ with state s. Then $\mathcal{M}, s \models_I \alpha$ if and only if $\mathcal{M}, s \models_M \alpha_{GT}$.*

---

[1] The satisfiable formulas in intuitionistic logic are the same as in classical propositional logic.

Model Checking Problems. This paper examines the model checking problems L-Mc for logics L whose formulas are evaluated on Kripke models with different properties.

Problem:	L-Mc
Input:	$\langle \varphi, \mathcal{M}, s \rangle$, where φ is an L-formula, $\mathcal{M} = (U, R, \xi)$ is a Kripke model for L, and $s \in U$ is a state
Question:	Is φ satisfied by $\mathcal{M}$ in state s ?

We assume that formulas and Kripke models are encoded in a straightforward way. This means, a formula is given as a text, and the graph (U, R) of a Kripke model is given by its adjacency matrix that takes $|U|^2$ bits. Therefore, only finite Kripke models can be considered.

Notice that all instances $\langle \varphi, \mathcal{M}, s \rangle$ of IPC-Mc have a graph (U, R) contained in $\mathcal{M}$ that is a preorder. Instances without this property can be assumed to be rejected. The same holds for S4-Mc and S4$_1$-Mc. Accordingly, KC-Mc, S4.2-Mc, and S4.2$_1$-Mc (resp. LC-Mc and S4.3-Mc) have instances only where the graph underlying the model is a directed preorder (resp. linear preorder). Since we only consider finite models, every directed preorder must have a maximal element. Therefore, it can be easily decided whether the model has the order property under consideration.

Complexity. We assume familiarity with the standard notions of complexity theory as, e.g., defined in [13]. In particular, we will show results for the classes LOGDCFL and P. The notion of reducibility we use is the logspace many-one reduction $\leq_m^{\log}$. The Gödel-Tarski translation can be seen as a reduction between the model checking problems for intuitionistic logics and their modal companions, namely BPL-Mc $\leq_m^{\log}$ K4-Mc, IPC-Mc $\leq_m^{\log}$ S4-Mc, KC-Mc $\leq_m^{\log}$ S4.2-Mc, LC-Mc $\leq_m^{\log}$ S4.3-Mc, and PC-Mc $\leq_m^{\log}$ S5-Mc. The respective reducibilities also hold for the model checking problems for formulas with any restricted number of variables.

LOGDCFL is the class of sets that are $\leq_m^{\log}$-reducible to deterministic context-free languages. It is also characterized as sets decidable by deterministic Turing machine in polynomial-time and logarithmic space with additional use of a stack. The inclusion structure of the classes under consideration is as follows.

$$\text{NC}^1 \subseteq \text{L} \subseteq \text{LOGDCFL} \subseteq \text{AC}^1 \subseteq \text{P}$$

L denotes logspace, the formula value problem for propositional logic is complete for NC^1 (= alternating logarithmic time) [5], and the model checking problem for IPC$_1$ is complete for AC^1 (= alternating logspace with logarithmically bounded number of alternations) [10].

P-complete problems. Chandra, Kozen, and Stockmeyer [11] have shown that the Alternating Graph Accessibility Problem AGAP is P-complete. In [12] it is mentioned that P-completeness also holds for a bipartite version.

An *alternating graph* $G = (V, E)$ is a bipartite directed graph where $V = V_\exists \cup V_\forall$ are the partitions of V. Nodes in $V_\exists$ are called *existential* nodes, and nodes in $V_\forall$ are called *universal* nodes. The property $apath_G(x,y)$ for nodes $x,y \in V$ is defined as follows.

1) $apath_G(x,x)$ holds for all $x \in V$
2a) for $x \in V_\exists$: $apath_G(x,y)$ iff $\exists z \in V_\forall : (x,z) \in E$ and $apath_G(z,y)$
2b) for $x \in V_\forall$: $apath_G(x,y)$ iff $\forall z \in V_\exists :$ if $(x,z) \in E$ then $apath_G(z,y)$

The problem AGAP consists of directed bipartite graphs G and nodes s,t that satisfy the property $apath_G(s,t)$. Notice that in bipartite graphs existential and universal nodes are strictly alternating.

> Problem: AGAP
> Input: $\langle G,s,t \rangle$, where G is a directed bipartite graph
> Question: does $apath_G(s,t)$ hold?

Theorem 1. *[11,12]* AGAP *is P-complete under $\leq_m^{\log}$-reductions.*

For our purposes, we need an even more restricted variant of AGAP. We claim that the graph is *sliced*. An *alternating slice graph* $G = (V,E)$ is a directed bipartite acyclic graph with a bipartitioning $V = V_\exists \cup V_\forall$, and a further partitioning $V = V_1 \cup V_2 \cup \cdots \cup V_m$ (m *slices*, $V_i \cap V_j = \emptyset$ if $i \neq j$) where $V_\exists = \bigcup_{i \leq m, i \text{ odd}} V_i$ and $V_\forall = \bigcup_{i \leq m, i \text{ even}} V_i$, such that $E \subseteq \bigcup_{i=1,2,\ldots,m-1} V_i \times V_{i+1}$ — i.e. all edges go from slice V_i to slice V_{i+1} (for $i = 1, 2, \ldots, m-1$). Finally, we claim that all nodes in a slice graph excepted those in the last slice V_m have outdegree > 0.

> Problem: AsAGAP
> Input: $\langle G,s,t \rangle$, where $G = (V_\exists \cup V_\forall, E)$ is a slice graph with slices $V_1, \ldots, V_m$, and $s \in V_1 \cap V_\exists$, $t \in V_m \cap V_\forall$
> Question: does $apath_G(s,t)$ hold?

It is not hard to see that this version of the alternating graph accessibility problem remains P-complete.

Lemma 2. AsAGAP *is P-complete under $\leq_m^{\log}$-reductions.*

Sketch of Proof. AsAGAP is in P, since it is a special case of AGAP, that is known to be in P, and since instances $\langle G,s,t \rangle$ where G is not a slice graph or $s \notin V_1 \cap V_\exists$ or $t \notin V_m \cap V_\forall$ can easily be identified.

In order to show P-hardness of AsAGAP, it suffices to find a reduction AGAP $\leq_m^{\log}$ AsAGAP. For an instance $\langle G,s,t \rangle$ of AGAP where G has n nodes it is straightforward to construct an instance $\langle G_n, s', t' \rangle$ of AsAGAP using the considerations from above. If $\langle G_n, s', t' \rangle \in$ AsAGAP, then there exists a tree being a subgraph of G_n, that witnesses this fact. This tree can directly be transformed to a witness for $\langle G,s,t \rangle \in$ AGAP. If $\langle G,s,t \rangle \in$ AGAP, this is also be witnessed by a (finite) tree T that can be seen to consist of copies of nodes and edges of G. This tree can be trimmed in a way that on every path from the root to a leaf, every node appears at most once. Hence T induces a tree that witnesses $\langle G_n, s', t' \rangle \in$ AsAGAP. □

3   Lower Bounds

We now give hardness results for the model checking problem. The P-hardness proofs use logspace reductions from the P-hard problem AsAGAP (Lemma 2). The slice graph is transformed to a frame to be used in an instance of the model checking problem. Since the semantics of the logics under consideration are defined by Kripke models with frames that are transitive (and reflexive), we need to produce frames that are transitive (and reflexive). The straightforward way would be to take the transitive closure of a slice graph. But we cannot compute the transitive closure of a directed graph in logspace. Fortunately, slice graphs can easily be made transitive by adding all edges that "jump" from a node to a node that is at least two slices higher. Clearly, the resulting graph is not anymore a slice graph, but it is a transitive supergraph of the transitive closure of the slice graph. We then will use the valuation function in order to let us rediscover in which slice a state is.

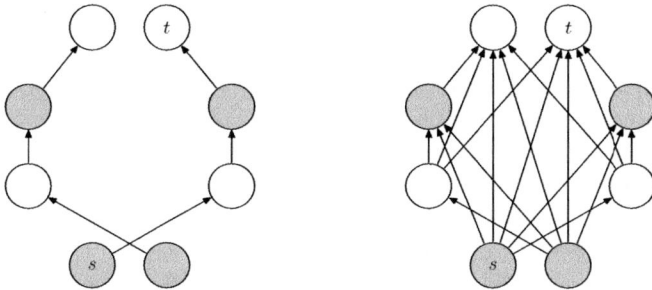

Fig. 3. A slice graph and its pseudo-transitive closure

Definition 1. Let $V_{\geq i} := \bigcup_{j=i,i+1,\ldots,m} V_j$, and $V_{\leq i} := \bigcup_{j=1,2,\ldots,i} V_j$. The pseudo-transitive closure of a slice graph $G = (V, E)$ with $V = V_1 \cup \ldots \cup V_m$ is the graph $G' = (V, E')$ where

$$E' \quad := \quad E \ \cup \ \bigcup_{i=1,2,\ldots,m-2} V_i \times V_{\geq i+2} \ .$$

The reflexive and pseudo-transitive closure of G is the graph $G'' = (V, E'')$ where

$$E'' \quad := \quad E' \ \cup \ V \times V.$$

An example for a slice graph and its pseudo-transitive closure is shown in Figure 3.

Theorem 2. KC-MC — *i.e. the model checking problem for* KC — *is* P-*hard.*

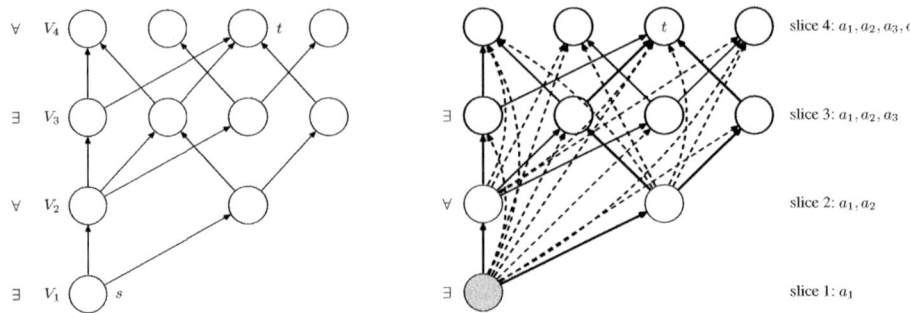

Fig. 4. A slice graph G, and the model $\mathcal{M}_G$ as constructed in the proof of Theorem 2. Pseudo-transitive edges are drawn dashed, and reflexive edges are not drawn for simplicity.

Sketch of Proof. We show ASAGAP $\leq_m^{\log}$ KC-MC. The P-hardness of KC-MC then follows from Lemma 2.

For simplicity, we informally sketch the ideas for the reduction ASAGAP $\leq_m^{\log}$ IPC-MC. Given an ASAGAP instance $\langle G, s, t \rangle$ where G has m slices, let (U, R) be its reflexive and pseudo-transitive closure. The valuation function ξ is defined for variables $t, a_1, \ldots, a_m$ as follows. t holds exactly in the state t of the graph ($\xi(t) = \{t\}$), and the variables $a_1, \ldots, a_i$ hold in slice i (for $i = 1, 2, \ldots, m$) ($\xi(a_i) = V_{\geq i}$) This yields the Kripke model $\mathcal{M}_G = (U, R, \xi)$. Figure 4 shows a slice graph G with $m = 4$ slices and Kripke model $\mathcal{M}_G = (U, R, \xi)$ that is transformed from it. The fat lines indicate that $apath_G(s, t)$ holds. The graph (U, R) is the reflexive and pseudo-transitive closure of G. The blue lines in Figure 4 are the pseudo-transitive edges, the reflexive edges are not depicted. The valuation function ξ is defined so that variable t holds exactly in the state t of the graph, and additionally the variables $a_1, \ldots, a_i$ hold in slice i (for $i = 1, 2, \ldots, m$).

The formulas $\psi_1, \ldots, \psi_m, \psi_{m+1}$ are inductively defined as follows.

1. $\psi_{m+1} := t$, and
2. $\psi_j := \psi_{j+1} \rightarrow a_{j+1}$ for all $j = m, m-1, \ldots, 1$.

Notice that $\psi_i = (\cdots((t \rightarrow a_{m+1}) \rightarrow a_m) \rightarrow \cdots \rightarrow a_{i+2}) \rightarrow a_{i+1}$. Therefore, ψ_i is satisfied in all slices where a_{i+1} is satisfied, i.e. the slices $V_{\geq i+1}$. In slice V_i, ψ_i and ψ_{i+1} behave like the mutual complement. Say that a state v is *good*, if $apath_G(v, t)$ holds, and otherwise it is *bad*. It turns out, that the good and the bad states can be distuinguished using the formulas ψ_i as follows.

Claim. For all $i = 1, 2, \ldots, m$ and all $w \in V_i$ holds:

1. if i is odd: $apath_G(w, t)$ iff $\mathcal{M}_G, w \not\models_I \psi_{i+1}$, and
2. if i is even: $apath_G(w, t)$ iff $\mathcal{M}_G, w \not\models_I \psi_i$.

For our example, this means the following.

slice(s):	in every good state holds:	in every bad state holds:
4,3:	$\not\models_I t \to a_5$	$\models_I t \to a_5$
3,2:	$\models_I (t \to a_5) \to a_4$	$\not\models_I (t \to a_5) \to a_4$
2,1:	$\not\models_I ((t \to a_5) \to a_4) \to a_3$	$\models_I ((t \to a_5) \to a_4) \to a_3$
1:	$\models_I (((t \to a_5) \to a_4) \to a_3) \to a_2$	$\not\models_I \ldots$

Since $\langle G, s, t \rangle \in \text{AsAgap}$ iff s is a good state, it now follows that $\langle G, s, t \rangle \in \text{AsAgap}$ if and only if $\mathcal{M}_G, s \models_I \psi_1$, i.e. $\langle \psi_1, \mathcal{M}_G, s \rangle \in \text{IPC-Mc}$. By the simplicity of the construction it follows that $\text{AsAgap} \leq_m^{\log} \text{IPC-Mc}$.

In order to make this reduction work for KC-Mc, we add an additional *top-state*, to which every state is related and in which every variable is satisfied.   □

It follows immediately from Lemma 1 that the model checking problem for S4.2—the modal companion of KC—is P-hard, too. In fact, we can improve the result and obtain P-hardness for the model checking problem for $S4_1$—i.e. the fragment of S4 with formulas with one variable only. This result is optimal in the sense that the model checking problem for $S4_0$ is easy to solve. A formula without any variables is either satisfied by every model w.r.t. S4, or it is satisfied by no model. This is because $\Diamond\top$ (resp. $\Box\top$) is satisfied by every state in every model, and $\Diamond\bot$ (resp. $\Box\bot$) is satisfied by no state in every model. Essentially, the modal operators can be ingnored and the remaining formula can be evaluated like a classical propositional formula—this problem is in NC^1 [5].

Theorem 3. $S4.2_1$-Mc *is* P-*hard—i.e. the model checking problem for* S4.2 *is* P-*hard, even if we consider modal formulas with one variable only.*

Sketch of Proof. We show that $\text{AsAgap} \leq_m^{\log} S4.2_1$-Mc. Since AsAgap is P-hard (Lemma 2), the P-hardness of $S4.2_1$-Mc follows. For space reasons, we informally sketch the ideas for the reduction $\text{AsAgap} \leq_m^{\log} S4.2_1$-Mc below.

Let $\langle G, s, t \rangle$ be an instance of AsAgap with a slice graph G with m slices (m even). First, we define the valuation function so that a holds in all nodes in all even slices. In order to be able to distinguish the goal node t from the other nodes, t gets a successor t', and t' is the only node in the new $m + 1$st slice. Finally, we add a slice V_{m+2} with some nodes between which we also have edges. For all nodes in the other slices we add edges to all nodes in V_{m+2}. By the choice of edges in V_{m+2} there is now a node h that is the top node of this construction. We chose the valuation ξ for the nodes in V_{m+2} in a way that a certain formula γ' is satisfied in all states in V_{m+2}, and in all other states it is not satisfied. For the remaining slices $V_1, \ldots, V_{m+1}$ it holds that $V_i \subseteq \xi(a)$ iff i is odd. Using this alternation of slices that satisfy a and that satisfy $\neg a$, we can estimate the slice to which a state belongs as follows using the inductively defined formulas δ_i (for $i = 1, 2, \ldots, m$).

1. $\delta_m := \Diamond(a \land \neg\gamma')$
2. for odd i, $1 \leq i < m$: $\delta_i := \Diamond(\neg a \land \delta_{i+1})$
   for even i, $1 \leq i < m$: $\delta_i := \Diamond(a \land \delta_{i+1})$

For $x \in V_{\leq m}$ we now have that $\mathcal{M}_G, x \models_M \delta_i$ iff $x \in V_{\leq i}$.

The goal state t is the only state in V_m that satisfies $a \wedge \Diamond(\neg a \wedge \gamma')$. Using the δ_i formulas to verify an upper bound for the slice of a state, we can now simulate the alternating graph accessibility problem by the following formulas.

1. $\lambda_m := a \wedge \Diamond(\neg a \wedge \neg \gamma')$
2. for odd $i < m$: $\lambda_i := \neg a \wedge \Diamond(\delta_{i+1} \wedge \lambda_{i+1})$
   for even $i < m$: $\lambda_i := a \wedge \Box(\delta_{i+1} \rightarrow \lambda_{i+1})$

It follows that $\langle G, s, t \rangle \in \text{ASAGAP}$ iff $\mathcal{M}_G, s \models_M \lambda_1$, i.e. $\langle \lambda_1, \mathcal{M}_G, s \rangle \in \text{S4.2}_1\text{-MC}$. Since the construction of $\mathcal{M}_G$ and λ_1 from G can be computed in logarithmic space, it follows that $\text{ASAGAP} \leq^{\log}_m \text{S4.2}_1\text{-MC}$.   □

The reduction in the proof of Theorem 3 is not suitable for intuitionistic logics, since the constructed Kripke model lacks the monotonicity property of the variables. Moreover, in that proof we make extensive use of negation, that would have a very different meaning in intuitionistic logics.

In Theorem 4 we show P-hardness of the model checking problem for the modal logic K4, even if we consider formulas without any variables.

Theorem 4. $\text{K4}_0\text{-MC}$ *is P-hard.*

Sketch of Proof. The P-hardness of the model checking problem for the modal logic K4_0 can easily be obtained using the P-hardness of ASAGAP from Lemma 2. The reduction from ASAGAP to K4-MC works as follows. Let $\langle G, s, t \rangle$ be an instance of ASAGAP where G is a slice graph with m slices. Define $\mathcal{M}_G = (U, R, \xi)$ as follows.

– (U, R') is the pseudo-transitive closure of G.
– $R := R' \cup \{(v, v) \mid$ *for every vertex* $v \neq t$ *in the top slice* V_m *of* $G\}$.

Informally spoken, the model $\mathcal{M}_G$ is the pseudo-transitive closure of G and every state in the last slice except the state t has an edge to itself. We define φ_G as follows.

– $\alpha_i := \Diamond \ldots \Diamond \Box \bot$ with $m - i$ $\Diamond$s for $i \in \{2, \ldots, m - 1\}$.
– $\varphi_{m-1} := \Diamond \Box \bot$
   for odd i, $m - 1 > i \geq 1$: $\varphi_i := \Diamond(\alpha_{i+1} \wedge \varphi_{i+1})$
   for even i, $m > i > 1$: $\varphi_i := \Box(\alpha_{i+1} \rightarrow \varphi_{i+1})$
– $\varphi_G := \varphi_1$

Notice that $\Box \bot$ is satisfied only in t because t is the only state without any successor. The subformula α_i is satisfied in state w, if there is a path in G from w to t with $m - i$ vertices. For this reason $\mathcal{M}, w \models_M \alpha_i$ implies $w \in V_{\leq i}$. With a straightforward induction it can be shown that for all $w \in V_{\leq i}$ holds: $\mathcal{M}_G, w \models_M \varphi_i$ iff $apath_G(w, t)$. Hence it follows that $\langle G, s, t \rangle \in \text{ASAGAP}$ iff $\mathcal{M}_G, s \models_M \varphi_G$.   □

4   Upper Bounds

We give upper bounds for the complexity of the model checking problem for the logics under consideration. For S4, the model checking problem is in P [3]. By the properties of the Gödel-Tarski embedding of IPC into S4 (Lemma 1), the same upper bound follows immediately for IPC. The same holds for the more common fragments BPL and K4.

Theorem 5. *[3] The model checking problem for K4 and for BPL is in* P.

Consequently, the model checking problems for the superintuitionistic logics and their modal companions can also be solved in polynomial time. We now consider logics for which this goes even better.

Theorem 6. *The model checking problem for LC is in* LOGDCFL.

Proof. The idea is as follows. Let $\mathcal{M} = (U, \leqslant, \xi)$ be an LC-model. This means that ξ is monotone and $(U, \leqslant)$ is a total preorder. For simplicity of notation we assume that $U = \{1, 2, \ldots, n\}$ and $\leqslant$ orders these states in the intuitive way, namely $1 \leqslant 2 \leqslant 3 \leqslant \ldots \leqslant n$. Because of the monotonicity of intuitionistic logic, for every formula α there exists an $i_\alpha \in \{1, 2, \ldots, n, n+1\}$ such that α is not satisfied in states $1, 2, \ldots, i_\alpha - 1$ and α is satisfied in states $i_\alpha, i_\alpha + 1, \ldots, n$. If $i_\alpha = n + 1$, then α is not satisfied in states $1, 2, \ldots, n$. We define a function g that maps formulas to this value. This function can inductively be defined as follows.

(1) $g(\bot) = n + 1$

(2) for atoms $\alpha = a$: $\quad g(a) = \min\left(\{i \mid i \in \xi(a)\} \cup \{n+1\}\right)$

(3) for $\alpha = \beta \wedge \gamma$: $\quad g(\beta \wedge \gamma) = \max(g(\beta), g(\gamma))$

(4) for $\alpha = \beta \vee \gamma$: $\quad g(\beta \vee \gamma) = \min(g(\beta), g(\gamma))$

(5) for $\alpha = \beta \rightarrow \gamma$: $\quad g(\beta \rightarrow \gamma) = \begin{cases} g(\gamma), & \text{if } g(\beta) < g(\gamma) \\ 1, & \text{otherwise} \end{cases}$

In order to decide $\mathcal{M}, 1 \models_I \alpha$ we calculate $g(\alpha)$ and decide whether this value equals 1. The calculation of $g(\alpha)$ can be done by a depth first search through the formula that we consider here as a tree. The "leaves" of this tree are variables resp. $\bot$. The g-values of these leaves can easily be computed in logarithmic space by inspecting the valuation function ξ. Every internal node of this tree represents a subformula of α. The g-value of each of these nodes can be computed using the g-values of its sons as described by the inductive definition of g above. Altogether, this search can be performed deterministically in polynomial time within logarithmic space and an additional stack. This shows that the model checking problem for LC is in LOGDCFL. □

The model checking problem for KC_1 can be reduced to that of LC_1, and by Theorem 6 it also has LOGDCFL as upper bound. The reduction relies on algebraic properties of KC_1 according to [14,15] and is left out here for space reasons.

Theorem 7. *The model checking problem for* KC_1 *is in* LOGDCFL.

We obtain the same upper bound for S5-MC.

Proposition 1. *The model checking problem for* S5 *is in* LOGDCFL.

Sketch of Proof. Let $\langle \varphi, \mathcal{M}, s \rangle$ be an instance of S5-MC for $\mathcal{M} = (U, R, \xi)$. Then R is a total relation on U. Therefore, every subformula of φ that begins with a modal operator (i.e. a subformula of the form $\Box \alpha$ or $\Diamond \alpha$) is either satisfied in all states of U or in no state of U. Now, φ can be evaluated as follows. First, evaluate the subformulas $\Box \alpha$ and $\Diamond \alpha$, where α is a propositional formula without any modal operators. In order to do this, check whether α is satisfied in every resp. in one state of U. This can be done in logspace. Replace these evaluated subformulas in φ by the propositional constants according to their satisfaction and evaluate the resulting formula. This must be repeated until one obtained a propositional formula that can straightforwardly be evaluated in the actual state.

This process can be implemented using a top down search through the formula, during which propositional formulas have to be evaluated in the states of U. The whole process then takes polynomial time, logarithmic space, and uses a stack for the top down search. This shows that S5-MC can be solved in LOGDCFL. □

In Theorem 8 we show NC^1-completeness of the model checking problem for the modal logic S4, even if we consider formulas without any variables. We sketch a proof for the upperbound. The NC^1-hardness follows immediately from [5].

Theorem 8. *The model checking problem for* $S4_0$ *is* NC^1*-complete.*

Sketch of Proof. Notice that the S4 frames are reflexive and transitive. It is not possible to distinguish differents states in a reflexive and transitive frame with a variable free formula. Hence $S4_0$ contains exactly all variable free formulas that can be satisfied by a reflexive and transitive Kripke model. For an $S4_0$-MC instance $\langle \mathcal{M}, \varphi \rangle$ it suffices to check whether $\varphi \in S4_0$. Because we can not distinguish differents states, modal operators can be ignored. We define the operator free version φ_{of} of the $S4_0$ formula φ as follows.

$-\ p_{of} = p$ for $p \in \{\bot, \top\}$
$-\ (\alpha \rightarrow \beta)_{of} = \alpha_{of} \rightarrow \beta_{of}$
$-\ (\Diamond \alpha)_{of} = \alpha_{of}$

It holds for an arbitrary $\mathcal{M}$ that $\langle \mathcal{M}, \varphi \rangle \in S4_0$-MC iff φ_{of} evaluates to true. Hence from [5] follows directly that $S4_0$-MC is NC^1-complete. □

5   Conclusion

The upper and lower bounds from the last sections (Theorems 2, 3, 4, and 5) combine to the following completeness results.

Theorem 9. *The following problems are P-complete.*

1. $K4_0$-MC—*i.e. the model checking problems for K4 and formulas without variables.*
2. $K4_1$-MC, $S4_1$-MC, $S4.2_1$-MC—*i.e. the model checking problems for K4, S4 resp. S4.2 and formulas with one variable only.*
3. KC-MC, IPC-MC, BPL-MC, S4.2-MC, S4-MC, K4-MC—*i.e. the model checking problems for KC, IPC, BPL, S4.2, S4, and K4.*

The one variable fragment IPC_1 of IPC is already deeply studied (see [16]). Recently it was shown that model checking for IPC_1 is AC^1-complete [10]. Our P-hardness proof of model checking for IPC uses an arbitrary number of variables. Rybakov [17] has shown that the tautology problem for the two variable fragment IPC_2 of IPC is already PSPACE-complete. This indicates that it is interesting to study whether model checking for IPC_2 is already P-complete.

O'Connor [18] gives a tautology-preserving translation from IPC formulas to those with two variables only. It is an open problem, whether such a translation to IPC_1 exists. From Theorem 2 and Proposition 7 follows, that we can exclude this for model checking for KC.

Theorem 10. KC-MC $\not\leq_m^{\log}$ KC_1-MC, *unless* P $\subseteq$ LOGDCFL.

The Gödel-Tarski translation from intuitionistic logic into S4 and the PSPACE-hardness of the tautology problem for IPC brought up the question for a "translation" from S4 into intuitionistic logic. In fact, this translation is expressed in terms of a reduction in [19]. Our results on the P-hardness of the model checking problem for S4.2 for formulas with one variable only (Theorem 3) and the contrasting LOGDCFL upper bound for KC_1 (Proposition 7) shows that those translations cannot omit the use of additional variables (unless P $\subseteq$ LOGDCFL).

Theorem 11. $S4.2_1$-MC $\not\leq_m^{\log}$ KC_1-MC, *unless* P $\subseteq$ LOGDCFL.

At all, the LOGDCFL upper bounds for the model checking for LC, KC_1, and S5 are not really satisfactory. A LOGDCFL computation (polynomial time and logarithmic space with an additional stack) allows to explore a formula in a top down manner. This seems to be a very natural way to evaluate a formula. It is very surprising, that for classical propositional logic the stack is not needed [4,5]. We conjecture that this is also possible for S5, and Proposition 1 could accordingly be improved. For KC_1, one can conclude from [14,15] that there are only 7 equivalence classes of formulas, and only 3 types of models–all states of the model satisfy a, no state satisfies a, resp. all others. The third type is the type that makes the difference to classical propositional logic. Nevertheless, we expect that the LOGDCFL upper bound for KC_1 (Proposition 7) can be improved.

Notice that the logics KC_1 and LC_1 are the same. In [15] it is shown that $S4.3_1$—their modal companion—has infinitely many equivalence classes of formulas. Therefore it seems possible to find a lower bound for model checking for $S4.3_1$ that is above the upper bound for KC_1 and LC_1.

Acknowledgements. The authors thank Steve Awodey for his introduction to intuitionistic logic and many helpful discussions, Matthias Kramer for discussing predecessors of the proofs of Theorems 2 and 6, Vitezslav Svejdar for helpful discussions about intuitionistic logic, and Thomas Schneider for his support. The authors specially thank an anonymous referee for her/his idea to improve Theorem 3 by saving one variable.

References

1. van Dalen, D.: Logic and Structure, 4th edn. Springer, Heidelberg (2004)
2. Chagrov, A., Zakharyaschev, M.: Modal Logic. Clarendon Press, Oxford (1997)
3. Fischer, M.J., Ladner, R.E.: Propositional dynamic logic of regular programs. J. Comput. Syst. Sci. 18(2), 194–211 (1979)
4. Lynch, N.A.: Log space recognition and translation of parenthesis languages. J. ACM 24(4), 583–590 (1977)
5. Buss, S.R.: The Boolean formula value problem is in ALOGTIME. In: Proc. 19th STOC, pp. 123–131. ACM Press, New York (1987)
6. Dummett, M., Lemmon, E.: Modal logics between S4 and S5. Zeitschrift für Mathematische Logik und Grundlagen der Mathematik 14(24), 250–264 (1959)
7. Visser, A.: A propositional logic with explicit fixed points. Studia Logica 40, 155–175 (1980)
8. Ladner, R.: The computational complexity of provability in systems of modal propositional logic. SIAM Journal on Computing 6(3), 467–480 (1977)
9. Spaan, E.: Complexity of Modal Logics. PhD thesis, Department of Mathematics and Computer Science. University of Amsterdam (1993)
10. Mundhenk, M., Weiß, F.: The model checking problem for intuitionistic logic with one variable is AC^1-complete (2010) (unpublished manuscript)
11. Chandra, A.K., Kozen, D., Stockmeyer, L.J.: Alternation. Journal of the Association for Computing Machinery 28, 114–133 (1981)
12. Greenlaw, R., Hoover, H.J., Ruzzo, W.L.: Limits to Parallel Computation: P-Completeness Theory. Oxford University Press, New York (1995)
13. Papadimitriou, C.H.: Computational Complexity. Addison-Wesley, Reading (1994)
14. Nishimura, I.: On formulas of one variable in intuitionistic propositional calculus. J. of Symbolic Logic 25, 327–331 (1960)
15. Makinson, D.: There are infinitely many Diodorean modal functions. J. of Symbolic Logic 31(3), 406–408 (1966)
16. Gabbay, D.M.: Semantical investigations in Heyting's intuitionistic logic. D.Reidel, Dordrecht (1981)
17. Rybakov, M.N.: Complexity of intuitionistic and Visser's basic and formal logics in finitely many variables. In: Papers from the 6th conference on "Advances in Modal Logic", pp. 393–411. College Publications (2006)
18. O'Connor, M.: Embeddings into free Heyting algebras and translations into intuitionistic propositional logic. In: Artemov, S., Nerode, A. (eds.) LFCS 2007. LNCS, vol. 4514, pp. 437–448. Springer, Heidelberg (2007)
19. Fernandez, D.: A polynomial translation of S4 into intuitionistic logic. J. of Symbolic Logic 71(3), 989–1001 (2005)

Depth Boundedness in Multiset Rewriting Systems with Name Binding*

Fernando Rosa-Velardo

Dpto. de Sistemas Informáticos y Computación
Universidad Complutense de Madrid
fernandorosa@sip.ucm.es

Abstract. In this paper we consider ν-MSR, a formalism that combines the two main existing approaches for multiset rewriting, namely MSR and CMRS. In ν-MSR we rewrite multisets of atomic formulae, in which some names may be restricted. ν-MSR are Turing complete. In particular, a very straightforward encoding of π-calculus process can be done. Moreover, $p\nu$-PN, an extension of Petri nets in which tokens are tuples of pure names, are equivalent to ν-MSR. We know that the monadic subclass of ν-MSR is a Well Structured Transition System. Here we prove that depth-bounded ν-MSR, that is, ν-MSR systems for which the interdependance of names is bounded, are also Well Structured, by following the analogous steps to those followed by R. Meyer in the case of π-calculus. As a corollary, also depth-bounded $p\nu$-PN are WSTS, so that coverability is decidable for them.

1   Introduction

In [16] we revised multiset rewriting with name binding, by combining the two main existing approaches to the study of concurrency by means of multiset rewriting: multiset rewriting with existential quantification and constrained multiset rewriting. The paper [6] presents a meta-notation for the specification and analysis of security protocols. This meta-notation involves facts and transitions, where facts are first-order atomic formulae and transitions are given by means of rewriting rules, with a precondition and a postcondition. For instance, $A_0(k), Ann(k') \rightarrow \exists x.(A_1(k, x), N(enc(k', \langle x, k \rangle)), Ann(k'))$ specifies the first rule of the Needham-Schroeder protocol. This notation gave rise to the specification language for security protocols MSR [5].

In [8] *Constraint Multiset Rewriting Systems* (CMRS) are defined. As in [6], facts are first-order atomic formulae, but the terms that can appear as part of such formulae must belong to a *constraint system*. For instance, the rule $count(x), visit \rightarrow count(x + 1), enter(x + 1)$ could be used to count the number of visits to a web site. For a comprehensive survey of CMRS see [9]. In CMRS, there is no mechanism for name binding or name creation, so that it has to be

---

* Research supported by the MEC Spanish project DESAFIOS10 TIN2009-14599-C03-01, and Comunidad de Madrid program PROMETIDOS S2009/TIC-1465.

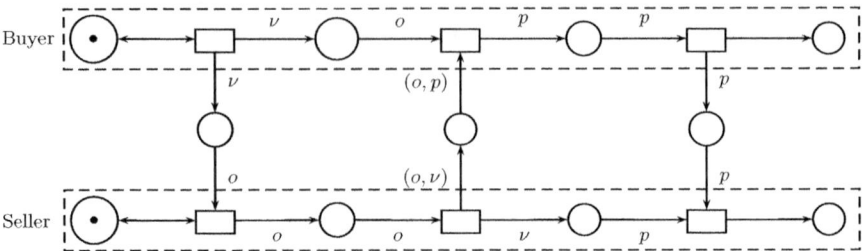

Fig. 1. Interconnection model between a buyer and a seller

simulated using the order in the constraint system (e.g., simulating the creation of a fresh name by taking a value greater than any of the values appeared so far). Thus, in an unordered version of CMRS, in which only the equality predicate between atoms is used, there is no way of ensuring that a name is fresh.

In [16] we combined the features in MSR and CMRS, obtaining ν-MSR. On the one hand, we maintain the existential quantifications in [6] to keep a compositional approach, closer to that followed in process algebrae with name binding. On the other hand, we restrict terms in atomic formulae to be pure names, that can only be compared with equality or inequality, unlike the arbitrary terms over some syntax, as in [6], or terms in a constraint system, as in CMRS.

We know [16] that ν-MSR is equivalent to $p\nu$-PN [18], an extension of Petri nets in which tokens are tuples of pure names, that can only be compared with each other by equality or inequality by using matching variables in the arcs of the net. $p\nu$-PN are Turing complete [18], so that so are ν-MSR. Moreover, the subclass of monadic ν-MSR is equivalent to ν-PN [17], the monadic version of $p\nu$-PN, for which tokens are just pure names. In [19] we proved that ν-PN are strictly Well Structured Transition Systems (WSTS) [10,2], which allows us to conclude that so are monadic ν-MSR, and coverability, boundedness and termination are decidable for them. However, reachability is still undecidable for ν-PN [19]. Finally, processes of the π-calculus [20] can be simulated within ν-MSR in a very natural way. This translation was inspired by the results about *structural stationary* π-calculus processes [14], that can be mapped to P/T nets.

Though ν-PN have better decidability properties than $p\nu$-PN, some works need to use the model of $p\nu$-PN to model things like instance isolation in architectures with multiple concurrent conversations [7] or transactions in data bases [21]. The example in Fig. 1 is taken from [7]. The subnet inside the dashed line in the top represents buyer processes, and the subnet inside the dashed line in the bottom represents seller processes. The places outside the dashed lines are *interface* processes used for communication purposes.

Thus, it is interesting to find subclasses of $p\nu$-PN in which some interesting properties are decidable. In the field of process algebra, there are many recent works that look for subclasses of the π-calculus for which some properties, such as termination, are decidable [4,14,13,15,3]. In this paper we will consider the results in [13] about depth-bounded π-calculus processes. Depth-boundedness is a semantic restriction on π-calculus processes. Intuitively, a process is depth-bounded whenever the interdependance of names is bounded in any process reachable from it. As a simple example, and assuming that the reader is familiar with the following π-calculus syntax, if starting from some process P the processes $\nu a_1. \ldots . a_n.(a_1\langle a_2\rangle \mid a_2\langle a_3\rangle \mid \cdots \mid a_i\langle a_{i+1}\rangle \mid \cdots \mid a_{n-1}\langle a_n\rangle) \mid Q_n$ are reachable for every $n > 0$, then P is a depth-unbounded process. However, the fact that processes $\nu a.a_1. \ldots . a_n.(a\langle a_1\rangle \mid a\langle a_2\rangle \mid \cdots \mid a\langle a_i\rangle \mid \cdots \mid a\langle a_n\rangle) \mid Q_n$ can be reached from P for every n does not allow us to conclude that P is depth-unbounded, since though an unbounded number of names can appear in reachable processes, those names do not depend one another, as happened in the previous example. Meyer proved in [13] that depth-bounded processes are WSTS. In this paper we adapt those results to ν-MSR. More precisely, we will consider depth-bounded ν-MSR, that is, ν-MSR for which the interdependance of bound names is bounded in every reachable term. We will prove that this subclass of ν-MSR is well structured by following the same steps followed in [13]. As a corollary, we obtain the analogous result not only for the π-calculus (which is already known) but also for $p\nu$-PN.

The rest of the paper is organized as follows. In Section 2 we introduce some basic definitions and notations we will use in the rest of the paper. Section 3 defines ν-MSR. Section 4 contains our main results: well structuredness of depth-bounded ν-MSR, which implies decidability of coverability for $p\nu$-PN. Finally, Section 5 presents our conclusions and some directions for future work.

2   Preliminaries

We denote by $\mathcal{MS}(A)$ the set of finite multisets over A. A quasi order in A is a reflexive and transitive binary relation on A. Every quasi order $\leq$ defined in A induces a quasi order $\sqsubseteq$ in $\mathcal{MS}(A)$, given by $\{a_1, \ldots, a_n\} \sqsubseteq \{b_1, \ldots, b_m\}$ if there is some $h : \{1, \ldots, n\} \to \{1, \ldots, m\}$ injective st $a_i \leq b_{h(i)}$ for all $i \in \{1, \ldots, n\}$. A quasi order $\leq$ is said to be a well-quasi order (wqo) if for every infinite sequence $s_0, s_1, \ldots$ there are i and j, with $i < j$, st $s_i \leq s_j$. Equivalently, it is a wqo if every infinite sequence has an increasing subsequence. It is a well known fact that the multiset order $\sqsubseteq$ induced by a wqo $\leq$ is also a wqo.

The set $\mathcal{T}(A)$ of trees over $(A, \leq)$ is defined by

$$T ::= a \mid (a, \{T_1, \ldots, T_n\})$$

where a ranges over A. We define the order $\preceq$ relating trees by $a \preceq a'$ if $a \leq a'$, and $(a, \mathcal{A}) \preceq (a', \mathcal{A}')$ if $a \leq a'$ and $\mathcal{A} \sqsubseteq \mathcal{A}'$, where $\sqsubseteq$ is the multiset order induced by $\preceq$. The mapping $height(T)$ is defined as $height(a) = 0$ and $height(a, \{T_1, \ldots, T_n\}) = 1 + max\{height(T_i) \mid i = 1, \ldots, n\}$. If we denote by $\mathcal{T}(A)_n$ the set of trees of height less or equal than n, then $(\mathcal{T}(A)_n, \preceq)$ is a wqo provided $(A, \leq)$ is a wqo.

A hypergraph is a tuple $\mathcal{G} = (V, E, inc)$, where V is the set of vertices, E is the set of edges and for each $e \in E$, $inc(e)$ is the set of vertices that incide in e. There is an arc between $v \in V$ and $e \in E$ whenever $v \in inc(e)$.

A transition system is a tuple $(S, \rightarrow, s_0)$, where S is a (possibly infinite) set of states, $s_0 \in S$ is the initial state and $\rightarrow \subseteq S \times S$. We denote by $\rightarrow^*$ the reflexive and transitive closure of $\rightarrow$. The reachability problem in a transition system consists in deciding for a given states s_f whether $s_0 \rightarrow^* s_f$. The termination problem consists in deciding whether there is an infinite trace $s_0 \rightarrow s_1 \rightarrow s_2 \rightarrow \cdots$. The boundedness problem consists in deciding whether the set of reachable states is finite. For any transition system $(S, \rightarrow, s_0)$ endowed with a quasi order $\leq$ we can define the coverability problem, that consists in deciding, given a state s_f, whether there is $s \in S$ reachable st $s_f \leq s$.

A Well Structured Transition System (WSTS) is a tuple $(S, \rightarrow, \leq)$, where $(S, \rightarrow)$ is a transition system, $\leq$ is a decidable wqo compatible[1] with $\rightarrow$ (meaning that $s_1' \geq s_1 \rightarrow s_2$ implies that there is $s_2' \geq s_2$ with $s_1' \rightarrow s_2'$), and so that for every s we can compute (a finite representation of) the set $\{s' \mid s' \rightarrow s'' \geq s\}$. We will refer to these properties as monotonicity of $\rightarrow$ with respect to $\leq$, and computability of the set of predecessors, respectively.[2] For WSTS, the coverability and the termination problem are decidable [2,10]. A WSTS is said to be strict if it satisfies the following strict compatibility condition: $s_1' > s_1 \rightarrow s_2$ implies that there is $s_2' > s_2$ with $s_1' \rightarrow s_2'$. For strict WSTS, also the boundedness problem is decidable [10].

3 ν-MSR

We fix a finite set of predicate symbols $\mathcal{P}$, a denumerable set Id of names and a denumerable set Var of variables. We use $a, b, c, \ldots$ to range over Id, $x, y, \ldots$ to range over Var, and $\eta, \eta' \ldots$ to range over $Id \cup Var$.

An atomic formula over $\mathcal{P}$ and Var has the form $p(\eta_1, \ldots, \eta_n)$, where $p \in \mathcal{P}$ and $\eta_i \in Var \cup Id$ for all i. A ground atomic formula has the form $p(a_1, \ldots, a_n)$, where $p \in \mathcal{P}$ and $a_i \in Id$ for all i. We use $X, Y, \ldots$ to range over atomic formulae and $A, B, \ldots$ to range over atomic ground formulae. We denote by $Var(X)$ and $Id(X)$ the set of variables and names appearing in X, respectively. We will write $\tilde{x}$ and $\tilde{a}$ to denote finite sequences of variables and names, respectively, so that we will sometimes write $p(\tilde{x})$ or $p(\tilde{a})$. We sometimes use set notation with these sequences and write, for instance, $x \in \tilde{x}$ or $\tilde{x}_1 \cup \tilde{x}_2$. A ν-MSR term is given by the following grammar:

$$M ::= \mathbf{0} \mid A \mid M_1 + M_2 \mid \nu a.M$$

We denote $\mathcal{M}$ the set of ν-MSR terms, ranged over by $M, M' \ldots$ We define $fn(M)$ the set of free names in M as follows: $fn(\mathbf{0}) = \emptyset$, $fn(A) = Id(A)$, $fn(M_1 + M_2) = fn(M_1) \cup fn(M_2)$, and $fn(\nu a.M) = fn(M) \setminus \{a\}$. A rule t is an expression of the form

$$t : X_1 + \ldots + X_n \rightarrow \nu\tilde{a}.(Y_1 + \ldots + Y_m)$$

---

[1] Different compatibility conditions are discussed in [10].

[2] Strictly speaking, decidability of the wqo and computability of the set of predecessors, are not part of the definition of WSTS, but of the so called *effective* WSTS. These properties are needed to ensure decidability of coverability and termination.

st $post(t) \subseteq pre(t)$, where $pre(t) = \bigcup_{i=1}^{n} Var(X_i)$, $post(t) = \bigcup_{j=1}^{m} Var(Y_m)$, and $Var(t) = pre(t) \cup post(t)$. A ν-MSR is a pair $\langle \mathcal{R}, M_0 \rangle$, where M_0 is the initial ν-MSR term and $\mathcal{R}$ is a finite set of rules.

Sometimes in examples, we will use commas instead of the symbol $+$. For instance, we will write $p(x,y), q(y,y) \rightarrow \nu a.q(x,a)$ instead of $p(x,y) + q(y,y) \rightarrow \nu a.q(x,a)$. We will identify ν-MSR terms up to $\equiv$, the least congruence on $\mathcal{M}$ where α-conversion of bound names is allowed, st $(\mathcal{M}, +, \mathbf{0})$ is a commutative monoid and:

$$\nu a.\nu b.M \equiv \nu b.\nu a.M \qquad \nu a.\mathbf{0} \equiv \mathbf{0}$$

$$\nu a.(M_1 + M_2) \equiv \nu a.M_1 + M_2 \quad if \quad a \notin fn(M_2)$$

The first rule justifies our notation $\nu \tilde{a}.M$. The last rule is called name extrusion when applied from right to left. A mode for $t : X_1 + \ldots + X_n \rightarrow \nu \tilde{a}.(Y_1 + \ldots + Y_m)$ is any substitution $\sigma : Var(t) \rightarrow Id$. We write $pre_t(\sigma) = \sigma(X_1) + \ldots + \sigma(X_n)$, where $\sigma(p(\eta_1, \ldots, \eta_n)) = p(a_1, \ldots, a_n)$, with $a_i = \sigma(x_i)$ if $\eta_i \in Var$, or $a_i = \eta_i$ if $\eta_i \in Id$. To define $post_t(\sigma)$ we consider a sequence of pairwise different names $\tilde{b}$ (of the same length as $\tilde{a}$) with $\sigma(Var(t)) \cap \tilde{b} = \emptyset$. Then, we take $\sigma' = \sigma \circ \{\tilde{a}/\tilde{b}\}$ and $post_t(\sigma) = \nu \tilde{b}.(\sigma'(Y_1) + \ldots + \sigma'(Y_m))$, where $\{\tilde{a}/\tilde{b}\}$ denotes the simultaneous substitution of each $a_i \in \tilde{a}$ by the corresponding $b_i \in \tilde{b}$. The transition system $(\mathcal{M}, \rightarrow, M_0)$, is given by

$$(t) \quad \frac{\sigma \; mode \; for \; t}{pre_t(\sigma) \xrightarrow{t} post_t(\sigma)} \qquad \frac{M_1 \equiv M_1' \xrightarrow{t} M_2' \equiv M_2}{M_1 \xrightarrow{t} M_2} \; (\equiv)$$

$$(+) \quad \frac{M_1 \xrightarrow{t} M_2}{M_1 + M \xrightarrow{t} M_2 + M} \qquad \frac{M_1 \xrightarrow{t} M_2}{\nu a.M_1 \xrightarrow{t} \nu a.M_2} \; (\nu)$$

Rules $(+)$ and (ν) state that transitions can happen inside a sum or inside a restriction, respectively. Rule $(\equiv)$ is also standard, and formalizes that we are rewriting terms modulo $\equiv$. Then we have a rule schema (t) for each $t \in \mathcal{R}$. We will write $M \rightarrow M'$ if there is $t \in \mathcal{R}$ such that $M \xrightarrow{t} M'$. As an example, let $t : p(x), q(x) \rightarrow \nu b.p(b)$ be a rule in $\mathcal{R}$. The rewriting $p(a), q(a) \rightarrow \nu b.p(b)$ can take place by taking $\sigma(x) = a$, which satisfies the conditions for modes and $pre_t(\sigma) = p(a), q(a)$ and $post_t(\sigma) = \nu b.p(b)$. In order to apply the rule t starting from $p(b), q(b)$ we need to rename b in the right handside of the rule, obtaining (e.g. if we replace b by a) $\nu a.p(a)$. We denote by $\rightarrow_{\not\equiv}$ the transition relation obtained by considering only rules (t), $(+)$ and (ν) above (that is, without $(\equiv)$).

As in the π-calculus [20], we can consider several normal forms, that force a certain rearrangement of bound names. M is said to be in *standard normal form* if $M = \nu \tilde{a}.(A_1 + \ldots + A_n)$. Every term is equivalent to some term in standard form, that can be obtained by applying the extrusion rule and α-conversion as much as necessary. The standard form is unique up to commutativity and associativity of $+$, and α-conversion and commutativity of the names in $\tilde{a}$. Moreover, the transition relation is compatible with respect to the standard form, that is, if $M_1 \equiv M_2$, M_2 is in standard form and $M_1 \xrightarrow{t}_{\not\equiv}$ then $M_2 \xrightarrow{t}_{\not\equiv}$ [16, Prop. 1].

Let us now define *restricted normal forms*, which will help us to characterize depth-bounded terms. A term is in restricted form if the scope of its restrictions is minimal, that is, if all its subterms $\nu a.(A_1 + \ldots + A_m)$ satisfy $a \in fn(A_i)$ for all i, so that no extrusion rule can be applied from left to right. Therefore, restricted forms can be seen as the opposite concept to standard forms.

Definition 1. *Let us define* $\hat{\equiv}$ *as the least congruence on* $\mathcal{M}$ *st* $+$ *is commutative and associative with* **0** *as identity, and* $\leadsto$ *as the least binary relation on* $\mathcal{M}$ *st:*

$$\frac{a \notin fn(M_2)}{\nu a.(M_1 + M_2) \leadsto \nu a.M_1 + M_2} \qquad \frac{M_1 \hat{\equiv} M_1' \leadsto M_2' \hat{\equiv} M_2}{M_1 \leadsto M_2}$$

$$\frac{M_1 \leadsto M_2}{M_1 + M \leadsto M_2 + M} \qquad \frac{M_1 \leadsto M_2}{\nu a.M_1 \leadsto \nu a.M_2}$$

M *is in restricted form if there is no* M' *with* $M \leadsto M'$. *We say a term* M *in restricted form is a* fragment *if it cannot be decomposed as* $M = M_1 + M_2$.

Any M in restricted form satisfies $M = F_1 + \ldots + F_n$ with F_i fragments, and any fragment is either an atomic formula or a term of the form $\nu a.(F_1 + \ldots + F_m)$, with F_i fragments st $a \in fn(F_i)$, for all i. For instance, $M = \nu a.\nu a_1.\ldots.\nu a_n.(p(a, a_1), \ldots, p(a, a_n)) \leadsto F = \nu a.(\nu a_1.p(a, a_1), \ldots, \nu a_n.p(a, a_n))$. Notice that F and each $\nu a_i.p(a, a_i)$ are fragments. The relation $\leadsto$ is confluent, up to $\hat{\equiv}$. Moreover, if $M \leadsto M'$ then $M \equiv M'$. Unlike the standard normal form, the restricted normal form is not compatible with the transition relation. For instance, for M and F above, the rule $t : p(x, y_1), p(x, y_2) \to q(x)$ satisfies $M \xrightarrow{t}_{\not\equiv}$ but not $F \xrightarrow{t}_{\not\equiv}$. However, restricted normal forms give more insight about the topology of pure names in terms. In particular, they are the basis of the proof that depth-bounded ν-MSR terms yield WSTS.

4   Depth-Bounded ν-MSR

We now consider depth-bounded ν-MSR. Intuitively, a ν-MSR is depth-bounded if names cannot appear *linked* in an arbitrarily long way. Thus, if every term of the form $\nu a_1, \ldots, \nu a_n.(p(a_1, a_2), p(a_2, a_3), \ldots, p(a_{n-1}, a_n))$ can be reached, then the ν-MSR is not depth-bounded. However, reaching all terms of the form $\nu a_1, \ldots, \nu a_n, \nu a.(p(a, a_1), \ldots, p(a, a_n))$ does not allow us to conclude that the ν-MSR is depth-unbounded. In order to define depth-bounded ν-MSR, we define a function $nest_\nu$, that measures the nesting of restrictions (occurrences of the operator ν) in a term.

Definition 2. *We define* $nest_\nu(M)$ *by structural induction on* M:

- $nest_\nu(A) = nest_\nu(0) = 0$,
- $nest_\nu(M_1 + M_2) = max(nest_\nu(M_1), nest_\nu(M_2))$,
- $nest_\nu(\nu a.M) = 1 + nest_\nu(M)$.

We take depth$(M) = min\{nest_\nu(M') \mid M \equiv M'\}$. *A ν-MSR is k-bounded if depth*$(M) \le k$ *for any reachable M, and depth-bounded if it is k-bounded for some $k \ge 0$.*

As explained in [13], *depth* measures the interdependence of restricted names. The fragment $F = \nu a_1 \ldots \nu a_n.\nu a.(p(a,a_1), \ldots, p(a,a_n))$, satisfies $nest_\nu(F) = n+1$ and is equivalent to $F' = \nu a.(\nu a_1.p(a,a_1), \ldots, \nu a_n.p(a,a_n))$, which satisfies $nest_\nu(F') = 2$. In fact, it can be easily checked that $depth(F) = 2$.

Lemma 1. *If $F \hat{\equiv} G$ then $nest_\nu(F) = nest_\nu(G)$.*

Proof. Obvious.

We said above that the relation $\rightsquigarrow$ is confluent up to $\hat{\equiv}$. However, it would not be confluent if the congruence $\hat{\equiv}$ also allowed reordering of bound names. For instance, the term $M = \nu a.\nu a_1 \ldots \nu a_n.(p(a,a_1), \ldots, p(a,a_n))$ satisfies $M \rightsquigarrow \nu a.(\nu a_1.p(a,a_1), \ldots, \nu a_n.p(a,a_n))$, but $F = \nu a_1 \ldots \nu a_n.\nu a.(p(a,a_1), \ldots, p(a, a_n))$ is in restricted normal form, that is, $F \not\rightsquigarrow$. Therefore, restricted forms are not enough to characterize the interdependance of bound names. Next, we will define for each fragment F another fragment that we denote by $nf(F)$ equivalent to F with respect to $\equiv$. Intuitively, $nf(F)$ is a representation of F that gives a better insight about the interdependance of names in F. In order to obtain $nf(F)$ from F we rearrange the whole set of bound names in F. For that purpose, as the first step we will consider *the* standard normal form of F. Then, we will split the set of bound names in those that appear both in A_1 and outside A_1, those that appear only in A_1 and the rest of names.

Definition 3. *Given a fragment F, we define $nf(F)$ in the following steps:*

1. *Let $F \equiv \nu \tilde{a}.(A_1 + \ldots + A_n)$ in standard form.*
2. *Split $\tilde{a}$ into $\tilde{a}_1$, $\tilde{a}_2$ and $\tilde{a}_3$ so that $\tilde{a}_1 = fn(A_1) \cap fn(A_2 + \ldots + A_n)$, $\tilde{a}_2 = fn(A_1) \setminus fn(A_2 + \ldots + A_n)$ and $\tilde{a}_3 = fn(A_2 + \ldots + A_n) \setminus fn(A_1)$. Then, $F \equiv \nu \tilde{a}_1.(\nu \tilde{a}_2.A_1 + \nu \tilde{a}_3.(A_2 + \ldots + A_n))$.*
3. *Let $\nu \tilde{a}_3.(A_2 + \ldots + A_m) \rightsquigarrow G_1 + \ldots + G_m$ in restricted form.*
4. *Compute $nf(G_i) = F_i$*
5. *Let $\nu \tilde{a}_1.(\nu \tilde{a}_2.A_1 + F_1 + \ldots + F_m) \rightsquigarrow nf(F)$.*

Whenever $F \equiv \nu \tilde{a}.A$ (that is, whenever $n = 1$ above) then $nf(F)$ is again F. Let us see how the procedure works (with $n > 1$) in the following example.

Example 1. Let $F = \nu a_1 \ldots \nu a_n.\nu a.(p(a,a_1), \ldots, p(a,a_n))$.

1. F is already in standard normal form.
2. We split $\{a, a_1, \ldots, a_n\}$ into $\tilde{a}_1 = a$, $\tilde{a}_2 = a_1$ and $\tilde{a}_3 = \{a_2, \ldots, a_n\}$, so that $F \equiv \nu a.(\nu a_1.p(a,a_1) + \nu \tilde{a}_3.(p(a,a_2) + \ldots + p(a,a_n))$.
3. Let $\nu \tilde{a}_3.(p(a,a_2) + \ldots + p(a,a_n)) \rightsquigarrow \nu a_2.p(a,a_2) + \ldots + \nu a_n.p(a,a_n)$.
4. As we have said above, $nf(\nu a_i.p(a,a_i)) = \nu a_i.p(a,a_i)$.
5. We obtain $F' = \nu a.(\nu a_1.p(a,a_1) + \nu a_2.p(a,a_2) + \ldots + \nu a_n.p(a,a_n))$, which is already is restricted form, so that F' is $nf(F)$.

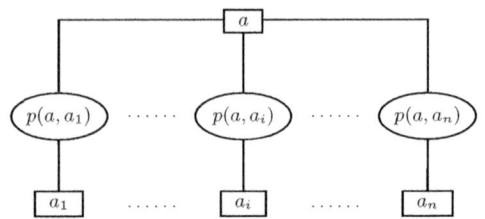

Fig. 2. Hypergraph of the fragments in Example 1

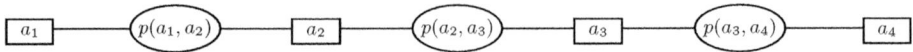

Fig. 3. Hypergraph of the fragments in Example 2

In this example we start building $nf(F)$ starting from the standard normal form $\nu a_1 \ldots \nu a_n.\nu a.(p(a, a_1), \ldots, p(a, a_n))$, but we could have also started from another term in standard normal form in which the atomic formulae $p(a, a_i)$ were given in a different order. It can be checked that in this particular example such order does not make any difference, so that the $nf(F)$ obtained is always the same (up to $\cong$). However, in general this is not the case, that is, the fragment $nf(F)$ defined above is not unique. More precisely, it is only unique (up to $\cong$), after fixing a given representative of the standard normal form.

The fragments of the form $nf(F)$ are called *anchored fragments* in [13]. Such fragments have an *anchor*, an atomic formula that contains the names that are bound. More precisely, in an anchored fragment $\nu a.(F_1 + \ldots + F_m)$ it is not only true that a is free in each F_i, but it is also free in the anchor of F_i. This fact will be used in Lemma 4 to characterize the nesting of restrictions in such fragments.

Example 2. Let

$$F_1 = \nu a_1, a_2, a_3, a_4.(p(a_1, a_2), p(a_2, a_3), p(a_3, a_4))$$

$$F_2 = \nu a_1, a_2, a_3, a_4.(p(a_2, a_3), p(a_1, a_2), p(a_3, a_4))$$

be two fragments in standard normal form, equivalent up to $\cong$. If we compute $nf(F_i)$ starting from F_i for $i = 1, 2$, then it can be checked that

$$nf(F_1) = \nu a_2.(\nu a_1.p(a_1, a_2) + \nu a_3.(p(a_2, a_3) + \nu a_4.p(a_3, a_4)))$$

$$nf(F_2) = \nu a_2, a_3.(p(a_2, a_3) + \nu a_1.p(a_1, a_2) + \nu a_4.p(a_3, a_4))$$

Therefore, as we have seen in the previous example, $nf(F)$ is not uniquely determined. Let us now prove some results that we will need to prove well structuredness of depth-bounded ν-MSR.

Lemma 2. *The two following facts hold:*

- $F \equiv nf(F)$ *for every fragment F.*
- *If $F_1 \equiv F_2$ then there are $nf(F_1)$ and $nf(F_2)$ st $nf(F_1) \cong nf(F_2)$.*

Proof. $F \equiv nf(F)$ because all the steps in Def. 3 preserve $\equiv$. Let us now take F_1 and F_2 st $F_1 \equiv F_2$. In that case, there is F in standard normal form st $F_i \widehat{\equiv} F$. Then, steps 2 to 5 in Def. 3 coincide for F_1 and F_2, so that $nf(F_1) \widehat{\equiv} nf(F_2)$.

As in [13], we use the graph-theoretic interpretation of fragments. A fragment can be seen as a hypergraph with its atomic formulae as nodes and its names as arcs, that link all the formulae that contain that name.

Definition 4. *For a term* $M \equiv \nu\tilde{a}.(A_1 + \ldots + A_m)$ *we define the hypergraph* $\mathcal{G}(M) = (V, E, inc)$, *where* $V = \{A_1, \ldots, A_m\}$, $E = \tilde{a}$ *and for* $e \in E$, $inc(e)$ *is the set of atomic formulae in* V *in which* e *occurs.*

Fragments correspond to connected components. $M_1 \equiv M_2$ implies that $\mathcal{G}(M_1)$ and $\mathcal{G}(M_2)$ are isomorphic hypergraphs. For the two fragments $F = \nu a_1 \ldots \nu a_n \nu a.(p(a, a_1), \ldots, p(a, a_n))$ and $F' = \nu a.(\nu a_1.p(a, a_1), \ldots, \nu a_n(p(a, a_n)))$ seen in Example 1, since $F \equiv F'$ the hypergraphs obtained for them are isomorphic (see Fig. 2). The ones in Example 2 are shown in Fig. 3.

   A *path* is a finite sequence $\rho = A_1 a_1 A_2 a_2 \cdots a_n A_{n+1}$ with $A_i, A_{i+1} \in inc(a_i)$. The length of ρ is $|\rho| = n$, and ρ is *simple* whenever $a_i \neq a_j$ for $i \neq j$. A simple path in the hypergraph in Fig. 2 is for instance

$$\rho_1 = p(a, a_1) \ a_1 \ p(a, a_1) \ a \ p(a, a_2) \ a_2 \ p(a, a_2)$$

with length 3. Any attempt to extend that simple path results in a path that is no longer simple (since a and a_2 alread occur in it). Indeed, it can be checked that the length of every single path is at most 3. In the case of the hypergraph in Fig. 3 the longest simple path, with length 4, is

$$\rho_2 = p(a_1, a_2) \ a_1 \ p(a_1, a_2) \ a_2 \ p(a_2, a_3) \ a_3 \ p(a_3, a_4) \ a_4 \ p(a_3, a_4)$$

In the first place, let us see that the length of any simple path in $\mathcal{G}(F)$ is bounded by a value that depends only on $nest_\nu(F)$.

Lemma 3. *If* F *is a fragment and* ρ *is a simple path in* $\mathcal{G}(F)$, *then* $|\rho| \leq 2^{nest_\nu(F)} - 1$.

Proof. We prove it by structural induction on F. If $F = A$ then $p = A$, so that $nest_\nu(F) = 0$ and $|p| = 0 = 2^{nest_\nu(F)} - 1$. Let now $F = \nu a.(F_1 + \ldots + F_n)$ and let p be a simple path in $\mathcal{G}(F)$. Then one of the following holds:

– p is a simple path in $\mathcal{G}(F_k)$ for some k, so that the hypothesis induction tells us that $|p| \leq 2^{nest_\nu(F_k)} - 1 \leq 2^{nest_\nu(F)} - 1$, or
– $p = p_i a p_j$ with p_i simple path of $\mathcal{G}(F_i)$ and p_j simple path in $\mathcal{G}(F_j)$, so that by induction we know that $|p_i| \leq 2^{nest_\nu(F_i)} - 1$ and $|p_i| \leq 2^{nest_\nu(F_i)} - 1$. Let m st $nest_\nu(F_m) = max\{nest_\nu(F_l) \mid l = 1, \ldots, n\}$. Then, $|p| = |p_i| + |p_j| + 1 \leq 2^{nest_\nu(F_i)} - 1 + 2^{nest_\nu(F_j)} - 1 + 1 \leq 2 \cdot 2^{nest_\nu(F_m)} - 1 = 2^{nest_\nu(F_m)+1} - 1 = 2^{nest_\nu(F)} - 1$.

For the fragments F and $F' = nf(F)$ in Example 1 we saw that $nest_\nu(F) = n+1$ and $nest_\nu(F') = 2$. A maximal simple path in $\mathcal{G}(F')$ is ρ_1, with $|\rho_1| = 3$, which satisfies $|\rho_1| \leq 2^{nest_\nu(F')} - 1 = 3$. In the case of the fragments seen in Example 2, both $nest_\nu(F_1) = nest_\nu(F_2) = 4$ and $nest_\nu(nf(F_1)) = nest_\nu(nf(F_2)) = 3$. Moreover, the length of the maximal simple path ρ_2 is $|\rho_2| = 4$, wich satisfies $|\rho_2| \leq 2^3 - 1$. Next let us see that $nest_\nu(nf(F))$ coincides with the length of some simple path in $\mathcal{G}(F)$.

Lemma 4. $nest_\nu(nf(F)) = |\rho|$ *for some simple path ρ in $\mathcal{G}(F)$.*

Proof. Any $nf(F)$ is of the form A or $\nu a.(F_1 + \ldots + F_n)$ with $a \in anc(F_i)$ for all i, where $anc(A) = A$ and $anc(\nu a.(F_1 + \ldots + F_n)) = anc(F_1)$. Therefore, it is enough to see that for such a fragment F, there is a simple path p in $\mathcal{G}(F)$ with $nest_\nu(F) = |p|$. We will also prove that p starts in $anc(F)$. We proceed by induction on F. If $F = A$ the path $p = A$ starts in $anc(A) = A$ and satisfies $nest_\nu(A) = 0 = |p|$. Let us now consider $F = \nu a.(F_1 + \ldots + F_n)$. By definition, $nest_\nu(F) = 1 + max\{nest_\nu(F_1), \ldots, nest_\nu(F_n)\}$. The induction hypothesis tells us that there are anchored paths $p_1, \ldots, p_n$ st p_i starts at $anc(F_i)$ and $nest_\nu(F_i) = |p_i|$. Let p_m the path with maximun length, so that $nest_\nu(F) = 1 + |p_m|$. Since p_m starts in $anc(F_m)$ and a is free both in $anc(F_1)$ and $anc(F_m)$, $p = anc(F_1)ap_m$ is an anchored path that starts in $anc(F) = anc(F_1)$ with length $|p| = 1 + |p_m| = nest_\nu(F)$.

The proof of the previous result builds a path in $\mathcal{G}(F)$, whose arcs correspond to the bound names traversed when computing $nest_\nu(nf(F))$. For instance, for the fragment F in Example 1 and $nf(F) = \nu a.(\nu a_1.p(a, a_1), \ldots, \nu a_n.p(a, a_n))$ the proof builds the path $p(a, a_1)$ a $p(a, a_i)$ a_i $p(a, a_i)$ $(i > 1)$, with length $2 = nest_\nu(nf(F))$. For the fragments F_1 and F_2 in Example 2 it builds

$$p(a_2, a_3)\ a_2\ p(a_2, a_3)\ a_3\ p(a_3, a_4)\ a_4\ p(a_3, a_4)$$

$$p(a_2, a_3)\ a_2\ p(a_2, a_3)\ a_3\ p(a_1, a_2)\ a_1\ p(a_1, a_2)$$

respectively, both having length 3. The previous results can be combined to prove the following proposition.

Proposition 1. $nest_\nu(nf(F)) \leq 2^{depth(F)} - 1$

Proof. Let G st $F \equiv G$ and $depth(F) = nest_\nu(G)$. Since $F \equiv G$, the hypergraphs $\mathcal{G}(F)$ and $\mathcal{G}(G)$ are isomorphic. By Lemma 4 there is a simple path p in $\mathcal{G}(F)$ st $nest_\nu(nf(F)) = |p|$. By Lemma 3, $|p| \leq 2^{nest_\nu(G)} - 1 = 2^{depth(F)} - 1$, and the thesis follow.

We have obtained a bound on the nesting of restrictions in every fragment of the form $nf(F)$, that only depends on $depth(F)$. Next we define an order over terms, that will endow ν-MSR with a well-structure.

Definition 5. *We define $\sqsubseteq_F$ as the least binary relation over fragments st $A \sqsubseteq_F A$, $\nu a.(\sum_{i=1}^{n} F_i) \sqsubseteq_F \nu a.(\sum_{i=1}^{n} G_i + \sum_{i=1}^{n'} G_i')$ provided $F_i \sqsubseteq_F G_i$ for all $i \in \{1, \ldots, n\}$, and $F \sqsubseteq_F G$ provided $F \equiv F' \sqsubseteq_F G' \equiv G$. We also define $M_1 \sqsubseteq M_2$ if $M_i \equiv \sum_{j=1}^{n_i} F_j^i$, $n_1 \leq n_2$ and $F_i^1 \sqsubseteq_F F_i^2$ for $i \in \{1, \ldots, n_1\}$.*

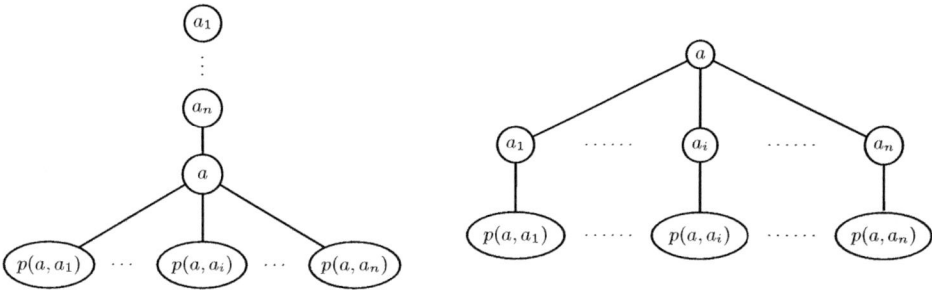

Fig. 4. Trees of the fragments F (left) and F' (right) in Example 1

The order $\sqsubseteq$ over terms can be seen as the multiset order induced by $\sqsubseteq_F$ over fragments. In turn, $\sqsubseteq_F$ can be intuitively characterized using standard forms.

Lemma 5. *Given two fragments F and G, $F \sqsubseteq_F G$ holds if and only if $F \equiv \nu\tilde{a}.(A_1 + \ldots + A_m)$ and $G \equiv \nu\tilde{a}.(A_1 + \ldots + A_m + M)$.*

Proof. Let F and G st $F \sqsubseteq_F G$. We proceed by induction on the rules used to derive $F \sqsubseteq_F G$. For $F = A \sqsubseteq_F A = G$ it is trivial. Suppose now that $F = \nu a.(F_1 + \ldots + F_n)$ and $G = \nu a.(G_1 + \ldots + G_n + G'_1 + \ldots + G'_m)$ with $F_i \sqsubseteq_F G_i$. The induction hypothesis tells us that $F_i \equiv \tilde{a}_i.(\sum A^i_j)$ and $G_i \equiv \tilde{a}_i.(\sum A^i_j + M_i)$. Then, $F \equiv \nu a, \tilde{a}_1, \ldots, \tilde{a}_n.(\sum A^i_j)$ and $G \equiv \nu a, \tilde{a}_1, \ldots, \tilde{a}_n.(\sum A^i_j + \sum G'_i + \sum M_i)$, which satisfy the thesis. Finally, if $F \equiv F' \sqsubseteq_F G' \equiv G$ the induction hypothesis tells us that $F' \equiv \nu\tilde{a}.(A_1 + \ldots + A_m)$ and $G' \equiv \nu\tilde{a}.(A_1 + \ldots + A_m + M)$ and because $\equiv$ is transitive, the same holds for F and G.

Conversely, if $F \equiv \nu\tilde{a}.(A_1 + \ldots + A_m)$ and $G \equiv \nu\tilde{a}.(A_1 + \ldots + A_m + M)$, trivially $A_i \sqsubseteq_F A_i$, so that $\nu\tilde{a}.(A_1 + \ldots + A_m) \sqsubseteq_F \nu\tilde{a}.(A_1 + \ldots + A_m + M)$ and we can conclude by rule ($\equiv$) that $F \sqsubseteq_F G$.

Let us see that depth-bounded ν-MSR are WSTS with respect to that order. In order to see that the order is a wqo, we map fragments to trees as follows.

Definition 6. *Let Δ be the set of names and atomic formulae. We define $\mathcal{T}$ that maps fragments to trees in $\mathcal{T}(\Delta)$ as follows:*

- $\mathcal{T}(A) = A$,
- $\mathcal{T}(\nu a.(F_1 + \ldots + F_n)) = (a, \{\mathcal{T}(F_1), \ldots, \mathcal{T}(F_n)\})$.

Figure 4 and Fig. 5 show the trees corresponding to the fragments considered in Example 1 and Example 2, respectively. The following lemma is easy to prove.

Lemma 6. $nest_\nu(F) = height(\mathcal{T}(F))$

Proof. Clearly, $nest_\nu(A) = 0 = height(A) = height(\mathcal{T}(A))$. For a fragment $F = \nu a.(F_1 + \ldots + F_n)$, $nest_\nu(F) = 1 + max\{nest_\nu(F_i) \mid i = 1, \ldots, n\}$. By the induction hypothesis, $nest_\nu(F_i) = height(\mathcal{T}(F_i))$. Then, $nest_\nu(F) = 1 + max\{height(\mathcal{T}(F_i)) \mid i = 1, \ldots, n\} = height((a, \{\mathcal{T}(F_1), \ldots, \mathcal{T}(F_n)\})) = height(\mathcal{T}(F))$.

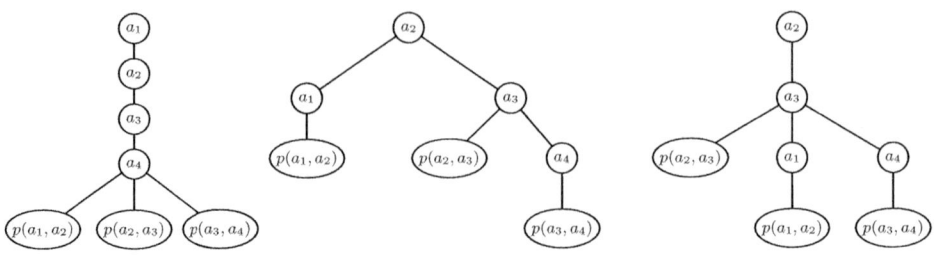

Fig. 5. Trees of the fragments F_1 (left), $nf(F_1)$ (center) and $nf(F_2)$ (right) in Example 2

Moreover, the corresponding orders are preserved by $\mathcal{T}$ in the following sense:

Proposition 2. *If* $\mathcal{T}(F_1) \preceq \mathcal{T}(F_2)$ *then* $F_1 \sqsubseteq_F F_2$.

Proof. We proceed by induction on the rules used to derive $\mathcal{T}(F_1) \preceq \mathcal{T}(F_2)$. If $\mathcal{T}(F_1) = A \preceq A = \mathcal{T}(F_2)$ then $F_1 = F_2 = A$ and trivially, $F_1 \sqsubseteq_F F_2$. Otherwise, $\mathcal{T}(F_1) = (a, \{T_1, \ldots, T_n\}) \preceq (a, \{T_1', \ldots, T_{n'}'\}) = \mathcal{T}(F_2)$ and $\{T_1, \ldots, T_n\} \sqsubseteq \{T_1', \ldots, T_{n'}'\}$, so that we can assume without loss of generality that $T_i \preceq T_i'$ for all $i \in \{1, \ldots, n\}$. Then, $F_1 = \nu a.(F_1^1 + \ldots + F_n^1)$ with $\mathcal{T}(F_i^1) = T_i$, and $F_2 = \nu a.(F_1^2 + \ldots + F_{n'}^2)$ with $\mathcal{T}(F_i^2) = T_i'$. The induction hypothesis tells us that $F_i^1 \sqsubseteq_F F_i^2$, which allows us to conclude that $F_1 \sqsubseteq_F F_2$.

We denote by $\mathcal{F}_n$ the set of fragments with depth less or equal than n, i.e., $\mathcal{F}_n = \{F \text{ fragment} \mid depth(F) \leq n\}$, and analogously, we define $\mathcal{M}_n$ as the set of terms with depth less or equal than n. Then we can prove the following lemma.

Lemma 7. $(\mathcal{F}_n, \sqsubseteq_F)$ *and* $(\mathcal{M}_n, \sqsubseteq)$ *are wqos.*

Proof. Let (F_i) be an infinite sequence of fragments, and let us consider the sequence of trees $(\mathcal{T}(nf(F_i)))$. Because every fragment is in $\mathcal{F}_n$, $height(\mathcal{T}(nf(F_i))) = nest_\nu(nf(F_i)) \leq 2^{nest(F_i)} - 1 \leq m = 2^n - 1$, thanks to Lemma 6 and Prop. 1. If $(\mathcal{T}(\Delta)_m, \preceq)$ is a wqo then there are $i < j$ st $\mathcal{T}(nf(F_i)) \preceq \mathcal{T}(nf(F_j))$. By Prop. 2, $nf(F_i) \sqsubseteq_F nf(F_j)$. Finally, because $F_i \equiv nf(F_i)$ and $F_j \equiv nf(F_j)$ we can conclude that $F_i \sqsubseteq_F F_j$. Indeed, $(\mathcal{T}(\Delta)_m, \preceq)$ is a wqo. To see it is enough to check that we can take Δ to be a finite set. Indeed, since fragments are depth-bounded, we can choose a finite set of names so that every name in Δ and every name in a formula in Δ is taken from that set. $(\mathcal{M}_n, \sqsubseteq)$ is also a wqo because $\sqsubseteq_F$ is and $\sqsubseteq$ is the multiset order induced by $\sqsubseteq_F$.

The proof of the previous result makes use of the fact that the order $\preceq$ in trees is a wqo. Therefore, if a ν-MSR is depth-bounded by n, then the set of reachable terms is contained in $\mathcal{M}_n$, which is a wqo with its order. In order to see that they are a WSTS, we still have to see that the transition relation is monotonic with respect the considered order, and that we can compute a finite representation of the set of predecessors of a given term.

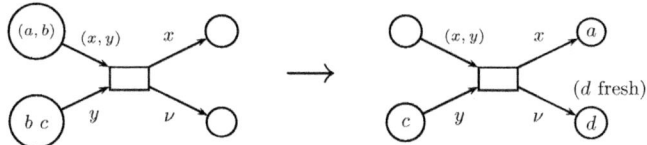

Fig. 6. A simple $p\nu$-PN

Theorem 1. *Depth-bounded ν-MSR are strict WSTS.*

Proof. We have to see that the defined order is monotonic with respect the rewriting relation, and that we can compute a finite representation of the set of predecessors of a given term. The former follows from the compatibility of the transition relation with respect to the standard normal form and Lemma 5. The latter follows from the fact that ν-MSR are finitary, that is, for a given M there are finitely many terms M' up to $\equiv$ st $M \rightarrow M'$.

Since coverability, termination and also boundedness are decidable for strict WSTS [10,2], we obtain the following result as a corollary.

Corollary 1. *Coverability, boundedness and termination are decidable for the class of depth-bounded ν-MSR.*

In [16] we proved that π-calculus processes can be directly encoded into ν-MSR. Moreover, depth-bounded π-calculus processes correspond to depth-bounded ν-MSR.

Proposition 3 ([16]). *For all π-calculus process P there is a ν-MSR $H(P)$ (with H computable) st the transition systems induced by P and $H(P)$ are isomorphic.*

Moreover, if P is a depth-bounded process then $H(P)$ is a depth-bounded ν-MSR. Then, thanks to the previous result, and as a corollary of Prop. 1 we can obtain the following result (that was already obtained in [13]).

Corollary 2. *Depth-bounded π-calculus processes are strict WSTS. Therefore, coverability, termination and boundedness are decidable for depth-bounded π-calculus processes.*

The novelty of our results lies in the fact that we can apply Prop. 1 to other formalisms that can be easily encoded within ν-MSR. This is the case for $p\nu$-PN. A $p\nu$-PN is a Petri net that manages tuples of pure names. More precisely, tokens in a $p\nu$-PN are of the form $(a_1, \ldots, a_n)$, where each a_i is a pure name [12], taken from a set Id. In order to handle names, arcs are labelled by tuples of variables, taken from a set Var. Moreover, transitions can create fresh names, which is formalized by means of a special variable $\nu \in Var$, that can only be instantiated to names that do not occur in the current state. Fig. 6 depicts a simple $p\nu$-PN and the firing of its only transition. See [18] for more details on $p\nu$-PN.

In [16] we proved that ν-MSR and $p\nu$-PN are actually the same thing, so that $p\nu$-PN can be seen as a graphical representation of ν-MSR that work in their standard normal form.

Proposition 4 ([16]). *For every $p\nu$-PN N there is a ν-MSR $K(N)$ (with K computable) st the transition systems induced by N and $K(N)$ are isomorphic.*

We say a $p\nu$-PN is depth-bounded if there is k st for any reachable state M and for any sequence $A_1, \ldots, A_n$ of tokens in M st for every i, there is a different name a_i in A_i and A_{i+1}, then necessarily $n \leq k$. Depth-bounded ν-PN correspond to depth-bounded ν-MSR [16]. Moreover, one can check that ordinary Petri nets correspond to 0-bounded ν-MSR and ν-PN (the monadic subclass of $p\nu$-PN) to 1-bounded ν-MSR.

Corollary 3. *Depth-bounded $p\nu$-PN are strict WSTS. Therefore, coverability, boundedness and termination are decidable for the class of depth-bounded $p\nu$-PN.*

5   Conclusions and Future Work

In this paper we consider a variation of the existing formalisms of concurrency based on multiset rewriting, that we call ν-MSR. We proved in [16] that they are Turing-complete, so that no interesting problem can be decided for them. Now we adapt the results in [13] in order to prove that a subclass of ν-MSR, that in which the interdependance of restricted names is bounded, is a strict Well Structured Transition System. This yields decidability of coverability, termination and also boundedness.

These results can be transferred to any formalism that can be encoded within ν-MSR. We know that π-calculus processes can be easily translated to a ν-MSR system, so that depth-bounded π-calculus processes are WSTS. This was already proved in [13]. However, we can also obtain as a corollary the strict well structuredness of depth-bounded $p\nu$-PN. Moreover, we claim that the same result holds for spi-calculus processes [1], with an encoding analogous to the one used for the π-calculus.

We have seen that the class of depth-bounded ν-MSR has decidable coverability. However, in order to obtain such decidability result, one needs to know a priori a bound on the nesting of restrictions in every reachable state. The paper [22] establishes how the algorithmic schema in [11] can be used to decide coverability using a forward analysis. This approach has the advantage that we do not need to know a bound on the nesting of restrictions a priori.

As an immediate future work, it would be interesting to find (structural) sufficient conditions for depth-boundedness of ν-MSR. In that sense, it would be useful to strengthen the bound found in Prop. 1 on the nesting of a fragment.

References

1. Abadi, M., Gordon, A.D.: A Calculus for Cryptographic Protocols: The spi Calculus. Inf. Comput. 148(1), 1–70 (1999)
2. Abdulla, P.A., Cerans, K., Jonsson, B., Tsay, Y.K.: Algorithmic analysis of programs with well quasi-ordered domains. Inf. Comput. 160(1-2), 109–127 (2000)

3. Baldan, P., Bonchi, F., Gadducci, F.: Encoding asynchronous interactions using open Petri nets. In: Bravetti, M., Zavattaro, G. (eds.) CONCUR 2009. LNCS, vol. 5710, pp. 99–114. Springer, Heidelberg (2009)
4. Busi, N., Gorrieri, R.: Distributed semantics for the pi-calculus based on Petri nets with inhibitor arcs. J. Log. Algebr. Program. 78(3), 138–162 (2009)
5. Cervesato, I.: Typed MSR: Syntax and Examples. In: Gorodetski, V.I., Skormin, V.A., Popyack, L.J. (eds.) MMM-ACNS 2001. LNCS, vol. 2052, pp. 159–177. Springer, Heidelberg (2001)
6. Cervesato, I., Durgin, N.A., Lincoln, P., Mitchell, J.C., Scedrov, A.: A meta-notation for protocol analysis. In: CSFW, pp. 55–69 (1999)
7. Decker, G., Weske, M.: Instance isolation analysis for service-oriented architectures. In: IEEE SCC, vol. (1), pp. 249–256. IEEE Computer Society, Los Alamitos (2008)
8. Delzanno, G.: An overview of MSR(C): A CLP-based framework for the symbolic verification of parameterized concurrent systems. Electr. Notes Theor. Comput. Sci, vol. 76 (2002)
9. Delzanno, G.: Constraint multiset rewriting. Technical Report DISI-TR-05-08, University of Genova (2005)
10. Finkel, A., Schnoebelen, P.: Well-structured transition systems everywhere? Theor. Comput. Sci. 256(1-2), 63–92 (2001)
11. Geeraerts, G., Raskin, J.F., Begin, L.V.: Expand, enlarge and check: New algorithms for the coverability problem of wsts. J. Comput. Syst. Sci. 72(1), 180–203 (2006)
12. Gordon, A.D.: Notes on nominal calculi for security and mobility. In: Focardi, R., Gorrieri, R. (eds.) FOSAD 2000. LNCS, vol. 2171, pp. 262–330. Springer, Heidelberg (2001)
13. Meyer, R.: On boundedness in Depth in the pi-calculus. In: Ausiello, G., Karhumäki, J., Mauri, G., Ong, C.H.L. (eds.) IFIP TCS. IFIP, vol. 273, pp. 477–489. Springer, Heidelberg (2008)
14. Meyer, R.: A theory of structural stationarity in the pi-calculus. Acta Inf. 46(2), 87–137 (2009)
15. Meyer, R., Gorrieri, R.: On the relationship between pi-calculus and finite place/transition Petri nets. In: Bravetti, M., Zavattaro, G. (eds.) CONCUR 2009. LNCS, vol. 5710, pp. 463–480. Springer, Heidelberg (2009)
16. Rosa-Velardo, F.: Multiset rewriting: a semantic framework for concurrency with name binding. In: 8th International Workshop on Rewriting Logic and its Applications, WRLA 2010. Springer, Heidelberg (to appear, 2010)
17. Rosa-Velardo, F., de Frutos-Escrig, D.: Name creation vs. replication in Petri net systems 88(3), 329–356 (2008)
18. Rosa-Velardo, F., de Frutos-Escrig, D.: Decidability problems in Petri nets with name creation and replication (submitted)
19. Rosa-Velardo, F., de Frutos-Escrig, D., Alonso, O.M.: On the expressiveness of Mobile Synchronizing Petri Nets. Electr. Notes Theor. Comput. Sci. 180(1), 77–94 (2007)
20. Sangiorgi, D., Walker, D.: The pi-calculus: a Theory of Mobile Processes. Cambridge University Press, Cambridge (2001)
21. van Hee, K.M., Sidorova, N., Voorhoeve, M., van der Werf, J.M.E.M.: Generation of database transactions with petri nets. Fundam. Inform. 93(1-3), 171–184 (2009)
22. Wies, T., Zufferey, D., Henzinger, T.A.: Forward analysis of depth-bounded processes. In: Ong, L. (ed.) FOSSACS 2010. LNCS, vol. 6014, pp. 94–108. Springer, Heidelberg (2010)

Efficient Construction of Semilinear Representations of Languages Accepted by Unary NFA

Zdeněk Sawa[⋆]

Center for Applied Cybernetics, Department of Computer Science
Technical University of Ostrava
17. listopadu 15, Ostrava-Poruba, 708 33, Czech republic
zdenek.sawa@vsb.cz

Abstract. Chrobak (1986) proved that a language accepted by a given nondeterministic finite automaton with one-letter alphabet, i.e., a unary NFA, with n states can be represented as the union of $O(n^2)$ arithmetic progressions, and Martinez (2002) has shown how to compute these progressions in polynomial time. To (2009) has pointed out recently that Chrobak's construction and Martinez's algorithm, which is based on it, contain a subtle error and has shown how they can be corrected. In this paper, a new simpler and more efficient algorithm for the same problem is presented. The running time of the presented algorithm is $O(n^2(n+m))$, where n is the number of states and m the number of transitions of a given unary NFA.

1 Introduction

It is well known that Parikh images of regular (and even context-free) languages are semilinear sets [7,4]. In *unary* languages, i.e., languages over a one-letter alphabet, words can be identified with their lengths (i.e., a^n can be identified with n), so the Parikh image of a unary language is just the set of lengths of words of the language, and it can be identified with the language itself. It can be easily shown that each regular unary language can be represented as the union of a finite number of arithmetic progressions of the form $\{c + di \mid i \in \mathbb{N}\}$ where c and d are constants specifying the offset and the period of a progression.

A unary nondeterministic finite automaton (a unary NFA) is an NFA with a one-letter alphabet. Given a unary NFA $\mathcal{A}$, a set of arithmetic progressions representing the language accepted by $\mathcal{A}$ can be computed by determinization of $\mathcal{A}$; however, this straightforward approach can produce an exponential number of progressions. Chrobak [1] has shown that this exponential blowup is avoidable and that a language accepted by a unary NFA with n states can be represented as the union of $O(n^2)$ progressions of the form $\{c + di \mid i \in \mathbb{N}\}$ where $c < p(n)$ for some $p(n) \in O(n^2)$ and $0 \leq d \leq n$. The computational complexity of the

---

⋆ Supported by the Czech Ministry of Education, Grant No. 1M0567.

A. Kučera and I. Potapov (Eds.): RP 2010, LNCS 6227, pp. 176–182, 2010.

construction of these progressions was not analyzed in [1], but it can be easily seen that a naive straightforward implementation would require exponential time. Later, Martinez [5,6] has shown how the construction described in [1] can be realized in polynomial time. The exact complexity of Martinez's algorithm is $O(kn^4)$ where n is the number of states of the automaton and k the number of strongly connected components of its graph. The result was recently used for example in [3,2] to obtain more efficient algorithms for some problems in automata theory and the verification of one-counter processes.

In [8], To pointed out that Chrobak's construction and Martinez's algorithm (whose correctness relies on correctness of Chrobak's construction) contain a subtle error, and he has shown modifications that correct this error.

In this paper, we give a simpler and more efficient algorithm for the same problem, i.e., for computing of a corresponding set of arithmetic progressions for a given unary NFA. The time complexity of the algorithm is $O(n^2(n + m))$ and its space complexity $O(n^2)$, where n is the number of states and m number of transitions of the unary NFA.

Section 2 gives basic definitions and formulates the main result, Section 3 describes the algorithm and proofs of its correctness, and Section 4 contains a description of an efficient implementation of the algorithm and an analysis of its complexity.

2   Definitions and Main Result

The set of natural numbers $\{0, 1, 2, \ldots\}$ is denoted by $\mathbb{N}$. For $i, j \in \mathbb{N}$ such that $i \leq j$, $[i, j]$ denotes the set $\{i, i + 1, \ldots, j\}$, and $[i, j)$ denotes the (possibly empty) set $\{i, i + 1, \ldots, j - 1\}$. Given $c, d \in \mathbb{N}$, an *arithmetic progression* is the set $\{c + d \cdot i \mid i \in \mathbb{N}\}$, denoted $c + d\mathbb{N}$, where c is called the *offset* and d the *period* of the progression.

The following definitions are standard (see e.g. [4]), except that they are specialized to the case where a one-letter alphabet is used. In such an alphabet, words can be identified with their lengths.

A *unary nondeterministic finite automaton (a unary NFA)* is a tuple $\mathcal{A} = (Q, \delta, I, F)$ where Q is a finite set of *states*, $\delta \subseteq Q \times Q$ is a *transition relation*, and $I, F \subseteq Q$ are sets of *initial* and *final* states respectively. A *path* of length k from q to q', where $q, q' \in Q$, is a sequence of states $q_0, q_1, \ldots, q_k$ from Q where $q = q_0$, $q' = q_k$, and $(q_{i-1}, q_i) \in \delta$ for each $i \in [1, k]$. We use $q \xrightarrow{k} q'$ to denote that there exists a path of length k from q to q'. A word $x \in \mathbb{N}$ is *accepted* by $\mathcal{A}$ if $q_0 \xrightarrow{x} q_f$ for some $q_0 \in I$ and $q_f \in F$. The language $L(\mathcal{A})$ accepted by a unary NFA $\mathcal{A}$ is the set of all words accepted by $\mathcal{A}$.

We consider the following problem:

PROBLEM: UNFA-Arith-Progressions
INPUT: A unary NFA $\mathcal{A}$.
OUTPUT: A set $\{(c_1, d_1), (c_2, d_2), \ldots, (c_k, d_k)\}$ of pairs of natural
numbers such that $L(\mathcal{A}) = \bigcup_{i=1}^{k}(c_i + d_i\mathbb{N})$.

The main result presented in this paper is:

Theorem 1. *There is an algorithm solving* UNFA-Arith-Progressions *with time complexity* $O(n^2(n+m))$ *and space complexity* $O(n^2)$ *where n is the number of states and m the number of transitions of a given unary NFA. The algorithm constructs $O(n^2)$ pairs of numbers and each constructed pair (c_i, d_i) satisfies $c_i < 2n^2 + n$ and $d_i \leq n$.*

3 $L(\mathcal{A})$ as Union of Arithmetic Progressions

In this section, we describe the algorithm for UNFA-Arith-Progressions and prove its correctness.

In the rest of the section, we assume a fixed unary NFA $\mathcal{A} = (Q, \delta, I, F)$ with $|Q| = n$.

3.1   The Algorithm

The algorithm works as follows. It computes the resulting set $\mathcal{R}$ of pairs of numbers that represent arithmetic progressions as the union of the following sets $\mathcal{R}_1$ and $\mathcal{R}_2$ where:

- $\mathcal{R}_1$ is the set of all of pairs $(x, 0)$ where $x \in L(\mathcal{A})$ and $x \in [0, 2n^2 + n)$, and
- $\mathcal{R}_2$ is the set of all of pairs (c, d) where $d \in [1, n]$, $c \in [2n^2 - d, 2n^2)$, and where for some $q_0 \in I$, $q \in Q$, and $q_f \in F$ we have $q_0 \xrightarrow{n} q$, $q \xrightarrow{d} q$, and $q \xrightarrow{c-n} q_f$ (note that $c \geq n$).

To compute $\mathcal{R}_1$, it is sufficient to test for each $x \in [0, 2n^2 + n)$ if $x \in L(\mathcal{A})$, and to compute $\mathcal{R}_2$, it is sufficient to test for each of $O(n^2)$ pairs (c, d), where $d \in [1, n]$ and $c \in [2n^2 - d, 2n^2)$, if the required conditions are satisfied. All these tests can be easily done in polynomial time and we can also see that $|\mathcal{R}| \in O(n^2)$. An efficient implementation of the algorithm, which avoids some recomputations by precomputing certain sets of states, is described in Section 4 together with a more detailed analysis of its complexity.

The correctness of the algorithm is ensured by the following crucial lemma and its corollary; the proof of the lemma is postponed to the next subsection.

Lemma 2. *Let $x \geq 2n^2 + n$. If $x \in L(\mathcal{A})$ then $x \in c + d\mathbb{N}$ for some $(c, d) \in \mathcal{R}_2$.*

Corollary 3. *Let $x \in \mathbb{N}$. Then $x \in L(\mathcal{A})$ iff $x \in c + d\mathbb{N}$ for some $(c, d) \in \mathcal{R}$.*

Proof. ($\Rightarrow$) Assume $x \in L(\mathcal{A})$. Either $x < 2n^2 + n$ and then $(x, 0) \in \mathcal{R}_1$ and $x \in (x + 0\mathbb{N}) = \{x\}$, or $x \geq 2n^2 + n$ and then $x \in c + d\mathbb{N}$ for some $(c, d) \in \mathcal{R}_2$ by Lemma 2.

($\Leftarrow$) It can be easily checked that $c + d\mathbb{N} \subseteq L(\mathcal{A})$ for each $(c, d) \in \mathcal{R}$. For $(c, d) \in \mathcal{R}_1$ this follows from the definition, and for $(c, d) \in \mathcal{R}_2$ from the observation that if $q_0 \xrightarrow{n} q$, $q \xrightarrow{d} q$, and $q \xrightarrow{c-n} q_f$ for some $q_0 \in I$, $q \in Q$, and $q_f \in F$ (where $c \geq n$), then $\mathcal{A}$ accepts each word from $c + d\mathbb{N}$.   □

3.2   Proof of Lemma 2

The rest of this section is devoted to the proof of Lemma 2, which is done by the following sequence of simple propositions.

The basic idea of the proof is that there exists a polynomial $p(n) \in O(n^2)$ such that if $q_1 \xrightarrow{x} q_2$ for some $q_1, q_2 \in Q$ and $x \geq p(n)$ then there is a path α of length x from q_1 to q_2 of the following form: α goes from q_1 to some state q by c_1 steps, then goes through a cycle of length $d \in [1, n]$ several times, and then goes from q to q_2 by c_2 steps. Obviously $x = c_1 + k \cdot d + c_2$ for some $k \in \mathbb{N}$, and it will be also ensured that $c_1 + c_2 < p(n)$.

Every path α of length x from q_1 to q_2 can be transformed into the described form by the following construction: we can decompose α into *elementary cycles*, i.e., cycles where no state is repeated, and a *simple path*, i.e., a path where no state is repeated, from q_1 to q_2. We can do this by repeatedly removing elementary cycles from α. Using this decomposition, we can construct a path of the required form by selecting one elementary cycle of some length, say d, and by repeatedly "cutting-out" some subsets of the remaining elementary cycles, such that the sums of lengths of cycles in these subsets are multiples of d, which means that they can be replaced with iterations of the selected cycle of length d.

However, when we "cut-out" cycles, we must be careful, because by cutting-out some cycles, some other cycles can become unreachable. An error of this kind was made by Chrobak in [1] as pointed out by To in [8].

To ensure that none of the cycles becomes unreachable, we divide elementary cycles into two categories — *removable* and *unremovable*. Only removable cycles will be cut-out, and it will be ensured that it is safe to remove any subset of removable cycles.

We say a sequence $\beta_0, \beta_1, \ldots, \beta_r$, where β_0 is a simple path from q_1 to q_2 and where $\beta_1, \beta_2, \ldots, \beta_r$ are elementary cycles, is *good* if for each $i \in [1, r]$ there is some $j \in [0, i)$, such that β_i and β_j share at least one state q. Note that from such good sequence we can construct a path from q_1 to q_2, whose length is the sum of lengths of all β_i, by starting with β_0 and repeatedly "pasting-in" $\beta_1, \beta_2, \ldots, \beta_r$ (in this order). Each cycle β_i can be "pasted-in" since it shares some state q with some β_j where $j < i$ (β_i can be pasted in by splitting it in q).

Note that a decomposition $\beta_0, \beta_1, \ldots, \beta_r$ of an original path α, where β_0 is a simple path from q_1 to q_2 and where $\beta_1, \beta_2, \ldots, \beta_r$ are elementary cycles in the reverse order, in which they were removed from α (i.e., β_r was removed first and β_1 last), is good. We say a cycle β_i, where $i \in [1, r]$, is *removable* if for each state q of β_i there is some $j \in [0, i)$ such that β_j contains q. Cycle β_i that is not removable is *unremovable*. It can be easily checked that a sequence obtained from $\beta_0, \beta_1, \ldots, \beta_r$ by removing some arbitrary subset of removable cycles is also good.

The following proposition is the main "tool" that allows us to find a subset of removable cycles such that the sum of lengths of cycles in this subset is a multiple of d.

Proposition 4. *Let $d \geq 1$. Every sequence $x_1, x_2, \ldots, x_r$ of natural numbers, where $r \geq d$, contains a non-empty subsequence $x_i, x_{i+1}, \ldots, x_j$ (where $1 \leq i \leq j \leq r$) such that $(x_i + x_{i+1} + \cdots + x_j) \equiv 0 \pmod{d}$.*

Proof. Consider a sequence $s_0, s_1, \ldots, s_r$ where $s_i = x_1 + x_2 + \cdots + x_i$ for $i \in [0, r]$. There are at most d different values of s_i modulo d. Since $r \geq d$, by the pigeonhole principle we have $s_i \equiv s_j \pmod{d}$ for some i, j such that $0 \leq i < j \leq r$. The nonempty sequence $x_{i+1}, x_{i+2}, \ldots, x_j$ has the required property $(x_{i+1} + x_{i+2} + \cdots + x_j) \equiv 0 \pmod{d}$, since $s_j - s_i \equiv 0 \pmod{d}$. □

Proposition 5. *Let $q_1, q_2 \in Q$, $x \in \mathbb{N}$, and $d \in [1, n]$. If $q_1 \xrightarrow{x} q_2$ then $q_1 \xrightarrow{y} q_2$ for some $y \in [0, 2n^2 - n)$ such that $y \leq x$ and $y \equiv x \pmod{d}$.*

Proof. Let us assume $q_1 \xrightarrow{x} q_2$ and let $y \in \mathbb{N}$ be the smallest number such that $y \equiv x \pmod{d}$ and $q_1 \xrightarrow{y} q_2$ (such y exists, since $y = x$ satisfies these properties). Let $\beta_0, \beta_1, \ldots, \beta_r$ be a good decomposition of a path of length y from q_1 to q_2 (β_0 is a simple path from q_1 to q_2 and β_i for $i \in [1, r]$ are elementary cycles). Let us assume that there are at least d removable cycles in this decomposition. Then, by Proposition 4, there is a nonempty subset of these removable cycles such that the sum of lengths of the cycles in this subset is a multiple of d. By removing the cycles in this subset we obtain a good sequence, from which we can construct a path from q_1 to q_2 of length $y' < y$ where $y' \equiv y \pmod{d}$. So $q_1 \xrightarrow{y'} q_2$ and $y' \equiv x \pmod{d}$, which is a contradiction, since we have assumed that y is the smallest such number. This implies that in the sequence $\beta_0, \beta_1, \ldots, \beta_r$ there are at most $d - 1$ removable cycles.

A cycle β_i is unremovable iff it contains a state q that does not belong to any β_j with $j < i$, which implies that there are at most $n - 1$ unremovable cycles (note that there is at least one state in β_0). The length of β_0 is at most $n - 1$ and a length of each elementary cycle is at most n, which implies

$$y \leq (n - 1) + (n - 1 + d - 1) \cdot n < 2n^2 - n,$$

since $d \leq n$. □

Corollary 6. *Let $q_1 \xrightarrow{x} q_2$ for some $q_1, q_2 \in Q$ and $x \in \mathbb{N}$. If $x \geq n$ then there exist $q \in Q$, $c_1 \in [0, n)$, $d \in [1, n]$, and $c_2 \in [0, 2n^2 - n)$ such that $q_1 \xrightarrow{c_1} q$, $q \xrightarrow{d} q$, $q \xrightarrow{c_2} q_2$, and $x \in (c_1 + c_2) + d\mathbb{N}$.*

Proof. By the pigeonhole principle, some $q \in Q$ must be visited twice in the first n steps of a path from q_1 to q_2 of length $x \geq n$, and so for some $c_1 \in [0, n)$, $d \in [1, n]$, and $c_2' \in \mathbb{N}$ we have $q_1 \xrightarrow{c_1} q$, $q \xrightarrow{d} q$, $q \xrightarrow{c_2'} q_2$, and $x = c_1 + d + c_2'$. By Proposition 5, there is some $c_2 \in [0, 2n^2 - n)$ satisfying $c_2 \leq c_2'$, $q \xrightarrow{c_2} q_2$, and $c_2 \equiv c_2' \pmod{d}$. So $c_2' = c_2 + k \cdot d$ for some $k \in \mathbb{N}$, and $x = c_1 + d + c_2' = (c_1 + c_2) + (k + 1) \cdot d$, which means that $x \in (c_1 + c_2) + d\mathbb{N}$. □

Proposition 7. *Let $q_1 \xrightarrow{x} q_2$ for some $q_1, q_2 \in Q$ and $x \in \mathbb{N}$. If $x \geq 2n^2 + n$ then there exist $q \in Q$, $c \in [0, 2n^2 - n)$, and $d \in [1, n]$, such that $q_1 \xrightarrow{n} q$, $q \xrightarrow{d} q$, $q \xrightarrow{c} q_2$, and $x \in (n + c) + d\mathbb{N}$.*

Proof. Assume $q_1 \xrightarrow{x} q_2$ where $x \geq 2n^2 + n$. By Corollary 6, there are some $q' \in Q$, $c_1 \in [0, n)$, $d \in [1, n]$, $c_2 \in [0, 2n^2 - n)$, and $k \in \mathbb{N}$ such that $q_1 \xrightarrow{c_1} q'$, $q' \xrightarrow{d} q'$, $q' \xrightarrow{c_2} q_2$, and $x = (c_1 + c_2) + k \cdot d$. Let α be a path of length x from q_1 to q_2 that goes from q_1 to q' by c_1 steps, then goes k times through a cycle β of length d, and then goes from q' to q_2 by c_2 steps, and let q be the state reached after the first n steps of α. Note that since $(c_1 + c_2) + k \cdot d = x \geq 2n^2 + n$ and $c_1 + c_2 < 2n^2$ (because $c_1 < n$ and $c_2 < 2n^2 - n$), we have $k \cdot d \geq n$. Together with $c_1 < n$ this ensures that the state q is on the cycle β, which implies $q_1 \xrightarrow{n} q$, $q \xrightarrow{d} q$, and $q \xrightarrow{x-n} q_2$. By Proposition 5, there is some $c \in [0, 2n^2 - n)$ such that $c \leq x - n$, $q \xrightarrow{c} q_2$, and $c \equiv x - n \pmod{d}$. This means that $n + c \equiv x \pmod{d}$, and since $c \leq x - n$ implies $n + c \leq x$, we have $x \in (n + c) + d\mathbb{N}$. $\qquad\square$

Now we can prove Lemma 2.

Proof (of Lemma 2). Assume that $x \geq 2n^2 + n$ and $x \in L(\mathcal{A})$, so there are some $q_0 \in I$ and $q_f \in F$ such that $q_0 \xrightarrow{x} q_f$. By Lemma 7, there exist $q \in Q$, $c' \in [0, 2n^2 - n)$, and $d \in [1, n]$, such that $q_0 \xrightarrow{n} q$ $q \xrightarrow{d} q$, $q \xrightarrow{c'} q_f$, and $x \in (n + c') + d\mathbb{N}$. This means that for each $c \in (n + c') + d\mathbb{N}$, such that $c \leq x$, we have $q \xrightarrow{c-n} q_f$ and $x \in c + d\mathbb{N}$. In particular, there is one such c in the interval $[2n^2 - d, 2n^2)$, since $n + c' \in [n, 2n^2)$. $\qquad\square$

4   Efficient Implementation

To avoid recomputations, the algorithm precomputes some sets. For $i \in \mathbb{N}$ we define $S_i = \{q \in Q \mid \exists q_0 \in I : q_0 \xrightarrow{i} q\}$ and $T_i = \{q \in Q \mid \exists q_f \in F : q \xrightarrow{i} q_f\}$, and for $q \in Q$ we define $Periods(q) = \{d \in [1, n] \mid q \xrightarrow{d} q\}$. In particular, the algorithm precomputes the sets S_n, T_i for $i \in [2n^2 - 2n, 2n^2 - n)$, and $Periods(q)$ for $q \in S_n$. To test for a given q if $q_0 \xrightarrow{n} q$ for some $q_0 \in I$, the algorithm tests if $q \in S_n$, to test if $q \xrightarrow{c-n} q_f$ for some $q_f \in F$, it tests if $q \in T_{c-n}$, and to test if $q \xrightarrow{d} q$, it tests if $d \in Periods(q)$.

All these sets can be implemented as bit arrays, so operations like adding an element to a set, testing if an element is member of a set, and so on, can be performed in a constant time. It is also obvious that for $Q' \subseteq Q$, the sets $Succ(Q') = \{q \in Q \mid \exists q' \in Q' : (q', q) \in \delta\}$ and $Pre(Q') = \{q \in Q \mid \exists q' \in Q' : (q, q') \in \delta\}$ can be computed in time $O(n + m)$ where m is the number of transitions (i.e., $|\delta| = m$). Using subroutines for computing Pre and $Succ$, the precomputation of all necessary sets can be done in time $O(n^2(n + m))$. For example, S_n can be precomputed by computing sequence $S_0, S_1, \ldots, S_n$ where $S_0 = I$, and $S_{i+1} = Succ(S_i)$ for $i \geq 0$, T_i can be computed by $T_0 = F$, and $T_{i+1} = Pre(T_i)$ for $i \geq 0$, etc. Also all $x < 2n^2 + n$ such that $x \in L(\mathcal{A})$ can be found in time $O(n^2(n + m))$ by computing the sequence $S_0, S_1, \ldots, S_{2n^2+n-1}$ and checking if $S_x \cap F \neq \emptyset$ for $x \in [0, 2n^2 + n)$.

There are $O(n^2)$ pairs (c, d) such that $d \in [1, n]$ and $c \in [2n^2 - d, 2n^2)$, and for each of them, at most n states are tested. Since the corresponding tests for one triple c, d, q can be done in a constant time as described above, all triples can be tested in time $O(n^3)$. We see that the overall running time of the algorithm is $O(n^2(n + m))$.

During the computation, only the values of S_n, T_i for $i \in [2n^2 - n - d, 2n^2 - n)$, and $Periods(q)$ for $q \in S_n$ need to be stored. Obviously, $O(n^2)$ bits are sufficient to store these values. Other values are used only temporarily, can be discarded after their use, and do not take more than $O(n^2)$ bits, so the overall space complexity of the algorithm is $O(n^2)$.

References

1. Chrobak, M.: Finite automata and unary languages. Theoretical Computer Science 47(2), 149–158 (1986)
2. Göller, S., Mayr, R., To, A.W.: On the computational complexity of verifying one-counter processes. In: LICS'09, pp. 235–244. IEEE Computer Society, Los Alamitos (2009), http://dx.doi.org/10.1109/LICS.2009.37
3. Gruber, H., Holzer, M.: Computational complexity of NFA minimization for finite and unary languages. In: Martín-Vide, C., Otto, F., Fernau, H. (eds.) LATA 2008. LNCS, vol. 5196, pp. 261–272. Springer, Heidelberg (2008)
4. Kozen, D.C.: Automata and Computability. Springer, Heidelberg (1997)
5. Martinez, A.: Efficient computation of regular expressions from unary nfas. In: Descriptional Complexity of Formal Systems, DFCS (2002)
6. Martinez, A.: Topics in Formal Languages: String Enumeration, Unary NFAs and State Complexity. Master's thesis, University of Waterloo (2002)
7. Parikh, R.J.: On context-free languages. J. ACM 13(4), 570–581 (1966)
8. To, A.W.: Unary finite automata vs. arithmetic progressions. Information Processing Letterss 109(17), 1010–1014 (2009),
http://dx.doi.org/10.1016/j.ipl.2009.06.005

Efficient Graph Reachability Query Answering Using Tree Decomposition

Fang Wei

Computer Science Department, University of Freiburg, Germany

Abstract. Efficient reachability query answering in large directed graphs has been intensively investigated because of its fundamental importance in many application fields such as XML data processing, ontology reasoning and bioinformatics.

In this paper, we present a novel indexing method based on the concept of tree decomposition. We show analytically that this intuitive approach is both time and space efficient. We demonstrate empirically the efficiency and the effectiveness of our method.

1 Introduction

Querying and manipulating large scale graph-like data has attracted much attention in the database community, due to the wide application areas of graph data, such as GIS, XML databases, bioinformatics, social network, and ontologies.

The problem of reachability test in a directed graph is among the fundamental operations on the graph data. Given a digraph $G = (V, E)$ and $u, v \in V$, a reachability query, denoted as $u \to v$, ask: is there a path from u to v? One of the fundamental queries on biological networks is for instance, to *find all genes whose expressions are directly or indirectly influenced by a given molecule* [15]. Given the graph representation of the genes and regulation events, the question can also be reduced to the reachability query in a directed graph.

Recently, tree decomposition methodologies have been successfully applied to solving shortest path query answering over undirected graphs [17]. Briefly stated, the vertices in a graph G are decomposed into a tree in which each node contains a set of vertices in G. Different from other partitioning based methods, there are overlapping between the tree nodes, i.e., for any vertex v in G, there could be more than one node in the tree which contains v. However, it is required that all these nodes constitute a connected subtree (see Definition 1 for the formal definition). Based on this decomposed structure, many otherwise intractable problems can be solved if the underlying tree decomposition has bounded treewidth.

In this paper we make an attempt to solve reachability problems over directed graphs by using tree decomposition based index structures. In comparison to shortest path queries, reachability query answering enjoys some nice properties. For instance, the existing BFS or DFS algorithms are highly efficient. However, these properties might cause challenging problems to occur, if

A. Kučera and I. Potapov (Eds.): RP 2010, LNCS 6227, pp. 183–197, 2010.

substantial improvement on time complexity is desired. Note that one extreme scheme is to store all the transitive closures in the pre-processing stage, thus the reachability queries can be answered in constant time. However this requires an index of size $O(n^2)$, which is unrealistic for large scale graphs. Therefore, finding a better trade-off between time and storage is the ultimate goal of many reachability query answering algorithms. Surprisingly, we have found that the tree decomposition-based methodology can be adapted on directed graphs and moreover, the efficiency of the query algorithm is substantially improved, based on the index which is much smaller than $O(n^2)$. Our main contributions are the following:

- **Linear time tree decomposition algorithm.** In spite of the theoretical importance of the tree decomposition concept, many results are practically useless due to the fact that finding a tree decomposition with optimal treewidth is an NP-hard problem, w.r.t. the size of the graph. To overcome this difficulty, we propose a simple heuristics to achieve a linear time tree decomposition algorithm.
- **Flexibility of balancing the time and space efficiency.** From the proposed tree decomposition algorithm, we discover an important correlation between the query time and the index size. This flexibility enables the users to choose the best time/space trade-off according to the system requirements.

1.1   Related Work

Most of the current research of reachability query answering concentrates on methods that first build an index structure to store part of the transitive closures, then speed up the query answering process, thus to find better trade-offs of index size and the query answering time. They can be categorized into the two main groups. The first group of algorithms are based on the 2-Hop approach first proposed by Cohen et al. [6]. The second are based on the *interval labeling* approach by Agrawal et al. [1].

2-Hop based algorithms. The basic idea of the 2-Hop approach is to assign for each vertex v a list of vertices which are reachable from v, denoted as $L_{in}(v)$, and a list of vertices to which v can reach, denoted as $L_{out}(v)$, so that for any two vertices u and v, $u \rightarrow v$ if and only if $L_{out}(u) \cap L_{in}(v) \neq \emptyset$. The ultimate goal of the algorithm is to minimize the index size of the form $\sum_{v \in V} L_{out}(v) + L_{in}(v)$. Clearly if the index is available, the reachability query answering requires only two lookups. However, this optimization problem is NP-hard. Improvements on the 2-Hop algorithm can be found in [13,14] Generally 2-Hop based algorithms do not scale for large size graphs.

Interval labeling based algorithms. Interval labeling based approaches utilize the efficient method of indexing and querying trees which was applied to XML query processing in recent years [18]. It is well known that given a tree, we can label each node v by an interval $[start(v), end(v)]$. Thus the reachability query can be answered by comparing the start and the end labels of u and v

in constant time. The labeling process takes linear time and space. The Dual Labeling algorithm proposed by Wang et al. [16] achieved to answer reachability queries in constant time. They first identify a spanning tree from the graph and label the vertices in the tree with pre- and post-order values. Then the transitive closure for the rest of the edges is stored. Clearly, the price for the constant query time is paid by the storage cost of t^2 where t is number of the non-tree edges in the graph. Therefore the Dual Labeling approach achieves good performance only if the graph is extremely sparse where $t \ll n$.

Jin et al. [9] proposed a different index structure called Path Tree. Like other interval labeling based methods, they extract a tree from the original graph. But every node in the tree contains a path, instead of a single vertex. This index structure is superior to the previous ones since it can encode some non-tree structures such as grid in an elegant way.

All of these algorithms in common is that the performance deteriorate for non-sparse graphs. In contrast, the index structure proposed in this paper scales for dense graphs as well.

2   Graph Indexing with Tree Decomposition

2.1   Tree Decomposition of Directed Graphs

A directed graph is defined as $G = (V, E)$, where $V = \{0, 1, \ldots, n-1\}$ is the vertex set and $E \subseteq V \times V$ is the edge set. Let $n = |V|$ be the number of vertices and $m = |E|$ be the number of edges.

For each directed graph, its tree decomposition is defined as follows:

Definition 1. *A tree decomposition of $G = (V, E)$, denoted as T_G, is a pair $(\{X_i \mid i \in I\}, T)$, where $\{X_i \mid i \in I\}$ is a collection of subsets of V and $T = (I, F)$ is a tree such that:*

1. $\bigcup_{i \in I} X_i = V$.
2. *for every $(u, v) \in E$, there is $i \in I : u, w \in X_i$.*
3. *for all $v \in V$, the set $\{i \mid v \in X_i\}$ induces a subtree of T.*

A tree decomposition contains a set of tree nodes, where each node contains a set of vertices in V. We call the sets X_i *bags*. It is required that every vertex in V should occur in at least one bag (condition 1), and for every edge in E, both vertices of the edge should occur together in at least one bag (condition 2). The third condition is usually referred to as the *connectedness condition*, which requires that given a vertex v in the graph, all the bags which contain v should be connected.

Note that from now on, the node in the directed graph G is referred to as *vertex*, and the node in the tree decomposition is referred to as *tree node* or simply *node*. For each tree node i, there is a bag X_i consisting of vertices. To simplify the presentation, we will sometimes use the term *node* and its corresponding *bag* interchangeably.

Given any graph G, there may exist many tree decompositions which fulfill all the conditions in Definition 1. However, we are interested in those tree decompositions with smaller bag sizes. The *width* of a bag is the cardinality of the bag. The *width* of a tree decomposition $(\{X_i \mid i \in I\}, T)$ is defined as $\max\{|X_i| \mid i \in I\}$[1]. The *treewidth* of G is the minimal width of all tree decompositions of G. It is denoted as $tw(G)$. Note that trees and forests are precisely the structures with treewidth 2.

Example 1. Consider the graph illustrated in Figure 1(a). One of the tree decompositions is shown in Figure 1(b) . Recall that only trees and forests have treewidth 2, therefore this tree decomposition is optimal and we have $tw(G) = 3$.

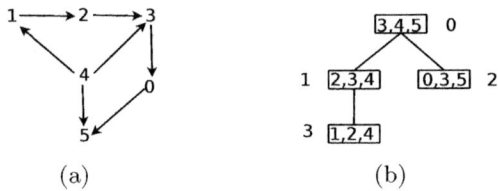

(a)   (b)

Fig. 1. The graph G (a) and one tree decomposition T_G (b) with $tw(G) = 3$

Let $G = (V, E)$ be a graph and $T_G = (\{X_i \mid i \in I\}, T)$ its tree decomposition. Due to the third condition in Definition 1, for any vertex v in V there exists an induced subtree of T_G in which every bag contains v. We call it the *induced subtree* of v and denote it as T_v. Furthermore, we denote the root of T_v as r_v and its corresponding bag as X_{r_v}. For instance, the induced subtree of vertex 3 in Figure 1(b) contains the bags X_0, X_1 and X_2, where $r_3 = 0$.

2.2   Tree Path

Let $G = (V, E)$ be a directed graph, and $u, v \in V$. We say v is reachable from vertex u, denoted as $u \to v$, if there is a path starting from u and ending at v with the form $(u, v_1, \ldots, v_n, v)$, where $(u, v_1), (v_i, v_{i+1}), (v_n, v) \in E$. Note that in this paper, we consider the more general definition of path, that is, a path is not necessarily a simple path.

Let us consider the graph vertices in the tree nodes. Since each vertex occurs in more than one bag, a vertex can be identified with $\{v, i\}$, where v is a vertex and i the node in the tree, meaning that vertex v is located in the tree node i. We denote it as *tree vertex*. Now we define the so-called *inner edge* and *inter edge* in the tree decomposition.

Definition 2 (Inner edge, Inter edge, Tree path). *Let $G = (V, E)$ be a directed graph and $T_G = (\{X_i \mid i \in I\}, T)$ its tree decomposition.*

---

[1] The original definition of the width is $max\{|X_i| \mid i \in I\} - 1$, due to esthetic reasons.

- *The* inner edges *of T_G are precisely the pairs of tree vertices defined as follows:* $\{(\{u, i\}, \{v, i\}) \mid (u, v) \in E, u, v \in X_i (i \in I)\}$.
- *The* inter edges *of T_G are the pairs of tree vertices with the form $(\{v, i\}, \{v, j\})$ where $v \in X_i$ and $v \in X_j$, and either $(i, j) \in F$ or $(j, i) \in F$ holds.*
- *A tree path from $\{u, i\}$ to $\{v, j\}$ is a sequence of tree vertices connected with either inter or inner edges.*

Intuitively, the set of inner edges consists precisely of those edges in E, with the extra information of the bags in which the edges are located. For instance, the inner edges of the tree decomposition of the graph in Example 1 are: $(\{0, 2\}, \{5, 2\})$, $(\{1, 3\}, \{2, 3\})$, $(\{2, 1\}, \{3, 1\})$, $(\{3, 2\}, \{0, 2\})$, ... Note that it happens that the same pair of vertices occurs in more than one bag. For instance, the edge $(4, 3)$ occurs in both bags X_0 and X_1. Thus there are two inner edges: $(\{4, 1\}, \{3, 1\})$ and $(\{4, 0\}, \{3, 0\})$ For instance, in Example 1, $(\{5, 0\}, \{5, 2\})$ is an inter edge, as well as $(\{5, 2\}, \{5, 0\})$.

Lemma 1. *Let $G = (V, E)$ be a directed graph and $T_G = (\{X_i \mid i \in I\}, T)$ its tree decomposition. Let $u, v \in V$. Let further $\{u, i\}$ and $\{v, j\}$ be tree vertices in T_G. There is a path from u to v in G if and only if there is a tree path from $\{u, i\}$ to $\{v, j\}$.*

Example 2. Consider the graph in Figure 1(a). Vertex 4 reaches vertex 0 with the path $\{4, 1, 2, 3, 0\}$. In the tree decomposition in Figure 1(b), there is a tree path from $\{4, 1\}$ to $\{0, 2\}$ as follows: { $\{4, 1\}$, $\{4, 3\}$, $\{1, 3\}$, $\{2, 3\}$, $\{2, 1\}$, $\{3, 1\}$, $\{3, 0\}$, $\{3, 2\}$, $\{0, 2\}$ }.

2.3   Reachability Test on Tree Decomposition

With the definition of tree path, to find a path from u to v, we can simply search in the tree decomposition for a corresponding tree path. Moreover, over the tree decomposition, we only need to concentrate on the simple path between the corresponding tree vertices. There is a well known property of trees that says for any two nodes i and j in a tree, there exists a unique simple path, denoted as $SP_{i,j}$, such that every path from i to j contains all the nodes in $SP_{i,j}$.

Proposition 1. *Let $G = (V, E)$ be a directed graph and $T_G = (\{X_i \mid i \in I\}, T)$ its tree decomposition. Let $u, v \in V$. Let further r_u (resp. r_v) be the root node of the induced subtree of u (resp. v). Then $u \to v$ if and only if for every node n in SP_{r_u, r_v}, there is at least one vertex $t \in X_n$, such that $u \to t$ and $t \to v$.*

Proof. The "if" direction is trivial: given a tree path from $\{u, i\}$ to $\{v, j\}$, we only need to consider the inner edges. Since for each inner edge $\{u, i\}, \{v, i\}$, there is an edge $(u, v) \in E$, the path from u to v can be easily constructed.

Now we prove the "only if" direction: assume that there is a path from u to v in G. We prove it by induction on the length of the path.

– Basis: if u reaches v with a path of length 1, that is, $(u,v) \in E$. Then there exists a node k in the tree decomposition, s.t. $u \in X_k$ and $v \in X_k$. We start from $\{u,i\}$, traverse along the induced subtree of u, till we reach $\{u,k\}$. Since the induced subtree is connected, the path from $\{u,i\}$ to $\{u,k\}$ can be constructed with inter edges. Then we reach from $\{u,k\}$ to $\{v,k\}$ with an inner edge. Now we traverse from $\{v,k\}$ to $\{v,j\}$ along the induced subtree of v, which can again be constructed with inter edges. The tree path from $\{u,i\}$ to $\{v,j\}$ is thus completed.

– Induction: assume that the lemma holds with paths whose length is less than or equal to $n-1$, we prove that it holds for paths with length of n. Assume that there is a path from u to v with length n, where u reaches w with length $n-1$ and $(w,v) \in E$. From induction hypothesis, we know that there is a tree path form $\{u,i\}$ to $\{w,l\}$ in the tree decomposition, where l is a node in the induced subtree of w. Since $(w,v) \in E$, there is a node n such that $w \in X_n$ and $v \in X_n$. Thus $\{w,n\}$ can be reached from $\{w,l\}$ with inter edges. Then $\{w,n\}$ can reach $\{v,n\}$ with an inner edge. Finally $\{v,n\}$ can reach $\{v,j\}$ with a sequence of inter edges. This completes the proof. □

Proposition 1 shows that for the reachability test from u to v, although the tree path from $\{u,r_u\}$ to $\{v,r_v\}$ may possibly visit any node in the tree, we only need to concentrate on the reachability test for those vertices which occur in the simple path SP_{r_u,r_v}. More precisely, we can simply take *any* node n from SP_{r_u,r_v}, and check whether there is a vertex $t \in X_n$, such that $u \to t$ and $t \to v$ hold. In order to further accelerate the query process, we can execute the reachability test along the path tree in a bottom-up manner, as shown in Figure 2. In order to enable the bottom up operation, we need to store the transitive closure for each bag in the tree decomposition. That is, in every bag X, for every pair of vertices $x,y \in X$, the boolean values of $x \to y$ and $y \to x$ are pre-computed. We show in the following proposition how the reachability queries from u to all the vertices in $SP_{r_u,k}$ can be answered.

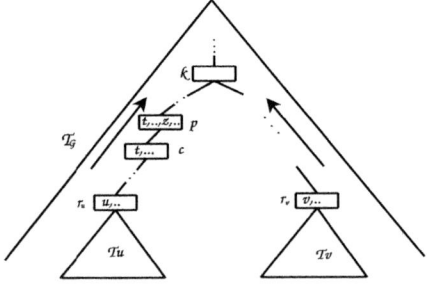

Fig. 2. Bottom-up processing on the simple tree path

Proposition 2. *Let $G = (V,E)$ be a directed graph and $T_G = (\{X_i \mid i \in I\}, T)$ its tree decomposition. Let $u,v \in V$. Let k be the lowest common ancestor of*

r_u and r_v. The reachability queries from u to all the vertices in $SP_{r_u,k}$ can be answered in $O(w^2h)$, where $h = |SP_{r_u,k}|$ and w is the maximal width of the bags in $SP_{r_u,k}$.

Proof. Assume that the transitive closure in every bag from $SP_{r_u,k}$ is available. The reachability test starts with node r_u. From the information of transitive closure, we can simply obtain the set $Y_{r_u} \subseteq X_{r_u}$ such that every vertex in Y_{r_u} can be reached from u. Next, we consider r_u as the child node and process its parent node, with the available reachability information. This process is recursively executed h times, until k is reached.

Next we show that at each step of the processing, all the vertices in the current bag reachable from u can be found in w^2 time, where w is the width of the current bag. Assume p is the current node, c its child node, and we have obtained $Y_c \subseteq X_c$, where Y_c contains all the vertices reachable from u. Now we have to decide the set $Y_p \subseteq X_p$, i.e. identify all the vertices reachable from u in X_p.

Let z be a vertex in X_p. We want to decide whether $u \to z$. We have the following two cases:

1. $z \in X_p$ and $z \in X_c$. Since at the child node we know whether $z \in Y_c$, we set $z \in Y_p$ if $z \in Y_c$.
2. $z \in X_p$ and $z \notin X_c$. This is a more complex case. We show that $z \in Y_p$ (i.e. z is reachable from u) if and only if there exists a vertex t, such that $t \in X_p$, $t \in Y_c$ and $t \to z$ holds.
   (a) "if" direction is trivial.
   (b) "only if: Assume that $u \to z$ holds. Since z does not occur in X_c, according to the connectedness condition, z does not occur in any bag in the subtree rooted with c. Thus the induced subtrees of u and z do not share any common node in T_G. Since $u \to z$, there is a tree path from $\{u, r_u\}$ to $\{z, r_z\}$, and $c, p \in SP_{r_u,r_z}$. The tree path from $\{u, r_u\}$ to $\{z, r_z\}$ must contain an inter edge of the form $(\{t, c\}, \{t, p\})$, where $t \in X_p, X_c$, because this is the only possible edge to traverse from c to p. Clearly $u \to t$ holds. From the assumption $u \to z$, we obtain that $t \to z$ must hold.
   Given the set $Y_c \subseteq X_c$ and the transitive closure in X_p, we can obtain Y_p as follows: First set Y_p as $Y_c \cap X_p$. Then for each vertex $t \in Y_p$, we add the vertex s into Y_p, if $t \to s$ holds. Clearly the time consumption is in the worst case $O(w^2)$ where w is the width of X_p.   □

3   Algorithms and Complexity Results

In this section, we present the detailed algorithms for both the index construction and the reachability query answering. In Section 3.1 we begin with the introduction of algorithmic issues on the tree decomposition from a complexity theory perspective, and then justify our choice of an efficient but suboptimal decomposing algorithm. In Section 3.2 we first analyze the reachability query answering algorithm proposed in Theorem 2 from the previous section. Then, we point out that the time and space improvement can be made to achieve higher efficiency of our algorithm.

3.1   Index Construction via Tree Decomposition

Since its introduction by Robertson and Seymour [12], the concepts of tree decomposition has been proved to be of great importance in computational complexity theory [4]. The theoretical significance of the tree decomposition based approach lies in the fact that many intractable problems can be solved in polynomial time (or even in linear time) for graphs with treewidth bounded by a constant. Problems which can be dealt with in this way include many well known NP-complete problems, such as the Independent Set, the Hamiltonian Circuits, etc. Recent applications of tree decomposition based approaches can be found in Constraint Satisfaction [10] and database design [7].

However, the practical usefulness of tree decomposition based approaches has been limited due to the following two problems: (1) Calculating the treewidth of a graph is hard. In fact, determining whether the treewidth of a given graph is at most a given integer w is NP-complete [2]. Although for fixed w, linear time algorithms exist to solve the decision problem "treewidth $\leq w$" [3], there is a huge hidden constant factor, which prevents it to be useful in practice. There exist many heuristics and approximation algorithms for determining the treewidth, unfortunately few of them can deal with graphs containing more than 1000 nodes [11]. (2) The second problem lies in the fact that even if the treewidth can be determined, it still can not be guaranteed that good performance will be obtained since the time complexity of most of the algorithms is exponential to the treewidth. Therefore, to solve really hard problems efficiently by using the tree decomposition based approaches, we have to require that the underlying graphs have *bounded* treewidth (i.e. less than 10).

As far as the efficiency is concerned, we can only search for an approximate solution, which yields a tree decomposition whose width is greater than the treewidth. On the other hand, we can tolerate a tree decomposition whose treewidth is not bounded. As we have seen from Proposition 2, the time complexity is in the worst case quadratic of the maximal bag size. We will show later in this section that our query answering algorithm does not depend on the treewidth, but with some parameter which can be enforced to be bounded, due to the nice property of our dedicated decomposing algorithm, and the height of the tree.

Inspired from the so-called pre-processing methods by Bodlaender et al. [5], we apply the reduction rules on the graph by reducing stepwise a graph to another one with fewer vertices, due to the following simple fact.

Definition 3 (Simplicial). *A vertex v is simplicial in an undirected graph G if the set of neighbors of v form a clique in G.*

Figure 3 shows some special cases. If a vertex v has degree of one (Figure 3(a)), then we can remove v without increasing the treewidth. Figure 3(b), 3(c) illustrate the cases of degree 2 and 3 respectively.

The main idea of our decomposition algorithm is to reduce the graph by removing the vertices one by one from the graph, and at the same time push the removed vertices into a stack, so that later on the tree can be constructed

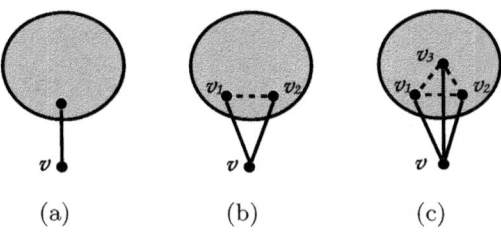

Fig. 3. A undirected graph containing a vertex v with degree 1 (a), 2 (b) and 3 (c)

with the information from the stack. First a vertex v with a specific degree is identified. We first check whether all its neighbors form a clique, if not, we add the missing edges to construct a clique. Then v together with its neighbors are pushed into the stack, which is followed by the deletion of v and its edges in the graph. See Algorithm 2.

Algorithm 1. $tree\_decomp(G)$
_____
Input: $G = (V, E)$ is a directed graph.
Output: return the tree decomposition T_G.
  1: Transform G into an undirected graph UG;
  2: $graph\_reduction(UG)$; {output the vertex stack S}
  3: $tree\_construction(S, G)$; {output the tree decomposition}
_____

The program begins with removing isolated vertices and vertices with degree 1. Then, the reduction process proceeds with the vertices with degree of 2, 3, ... We denote such procedure of removing all the vertices with degree x as *degree-x reduction*.

Example 3. Consider the undirected version of the graph in Example 1. Figure 4 illustrates the reduction process. The process starts with a degree-2 reduction by removing vertex 0 and its edges, after adding the edge between 3 and 5. Vertex 0 and its neighbors are then pushed in the stack. Next vertex 1 is removed, following the same principle as of 0. After vertex 2 is removed, a single triangle is then left.

The procedure $graph\_reduction$ will terminate when one of the following conditions is fulfilled. (1) The graph is reduced to an empty set. For instance, if the graph contains only simple cycles, it will be reduced to an empty set after degree-2 reductions. This is usually the case for extremely sparse graphs. (2) For graphs which are not sparse, one has to define a upper bound l for the reduction, so that the program stops after the degree-l reduction. Note that as the degree increases, the effectiveness of the reduction will decrease, because in the worst case, we need to add $x(x-1)/2$ edges in order to remove x edges.

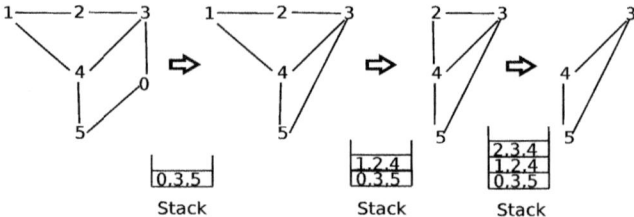

Fig. 4. The reduction process on the undirected graph of Example 1

Algorithm 2. *graph_reduction(UG)*

Input: UG is the undirected graph of G, l is the upper bound for the reduction.
Output: stack S and the reduced graph UG'
1: initialize stack S;
2: **for** $i = 1$ to l **do**
3:     *remove_upto(i)*;
4: **end for**
5: **return** S, UG;

6: **procedure** *remove_upto(x)*
7: **while** TRUE **do**
8:     **if** there exists a vertex v with degree less than x **then**
9:        $\{v_1, \ldots, v_x\}$ = neighbors of v;
10:       build a clique for $\{v_1, \ldots, v_x\}$;
11:       push $v, v_1, \ldots, v_x$ into S;
12:       delete v and all its edges from UG;
13:     **else**
14:       break;
15:     **end if**
16: **end while**

After the reduction process, the tree decomposition can be constructed as follows: (1) At first we collect all the vertices which were not removed by the reduction process and assign this set as the bag of the tree root. The size of the root depends on the structure of the graph (i.e. how many vertices are left after the reduction). (2) The rest of the tree is generated from the information stored in stack S. Let X_c be the set of vertices $\{v, v_1, \ldots, v_x\}$ which is popped up from the top of S. Here v is the removed vertex and $\{v_1, \ldots, v_x\}$ are the neighbors of v which form a clique. After the parent bag X_p which contains $\{v_1, \ldots, v_x\}$ is located in the tree, X_c is added as a child bag of X_p. This process proceeds until S is empty. Algorithm 3 illustrates the process.

The last step of the tree construction process is to generate the transitive closure for every bag.

The correctness of our tree decomposition algorithm can be shown by the induction on the reduction steps. Note that during the reduction process, edges

---

Algorithm 3. $tree\_construction(S, G, UG')$

Input: S is the stack storing the removed vertices and their neighbors, G is the directed
    graph, UG' is the reduced graph of UG.
Output: return tree decomposition T_G
 1: construct the root of T_G containing all the vertices of UG';
 2: **while** S is not empty **do**
 3:    pop up a bag $X_c = \{v, v_1, \ldots, v_x\}$ from S;
 4:    find the bag X_p containing $\{v_1, \ldots, v_x\}$;
 5:    add X_c into T as the child node of X_p;
 6: **end while**
 7: generate transitive closure in all bags;

---

are inserted into the original graph. Therefore, the tree decomposition we obtain
according to the algorithm is based on a graph consisting of extra edges. However,
this does not affect the correctness proof due to the following proposition.

Proposition 3. *Let $G = (V, E)$ and $G' = (V, E')$ be graphs where $E \subseteq E'$.
Then any tree decomposition of G' is a tree decomposition of G.*

Proof. Let $T_{G'}$ be the tree decomposition of G'. By checking the three properties
of Definition 1, it is obvious that $T_{G'}$ is also a tree decomposition of G.

3.2   Reachability Query Answering

Recall from Proposition 2 that the time complexity of the bottom-up query
answering is $O(w^2 h)$. This upper bound is optimal, only if the following two
conditions are fulfilled: (1) the treewidth of the underlying graph is bounded
(that is, $w^2 \ll n$), and (2) there is an efficient tree decomposition algorithm
for it. The first condition has to be fulfilled, since otherwise the linear time
BFS algorithm would be more efficient. Unfortunately, as we have seen in the
previous section, given an arbitrary graph, it is clear that neither (1) nor (2)
can be fulfilled. Therefore, we have to inspect the tree decomposition heuristics
applied in Section 3.1 for improvements.

From Treewidth to $|R|$ and l. According to Algorithm 2, a graph G can
be decomposed by the *degree-l reductions* by increasing x from 1 to l. As soon
as the *degree-l reduction* is done, all the vertices which are not yet removed
are the elements in R of the tree decomposition. Usually if the graph is not
extremely sparse, the relationship $l \ll |R|$ holds. In fact, we could even enforce
such a relationship by setting l to be small enough in the tree decomposition
algorithm. Hence, the resulting tree decomposition has the following properties:
(1) the root is of big size ($|R|$), and (2) the rest of the bags have smaller size
(the upper bound is l).

    If we inspect the bottom-up query processing more carefully, we could observe
that the quadratic time computation over the root can be *always* be avoided. To
see this, let us consider the vertices u and v and the lowest common ancestor of

r_u and r_v is the root R. Assume that X_1 (resp. X_2) is the child node of R which locates in the simple path from r_u (resp. r_v) to R. Consider now that for all $x \in X_1$, $reach(u, x)$ (resp. all $y \in X_2$, $reach(y, v)$) have been computed. Clearly, any path from u to v has to pass through a vertex in X_1 and X_2 respectively. Therefore, at the root node R, we can first calculate $X_1 \cap R$ and $X_2 \cap R$. Since all the paths from u to v has to pass one vertex in $X_1 \cap R$ and another vertex in $X_2 \cap R$, we only need to execute a nested loop on $X_1 \cap R$ and $X_2 \cap R$ to decide the reachability. Since both $|X_1|$ and $|X_2|$ have the upper bound of l, the overall time consumption is of $O(l^2 h)$, thus independent of $|R|$. Note that if both u and v are located in R, then the shortest path can be immediately obtained from the local shortest path from u to v, which are pre-computed.

Algorithm 4. $reach(T_G, u, v)$

Input: T_G is the tree decomposition of G and u, v vertices in G.
Output: return TRUE if $u \to v$, otherwise FALSE

1: $c = r_u$ = root of induced subtree of u; $c = r_v$ = root of induced subtree of v;
2: k = lowest common ancestor of r_u and r_v;
3: R_u = reachable vertices from u in X_c;
4: **while** $c.parent \neq k$ **do**
5:     $p = c.parent$; $R_u = R_u \cap X_c \cap X_p$;
6:     **for all** t in R_u **do**
7:         R_t= set of vertices reachable from t in X_p; $R_u = R_u \cup R_t$;
8:     **end for**
9:     $c = p$;
10: **end while**
11: R_v = all vertices that reach v in X_c;
12: **while** $c.parent \neq k$ **do**
13:     $p = c.parent$; $R_v = R_v \cap X_c \cap X_p$;
14:     **for all** t in R_v **do**
15:         R_t= set of vertices reach t in X_p; $R_v = R_v \cup R_t$;
16:     **end for**
17:     $c = p$;
18: **end while**
19: $R_u = R_u \cup X_k$; $R_v = R_v \cup X_k$;
20: **return** $(reach(x, y) \mid \exists x \in R_u \wedge \exists y \in R_v)$;

The algorithm for the reachability query answering is presented in Algorithm 4. Comparing with the bottom-up query processing shown in Proposition 2, Algorithm 4 is customized with respect to our dedicated tree decomposition algorithm, in the sense that the query time complexity is adapted to be related to l, instead of the treewidth.

3.3   Complexity

Index construction time. For the index construction, we have to (1) generate the tree decomposition, and (2) at each tree node, generate the local transitive closures. For (1), both of the reduction step and the tree construction procedure take time $O(n)$. For (2), we deploy the classic BFS algorithm, which costs in worst case $O(m)$. In fact, we need to run for each vertex in G exactly one BFS procedure. Therefore, the overall index construction time is $O(nm)$.

Index size. In each bag X, for each pair of vertices u, v in X, if u reaches v, we need to store a boolean value. Thus the index size is $|X|^2$, Since the relationship $l \ll |R|$ holds, the root size $(|R|)$ is dominant among all the bags. Therefore, the index size is $|R|^2$. The index size consists of the tree structure, constructed by using the tree decomposition algorithm. However, this space overhead is linear to n, thus can be ignored.

Query. The bottom-up query processing for reachability query answering takes time $O(l^2 h)$, where l is the number of the reductions and h is the height of the tree decomposition. Note that the proposed tree decomposition algorithm is independent of the treewidth of the underlying graph, since the reduction parameter l can be adjusted according to the property of the graph. On the other hand, there is no guarantee that the optimal tree decomposition can be obtained. In the worst case, if tree-width is approximately n, there are $\Theta(n^2)$ edges to be stored. So the running time of the query algorithm in the worst case is worse than the one of the BFS (or DFS): if $tw(G) = \Theta(|G|)$. Clearly our algorithm is not suitable for such graphs.

4 Experiments

In this section we evaluate the tree decomposition method on real datasets. We are interested in the following parameters: *Index size, Index construction time,* and *Query time*. Note that the index size is measured as the size of transitive closures, which takes up the major part of the overall index size. Besides the standard measurements, we are also interested in the structure of the tree decomposition, which may influence the performance of the algorithm. These are: the number of tree nodes (#TreeN), the number of all the vertices stored in the bags (#SumV), the height of the tree (h), the number of vertex reductions (l), and the root size of the tree $(|R|)$. Note that we have chosen the optimal l, in order to achieve the best query time performance.

We tested our algorithm over real large datasets with density being larger than or close to 2 used in [8]. All graphs are extracted from real-world large datasets with density being larger than or close to 2. Among them, arXiv is extracted from a dataset of citations among scientific papers from the arxiv.org website. Citeseer contains citations among scientific literature publications from the CiteSeer project, and pubmed was extracted from an XML registry of open access medical publications from the PubMed Central website. GO contains genetic terms and their relationships from the Gene Ontology project. Yago describes the structure of relationships among terms in the semantic knowledge database from the YAGO project. The details of the datasets can be found in [8]. All tests are run on an Intel(R) Core 2 Duo 2.4 GHz CPU, and 2 GB of main memory. All algorithms were implemented in C++ with the Standard Template

Library (STL). A query is generated by randomly picking a pair of nodes for a reachability test. We measure the query time by answering a total of 10000 randomly generated reachability queries. We make a comparison of the query time with the linear time Breadth First Search method (BFS).

Table 1. Statistics of real graphs, the properties of the index and query performance

Graph	#V	#E	#TreeN	#SumV	h	l	|R|	Index		Query Time	
								Time(s)	Size	TD (ms)	BFS (ms)
Arxiv	6000	66707	4713	28300	12	30	1288	12.5	362228	49.6	449.5
Citeseer	10720	44258	8291	33411	9	8	2430	3.6	91067	8.8	135.5
Go	6793	13361	5186	19262	9	5	1608	1.2	29674	5.8	77.1
Pubmed	9000	40028	6482	26746	6	9	2519	2.9	185065	5.8	127.4
Yago	6642	42392	6161	19677	8	8	482	1.2	11673	3.2	78.9

As shown in Table 1, the time costs for query answering are substantially improved with respect to the naive BFS algorithm. As expected, there is a correlation between the index size and the size of the root size of the tree decomposition $|R|$. Note that the size of the index structure should be approximately $|R|^2$. However, we can reduce the size by only store those pairs which are reachable from one to the other. We obtain a query time speedup with respect to the naive BFS approach between 11% (Arxiv) and 4% (Yago).

5   Conclusions and Future Work

In this paper, we introduced the tree decomposition as the index structure for large directed graphs to answer reachability queries efficiently. With both theoretical and empirical analysis, we demonstrated that our approach is intuitive and efficient. The algorithms achieve good transitive closure compression rates and scale well on large size graphs.

In the future we plan to investigate the following problems: (1) Development of scalable tree decomposition algorithms. We expect to investigate more heuristics and integrate them into our implementation. (2) How to update the of the index structure is the underlying graph is changed. Furthermore, we will consider on-disk algorithms for both index construction and query answering.

References

1. Agrawal, R., Borgida, A., Jagadish, H.V.: Efficient management of transitive relationships in large data and knowledge bases. In: SIGMOD (1989)
2. Arnborg, S., Corneil, D.G., Proskurowski, A.: Complexity of finding embeddings in a k-tree. SIAM J. Algebraic Discrete Methods 8(2), 277–284 (1987)
3. Bodlaender, H.L.: A linear time algorithm for finding tree-decompositions of small treewidth. In: STOC (1993)

4. Bodlaender, H.L.: A tourist guide through treewidth. Acta Cybernetica 11, 1–23 (1993)
5. Bodlaender, H.L., Koster, A.M.C.A., van den Eijkhof, F.: Pre-processing rules for triangulation of probabilistic networks. Computational Intelligence 21(3), 286–305 (2005)
6. Cohen, E., Halperin, E., Kaplan, H., Zwick, U.: Reachability and distance queries via 2-hop labels. SIAM J. Comput. 32(5), 1338–1355 (2003)
7. Gottlob, G., Pichler, R., Wei, F.: Tractable database design through bounded treewidth. In: PODS, pp. 124–133 (2006)
8. Jin, R., Xiang, Y., Ruan, N., Fuhry, D.: 3-hop: a high-compression indexing scheme for reachability query. In: SIGMOD (2009)
9. Jin, R., Xiang, Y., Ruan, N., Wang, H.: Efficiently answering reachability queries on very large directed graphs. In: SIGMOD (2008)
10. Kask, K., Dechter, R., Larrosa, J., Dechter, A.: Unifying tree decompositions for reasoning in graphical models. Artif. Intell. 166(1-2), 165–193 (2005)
11. Koster, A.M.C.A., Bodlaender, H.L., Hoesel, S.P.M.V.: Treewidth: Computational experiments. Electronic Notes in Discrete Mathematics (2001)
12. Robertson, P.D., Seymour, N.: Graph minors iii: Planar tree-width. Journal of Combinatorial Theory, Series B 36, 49–64 (1984)
13. Schenkel, R., Theobald, A., Weikum, G.: Hopi: An efficient connection index for complex xml document collections. In: Bertino, E., Christodoulakis, S., Plexousakis, D., Christophides, V., Koubarakis, M., Böhm, K., Ferrari, E. (eds.) EDBT 2004. LNCS, vol. 2992, pp. 237–255. Springer, Heidelberg (2004)
14. Schenkel, R., Theobald, A., Weikum, G.: Efficient creation and incremental maintenance of the hopi index for complex xml document collections. In: ICDE, pp. 360–371 (2005)
15. Trissl, S., Leser, U.: Fast and practical indexing and querying of very large graphs. In: SIGMOD (2007)
16. Wang, H., He2, H., Yang, J., Yu, P.S., Yu, J.X.: Dual labeling: Answering graph reachability queries in constant time. In: ICDE (2006)
17. Wei, F.: Tedi: Efficient shortest path query answering on graphs. In: SIGMOD (2010)
18. Zhang, C., Naughton, J.F., DeWitt, D.J., Luo, Q., Lohman, G.M.: On supporting containment queries in relational database management systems. In: SIGMOD Conference (2001)

Author Index

GPSR Compliance

*The European Union's (EU) General Product Safety Regulation (GPSR)
is a set of rules that requires consumer products to be safe and our
obligations to ensure this.*

*If you have any concerns about our products, you can contact us on
ProductSafety@springernature.com*

In case Publisher is established outside the EU, the EU authorized
representative is:

Springer Nature Customer Service Center GmbH
Europaplatz 3
69115 Heidelberg, Germany

Batch number: 09490872

Printed by Printforce, the Netherlands